ANCIENT ECONOMIC THOUGHT

This collection explores the interrelationship between economic practice and intellectual constructs in a number of ancient cultures. Each chapter presents a new, richer understanding of the preoccupation of the ancients with specific economic problems including distribution, civic pride, management and uncertainty and how they were trying to resolve them. The research is based around the different artifacts and texts of the ancient East Indian, Hebraic, Greek, Hellenistic, Roman and emerging European cultures which remain for our consideration today: religious works, instruction manuals, literary and historical writings, epigrapha and legal documents. In looking at such items it becomes clear what a different exercise it is to look forward, from the earliest texts and artifacts of any culture, to measure the achievements of thinking in the areas of economics, than it is to take the more frequent route and look backward, beginning with the modern conception of economic systems and theory creation.

Presenting fascinating insights into the economic thinking of ancient cultures, this volume will enhance the reawakening of interest in ancient economic history and thought. It will be of great interest to scholars of economic thought and the history of ideas.

B. B. Price is Professor of Ancient and Medieval History at York University, Toronto, and is currently doing research and teaching as visiting professor at Massachusetts Institute of Technology.

ROUTLEDGE STUDIES IN THE HISTORY OF ECONOMICS

ANCIENT ECONOMIC THOUGHT

Volume 1

Edited by B. B. Price

London and New York

First published 1997
by Routledge
11 New Fetter Lane, London EC4P 4EE

Simultaneously published in the USA and Canada
by Routledge
29 West 35th Street, New York, NY 10001

Phototypeset in Garamond by Intype London Ltd
Printed and bound in Great Britain by
Mackays of Chatham PLC, Chatham, Kent

British Library Cataloguing in Publication Data
A catalogue record for this book is available from the British Library

Library of Congress Cataloging in Publication Data
Ancient Economic Thought / edited by B.B. Price
p.   cm.
"Many of the chapters ... issued for a conference at Massachusetts
Institute of Technology in 1994" — Introd.
Includes bibliographical references and index.
1. Economics — History — Cross-cultural studies. 2. Economic
history — To 500. I. Price, B. B. (Betsey Barker).
HB77.A63   1996
330'.09 — dc20   96–33564
ISBN 0–415–14930–4

In memory of Barry Gordon

CONTENTS

vii

CONTENTS

CONTRIBUTORS

B. B. Price is Professor of Ancient and Medieval History at York University, Toronto, Canada, and is currently a visiting Professor at Massachusetts Institute of Technology.

S. Ambirajan is Professor Emeritus of Economics at the Indian Institute of Technology, Madras, India.

Kishor Thanawala is Professor of Economics at Villanova University, Villanova, Pennsylvania, USA.

Mark Perlman is Professor Emertius of Economics at the University of Pittsburgh, Pennyslvania, USA.

Ephraim Kleiman is Professor of Economics at The Hebrew University of Jerusalem, Jerusalem, Israel.

Bertram Schefold is Professor Doctor of Economics at the Johann Wolfgang Goethe Universität, Frankfurt am Main, Germany.

Louis Baeck is Professor of Economics at the Katholicke Universiteit Leuven, Leuven, Belgium.

Murray C. McClellan is Professor of Archeology at Boston University, Boston, Massachusetts, USA.

Gloria Vivenza is Professor of the History of Economics at the Universita di Verona, Verona, Italy.

Alan E. Samuel is Professor of Classics at the University of Toronto, Toronto, Canada.

INTRODUCTION

B.B. Price

It is clear from the endeavours of academics and the gatherings they have fostered in the most recent few years that interest and serious scholarship in the subject of economic ideas in antiquity are increasing. The academic excitement is also broadening to become virtually worldwide. In this volume alone are presented contributions from scholars in India, the United States, Israel, Germany, Belgium, Italy and Canada, each with a cross-cultural awareness of one or more traditions of economic thinking whose roots derive from antiquity. It is also clear just from the scholars here presented that the purview to undertake the requisite research in ancient economic ideas extends through the disciplinary boundaries of economics, archeology, classics and history. Appreciation of the benefits of the variety of approaches to the study of ancient economic ideas is clearly reflected by the scholars themselves. Also, accessibility to the research area is undoubtedly enhanced by this complementarity, for readers both in the academic community and in the greater world of general interest. It is acknowledged that lack of familiarity with a cultural setting and the theological or philosophical terminology or argumentation of a particular period can make the subject seem daunting. This volume hopes, however, to have so contextualized the ancient facet of the history of economic ideas as to sustain the breath of new life and interest growing in the previously relatively ignored esoteric connections between classical and archeological studies and ancient intellectual history, and economics.

It is, of course, a constant temptation, especially for economists, to see connecting links, if not direct continua, between the ancient thinkers and later writers of economics, such as Adam Smith. The editorial position for this volume has been, however, to recognize that the task to present the ideas of the ancients themselves is large enough, and that the necessary substantiation of the lineage in terms of evidence of direct transmission, let alone a significant parallelism or similarity of ideas, must await a different volume. The few references to modern economic thought figure as aids to a non-anachronistic understanding of the past, assuredly not as gratuitous arrows pointing to the relevance of earlier ideas.

This volume's exciting collection of documentary and analytical material, grounded in many respects in ancient economic history, is intended to

1

enhance the reawakening in ancient economic thought. The survey addresses ancient Indian, Hebraic, Greek and Roman economic ideas, supported by basic research in archival collections and field work. Analysis and insight are dedicated to written works significant to economic thought in each of the four historical spheres: the *Mahabharata* and *Arthasastra*, Pentateuch and other Biblical books, the Mishna, *Gemara*, *Midrash*, and *Geonica*, Homer's *Iliad* and *Odyssey*, the poetry of Hesiod, Tyrtaios, Sappho, Alkaios, Solon, and Pindar, the plays of Aeschylus, Sophocles, and Aristophanes, Plato's *Republic* and other dialogues, Aristotle's *Politics* and *Nicomachean Ethics*, Xenophon's *Oikonomikos*, and Seneca's *De beneficiis* and Cicero's *De officiis*. Material artifacts, such as urban excavations and numismatics, are also interpreted. Each chapter's author attempts to illustrate the leading edge of research and discussion in the economic component of a tradition's thought. Some are specifically designed in tenor to reflect an analytical perspective; others, a tighter treatment of existing texts.

Many of the chapters stem from the explicit request to give the *status quaestionis* of a specific area of ancient economic thought, issued for a conference at Massachusetts Institute of Technology in 1994. The conference, organized by O.F. Hamouda and B.B. Price, was intended to bring together the small but currently active group of scholars across the range of interest and research activity in ancient economic thought. In many respects it was a meeting of long-standing, well-published acquaintances whom circumstances had not otherwise brought together recently. It proved to be such an overwhelmingly successful response to the proposed opportunity to give and hear cutting-edge papers, that the decision to publish some of the papers, complemented by the research of others unable to attend or "discovered" during the conference, seemed most appropriate. The following chapters are thus the product of much thought, formal and informal discussion, some ruthless editing and careful rewriting.

The chapter by Professor of Economics S. Ambirajan of the Indian Institute of Technology in Madras, "The concepts of happiness, ethics, and economic values in ancient economic thought", opens the volume. Ambirajan sets forth a cross-cultural thesis for the earliest chronology in the collection. It concerns the essential interconnectedness of happiness, ethics and economic values as three aspects of human existence. The author postulates that their interconnectedness stems from the predicament perceived by ancient philosophers and poets of having to determine on the societal scale, thus "ethically", to what level individual material demand for goods, i.e. "economic" expression, was to be restricted to mere subsistence, to "happiness", or to extreme pleasure or abundance, in the early material cultures between 3000 BC and AD 500, in which the insufficient supply of the virtually uncontrollable physical environment made scarcity and distribution prime concerns. The systems of ethics, whether religious

2

(for example, Vedic, Upanishadic, Christian, Buddhist, or Jainist), philosophical (for example, Socratic or Aristotelian), or legal (for example, Roman or Manu, etc.) which developed, according to Ambirajan, to bring about orderly, stable economic organizations, all, quite understandably, embraced the precept that a level of defined or controlled material well-being is the highest material good to which human beings should strive. By both Greek and Indian philosophers, good, right, just and virtuous pleasures of the body, which must be left behind at death, were distinguished, however broadly, from the higher goals of the soul, "light", wisdom, heaven, bliss, and immortality. Ambirajan observes that across all ancient cultures, hedonistic advocates in search of extreme forms of pleasure appear to have been relatively few, and selfishness is presented as the confusion of body for true Self.

Ambirajan discusses, alluding to Greek and Roman models, the complex relationship of ancient Indian religious beliefs and ethical practices as constructs for the framing of standards for defining the ends and means of happiness and for the dissemination and/or codification of morally correct ideas and acts. He draws attention, amidst the prayers and sacrificial instructions of the earliest Indian writings of the Vedas and Upanishads, to references to correct behaviour. In subsequent historical periods, ethical codes, stating dos and don'ts and the qualities of the righteous, become more detailed and legalistic on the subject of *dharma*, the path of virtue enjoined by authority or conscience, and the requirements for an ideal, civilized and moral state of humanity. Dharma texts, as law codes, describe duties for each caste, for each life stage, and for different religious ceremonies, as well as rules about food, women, property, levirate, sin and penance. Buddhist and Jain writings offer systematic ethical teachings.

Again with reference to the Greeks, specifically to the presentation of Aristotle's economic ideas on household management, scarcity, and justice as the notion of sharing one's wealth, within his politics and ethics (and likewise, briefly, to medieval Christian thought), Ambirajan depicts Indian philosophers' economic ideas as similarly a subset of their ethics and politics. With legal sources, instead of a written tradition of philosophical discourses, ancient Indian economic thought appears somewhat formulaic on the four traditional Indian facets or ends of life. Ambirajan closes, however, by noting that none the less, good and bad, desire which provides the motivation for all action, operative or imperative self-restraint, and social and individual well-being are all addressed. The most prominent Indian "lawgiver" texts, the *Mahabharata* and *Arthasastra*, among his concluding textual examples, are thus described as emphasizing stress conservation, sharing and prevention of the injustice to which human nature is seen to be all too prone.

In Chapter 2 of the volume's opening section on ancient Indian economic thought, Kishor Thanawala, Professor of Economics at Villanova Univer-

sity in Villanova, Pennsylvania, focuses exclusively on the work with which
Ambirajan's discussion ends, the *Arthasastra*. As the starting point for his
chapter "Kautilya's *Arthasastra*", Thanawala applies Schumpeter's distinction between contributions in the history of economic thought and
contributions in the history of economic analysis to the fifteen-part Sanskrit work, *Arthasastra*. Like Spengler, whose 1971 original and insightful
interest in the *Arthasastra* first gave it importance in the eyes of historians
of economic thought, Thanawala directs his attention to those portions of
the *Arthasastra* that are relevant from the point of view of the history
of economic ideas. He has the advantage of the availability of the newer,
1963 presentation of the text by R.P. Kangle, who as its editor, translator
and commentator, attributes it with almost complete certainty to Kautilya,
advisor to the Indian king, Candragupta, and dates it to *circa* 320 BC.

Thanawala prefaces his discussion, reflecting that since most forms of
early Indian literature arose out of theology, any discussion of the history
of Indian economic thought must take into account its religious aspect.
He thus complements Ambirajan's discussion of the allied content of economic and religious ideas with an argument based upon the contextual
source of Indian economic thinking. For example, as explicitly noted in
the *Arthasastra*, economics is classified as one science, along with "reasoned
investigation of good and evil", "politics", and "philosophy". Referring to
discrete sections in the *Arthasastra*, Thanawala quotes numerous passages,
sometimes rephrasing them into simpler, non-literal translations of the
verse, to convey both the author's descriptions and views on seven different
topics pertaining to economic thought.

For his section on "The economy", Thanawala extracts texts reflecting
on the constituents of the economy, agriculture, trade, and cattle-rearing,
as well as the need for wealth in order to create more wealth and the role
of government or the King in the economic affairs of the country. A next
section, "The treasury", is replete with passages revealing the ancient
author's recognition of the importance of the treasury in economy management. In his section on "Economic administration", Thanawala provides
illustration of the significant degree of state control over the Arthasastrian
economy with lengthy, extracted descriptions of the responsibilities of
economic officers. For the section on the "Salaries of (State) Servants", the
author of the *Arthasastra* is cited as discussing the principles on which
salary structure for the various officers, explained in terms of cash payments although paid in kind, should be determined. Thanawala's next
section on "Rules and regulations" is a collection of some of the frequent
references in *Arthasastra* to the duties of the King (or government) toward
the people as well as similar rules and regulations governing activities of
several economic groups: artisans, weavers, washermen, metal workers,
physicians and actors. The last section (Section 15) of *Arthasastra* deals

with methodology, and so also does Thanawala's last brief section of extracts.

Thanawala closes his survey of the economic ideas in the *Arthasastra* with two general conclusions already alluded to in choice editorial comments and in the sections on administration, and rules and regulations. First, the economy as described in the *Arthasastra* is completely dominated by the state. Second, there is an implicit assumption by Kautilya, suggested by the large number of incentives and penalties prescribed in *Arthasastra*, that individual behavior could be controlled to a significant degree through economic rewards and penalties and that especially incentives can modify behavior insofar as it influences economic activity. Thanawala returns full circle to the title of *Arthasastra*, literally translated as "the science of wealth", to ponder the scientificity of its economic thought. While rejecting any attempt to see in *Arthasastra* systematic explanations supported by empirical data to provide rigorous, deductive theories of human economic action, Thanawala does conclude with the ironic reflection that for all its discussion of economic ideas, historians of science, such as George Sarton, have perhaps seen more of value in the work than economists other than Spengler, something which Thanawala's chapter is clearly intended to rectify.

Part II of this book is devoted to Hebraic economic thought. In Chapter 3 Professor Emeritus of Economics Mark Perlman of the University of Pittsburgh opens the section with his perspectival discussion entitled "Looking for ourselves in the mirror of our past: with what does economics cope? and the differences in the Jewish and Christian rationales for handling usury". With an eye to elaborating a past historiography focused on the differences between two separate elements in Western cultural tradition, the Hellenistic and the Hebraic, Perlman examines two parts of the pathway to the merger of the two strains of ideas into today's Western economic thought. His first part is found in the two contrasting traditions of analyzing the critical opening challenge in the Book of Genesis, human survival outside the Garden of Eden. The different interpretations turn on two exegetical questions: what was the sin of Adam and Eve? and what was the punishment? Accepting the pluralism of answers that the sin was something combining (1) the inability to follow directions, (2) a willingness to be tempted, (3) greed, (4) an inability to leave well enough alone, and (5) excessive curiosity, Perlman sees as well much lurking behind the answer to "what punishment?", "considerable pains and few pleasures". For him it is tied to two paradigms at the heart of the economics discipline: the Christian Hellenistic "scarcity" (the forced allocation between preferences) from Plato and Aristotle, noted by Ambirajan as predating even the Greeks, and the Hebraic "uncertainty" (the forced push beyond reason to opinion) of Maimonides. A corollary or lesser paradigm from the Christian tradition involves the individual as unit of account and the empirical observation of individual choice, from which, if one pushes into the modern era, have been derived economics' paradigmatic concepts of subjective individualism and materialistic utilitarianism. Perlman sees the general role of faith in knowledge addressed through a third group of economics paradigms: one geared to stable ethical imperatives, a second related to methods of testing for "truth", and a third confronting theological treatments of problems. Perlman finds the presence of these four sets of paradigms in virtually all areas of dominant economics today: welfare, individual choice theory, institutionalism, ethics, and theory-testing methodologies.

Perlman examines a second part of the pathway to the merger of Hellenistic and Hebraic ideas into today's Western economic thought, the grappling with specific issues, such as the treatment (and definition) of usury from two perspectives, the theory and the practices of market performance. He notes that in the Hebraic treatment, although usury was forbidden, by the biblical Books of Exodus, Leviticus and Deuteronomy, to be taken from those within the Peopledom of Israel, the history of the Jews clearly suggests that it was realized from early on that total prohibition would bring the economy to a standstill. Even during the period of the Talmud, the need for market interaction clearly dominated market practices and led to a theoretically interpreted loosening of the law. Perlman parallels the post-Talmudic period efforts in further loosening the anti-interest principle to similar evasion attempts by the Christian Fathers. He concludes that their differences can not be associated with the practical ways evasions were realized, but rather with the envisaged exploitation expressed in the actual prohibitory terms. Both, he emphasizes, the Christian Hellenistic logical reasoning for personal morality and the Hebraic sociological concerns for intra-group responsibility, are part of today's synthetic economic thought.

The second paper in the section on Hebraic economic thought, Chapter 4, opens by declaring itself a poor fit! Professor of Economics at The Hebrew University of Jerusalem, Ephraim Kleiman denies the value of any identification of a body of economic thought as ethnic Jewish or Hebraic. He adopts instead a classification under the rubric of Rabbinic economic thought, the study of the economics of the Hebrew Bible by Rabbinic authors in the Mishna by Post-Destruction of Tannaitic scholars, in the *Gemara* of later Amoraic Scholars, in homiletic literature of the *Midrash* books and the Mesopotamian *Geonica* or *responsa*, as well as in distillates, such as the works of Rashi and Maimonides. Beginning with Sombart's high praise of the economic ideas in the Talmud, Kleiman attempts to explain and to start to rectify the fact that although ancient and medieval Rabbinic economic thought entered the mainstream of Western economic thought, just as Perlman argues, due perhaps rightly to its inaccessibility and sheer volume it has received little analytical attention.

Kleiman concludes that there are inherent reasons for the Rabbinic literature not to yield an understanding of economics as a cohering system, in the facts that, since Palestine and Mesopotamia during the most prominent periods of Rabbinic literature were agricultural economics of endogenous provisioning, they had little comparative contact with and intellectual stimulus from other types of economics, and that the views expressed in the literature are the product of a social group never saddled with confronting the problems of macro-economic governance. He goes on, however, to assert that these are different grounds from the reasoning depicting the ancient and medieval economies as overly simplistic and of phenomena too commonplace to produce analysis, which scholars have used in the past in ignoring Rabbinic economic thought. Kleiman proposes a three-part methodology to do justice to the economic ideas within the vast Rabbinic literature: (1) decide on a list of basic concepts; (2) having distinguished between mainstream Rabbinic literature and the rest, study the mainstream, supplementing it with the thought of the periphery and opposition; and (3) try to establish the scope and detail of the literature's treatment of the selected concepts. Kleiman illustrates his proposed methodology with the example of the concept of usury (which also figures in Perlman's discussion), (a) as interest, (b) as a catalyst to the search for an absolute standard of value, (c) in connection with the notion of opportunity costs, and (d) in relation to extended ideas on compensation. He surveys ideas pertaining to each part of the list running through the mainstream from the Old Testament Leviticus' ban on usury to the Tannaitic and Amoraic commentaries and responsa. Due to the lack of research on Rabbinic economic thought in the post-Talmudic or medieval period, a brief section is devoted to speculation on just how a transfer of ideas into and throughout medieval Europe might have occurred at the interfaces between Jews and Gentiles. Kleiman turns in the end to the Renaissance and Nissim da Pisa (1507–1574) and Abraham Farrisol of Ferrara (b. 1451) for examples of marginal authors with strong views about usury and for testimonies to the transmission of Rabbinic thought through the Middle Ages and beyond.

Chapter 5 by Bertram Schefold, Professor Doctor of Economics at the Johann Wolfgang Goethe Universität in Frankfurt am Main, "Reflections of ancient economic thought in Greek poetry" opens the three-chapter section on Greek economic thought. Some of its ideas were presented at a session organized by B.B. Price at the 1994 International Medieval Congress in Leeds in a paper entitled "Aristotle as Systematizer of earlier Greek economic ideas". Schefold had already completed and published a much larger discussion of the earliest Greek economic thought (Schefold 1992). This volume includes a version of that article translated by Courtney Shiley and B.B. Price.

Schefold begins with a historiographic discussion, in which he queries whether it makes sense to draw upon literature for the thoughts of ancient Greeks on their particular economic circumstances. His aim is to establish affirmatively that from even the oldest Greek texts a clear picture of the ancients' economic life and a better understanding of the economic problem(s) they were trying to resolve can be acquired. He proceeds to trace various economic topoi in classical Greek poetry. He sees the poetry neither as the reflection of a developed economic theory nor as a systematizing device for unordered pieces of economic learning. He does, however, view it, as one might any form of ancient Greek art, as conveying directives, in this case, of economic life.

Greek poetry is set both in contrast and in symbiosis with Greek philosophy, particularly the works of Plato and Aristotle which present a systematic, though not a causal, economic analysis of the economy, state, and society, but also, to show philosophical variety, extracts of the pre-Socratics, who also express the economic ethics of Greek classical society. Schefold suspects the pure representativeness of Plato and Aristotle because their philosophical understanding of economics appears limited when set within the course of contemporary Greek economic history, in which are seen more money-economy and capitalistic activities than would be suggested by the philosophers' teachings about the collective life of the stably provisioned extended autarchic household in a politically and culturally autarchic polis. Schefold uses some quantitative details of the known economic realities in Athens during the height of its influence as a touchstone, contenting himself, however, cautiously with a representation of the Attic economy as a system of production by self-employed freemen, slaves, and paid workers, all enabled by the market.

Among the topoi and reports of economic happenings Schefold traces back to Homer's *Iliad* and *Odyssey*, Hesiod's *Works and Days*, Tyrtaios, Sappho, Alkaios, Solon, Pindar, Aeschylus, Sophocles, and Aristophanes are the individual household (from which Aristotelian politics takes its starting point), based at its core on agricultural self-sufficiency; profiteering, or the customary limits on the collection of wealth (of all the ideas of Greek economic philosophy the most clearly expressed in the Homeric epics), according to the maxim of "endeavour to live, rather than to live well"; devotion to the carefully made product (the artisan as the holy hero of Greek economic thought); and the idea of fair exchange, based on the maintenance of an ordered society (translated philosophically into Aristotle's concept of reciprocity as a part of right, and not as a part of rank and separated from right).

In conclusion, Schefold notes that it is a different exercise to look forward through early Greek literature to measure the achievements of Greek philosophical thinking in the area of economics rather than to look backward beginning with the modern conception of theory creation. Instead of ending up with a glass empty of utility theory and market self-

8

regulation, the thirsty will find a glass full of economics as ethical rights and duties.

Chapter 6, the second to address Greek economic thought, this time in a more breezy "modernizing air", is by Louis Baeck, Professor of Economics at Katholieke Universiteit Leuven. Since from the end of the nineteenth century a vast amount of scholarly research and studies has been published on the economic thought of ancient Greece (some of which has been referenced by Schefold in the previous chapter), Louis Baeck starts his analysis with the reminder that from about five thousand years ago, the Mediterranean region became the cradle to a number of civilizations, an earliest one of which was the classical Greek culture of humanized arts and philosophy. He prefaces his exposition of that culture's contribution to economic thought with a historical theory tracing the launching, by a spiritual and intellectual élite, of a re-interpretation of older ideas or a new tradition of thinking through four processes: (1) thematization, manifest in any intense wave of formulating fundamental themes, such as in treatises provoked by the crisis of the Athenian city state of the fourth century; (2) codification, whereby the results of thematization are formalized in written language; (3) institutionalization, in which institutions become the vehicles of an intellectual current, such as early medieval Latin monasteries for the Neoplatonic-Augustinian synthesis; and (4) canonization, the selective process of text-stabilization and theme-focusing.

Since Baeck sees Greek scholars as the first to write extensively on problems of practical philosophy, i.e. ethics, politics and economics, he asks in his chapter, "Greek economic thought: initiators of a Mediterranean tradition", by way of introducing the agenda of Greek economic thought, why and how the genre of *"peri oikonomias"* came to the fore in the fourth century BC in Athens. He concludes that from the critical mass for polemic debates and from deeper analyses, three major strands of economic discourse evolved: (1) essays on efficient, but gentlemanlike or honourable estate management, more particularly on the development of the natural economy, with emphasis on agriculture; (2) treatises on politics, ethics, social justice, economic value, exchange relations, the intermediary function of money, and on the practice of usury; (3) public debates and essays on the public economy, fiscal administration, and on the mobilisation of human and physical resources for the budgeting of the city state, and that several main schools of thought arose: the Socratic with written ethical norms for the city state, as in Xenophon's *Oikonomikos*; the Platonic, deriving from Plato's own original and penetrating chapter on the genesis of the state, emphasising the material base of society (*Republic*, 369b–371e); the pioneering Aristotelian from Aristotle's synthetic *Politics* on the political regimes of the Aegean and his practical *Nicomachean Ethics* with its keen focus on just behaviour; and the matter-of-fact Stoicism of Zeno, relayed into the Middle Ages through the Roman rhetorician, Cicero, and the pan-Hellenism of Isocrates.

Throughout the balance of his chapter, Baeck follows the legacy of the Greek economic tradition, its schools and modes of discourse, through subsequent cultural transformations in the Mediterranean: Roman, Islamic (from 750 to 1250) and Latin medieval. In his discussion of Islamic economic thought Baeck highlights the scholars al-Farabi (873–950), Ibn Rushd (1126–1198), and Ibn Khaldun (1332-1406), and the influence of *kalam* or scholastic theology on Greek discussions of a fluctuating money standard in service of commensurability, as well as on exchange relations generally. He turns lastly to the Latin West from its eleventh-century urban and economic revival on, to trace Greek impact on medieval practical philosophy and moral theology.

Chapter 7, by Murray C. McClellan, Professor of Archeology at Boston University, also traces the seminal role of the ancient Greeks, both as a source of inspiration in the development of economic theory and as a subject for scholarly inquiry by economic historians. As his title, "The economy of Hellenistic Egypt and Syria: an archeological perspective" reflects, however, his is an archeological approach with its historiographic starting point in the transformation of modern scholarship on early economic activities and economic thought by the epochal studies of ancient Greek and Roman economies of Sir Moses Finley and his predecessor at Cambridge, A.H.M. Jones. McClellan notes that in recent years the dialectics of scholarship fostered by Classical historians and archeologists have sought particularly to modify, if not to overturn, some aspects of Finley's model of the ancient economy. His chapter addresses the contributions that archeological evidence can provide in the reconstruction of economic activities and economic thought within the Hellenistic kingdoms of the Ptolemies and Seleucids. Archeology has real analytic value, he believes, in its potential to provide insights into what the Annales school has termed the *conjonctures* and *mentalités* – environmental, social, and economic constraints that operate on an extended time-scale.

He prefaces his exposition by noting that it is due in part to the dearth of archeological evidence and our incomplete knowledge of the pre-Hellenistic presence in Egypt and Syria that written documents have naturally loomed large in reconstructions of the economies of the Hellenistic world. The question of "Hellenization" itself – that is, the degree to which the indigenous peoples of Egypt or Syria absorbed Greek cultural patterns – has dominated scholarship. The traditional picture of the Greeks maintaining their culture in almost complete separation from the surrounding milieu of Egypt or Syria is now rejected by modern researchers, although no unanimity reigns in alternative explanations of how the Ptolemaic or the Seleucid economy functioned or the extent to which Greek settlers imposed their culture on their surroundings.

McClellan's perspective as an archeologist allows him to perceive potential avenues to finding conducive evidence for consensus. Already, evidence of Seleucid policy to promote trade and commerce, and establish settlements designed to control trade routes to the east, is being sought at Ai Khanoum in Afghanistan and Failaka in the Persian Gulf. An increase in the agrarian base and a shift in the mode of agricultural production during the Hellenistic period is being so born out by archeological sites, that with future palaeo-ethnobotanical studies there will be no reason to doubt there was an intensification of settlement and agriculture in Seleucid Syria. Excavation of urban centers may show new cities laid out on Greek lines as an intentional policy of the Seleucid kings. Numismatic finds from coin hoards and controlled excavations could help ascertain the role that money played in Ptolemaic Egypt. Establishment of a set of archeological traits characteristic of Greek or Egyptian ethnicity could probe further the interactions among Greeks and native Egyptians in the social and economic life of Ptolemaic Egypt. Evidence, not apparent in the papyri, of general economic activity could be interpreted in connection with policy statements to reveal perhaps an independent Egyptian network of production and exchange, taxed but not organized by the Ptolemaic bureaucracy. McClellan, in true *status quaestionis* fashion, concludes that much evidence still awaits unearthing.

This volume could not pretend to encompass ancient economic thought without at least one chapter devoted particularly to Roman economic ideas. The contribution by Professor Gloria Vivenza of the Universita of Verona, "The Classical roots of benevolence in economic thought", Chapter 8, does just that. Her study is the result of work she began a few years ago, starting from the intention to retrace the intellectual and historical background of the use of the term "benevolence" in economic contexts. In this portion of the research she has focused exclusively on its Greek and Roman roots, so important for their implications on economic as well as moral and political issues. Vivenza sees the origins of "economic" benevolence, as understood today, as more rightly attributable to beneficence than to benevolence. The classical approach to benevolence took into consideration the (beneficent) fact and put it in relation to a return (even if only of gratitude), not usually thus considering the ensuing benefits, charitable actions. Over time benevolence came to relate both to *euergesia/beneficium* (*beneficentia*), and *eunoia/benevolentia*, i.e. both to the fact and the intention.

Much of Vivenza's discussion is devoted thus to the different Greek and Roman understandings of the good deed, *euergesia/beneficium* (good deed), which has also received much attention in anthropological interpretations of ancient history. The economic historical setting is the victualling of the big towns or cities in the ancient world, such as Athens and Rome, about which a lot of evidence has survived. Vivenza asserts that, since the victualling of the ancient city was not a sort of public assistance, but rather a measure of civic administration, it involved, almost on equal ground, landowners having corn reserves, politicians (for example, a rich man who benefits the city while exercising a magistrature) and merchants (acting perhaps as private benefactors out of personal generosity), all of whom would draw from their actions valued rewards. For the merchant or trader (a profession scarcely appreciated in ancient society), a return for "saving" a whole city, such as the right to own land or exemption from taxes, was extremely desirable.

The virtue of beneficence seems in Greek antiquity to have come to encompass the feature of obligation: the rich man *had* to benefit both city and friends, whether through *proxenia* (a public hospitality or patronage, frequently representing the interests of a foreign community), or the "euergetic" *philia* of a bilateral relation between a powerful benefactor and a needy antagonist. The concept of *philia* entailed sentiment, although both Plato and Aristotle saw it as directed to action and potentially exercised by means of money, body, knowledge or speech. Since the benefactor was always in a position of superiority in relation to the benefited, the "beneficial" or utilitarian friendship had complex rules for returns, especially when related with family or hospitality connections, some of which allowed for its extension well beyond the economic realm to the point of presenting worship as the only possible return. Once the epithet *euergetes*, alone or coupled with *soter* (great or victorious), came, together with other "human" adjectives, to be applied to gods and vice versa, "for a man, to benefit others was a way to be divine", *euergesiai* took on a non-economically reciprocatable character that contributed to its shift toward a more abstract meaning.

In the Roman concept of beneficence, Vivenza sees emphasis on both a vertical and horizontal character of the relationship, in which the "patron" gives a *beneficium* and the "client" gives, in return, an *officium* or *gratia* and where public and private aspects are difficult to distinguish. This relation was "vertical", i.e. between unequal parties, and on a voluntary basis. As a "horizontal" relationship, it reflected a growing awareness, especially in the political and philosophical reasoning of Cicero, of the generalized human capability of collaboration in social relations. Vivenza records an ultimate shift of the beneficial perspective towards a specification of the difference between a "vertical" economic transaction with euergetic character, and a normal "horizontal" contract, which, having an impersonal character, put the contracting parts on the same level.

Chapter 9, "Assumptions, economics and the origins of Europe", by Alan E. Samuel, Professor of Classics at the University of Toronto, forms a fitting conclusion to this volume. Stimulated by the American Historical Association presidential address of 1987 by Katherine Fischer Drew, in which she complained of a tendency of historians to concentrate on detail at the expense of the larger view of events affecting the broad scope of history in the Western world, Alan E. Samuel has taken up the challenge. Unlike other historians also tweaked by the assessment, who were willing to consider exclusively ideas, rather than also material conditions, as playing the critical role in the evolutions and revolutions in human experience, Samuel risks running against the tide in his discussion, attempting, in terms of the material categories which inspired the arguments of Henri Pirenne, to locate the "change" from the Roman to the medieval world in Carolingian times and posing his questions in the terms Pirenne used to frame the issue. What, he asks, was the phenomenon which made life in Western Europe different after the Roman patterns were no longer in effect?

Samuel, as a Classics scholar, was already adjusted to the almost negligible data available for the fifth century BC in Greece, or even Ptolemaic Egypt, and felt confident that the comparatively plentiful intellectual and material sources of the Late Empire would offer the possibility to see how the effects of material culture on ideas, or, more accurately, on mental assumptions, played their part in generating economic and political decisions which ultimately remade the world of the Western Roman Empire. That the world of Francia in 900 was dramatically different from the Gaul of 400 is readily acknowledged. It is precisely the inability to assert a smooth, invisible transition in Northwestern Europe from the fifth to the eighth century that prompts the assertion of "change". Thus Samuel has tried here to move beyond the casual observation of change to respond to the need for greater specificity as concerns its causation.

Samuel believes that seeing the cause, as Pirenne had, in "the extent of trade" ought to be treated with scepticism, particularly since virtually all of the evidence in the form of reconstructions of economic activity and the purposes behind it ignore some fundamental questions: if the supposed trading existed on the large scale proposed, and if there was a trade-generated inflow of silver to Western Europe in Merovingian and early Carolingian times, who carried it on, and who got the money? Through these questions, his discussion focuses on several ostensibly contrasting characteristics of late Roman and Carolingian society: their involvement in trade, their use of money, and their conception of the role of the urban setting. In the case of trade Samuel concludes that actual evidence for long-range trade in Carolingian times is not so different from that of earlier times. As for the use of money as the root of social change, Samuel asserts that the segment of economic activity accounted for by the goods exchanged for money remains small, as a percentage of overall volume and value, throughout the Roman and early medieval periods. He sees instead the decline of antiquity's cities as the identifying difference between the Roman era and what followed. The early medievals did not see towns as centers of importance for trade, taxation, and public display as had the

Romans, and thus they let them decay. Samuel concludes that the disappearance of all cultural and economic activity which depended upon the existence of towns and cities is the major index of a change, and the absence of Roman assumptions of the economic benefit of their existence was the cause in bringing about the social and political changes associated with the beginning of medieval society.

Samuel's chapter thus introduces the Middle Ages at the close of this volume, which is most appropriate for more than one reason. First of all, it closes the collection of chapters here chronologically. With the Middle Ages, the context of ancient economic thought ceases to exist. A number of the chapters here strengthen this assertion with their examples. To make it further undeniable, this volume is complemented by another, devoted exclusively to medieval economic thought (forthcoming from Routledge). Together they will offer a very complete picture of current research and its findings on the existence, substance and context of ancient and medieval economic thought.

Of course, no amount of research (or editing), can preclude readers finding shortcomings in scope or insight in any volume's ideas or their presentation. It will be very clear upon reading this collection that no one thesis is promoted throughout, nor any one current of ideas traced through its entire history of transmission. This leaves the volume open, of course, to an assessment of lack of cohesion, uniformity or completeness in its focus. Better this, however, than a possibly stultifying historiographic or theoretical dogmatism. It is only hoped that any perceived lacks are accepted as part of the growing pains of the area of research and perhaps even as part of this volume's actual goal, to stimulate the reader to question, probe and pursue further assumptions and conclusions already formulating in the field of ancient economic thought.

The editor would like to thank all the contributors for their eagerness to figure in this volume. Their serious enthusiasm for the conference, the publication, and the aim to foster interest in further research in the area of ancient economic thought will be well remembered. Each has contributed significantly to the collection. The discussants of the conference papers, Professors Charles M.A. Clark of St Johns University, New York and Paul A. Heise of Lebanon Valley College, Pennsylvania also receive our thanks; their comments both during and following the gathering were very helpful in enhancing the quality of our endeavour. Our thanks extend as well to the Massachusetts Institute of Technology and the current Dean of the School of Humanities and Social Sciences, Professor of History, Philip Khoury, and the Undergraduate Research Opportunities Program, under whose auspices the initial conference and the volume's editing were made possible. Without the enthusiasm and help of Professor O.F. Hamouda of York University, Toronto, and Visiting Fellow of MIT in realizing the conference and in continuing his astute guidance in the preparation of this volume, neither would have come to pass; his part is formally acknowledged here with sincere appreciation. Thanks as well go to Alan Jarvis, Economics Editor at Routledge, for his strong support of this collection of esoteric ideas, and the production staff, including Sarah Brown and Alison Elks, who have brought it into print. Any difficulty the publisher has had in extracting the volume from my desk is not due in any way to reluctance on the contributors' side, nor to a lack of industry on the part of the manuscript's voluntary editors. Grace Kim and Christopher Yang worked unfailingly into many a long night of proofreading, Courtney Shiley honed her German to English translation skills, and Tony Celano standardized the Greek transliterations. In closing it is noted that there are, of course, scholars who were unable to contribute within this publication's timeframe, and their omission can only be regretted now and rectified in the future with the promise of more conferences and publications dedicated to the subject.

Part I

INDIAN ECONOMIC THOUGHT

1

THE CONCEPTS OF HAPPINESS, ETHICS, AND ECONOMIC VALUES IN ANCIENT ECONOMIC THOUGHT[1]

S. Ambirajan

INTRODUCTION

The three words in the title of this chapter, namely happiness, ethics and economics, signify different things, yet have strong interconnections. Happiness is essentially an affair of the individual self, a peculiar characteristic flowing from the emotional or spiritual experience and capacity of the individual, albeit influenced by external circumstances. Ethics, on the other hand, is normative and deals with conduct. Ethical norms prescribe the right conduct for individuals so that they can relate well to their fellow human being, individually and collectively. As the *Encyclopaedia of the Social Sciences* puts it: "Ethics is the organisation or criticism of conduct in terms of notions like good, right or welfare" (1931: vol. V, 602). In this sense, ethics is concerned not merely with actual conduct, but with conduct as it should be, i.e. ideals. Economic values involve the understanding of economic phenomena in addition to "the opinions and desires" (Schumpeter 1954: 38), concerning the way human beings organize their material, as opposed to spiritual life.

Although at first glance all three deal with seemingly unconnected things, there is the undoubted fact that throughout human history, people in their day-to-day living have been concerned with all these three aspects of existence, and have seen them all as parts of a whole. This nexus did not emerge suddenly, as it were. One has to be aware of a chronological sequence, i.e. concepts of happiness leading to ethical principles which in their turn influenced the structure and content of economic values. These issues have been discussed by philosophers separately for reasons of convenience, although their interconnectedness in actual life was understood by close observers. Classical Indian metaphysics, of course, went further and saw every aspect of existence as part of a unifying force. Thus, Sri Aurobindo, the foremost Indian philosopher in recent times, states:

19

the idea of transcendental unity, oneness, and stability behind all the flux and variety of phenomenal life ... is the pivot of all Indian metaphysics. ... And this unity, stability, unvarying fixity which reason demands, and ordinary experience points to is being ascertained slowly but surely by the investigations of science.

(Sri Aurobindo 1972: vol. XII, 1)

Even without entering into any deep philosophical speculations one can see clearly that a large intersecting set exists involving the three entities (happiness, ethics and economic values) and their relation to human existence. The nature of the economic organization determined – most certainly in the early stages – to a large extent the nature of economic thinking. During the early epochs (circa 3000 BC to AD 500), both in the East and the West, the production and exchange of material goods were uncomplicated affairs. The economy was basically composed of self-sustaining autarchic units. As custom determined most of the activities (including economic), there was hardly any scope for individual initiative. The slow progress in technology and capital accumulation, if any, also resulted in a restricted availability of consumption goods.

As material prosperity was essentially determined by nature, any minor differences in attitudes towards economic life could be explained by a reference to the physical environment. For example, in Greece, when an early writer, Hesiod, was speculating, the physical conditions with which he was familiar (notably the "inhospitable slopes of Mount Helicon") led him to discuss in detail the habitual scarcity and how one kept oneself from hunger and privation through the expenditure of relentless human effort.[2] But in the ancient Indian situation, with the inhabitants living in the fertile river valley areas blessed with copious periodic rains, the concerns were different. Unlike Hesiod, who accused the gods of keeping "hidden from men the means of life", the Rigvedic poets fervently prayed to their gods (especially the rain gods) to be regular and benign:

> Give us not as a prey to deaths, to be
> destroyed by thee in wrath,
> To thy fierce anger when displeased. ...
>
> (I. 25. 2)

> Waters which come from heaven, or those
> that wander dug from the earth, or
> flowing free by nature,
> Bright, purifying, speeding to the ocean, here
> let those waters, goddesses, protect me.
>
> (VII. 49. 2)[3]

With control over production being limited to one's physical labor and

20

propitiating gods,[4] distribution occupied a prime position in the thinking of ancient philosophers and poets because scarcity due to famine, floods or disease was always a possibility, even in fertile lands. Also, Marshall's dictum of the insatiability of wants was as much true in ancient times as it is for our times. That individuals desired the material and sensual things of life, which could not, however, be supplied in abundance to all given the state of technology, was a fact of life. When supply could not be increased, the demand had to be regulated in the interest of saving society from confusion, anarchy and disorder. No wonder then the quest was for order, fairness, and justice.

In this quest, the first task was to restrict demand for material goods. This was done by emphasizing the happiness to be derived from non-material things. But how to make the individual restrict his pleasures? That had to be accomplished by ethical systems which could provide both individual and social ideals to strive for. Economics in its turn was to provide the nitty-gritty of rules to achieve the restriction and fair distribution of goods in consonance with the ethical systems, in addition to providing directions as to how best to increase output under the difficult circumstances. Thus one can see how the three, happiness, ethical ideas and economic thinking were interconnected, and why the views on these subjects held by thinkers of the ancient world have to be seen in this light.

HAPPINESS

The Sanskrit exhortation made during almost all rituals in India means: "Let everyone fare well". This is but a weak translation, for the original *Sarve Janah Sukhino Bhavantu* cannot easily be translated, since the word *sukha* may mean pleasure, happiness, well-being, welfare and a lot more. All we can say is that it was for mankind a comfortable state to aspire for. This word is the opposite of *duhkha*, meaning sadness, deprivation, unhappiness and a lot more. The English words given as meanings for *sukha* and *duhkha* are not all synonymous: for example, one can be "happy" in a state of inebriation, but that may not be tantamount to one's real well-being. However, the ultimate aim of our economic activities has something to do with *sukha*, that is to say, as a result of all the labour, people should feel happy or fulfilled, or get a sense of well-being, or an amalgam of all three.

The idea that pleasure/happiness is the highest good that human beings should strive for was widely prevalent in the ancient and medieval worlds. Every one of the Greek thinkers had subscribed to one or other variants of this view. The ideas of Epicurus are well known, but he was not alone. There were others like the not well-known Callicles and Antiphon who also believed in this doctrine of the pursuit of pleasure. Great philosophers like Socrates, Plato, and Aristotle, not identified as Hedonists or Utilitarians as such, also believed in happiness as one of the goals, if not the ultimate one, of human existence. Even Stoics, popularly believed to be votaries of pain, were only indifferent to pain or pleasure and not against happiness *per se*. Much later, the foremost Christian theologian, St Augustine, was not against happiness if it could be achieved; only that, according to him, life was misery and happiness was impossible. The later medieval Christian theologian, St Thomas Aquinas, who had achieved a synthesis of Aristotle and Christian doctrine, held that *beatitudo* was the natural goal for human beings, even as Aristotle thought of *eudaimona* in similar terms.[5] Both these words are translated usually as "happiness" although they involve somewhat more, just as *sukha* does in Sanskrit.

Similarly, ancient Indian thinkers felt that happiness should be the ultmate goal for human beings. They thought in terms of pleasure (*priti*), happiness (*sukha*) and bliss (*ananda*). Pleasure was a desirable *rasa* or sentiment, as against other disagreeable experiences such as pain, desire and so on. Out of the four ideals (*Purusharthas*) posited by the Classical Indian world-view, *Dharma*, *Artha*, *Kama*, and *Moksha*, the last three involve the above-mentioned pleasure, happiness and bliss.

It is, of course, not difficult to understand why individuals everywhere in the past and present have preferred happiness, and think of it as the ideal to aspire to. It is, simply stated, a preferred mental state by definition, for even a masochist is "enjoying" pain, since *that* to him is happiness! What kind of happiness or pleasure should be the ideal? It is when we move from the comfortable all-purpose happiness/pleasure/well-being to the actual task of defining these in individual cases that all of our economic and philosophical problems arise, which is why there is so much difference of opinion. The most awkward of all these questions is: "Can there be happiness without pleasure?"

The one noticeable characteristic that cuts across national boundaries is that those who hold an extreme form of pleasure as the ultimate goal of human life seem to be few. In the Greek tradition, for example, we have an odd thinker like Callicles whose view was:

> luxury, wantonness and freedom from strength, constitute excellence (*arete*) and happiness; all the rest is fine talk. . . . Natural goodness and justice decree that the man who would live rightly must not check his desires but let them grow as great as possible, and by his courage and practical sense be capable of gratifying them to the full.[6]
>
> (Guthrie 1988: 105)

This type of hedonism, identifying unhampered individual pleasure with the good, has its counterpart in ancient India too. There were individuals who belonged to the so-called heretic sects like *Caravakas* and *Lokayatas* (*circa* 600–300 BC), who firmly believed that "*kama* or the fulfillment of desire" was the "*summum bonum* of human life" (Shastri 1969: vol. III,

178ff.).[7] At a later stage, material advantage (*Artha*) was added to this ideal of pleasure seeking. The droll *Kama Sutra* is but a treatise based on refined hedonism which seems to have had some following in the post-Buddhist era.

These exceptions apart, happiness did not mean something without definition or control, as it was realized that happiness was too general a concept. Aristotle had said, "when it comes to saying of what happiness consists, opinions differ", although everyone agrees that it should be the supreme good (Aristotle 1955, trans Thomson: 29). Even Epicurus, the so-called originator of unbridled hedonism, was not such a diehard pleasure-monger. As Drakopoulos points out, the Epicurean hedonism was more "of an enlightened hedonism" because it identified happiness with peace of mind (Drakopoulos 1991: 16). He distinguished between kinetic, or temporary, pleasures, and catastematic, or long-lasting pleasures, which ought to be the goal of human life.[8] Perhaps Plato had in mind a distinction like temporary and permanent pleasure when he went to the extent of claiming pleasure to be an actual enemy of happiness. Actually, it has been said that Epicureans, no less than Cynics and Stoics, were aware of the "need for spiritual liberation" (*Encyclopaedia of the social Sciences* 1931: 568). The spiritual liberation could be interpreted as transcending even pleasure and pain. Plato in his *Republic* (Book IX) makes a distinction between positive pleasure and positive pain, and seems to prefer a neutral restful state in between. The Epicureans similarly said that the highest stage of happiness is to be acquired, not by chasing fugitive pleasures, but by a neutral state of tranquility.[9]

The Greek philosophers were quite clear about the existence of good, right, just and virtuous pleasures and those that were not. They believed that the individual's happiness achieved by any means whatsoever was not acceptable if it failed to ensure social happiness. Even a Hedonist like Antiphon was clear in his mind that one man's pleasure should not go against another's happiness. In Guthrie's summary:

> One must plan to get the maximum pleasure and minimum of suf-
> fering from our brief and imperfect existence, and this could not be
> achieved in a completely anarchic society, where everyone was free
> to act on the impulse of the moment, and assaulted his neighbour at
> every opportunity.[10]

> (Guthrie 1988: 290)

The happiness an individual could enjoys, would be (a) external, (b) of the soul; and (c) of the body, should be good and long lasting.

The Indian philosophers seemed to have made a distinction between happiness in relation to the body and to the soul, in other words, happiness secured through material goods and services, and happiness as a result of non-material spiritual endeavours. The question to be asked is: which is the preferable and according to what standard of "better"? The thinkers of ancient India drew a distinction between the Good and the Pleasant, as the *Kathopanishad* says:

1 One thing is the good and quite another thing is the pleasant, and both seize upon a man with different meanings. Of these whosoever takes the good, it is well with him; he falls from the aim of life who chooses the pleasant.

2 The good and the pleasant come to a man and the thoughtful mind turns all around them and distinguishes. The wise chooses out the good from the pleasant, but the dull soul chooses the pleasant rather than getting of his good and its having.[11]

It is argued that, although these two are quite opposite to each other, they do not appear to many humans as being such. More intelligent people realise quickly that both cannot be pursued simultaneously for any length of time. Since the Vedic times in India, people have expressed their hankering after material things. There are many passages in the Vedic texts (the most ancient in the Indian context) referring to the search for material things, such as grain, cows, horses, chariots, gold and so on. But one must also remember that Vedic hymns are not only poetry but mystic poetry at that, and were perfected over a long process of meditation and reticulation. Therefore one has to be careful in interpreting them literally in terms of latter-day perceptions. As Jeanine Miller has said:

Uninspired translation, wholly missing the point of Vedic imagery which though it may appear mixed up yet shows consistency in significance, have given countenance to the erroneous idea that the Vedic rsis prayed only for material prosperity.

(Miller 1974: 112)

On the contrary, mortals are asked not to attach much importance to material wealth, but to aspire only to "light, wisdom, heaven, bliss, immortality". We need not go to the other extreme and suggest that the only concern of the people in the Vedic period was a non-material spiritual quest. It may have been so for the sages who composed the hymns, but ordinary people had to live, which was something well understood by the seers of the Vedas. They felt that man could indeed live a good and happy life, and did not need to seek an escape from this world. They emphasized the "wholeness of being, resulting from communion bringing about right living and subsequently all the boons of well-being, abundance" (Miller 1974: 118)[12] implied in the Vedic prayer: "Grant us those riches that cause prosperity for all" (*Rig Veda*, I, 79, 9 in McNicol 1938). The thinking of the Upanishads which came after the Vedas (*circa* 1000–500 BC) was similar. These authors said that happiness based solely on material goods was not attainable. The parable of Nachiketas in the *Kathopanishad* makes this clear:

23 Yama (God of Death) to Nachiketas: "Choose sons and grand-sons, choose much cattle and elephants and gold and horses; choose a mighty reach of earth and thyself live for as many years as thou listest"

25 Yea, all desires that are hard to win in the world of mortals, all demand at thy pleasure; lo these delectable women with their chariots and their bugles, whose like are not to be won by men, these I will give thee[13]

This is flagrant enticement and Nachiketas's reply is significant:

26 These things last till tomorrow, O Death, for they wear out this vigour of all the senses. Even the whole of life is short. Keep they horses, keep dance and song for thyself

27 No man can be made happy by wealth. Shall we possess wealth, when we see thee?

(McNicol 1938: 243)

Apart from the fact that man cannot enjoy these pleasures when he is dead, is infinite happiness possible at all in the living state? Summarizing the *Ishavasyopanishad*, Sri Aurobindo said:

so long as the difference between I and you exists, hatred cannot cease, covetousness cannot cease, war cannot cease, evil and sin cannot cease, and because sin cannot cease, sorrow and misery cannot cease. This is the eternal maya that makes a mock of all materialistic schemes for a materialistic Paradise upon earth. Paradise cannot be made upon the basis of food and drink, upon the equal division of goods or even upon the common possession of goods, for always the *mine* and *thine*, the greed, the hate, will return again if not between this man and that man, yet between this community and that community.

Then what should one do? The answer is to see oneself as an integral part of the society:

To see your Self in all creatures and all creatures in your Self – that is the unshakable foundation of all religion, love, patriotism, philanthropy, humanity, of everything which rises above selfishness and gross utility.

Selfishness was nothing but mistaking the body for the Self, and seeking its gratification in the form of "a gross narrow and transient pleasure, instead of the stainless bliss" of one's true Self (Sri Aurobindo 1972: Vol. XII, 484–485). Thus by emphasizing the "Self" as well as de-emphasizing the material basis of the individual, Indian philosophy of the ancient times pointed towards what Gopalan calls the "individual-in-society" approach. Thus classical Hindu ethics avoided the two extremes, i.e. considering society to be all-important, and over-emphasizing the importance of the individual by overlooking the effect society has on individual development (Gopalan 1979: 55).

The Vedic and Upanishadic texts determined the thinking of almost all later thinkers, philosophers and lawgivers, and these ideas, though set in deeply philosophical language, did percolate to the ordinary masses as well. Whether they consciously practised them or not, simple living remained an ideal even for the common man. Much later, as we approach the Gupta period (*circa* AD 320–540), references to luxuries and items of consumption increase, but only in connection with kings and merchant princes. For the common man, purity and simplicity remained the ideals. When Hiuen Tsang, the seventh century AD Chinese pilgrim visited India, he found that even Kshatriyas and Brahmins were clean-handed, unostentatious, simple and frugal in their lives. People lower in the socio-economic scale would not have been any different.[14]

HOW TO ACHIEVE HAPPINESS: ETHICAL SYSTEMS

Once it is granted that human beings cannot and should not purely pursue happiness egotistically, and that some conditions should be attached to the pursuit of happiness, ethical and moral systems start developing. Ethical systems arise because of the conviction that there is a genuine moral code – of divine or transcendental origin – ready to be discovered by philosophers. Ethical systems, or moral philosophy as it soon came to be called, sought to give general guidance regarding human behaviour, i.e. what to seek, what to do and how to relate to others. There is a vast body of writing – both in the West and the East – to show how human beings should lead a purposeful life. Whereas in ancient Greece it was in the form of philosophical texts, in India it was in the form of epics, hymns and sacred literature, all with one unique purpose – to make the individual realise his duties, potential and role in the society. In short, their aim was to tell man how to live out his life.

A question arises about the complex relationship of religious beliefs and ethical practices in ancient India. These two no doubt mutually interact but their origins are different. A religious system has to have three components, namely: a mystical experience which takes place at an emotional plane, a philosophical system that intellectualises the above, and finally a set of rituals. In this sense there were numerous religious sects, although differences were not significant. Even when reformist sects such as Buddhism and Jainism introduced substantial points of departure in philosophical tenets and forms of ritual with the rest, at the level of day-to-day living, followers of all the religious denominations believed in broadly similar ethical practices.

Invariably, the earlier writings generally tended to confine themselves to broad statements about good and bad, right and wrong. With the passages of time, and recognition of the complexities arising within societies, more specific dos and don'ts began to appear. One has only to compare the work of thinkers such as Plato, Aristotle, and Socrates, to the later parish-priest type of advice given during the early Christian period.[15] This is even more glaring when we compare the early Vedic and Upanishadic writings with the later *smritis*, *Dharmasastras*, Buddhist and Jain texts (*circa* 600 BC to AD 300)

Socrates was the first to understand the need to analyze the meaning of ideas such as good, right, just, and virtuous as well as the necessity to frame standards for defining these ends and means. Whereas Plato aimed at finding timeless ideals, such as prudence, justice, wisdom and fortitude, Aristotle tried to marry these with what was practical. Again and again, they all stressed right action, just laws, and virtuous character, as the means to achieve individual happiness and social well-being.[16] Their real aim was to change the crude and vulgar ideas they knew people held about happiness. They believed in distinguishing a hedonistic type of happiness that pleased their own self and the eudaemonistic type of happiness that stressed a life worth doing. Aristotle was sure that the goal of studying "the science of conduct" was to ensure that individuals would behave well in society. As he said, "it is not enough to know about goodness; we must endeavour to possess and use it" (Aristotle 1955, trans. Thomson: 309).[17] To make it clear, Aristotle lists twenty-seven vices to be avoided and fourteen virtues to be cultivated.[18] As Guthrie elaborates, Aristotle's practical aims are "inculcating good habits, of parental upbringing and good laws, including a system of punishments" (Guthrie 1981: 399).

While Greek thinkers seem to have felt that wide dissemination of what is good would result in the acceptance of morally correct ideas, the Roman view was to codify what was right in the form of legal systems.[19] The early Christian works on ethics also prescribed what is correct and what is wrong without any question of ambiguity. In India, during the early period when States had not yet come about, the dissemination of good ideas through preceptors was prevalent. In the later period (*circa* post 300 BC), systematic law codes were prepared to say what should be and what should not be done.

Amidst the thicket of prayers and sacrificial instructions, one does find in the earliest Indian writings references to correct behaviour. Among the ideals of living, charity received maximum support. Nowhere do we find accumulation of property castigated as a vice, but it was considered sinful not to share one's riches with others. The *Rig Veda's* advice is clear on this point:

27

The gods have not ordained hunger to be our death: even to the well-fed man comes death in varied shape.
The riches of the liberal never waste away, while he who will not give finds none to comfort him.

The man with food in store who, when the needy comes in miserable case begging for bread to eat,
Hardens his heart against him – even when of old he did him service – finds not one to comfort him.

Bounteous is he who gives unto the beggar who comes to him in want of food and feeble,
Success attends him in the shout of battle. He makes a friend of him in future troubles. . . .

All guilt is he who eats with no partaker.
(X, 117, 1–6. in McNicol 1938: 30)

The Upanishads that followed the Vedas were preoccupied with finding the Self, and with meditation and abstract speculation, although ethical precepts are also mentioned in passing. Take, for instance, the first stanza of the Isa Upanishad: "All this, whatsoever moves on earth, is to be hidden in the Self. When you have surrendered all this, enjoyment results. Do not covet the wealth of any man". The only place in the Upanishads when an individual is systematically advised about proper conduct of life is in *Taittriya Upanishad*, where the preceptor tells his departing student:

When the Master has declared Veda then he gives the commandments to his disciple. Speak truth, walk in the way of thy duty, neglect not the study of Veda. When thou has brought to thy Master the wealth he desires, thou shalt not cut short the long thread of thy race. Thou shalt not be negligent of truth; thou shalt not be negligent of welfare; thou shalt not be negligent towards thy increase in thy thriving.[20]

Once we move from the period of the Vedas and Upanishads, societies become complex, states are formed, the material basis of civilization is developed, and the ethical codes become more and more detailed. The Dharma*sutras*, and Dharma*sastras* associated with many lawgivers like Manu, Baudayana, Brihaspati, Katyayana, Gautama, Narada, Yajnavalkya, and others give very minute instructions as to daily life.[21] To give an example of the detail one finds in the texts:

Interest from money-lending paid at one time should not exceed double (the Principal), but on grain, produce, fleece, or draught animals it should not exceed five times (the Principal). Excessive interest above the customary rate is not legal, and they call this the path of money-lending; a man has a right to five per cent. He should not take interest that extends for more than a year or that is not recognized, nor compound interest, periodical interest, forced interest, or corporal interest.

(*The Laws of Manu* 1991, trans. Wendy Doniger: 168–169)

Some of them are very comprehensive as, for example, Bhatta Lakshmidhara's *Krtyakalpataru*, which expounds the "public and private duties of man" from birth to death (Rangaswami Aiyangar 1941: 27). Apart from these legal texts there are the Itihasas (Epics), the *Ramayana* and the *Mahabharata*, which contain detailed ethical statements. In *Mahabharata*, not only is there the *Bhagawat Gita* (the most influential of ethico-religious texts), but also a whole section, Santi Parva, which is nothing but advice on how people should organize their lives. Similarly, there is *Yogavasishta*, another philosophical-ethical text, full of similar advice. In addition to these, the reformist sects, like Buddhism and Jainism, produced detailed ethical manuals.

The literature is extensive but, in general, while the theory was that the *Srutis* (Vedas) were the ultimate source of all *Dharma*,[22] in practice it was the *Smritis* (legal texts) that became the ultimate authority on *Dharma*. The acceptance of the various *Smritis* by the common man was not mandatory.[23] The *Smritis* give general guidance to people and their rulers. The various legal texts were written by different people and at different times. The texts and their commentaries were used on particular occasions to arrive at decisions for specific problems.

While they all talked broadly about what they considered to be requirements of a civilized and moral state of what should be, they were not identical. The problem created by the existence of numerous legal codes was compounded by the different positions taken by the commentators of the original texts. If conflicts arose, which advice should be accepted was a question that worried many. Some attached importance to Manu, the most famous of all the law givers, but then which of his commentators should be followed? There were many of them, the most important being Medhatithi, Kulluka Bhatta and Govindaraja. Others suggested that a majority opinion from among the texts should be given credence. A third view suggested that which is "reasonable" given the times.

What should be noted here is that though the *Dharmasastras* are important, they were not static. The Indian law thinkers felt that *Dharma* should change with times, although some ideas were considered eternal, and accepted by everyone at all times. As Surendranath Dasgupta points out, barring minor variations, the "goals of life, their attitude towards the world, and the means for the attainment of the goal" are the same for all Indian ethical-philosophical systems. They all agreed "upon the general principles of ethical conduct which must be followed for the attainment of salvation. That all passions are to be controlled, no injury to life in any form should be done, and that all desire for pleasures should be checked" (Dasgupta 1922: vol. I, 77). What the right kind of behaviour is has been stated in terms of both the dos and don'ts, in addition to defining the qualities a righteous person should possess.

All the lawgivers believed in the caste system, which divided society in terms of hierarchy, ritual purity and exclusive duties. While not identical, since they differentiated individuals in a society according to birth, this was no different from Plato and Aristotle who also did not view all individuals in society as identical.[24] When the Indian lawgivers prescribed the duties and ideals of behaviour, specific injunctions were given to different caste segments. The duties were clearly demarcated, although some exceptions (*apadharma*) were allowed under extraordinary circumstances. For example, the Parasara Smriti declares that even *Brahmanas* could take up agriculture or trade if the circumstances dictate. By and large, there was a very real distinction between *Swadharma* (duties specific to the caste of which the individual is a member) and *Sadharanadharma* (duties that are universal in scope and eternal in nature that are obligatory for all).[25] The duties themselves are given in terms of *acara* (rites), *Vyavahara* (dealings) and *Prayaschitta* (expiation).

The law codes (*Dharmasutras* and *Dharmasastras*) describe the duties of the four castes, four stages of human existence, the different religious ceremonies (*Samskaras*) individuals have to go through, rules about food, women, property, levirate, sins, penances, and many more matters. In some cases, the public duties of castes are also highlighted. For example, there are detailed descriptions of the duties of monarchs, and rules relating to taxation, ownership, guardianship, inheritance, partition, monetary transactions, punishment for various crimes, and the way to utilize witnesses. Similarly, how one should conduct one's affairs within the caste is also discussed in great detail.

Quite apart from the specific injunctions (*swadharma*) to kings, commoners, learned scholars, women and other such groups, which at times border on the ridiculous, there are also the duties and ideals (*Sadharanadharma*) intended for everyone. The following is a tentative list, although every lawgiver has his own preferences.

1 To be controlled:

attachment	(*raga*)
antipathy	(*dvesa*)
ignorance	(*tamah*)
anger	(*krodha*)
pride	(*mada*)
jealousy	(*matsarya*)
lust	(*kama*)

greed   (*lobha*)

2 Virtues to be cultivated:

determination	(*vairagya*)
self-denial	(*Tapas*)
compassion	(*Daya*)
charity	(*Dana*)
purity	(*Shaucha*)
peace of mind	(*shama*)
restraint	(*dama*)
learning and knowledge	(*Vidya*)
patience	(*titiksha*)
self-adjustment	(*samadhana*)
steadiness	(*dhairya*)
forgiveness	(*ksama*)
truthfulness	(*satya*)
sincerity of mind	(*anupadha*)
non-injury/free of cruelty	(*ahimsa*)
forbearance	(*Santi*)
freedom from backbiting	(*apaisunyam*)
sweet speech	(*Priyavadita*)

Buddhist and Jain texts also attempt a systematic presentation of ethical teachings. Tachibana lists seventy-nine vices to be avoided as stated in the Buddhist canon. While many of them are repetitive, vices like covetousness, hatred and ignorance, come under different names. There are other injunctions against killing, stealing, committing adultery, lying, drinking alcohol. The positive virtues are to be encouraged and cultivated such as determination, ethicality, truthfulness, voluntary relinquishment of pleasures, patience, equanimity, generosity, loving kindness and wisdom (S. Tachibana, *The Ethics of Buddhism*: 73, cited in Dasgupta 1922: vol. II, 496–498). The Jaina ethics, too, are not dissimilar, except that non-violence occupies a central place. The Jain texts urge the aspirant to acquire humility by freeing him and herself from eight types of arrogance: (1) the possession of intelligence; (2) the ability to conduct grand types of temple worship; (3) noble family; (4) caste; (5) physical and mental strength; (6) magical powers; (7) Tapas or Yoga; and (8) the beauty of one's person. Besides this, the individual must practise *ahimsa*, *satya*, *asteya*, and *brahmacharya*, i.e. be free from cruelty, untruth, theft, unchastity and avarice. But in this list *ahimsa* (free of cruelty) overrides everything else (Chakravarti 1969: vol. I, 431).

In conclusion, the ancient Indian texts all proclaim the path of virtue or righteousness called *Dharma*. While the lawgivers have explained and specified the nature of *Dharma* in abundant and excruciating detail, it was understood that one should not depend upon them alone over and above the individual's conscience. As K.V. Rangaswamy Aiyangar pointed out, *Dharma* is "Whatever is enjoined by authority or the inward promptings of conscience" (1941: 26).

From the point of good behavior – although not in terms of philosophy, history or eschatology – there is a similarity to the codes of behaviour devised by Greek philosophers, Christian theologians or Indian lawgivers. One has only to compare the list given above with the Ten Commandments of Moses, the seven immortal Christian virtues (faith, hope, charity, justice, prudence, temperance and fortitude), or the four cardinal virtues of Plato (justice, wisdom, temperance and courage) to see that everywhere many of the same virtues have been encouraged and the same vices condemned in an effort to ensure an orderly and happy world.

ECONOMICS AS A SUBSET OF ETHICS

An interesting parallel between ancient Greek philosophers and the Indian lawgivers is that they both considered the study of economics as a subset of ethics and politics, as all of them were deeply concerned about the ultimate ideal of man, and his achievement of true happiness. Taking Aristotle first, as Guthrie has stated, "Ethics and politics (to give his words their established translation) constitute for Aristotle one continuous study which he calls the philosophy of human life" (Guthrie 1981: 331). In Aristotle's scheme, the issue of happiness and the pleasure/pain dichotomy are so vital to human life that the disciplines of ethics and politics are intimately connected. As he said, "In a word, moral virtue has to do with pains and pleasures" (Aristotle, 1955, trans. Thomson: 59).

Economics is an integral part of human life and almost all of Aristotle's writings on economics are to be found in his *Politics* and *Ethics*. While one can extract some analytical fragments and claim that he was the distant forerunner of this or that aspect of modern economic theory, it is doubtful whether theorizing was his central aim. Barry Gordon correctly observed that Aristotle's purpose in writing these two works was to help the "reconstruction of the existing social order which will salvage what he sees as valuable in the disintegrating structure of Greek civilization" (Gordon 1975: 24).[26] Such was indeed the ultimate aim of ancient Hebraic thinking as well. As Meir Tamari points out, one should not search for "economic theories in Judaism but rather for a code of economic conduct (Tamari 1979)". The main concern of the ancient Hebrew thinkers was not to understand the economic mechanism *per se* but to see "that it remained within the ethical and religious conceptual framework" (Tamari 1979).

The basic aim of Aristotle, and indeed of all other early economists, was to study household management and provide rules to tackle scarcity. They were certainly not trying to propound laws of economics. In a perceptive essay, Kurt Singer pointed out that the *"nomos"* part of *Oikonomia* (composed of *oikos*, meaning estate or household, and *nomos*) does not refer to law, but simply to the act of managing (Singer 1958: 29ff.). Ancient societies faced very serious scarcities, and during the period 800 BC to AD 400, different thinkers tried to solve the problem in different ways.[27] The Greek philosophers recommended moderation in matters economic, but more specifically, through the acquisition of wealth (Aristotle), or the reduction of the demand for goods (Epicurus) (Spiegel 1971: chapter 2). Both Plato and Aristotle realized that wealth was necessary, but only to "furnish foothold and room for the practice of virtue". Indeed they were convinced that the "progressive increase of wealth in a people" is "evil rather than good" (Bonar, 3rd ed. 1922: 47).

From the idea of moderation comes Aristotle's development of the concept of justice which enshrines the notion of sharing one's wealth.[28] This is because, for the sake of efficiency, gradation in society becomes necessary, and once gradation exists, it is necessary to prevent tyranny and exploitation of the weak. Plato, for example, thought that when a society is organized hierarchically, everyone is part of an ordered scheme, and can specialize to do his best. Yet we find profound concern expressed in his *Republic* about the possible unhealthy consequences. Hence his statement: "a man may neither take what is another's, nor be deprived of what is his own" (Plato, 3rd ed., 1936, trans. Benjamin Jowett: I: 433). Even without the notion of gradations, Christian theologian-economists understood the need to reduce the unequal distribution of wealth, to increase the general welfare of everyone concerned through "incorporating ethical judgements in their economic ideas".[29]

Mainstream medieval Christian thinking, represented by St Thomas Aquinas, while desirous of keeping in check unrestricted desire for material goods, did not go to the extent of some of the extreme positions – held for example by St Francis of Assisi about the total sinfulness of pursuing any kind of material prosperity.[30] A whole range of ideas associated with the economic thought prevalent in the Western world until the end of middle ages dealt with the changing of human action either through the dissemination of ethical/economic behaviour, or through specific directions and legal codes. Ideas about just price, usury regulation, private property, monopoly, profit making, etc. were developed as normative instructions to reduce the rigours of economic privation and dampen the individual's naturally selfish motives. In this sense, economics was but a handmaiden of ethics.

In the Indian tradition, economics and ethics are even more closely intertwined. A digression is necessary when we try to compare classical Western ideas on economics with ancient Indian thinkers' conclusions on the same subject. If Schumpeter could dismiss Aristotle as a mere purveyor of "more than slightly pompous commonsense" (Schumpeter 1954: 57) despite solid ethico-philosophical texts like the *Nicomachean Ethics* and *Politics*, one wonders what epithets he would have used to damn the simple sounding *sutras* contained in the various *Arthasastra* and *Dharmasastra* texts?

Students of ancient Indian economic thought regret the absence of the type of written tradition of philosophical discourses like those of Plato and Aristotle. Spengler, writing in general about ancient economic thought, says:

> Because we lack treatises such as Aristotle's, when dealing with extended periods we are limited in our understanding of the changes in economic thinking and practice that may have accompanied political and cultural change – information we have respecting Athens and Greece.
>
> (Spengler 1980: 30)

If we had such treatises, we would have an inkling of the speculative process by which certain conclusions were arrived at. The absence of such discussions does not mean that speculation and reasoning were lacking prior to the actual composition of the codes of behaviour. The absence of such philosophical texts in prose is explained by the prevailing oral tradition which communicated knowledge to succeeding generations. While the script system was well developed, it was also widely known that written materials could not be preserved for very long periods except when inscribed in stone tablets or copper plates. Palm (or Cadjan) leaves which were used for writing had a limited life. If sayings had to be memorized, they must not only have a systematic arrangement but also be brief and pithy. Hence materials were in the form of poetry (based on rigorous rules of composition and metre), or in the form of *sutras*. These, of course, are the end products of much reasoning, argumentation and discussion. This explains the lavish praise often heaped upon terse statements. The couplets of Thiruvalluvar (circa 50 BC to AD 50), for example, were described by a contemporary poetess Avvaiar as an achievement similar to boring a hole in the atom to make it a receptacle to hold the seven seas.

Many of the classical Indian writings on ethics, economics, law or philosophy are somewhat like mathematical theorems whose proofs have not been written out. Hence we have to work out how and why these terse statements came about either in the form of poetry or *sutras*. This is not easy, partly because of the inherent difficulties of fathoming the minds that considered these issues millenia ago, but also because of the numerous interpolations that have taken place since their original composition. Learning in the classical Indian style meant learning to memorize texts. This was not a mechanical process, because in the process of the rote learning, the meaning and context of the portions were explained with detailed cross-referencing. Everything was done from the teacher's memory.

In the very early days the authors of the texts were themselves teachers, and hence it is likely that they also gave the reasoning behind the terse statements to be memorized, as a sort of key to what was taught.[31] After a few centuries, the *sutras* remained intact but the explanations and context had been lost. Herein lies the origins of commentaries which, in their turn, often interpreted the sutras in line with the commentators' biasses.

The traditional ends of human life, *Dharma* (righteous living), *Artha* (material well-being), *Kama* (enjoyment of sensual and artistic things), and *Moksha* (freedom from the birth–death cycle) all go together, and enjoyment of a full life was thought to be impossible without any one of the above ends. Of these, *Artha* occupies a key position in human life. Like Aristotle, Kautialya, the foremost economic thinker of ancient India, treated economic topics along with political matters in his *Arthasastra*. Another source of ideas on economic matters was Santi Parva of the *Mahabharata*, the epic wherein advice concerning the accumulation and distribution of wealth was interspersed with advice on how to run a country.

While ancient Indian thinkers discussed the four facets/ends of human life distinctly in separate treatises, they knew quite clearly that these ends were in no sense totally autonomous. Thus one can find references to ethical well-being in treatises exclusively intended for the study of *Artha* or *Kama*. The sheet anchor of life was *Dharma*, which included codes of socio-economic relationships, and this is why "there is so little literature in the early period devoted exclusively to the discussion of political theories or economic ideas" (Maitra 1969: vol. V, 335). Even *Arthasastra* of Kautilya, supposedly a work uninfluenced by moral considerations because of the presence of many amoral policies at times bordering on the criminal, has a strong ethical element which comes through in many of its economic and political policy suggestions. K.V. Rangaswami Aiyangar has pointed out that to distinguish

> between Arthasastra and Dharmasastra on the plea that the former deals with real-politik and the latter with ideals, overlooks the fact that when judges and parties shared the same ideals, as expressed in smritis, ideals were translated into action, and that there was an idealistic element in Arthasastra.
>
> (Rangaswami Aiyangar 1941: 24)[32]

These ideals were "part and parcel of ideas concerning social well-being, whether this was to be achieved through the conduct of the individual or through the conduct of the king" (Maitra 1969: vol. V, 335). At the end of his treatise, the author of *Arthasastra* states categorically: "This science brings into being and preserves spiritual good, material well-being and pleasures, and destroys spiritual evil, material loss and hatred".[33] This treatise was composed during the time when Indian society was becoming increasingly complex, and political units were being formed when the methods of wealth gathering came into conflict with other objectives of human existence. Consequently, new rules were necessary to iron out the contradictions.

While discussing ancient Indian economic thinking, there is an avoidable confusion. In the fourfold classification of human ends, the second category, namely *Artha*, is translated as wealth. It has been variously described as wealth, profit, property, riches and so on. From Vedic times onwards, the word *varta* was in vogue to describe economics. We know that Aristotle used the word *Oeconomia* to describe household cum agricultural management, as explained by Kurt Singer on the basis of etymology. Similarly by looking at its etymology and usage, it is *varta* that comes closest to Aristotle's *Oeconomia*. K.V. Rangaswami Aiyangar and R.P. Kangle point out that the word *varta* comes from *vrtti*, meaning profession or livelihood, which at that time consisted mostly of agriculture, animal husbandry, handicrafts and barter.[34] When *Artha* is used in the fourfold classification of man's ideals, it is simply interpreted as the satisfaction of human (non-spiritual) desires. In this sense it involved attainment of riches, prosperity, matters relating to business and so on. In his *Kama Sutra*, Vatsyayana defines *Artha* as acquisition of arts, land, gold, cattle, riches, equipages, and friends. He also uses it to refer to the protection and further development of one's material possessions (Vatsyayana 1963: 3). But when Kautalya used the term as the title of his manual, it embraced a far wider field that included every aspect of economic, social and political life, including what we would call political economy and government policy.

The lawgivers did not recommend an ascetic mode of life for everyone regardless of the individual's circumstances because every human being, according to the four-stage prescription of life, has to take *Sanyasa* (the ascetic mode) in his old age anyway. Before he reaches that stage in his life, he has to go through three stages, all of which required ample resources to live in a purposeful way. The three stages, namely *Brahmacharya* (childhood and learning), *Grihastya* (household), and *Vanaprasta* (renunciation while still living as a householder), have to be gone through in one's life before one plans to renounce the world totally in preparation for the final stage of liberation (*Moksha*). During these first three stages, a person cannot entirely forsake income-generating and wealth-accumulating activities.[35] Indeed Dharmasastras advocate punishment to the householder by the State if he leaves his parents, wife and children in the lurch by seeking Sanyasa or renunciation.[36]

The teacher specifically advises his pupil (as we saw earlier) to ensure his well-being (*Kusala*), at the end of his *Brahmacharya* stage, which includes physical welfare as well. Material possessions are essential for the performance of a person's duties as a householder, such as keeping the household fires burning and contributing to charity. Any deliberate cultivation of poverty, except by a class of holy persons seeking the ultimate transcendent truth, was considered sinful. Thus the *Mahabharata*: "Poverty is a state of sinfulness.... From wealth springs all religious acts, all pleasures, and heaven itself, O, King! Without wealth, a man cannot find the very means of sustaining life."[37] Again and again, in both the sacred and secular writings, we see references to the need to cultivate riches, but with the proviso that it must be done by virtuous means. In the Vana Parva of the *Mahabharata*, it is asserted: "The individual seeking pleasure without virtue and riches will not last long, like a fish that happily indulges in the pleasures of swimming till the lake dries up. Hence men of wisdom understand that pleasure can arise only with virtue and riches." It goes on to say that riches are rooted in a virtuous life, while virtue cannot be practised without necessary wherewithal. The relationship is symbiotic, like that of monsoon and rain. A king or a householder has to cultivate virtue, riches and pleasure without going to extremes. While earning an income and accumulating riches, the means are important.[38] There are frequent references to the importance of acquiring wealth "without disregarding the requirements of virtue" (*the Mahabharata*, rpt. 1993: vol. VIII, 367). The lawgiver Narada clearly states that when the rules of *dharmasastra* and *arthasastra* come into conflict on particular issues, the King ought to discard the dictates of the science of wealth and follow the precepts of ethics.[39]

The very way wealth was classified indicated what the ancients considered good and bad. Wealth was described as white (*Sukla*), dark-white mixed (*sabala*) and black (*Krsna*). The first consisted of "what is acquired by sacred knowledge, valour in arms, the practice of austerities ... through (instructing) a pupil, by sacrificing and by inheritance". The second set consisted of "what is acquired by lending money at interest, tillage, commerce, in the shape of *sulka* (gift), by artistic performance, by servile attendance, or as a return for a benefit conferred on someone". The third category (obviously not preferred) consisted of "what is acquired as a bribe, by gambling, by bearing a message, through one afflicted with pain, by forgery, by robbery or by fraud" (Gopalan 1979: 76). This particular classification by Narada in his *Naradasutra* was by no means universally accepted, and as Kane warns us, the "enumeration of the means of acquiring property in the dharmasastra works is not exhaustive but only illustrative" (Kane 1968: vol. III, 550, fn.).[40]

An important link in the chain connecting virtue, wealth and happiness is desire, which provides the motivation for all action. We have already seen that in general terms desire is considered a vice in the ethical writings. This is surprising, when considered with reference to *Artha*, in which desire is not condemned outright. There are passages that even extol desire as a positive virtue. The author of the *Mahabharata* puts the following in the mouth of Bhima:

As butter represents the essence of curds, even so is Desire the essence of profit and virtue. It is under the influence of Desire that the very *Rishis* (sages who renounce the worldly life to seek spiritual truth) devote themselves to penances subsisting on fruits. Traders, agriculturists, keepers of cattle, artists and artisans, and those who are employed in rites of propitiation, all act from Desire. . . . A man outside the path of Desire never is, was or will be, seen in this world.

(*Mahabharata*, rpt. 1993: vol. VIII, 367)

Thus while the mainspring of all actions – virtuous or otherwise – was desire, almost all texts that have anything to do with economic issues stress the value of self-restraint. For example, the *Mahabharata* is firm: "Self-restraint, according to all virtuous persons, is the highest virtue in the world . . ., (it is the source) of the highest happiness both here and here-after." Generally speaking, restraint refers to the accumulation of material acquisitions. The Jain texts have a word, *Aparigraha*, which is explained as:

limiting one's attachment to wealth and other worldly possessions – *parimita parigraha*. Inordinate longing for worldly goods will never result in contentment and happiness. It prevents spiritual harmony and peace in life. Hence even a householder has to reduce his wants and limit his desires, if he is to pursue his spiritual career and not be altogether lost in the world.

(Chakravarti 1969: vol. I, 432)[41]

If desire is not tempered by self-restraint, it leads to egotism and finally to destruction. Uncontrolled desire degenerates into covetousness, which can have serious consequences both for the individual and society. How the act of covetousness destroyed whole kingdoms and societies are the subjects of both the great epics of India. In the *Ramayana*, it was the act of Ravana coveting another person's wife, and in the *Mahabharata* it was the case of one prince coveting the kingdom belonging to his cousins. What it all amounts to is that, according to the general economic opinion prevailing in the distant past, economic activities were necessary for material prosperity. However, as economic activities will take place only in the presence of strong motivations in individual behaviour, considerable self-restraint was also necessary.

So much for the ethico-economic views. But the Indian lawgivers had no illusions about human nature. Both Kautilya and Manu, to name two of the foremost lawgivers, thought ordinary men were generally depraved and only too anxious to get the better of their fellow human beings.[42] Hence the ordinary citizen could be kept well-behaved only through fear or threats of punishments.[43] But Bhishma, while advising Yudhishtira on statecraft in the *Mahabharata*, is explicit:

The man armed with the rod of chastisement governs all subjects and

protects them ... (it) protects Righteousness and Profit (*Artha*). ...
Corn and wealth are both protected. ... If the rod of chastisement
did not protect people, they would have sunk in the darkness of hell.

(*Mahabharata*, rpt. 1993: vol. VIII, 25)

The economics part of Kautilya's *Arthasastra* is nothing but a manual
of public finance with detailed descriptions of economic offences and
punishments.

In conclusion it can be confidently stated that economic ideas in India
– just as in Classical Greece – dealt with the improvement of human
behaviour through teachings and legal regulations which would contribute
to the emergence of an orderly and stable economic organization. The
stress was not on the growth of the economies as such, but rather conservation, sharing and the prevention of injustice through escape from the
rigors of scarcity caused by inhospitable geographical conditions, unexpected disasters, and above all by a fickle and basically greedy human
nature.

NOTES

1 I thank Professor K. Satchidanandamurthy, Professor A.W. Coats, Professor
Betsey Price and Professor Omar Hamouda for reading and commenting on
earlier drafts. They are not responsible for what I have made of their comments
and suggestions.

2 Gordon (1975), 3ff. See also his (1963) 147ff.

3 See McNicol (1938), 4, 19. Translated from original Sanskrit, the hymns of
Rigveda were composed during 2000–1000 BC.

4 "Prayers for success in agriculture are not infrequent" in the Vedas. See Altekar
(1958), vol. 228.

5 In Aristotle's words: "Well, so far as the name goes there is pretty general
agreement (as to what is the supreme good). It is happiness, say both intellectuals and the unsophisticated, meaning by happiness living well or faring well",
(1955), 28–29. For St Thomas Aquinas' concept of happiness, see Copleston
(1955), 180–183. See also McGill (1967), chapters 1–4, pp. 1–90.

6 Guthrie's summary of Callicles's view. We must also mention Aristippus, the
founder of Cyrenaic philosophy, who saw "pleasure of the moment as the chief
happiness and end of man". See Bonar (1922), 47. See also Drakopoulos (1991),
10–12. Adam Smith also refers to Aristippus in his *Theory of Moral Sentiments*
1976: 214, 294.

7 See also for a similar view, Rangaswami Aiyangar (1965), 38–39, Debiprasead
Chattopadhyaya has argued that the Lokayatas were not crude hedonists at all.
Far from it. Their ethics suggested moral values prevailing in the popular mind
as evidenced from the Caravaka episode in the *Mahabharata*. See his (1985),
30ff.

8 For a discussion of Epicurus' ideas on different kinds of pleasures, see Mitsis
(1988), 45ff.

9 It is interesting that the "neutral state of tranquility" of the Epicureans has an
analogue in Indian sacred writings. The *Mahabharata* states, "As between hot
and cold there is a point, a state which is neither, so is there somewhere between

S. AMBIRAJAN

pleasure and pain, a point, a state, which is neither; [this] has to be diligently striven after and realized", cited by Bhagwan Das (1924), ll.

10 For a discussion of Antiphon's views on happiness, see also Havelock (1957), Chapter X.

11 First Cycle: Second Chapter 1, 2, Sri Aurobindo's translation in *Sri Aurobindo.* (1972): vol. XII, 244.

12 See also Kunhan Raja (1969), vol. I, 199ff.

13 23 and 25 are Sri Aurobindo's translations from *Sri Aurobindo* (1972: vol. XII, 242–243).

14 See Ghoshal (1954), 570ff. It is interesting to find the Chinese traveller appreciating these virtues because in China Confucian tradition also set great store by simplicity and tradition. Confucianism tended to think wistfully of the ideal conditions that prevailed during Emperors Yao and Shun, considering them worthy of emulation: "When life was at its simplest and the needs of man were fewest". In general, as Lin Yutang, a modern interpreter of ancient Chinese life says, "The Chinese ideal of happiness was ... the enjoyment of this simple rural life, together with the harmony of social relationships" (Yutang [1938], 114–115). Confucius pointed out that happiness can be independent of poverty because one can find pleasure in contentment, pride and truth. See Huan-Chang (1911), vol. I, chapter xiii.

15 This is not to deny that specific advice was totally absent. In ethical texts advice cannot be totally avoided. One does find such advice in all ethical writings. Aristotle specifically refers to adultery, theft, and murder as evils to be avoided. Epicurus asked people to live a simple life which will involve not falling in love, not mixing in politics, not enjoying the pleasures of gluttony, and suppressing excessive desires.

16 Even Epicurus argued that the pursuit of pleasure demands the "cultivation of moral virtues". See Irwin (1989), 160.

17 See also Kenny (1992), 112.

18 See Aristotle's *Eudemian Ethics* (1992) No. 1220a, chapter 3: 17.

19 It must be pointed out that Greek thinkers also had attached importance to legislation but it was the Roman tradition to codify things precisely.

20 Sri Aurobindo's translation (in *Sri Aurobindo* 1972: vol. XII, 325).

21 See Kane (1968), vol. I, part 1, for a comprehensive introduction to the study of the ancient lawgivers. See also Chandra Banerji (1962), for a briefer account. A study of law and jurisprudence becomes essential if we are to comprehend fully the ethics–economics relationship in actual life. J.J. Spengler points out correctly that "Since many ties connect the economy and the legal system, the legal system may serve as a link between ethical and economic realms" (1980), 117 fn.

22 "The conception that *Rta*, which means both natural and moral law, controls even the action of gods, belongs to the Vedas", Raju (1941), 362.

23 See Altekar (1941), 18ff.

24 There are the exceptions. Stoics in Rome and Buddhists, Jains, Tamil poets of the Sangam age and Thiruvalluvar stressed universal brotherhood rather than hierarchical stratification of society. For an interesting comparison between Roman Stoic thought and ancient Tamil doctrine, see Xavier S. Thani Nayagam's inaugural lecture given in Kuala Lumpur at the University of Malaya, *Indian Thought and Roman Stoicism* (n.d.).

25 For a discussion of these kinds of *dharmas*, see Klimar Mastra (1925), Chapter 1.

26 For a reference to others who also have claimed that Aristotle's purpose was

not to build an economic theory of the market mechanism, see Worland (1984), 108–109.

27 See Gordon (1989).

28 For a detailed analysis of the Classical Greek concepts of economic justice, see Spengler 1980, chapter 5.

29 See for one particular Christian sect's views on the matter, Karayiannis (1994), 39ff.

30 See McKee (1987), 29, 145.

31 For a very original and perceptive account of the oral transmission of knowledge and its deeper purpose, see Sjoman (1986).

32 See also Rangaswami Aiyangar (1949) He says clearly that this work is firmly in the Indian ethical and religious tradition (p. 45). D.D. Kosambi (1977: 142) gives a diametrically opposite view of Kautilya's ethics, arguing that "There is not the least pretence at morality. . . . The work remains unique in all Indian literature because of its complete freedom from cant and absence of specious reasoning".

33 The Kautiliya Arthasastra (1972), vol. II, 516. It is no less interesting to note that Vatsyayana, author of a supposedly purely hedonistic manual on erotic love, Kama Sutra, upholds religious ideals. See Vatsyayana, Kama Sutra (1883, rpt 1963) 5.

34 Rangaswami Aiyangar (1965), 12ff. Kangle writes: "The word vartta is clearly derived from vrtti, 'livelihood' – visti, 'labour', i.e., labourers. The root in the word is vis, 'to be active' ". [Kautilya] The Kautiliya Arthasastra (1986), vol. II, 9, fn. See also "Economic Ideas of the Hindus" The Cultural Heritage of India, op.cit., vol. I, 655.

35 There is a statement in Ishavasyopanishad which says "Do thy deeds in this world and wish to live thy hundred years". This passage emphasizes that "we must do our deeds in the world and not avoid doing them". You can realize the Self by being part of this world rather than running off from life to achieve salvation. For a more detailed comment, see Sri Aurobindo (1972), vol. XII, 455.

36 See Kane (1968), vol. II, pt 1, 551–559. Kane quotes from Apasthamba, a lawgiver: a householder "who abandons his faultless wife should put on the skin of an ass with the hair outside and should beg for alms at seven houses for six months" (p. 569). Sukra in his Sukraniti (a latter-day adaptation of Kautilya's opus) lays down that if a householder neglects his family, the king "should manacle him, set him on the work of repairing roads, and out of the wage earned by him by such labour give one-half to the deserted family" (cited in Rangaswami Aiyangar [1965]: 148).

37 Santi Parva, section 8. The Mahabharata (1993), vol. VIII, 12.

38 There is no clear distinction between income and wealth in the literature. Both are used interchangeably. Obvious consumer goods like an ornament or a sack of grain and productive assets such as cows or land, are treated simply as possessions to satisfy our material wants and desires. In a transitional stage from nomadic to pastoral farming, the material basis of the civilization will have to be land, labour, and capital in the form of cattle. Hence it is not surprising that invariably land, children and cattle are mentioned in the Vedas when talking about material prosperity. It is only when the regions are becoming settled through the formation of societies and states (circa 300 BC to AD 300) that we begin to hear about capital, trade and interest more frequently in the Dharmasastra.

39 Original Sanskrit version cited in Kane (1968), vol. I, pt I, 471 fn. Similar

sentiments are expressed in other texts such as *Sukraniti* (IV, 5, 44, 274), *Yagnavalkya Smriti* (II, 21), and *Agnipurana* (253, 50). See also Bal Krishna, vol. II, 639. Ancient Chinese lawgivers, like Confucius too, were clear that "when the economic life and ethical life cannot both be preserved, economic life must be sacrificed", Huan-Chang (1911) vol. I, 101.

40 See also Kane (1968) vol. II, pt 1, 130.

41 See also the comprehensive study by Dayanand Bhargava (1968).

42 In this they are in the good company of Aristotle, because he too felt that if man were not trained by habit and instruction to rise, he is depraved by nature: "he is the most unholy and the most savage of animals, and the most full of lust and gluttony. But justice is the bond of men in states, for the administration of justice, which is the determination of what is just, is the principle of order in political society." Aristotle, *Politics*, (1947), 557.

43 See *The Laws of Manu* (1991), 130. See Kane (1968), vol. III, 238ff.) for several such citations from other lawgivers.

2

KAUTILYA'S *ARTHASASTRA*[1]

A neglected work in the history of economic thought[2]

Kishor Thanawala

INTRODUCTION

Men undoubtedly behaved economically for many centuries before they undertook to analyze economic behavior and arrive at explanatory principles. At first, this analysis was more implicit than explicit, more inarticulate than articulate, and more philosophical and political in mode than economic. But in the face of ubiquitous and inevitable scarcity, the study, in various forms and for various proximate purposes, went on.

(Spengler and Allen 1960: 2)

One meaning of the Sanskrit word *Artha* is wealth. *Sastra* means science. *Arthasastra* can therefore be translated to mean the science of wealth.[3] Along with *Dharma* (moral behavior), *Kama* (worldly pleasures) and *Moksha* (salvation), *Artha*, or wealth, is one of the four goals of human endeavor prescribed in the Hindu tradition. *Arthasastra* is the title of a treatise most probably written by Kautilya and probably written in the fourth century, BC.[4] It contains fifteen parts or sections and discusses a number of topics, including a code of law as well as conduct of foreign policy. There is discussion about the way in which the economy is organized, how taxation should be arranged and distributed, how war should be conducted and how ministers should be selected. Although Kautilya presents no overt philosophy, *Arthasastra* maintains that the State or government of a country has a vital role to play in maintaining the material status of both the nation and its inhabitants.

To appreciate *Arthasastra*, it may be helpful to know something about its author and the regime in which he lived. Kautilya, also known as Canakya and as Vishnugupta, was an adviser to King Candragupta, who ruled in northern India *circa* 322 to 298 BC. He has been credited as being the person who helped the King in overthrowing the Nanda dynasty and who installed Candragupta Maurya as the King of Magadha in northern

India. He is recognized as one of the earliest Indian philosophers to write about economics and politics. "All authorities agree that it was mainly because of Kautilya that the Mauryan Empire under Candragupta and later under Asoka (reigned *circa* 265 to 238 BC) became a model of efficient government" (*Encyclopaedia Britannica* 1974: Micropedia V, 733–734).

The historian Will Durant quotes Megasthenes[5] about life in India during the reign of King Candragupta, who ruled during the years 322 to 298 BC:

> The simplicity of their laws and their contracts is proved by the fact that they seldom go to law. They have no suits about pledges and deposits, nor do they require either seals or witnesses, but make their deposits and confide in each other.... Truth and virtue they hold alike in esteem.... The greater part of the soil is under irrigation, and consequently bears two crops in the course of the year.... It is accordingly affirmed that famine has never visited India, and that there has never been a general scarcity in the supply of nourishing food.
>
> (Durant 1954: 441)

According to Durant, in the regime of King Candragupta,

> The actual direction of government was in the hands of the crafty vizier. Kautilya was a brahman who knew the value of religion, but took no more guidance from it; like our modern dictators he believed that every means was justifiable if used in the service of the state. He was unscrupulous and treacherous, but never to his King ... by his wily wisdom [he] made the empire of his master the greatest that India had ever known. Like the author of *The Prince*, Kautilya saw fit to preserve in writing his formulas for warfare and diplomacy; tradition ascribes to him the *Arthasastra*, the oldest book in extant Sanskrit literature.
>
> (Durant 1954: 443)

Our interest here is in bringing attention to those portions of *Arthasastra* that are relevant from the point of view of history of economic thought.[6] For Schumpeter, economic thought meant "the sum total of all the opinions and desires concerning economic subjects, especially concerning public policy bearing upon these subjects that ... float in the public mind" (Schumpeter 1954: 38). He further observed that "The history of economic thought starts from the records of the national theocracies of antiquity whose economies presented phenomena that were not entirely dissimilar to our own." (Schumpeter 1954: 51). Kautilya's *Arthasastra* does contain some relevant records. It has been remarked by Ghosal that Kautilya was not the first to introduce us to a new field of inquiry dealing with the "acquisition and preservation of dominion" (Ghosal 1959: 80). Kautilya acknowledged this at the very beginning of *Arthasastra*:

This single [treatise on the] Science of Politics has been prepared by mostly bringing together [the teaching of] as many treatises on the Science of Politics as have been composed by ancient teachers for the acquisition and protection of the earth.

(Kautilya 1986: 1)

Most technical literature in India had its rise in theology, just as in most ancient cultures religion tended to play a central role in a person's thinking and lifestyle. Philosophy, developed in the Upanishads,[7] was not completely dissociated from theology. Any discussion dealing with the history of Indian economic thought must take into account the religious aspect. As Max Weber noted, oriental religions are characterized by "contemplative mysticism". Central to Hinduism according to Weber is the notion of a "caste-structured world thought to be eternal and unchangeable" (Weber 1967: 3). Although it may be difficult to give an exact definition of Hinduism because it contains the influences of many cultures, there is little doubt that the early Indian scriptures described material or worldly success not only as morally desirable but also as an essential stage in a full and civilized life. The rational and systematic pursuit of gain (including material gain) was, at the very least, not inconsistent with a moral life as long as such a pursuit did not violate basic moral norms.

RELEVANT TEXTS

In Chapter 2 of Book 1 of the *Arthasastra*, we read that there are four sciences, of which economics is one:

Investigating, by means of reasoning [what is] spirited good and evil in the Vedic lore, material gain and loss in economics, good policy and bad policy in the science of politics, as well as the relative strength and weakness of these [three sciences], [philosophy] confers benefit on the people, keeps the mind steady in adversity and in prosperity and brings about proficiency in thought, speech and action.

(Kautilya 1986: 6–7)

As already noted above, *Arthasastra* contains fifteen parts or sections. Although there may be a logic to the sequence in which various topics are introduced and discussed, and although economics is an important part of the treatise, one has to read back and forth to get a clear idea about the economic system prevailing in Kautilya's times. In the following sections we bring together his description and views on different topics pertaining to the economy.

The economy

In Chapter 4 of Book 1 we are told that

> Agriculture, cattle-rearing and trade, – these constitute economics, [which are] beneficial, as they yield grains, cattle, money, forest produce and labor. Through them, the [King] brings under his sway his own party of the enemies, by the [uses of the] treasury and the army.
>
> (Kautilya 1986: 9)

The idea that one needs wealth to create more wealth is expressed thus: "Men, without wealth, do not attain their objects even with hundreds of efforts; objects are secured through objects, as elephants are through elephants set to catch them" (ibid. 419).

Kautilya's views on the role of government or the King in economic affairs of the country are illustrated by the following excerpts from *Arthasastra*:

> In the happiness of the subjects lies the happiness of the King and in what is beneficial to the subjects his benefit. . . .
>
> Therefore, being ever active, the King should carry out the management of material well-being. The root of material well-being is activity, of material disaster its reverse.
>
> In the absence of activity, there is certain destruction of what is obtained and of what is not yet received. By activity reward is obtained, and one also secures abundance of riches.
>
> (ibid. 47–48)

Although Kangle's literal translation may sound wordy, the message is clear: the government or the King should be active in managing the economy because the source of material wealth is economic activity. Without economic activity, material well-being is not possible. In the absence of an active policy, economic prosperity and increased future material well-being are endangered.

The treasury

Kautilya recognized the importance of the treasury in the management of the economy.

> The King, the minister, the country, the fortified city, the treasury, the army and the ally are the constituent elements [of the state]. . . .
> Acquired lawfully by the ancestors or by oneself, consisting mostly of gold and silver, containing various kinds of big jewels and cash,

[one] that would withstand a calamity, even of a long duration in which there is no income, – these are the excellences of a treasury.

(ibid. 314–316)

The Director of Stores should cause to be built a treasury, a warehouse, a magazine–. Presiding over bureaus of experts for the different products, he should receive gems, articles of high value, articles of small value and forest produce, whether old or new.... He should accept money certified as genuine by the Examiner of Coins. He should cut counterfeit [coins].... He should accept corn that is clean, full [in measure] and new.... For one in charge of the treasury, execution [shall be the punishment] for robbing the treasury. For those who help them, [the punishment] shall be half the fines.... He should be conversant with receipts from outside and inside even after a hundred years, so that when asked he would not falter in respect of expenditure, balance and collections.

(ibid. 72–75)

All undertakings [activities] are dependent first on the treasury. Therefore, he [the King] should look to the treasury first.

(ibid. 85)

For, a king with a small treasury swallows up the citizens and the country people themselves.

(ibid. 56)

The treasury has its source in the mines; from the treasury the army comes into being. With the treasury and the army, the earth is obtained with the treasury as its ornament.

(ibid. 110)

The army, indeed, is rooted in the treasury. In the absence of a treasury, the army goes over to the enemy or kills the king. And the treasury, ensuring [the success of] all endeavors, is the means of deeds of piety and sensual pleasures. In conformity with the place, the time and the work, however, one of the two, treasury and army becomes important. For, the army is the means of acquiring and protecting the treasury, the treasury that of the treasury and the army.

(ibid. 388)

Therefore, he [the king] should keep the power of the treasury and the army in his own hands.

(ibid. 390)

The minister should take steps in case of a calamity of the king in the following manner: – He should cause the treasury and the army to be collected in one place, in the fortified city or on the frontier, in charge of trustworthy men, also [bring together] members of the [royal] family, princes and principal officers under some pretext.

(ibid. 310)

Prosperousness of activities, cherishing of customs, suppression of thieves, control over employees, luxuriance of crops, abundance of commodities, deliverance from trouble, reduction in exemptions, [and] presents in cash, – these are [the means of] increase in the treasury.

(ibid. 85)

Hinderance, lending, trading, concealment, causing loss, use, interchange and misappropriation, – these are [the causes of] depletion of the treasury.

(ibid. 86)

Internal [hindrance] is hindrance by the chiefs, external the hindrance caused by enemies or forest tribes.... Affected by those two [hindrances] and by the afflictions as described, appropriated by chiefs, impaired by exemptions, scattered, wrongfully collected, [and] carried off by neighboring kings and forest tribes, – these are stoppages of [payment to the] treasury. The [king] should strive to prevent the afflictions from arising and to overcome those that have arisen, as well as to destroy the hindrances and stoppages [of payment] for the sake of the country's prosperity.

(ibid. 401)

Looking after income and expenditure in this manner, he [the king] does not suffer a calamity of the treasury and the army.

(ibid. 305)

Kangle's literally correct or exact translation contained in this last verse could be restated for greater impact: The king will avoid financial difficulties if receipts and expenditures are properly managed as prescribed. According to Kautilya, the receipts or revenues of the treasury are derived from a variety of sources. These include taxes and tolls, income from property owned by the state, fines as well as fees and collections. The arrangement of topics in *Arthasastra* is such that neither revenues nor expenditures are discussed under a single heading. We do, however, find verses like these:

Price, share, surcharge, monopoly tax, fixed tax manufacturing charge and penalty constitute the heads of income. What is intended for the worship of gods and manes and for charity, gifts for benedictions received, the royal palace, the kitchen, the employment of envoys, the magazine, the armory, the warehouse, the store for forest produce, factories, laborers, maintenance of foot soldiers, horses, chariots and elephants, herds of cattle, enclosures for beasts, deer, birds and wild animals and stores of fuel and grass, – these constitute the corpus of expenditure. The king's [regnal] year, the month, the fortnight and the day, thus the date-entry, the third and seventh fortnights of the rainy season, winter and summer short by one day, the rest full [and] a separate intercalary month, – this is time

(ibid. 77)

A simple, non-literal translation of the verse containing the last sentence above would read like this: "Every transaction should be recorded in the account books with the appropriate date (of the transaction)." A reason for the complex sentence structure contained in the verse is the complicated lunar calendar prevailing in Kautilya's time in India. (A variation of the same complicated lunar calendar is used even today by millions of Hindus.) *Arthasastra* also contains several chapters detailing duties of government accountants and auditors.

Economic administration

It is clear from the above discussion that *Arthasastra* presupposes a significant degree of state control over the economy. Such control would not be possible without a well-defined and efficient administration. Kautilya describes a fairly elaborate administrative machinery. More than thirty different department heads and their duties are described in the treatise. Some official titles are: Superintendent of the Treasury, Master of the Mint, Director of Trade, Superintendent of Measurements, Textile Commissioner, Controller of Alcoholic Beverages, Controller of Shipping, Superintendent of Passports and Superintendent of Prisons. To illustrate the degree of detail about the officers' responsibilities, we quote from the description about the Director of Trade:

The Director of Trade should be conversant with the differences in the prices of commodities of high value and of low value and the popularity or unpopularity of goods of various kinds, whether produced on land or in water [and] whether they have arrived along land-routes or water-routes, also [should know about] suitable times for resorting to dispersal or concentration, purchase or sale. And that commodity which may be plentiful, he should collect in one place and raise the price.... He should not create a restriction as to time

49

or the evil of a glut in the market in the case of commodities constantly in demand.... He should encourage the import of goods produced in foreign lands by [allowing] concessions.... In foreign territory, however, he should ascertain the price and the value of the commodity [taken out] and the commodity to be brought in exchange and should calculate the profit after clearing expenses for duty, road-access, escort-charges, picket- and ferry-dues, food and fodder and share. Should there be no profit, he should see if there is any advantage in taking out goods or in bringing in goods in exchange for goods.

(ibid. 127–129)

This excerpt comprises less than half of the description of the responsibilities of one officer provided by Kautilya! And he describes in similar detail the duties of more than thirty similar office-holders! It is worth noting that in the process of describing the duties of the Director of Trade, Kautilya has also indicated what he thought were some principles of fair trading:

If there is glut of commodities, the Director of Trade should sell all goods in one place. So long as these are unsold, others shall not sell [those goods]. The [agents] shall sell those for a daily wage for the benefit of the subjects. In the case of commodities distant in place and time, however [he], expert in fixing prices, shall fix the price after calculating the investment, the production of goods, duty interest, rent and other expenses.

(ibid. 262)

The Merchant should fix, after calculating their total earnings for the day, what the [sales-agents] should live on with permission. What falls in between the purchaser and the seller becomes different from what is received. With that they may make stores of grains and commodities, when permitted to do so.

(ibid. 261)

Salaries of (State) servants

There is a section in Arthasastra which discusses the principles on which salaries of the various officers should be determined:

In accordance with the capacity of the fortified city and the country-side, he [the King] should fix [wages for] the work of servants at one quarter of the revenue, or by payment to servants that enables the carrying out of works. He should pay regard to the body [of income], not cause harm to spiritual good and material advantage. The sacrificial priest, the preceptor, the minister, the chaplain, the commander-in-chief, the crown prince, the king's mother and the crowned queen should receive forty-eight thousand [panas]. With this much remuneration, they become insusceptible to instigations and disinclined to revolt. The Chief Palace Usher, the Chief of Palace Guards, the Director [of labor corps], the Administrator and the Director of Stores should receive twenty-four thousand. With this much, they become efficient in their work. The princes, the mothers of princes, the commandant, the city-judge, the Director of Factories, the council of ministers, the provincial officer and the frontier officer should receive twelve thousand. For, with this much, they help in strengthening the entourage of the master. Heads of banded troops, commandants of elephants, horses and chariot corps, and magistrates should receive eight thousand. For, with this much, they are able to carry their groups with them. . . .

The fortune-teller, the soothsayer, the astrologer, the narrator of Puranas, the charioteer and the bard, the chaplain's men and all superintendents should receive one thousand. Foot-soldiers trained in the [fighting] arts and the groups of accountants, clerks and others should receive five hundred. But actors should receive two hundred and fifty, and makers of musical instruments should receive double the wage of these. . . .

Teachers and learned men should receive an honorarium as deserved, a minimum of five hundred and a maximum of one thousand. The average envoy should receive ten panas per yojana, a double wage beyond ten [yojanas] up to one hundred yojanas. . . .

Those moving about for spying should get two hundred and fifty or should have their wage increased according to their efforts. . . .

Of those dying while on duty, the sons and wives shall receive the food and wages. And their minor children, old and sick persons should be helped. And he should grant them money and do honor on occasions of death, illness and birth ceremonials. . . .

(ibid. 302–304)

Kautilya's proposed salary structure thus was explained in terms of cash payments. But salary could be paid in kind:

If he has a small treasury, he should give forest produce, cattle and fields and a little money. Or, if he has undertaken the settlement of new lands, he should give only money, not a village, in order that transactions that have taken place in the village may be stabilized.

(ibid. 304)

51

The king could also give an officer land which he could farm for his own benefit.

He [the King] should grant [lands] to priests, preceptors, chaplains and Brahmins learned in the Vedas [as] gifts to Brahmins, exempt from fines and taxes with inheritance passing on to corresponding heirs, [and] to heads of departments, accountants and others – [lands] without the right of sale or mortgage.

(ibid. 56)

Rules and regulations

There are frequent references in *Arthasastra* to the duties of the king (or government) toward the people. These include not just issues in the area of protection or defense but also in the sphere of the well-being of the people. Kautilya repeatedly uses the phrase "well-being and security" of the people in the context of the King's duties: "Kings bring about the well-being and security of the subjects" (ibid. 28). Protection of the people and of property requires the maintenance of a well-equipped police force and army. Kautilya uses the Sanskrit word, "Yogakshema," which implies well-being including the notion of happiness and prosperity. In order to further the well-being of the people, the King is expected, according to Kautilya, to engage in a number of different kinds of activity. These include regulating the work of various economic agents. Based on several different references, one can conclude that protection of consumers was an important priority for Kautilya:

In this manner the [King] should prevent thieves who are not known as thieves such as traders, artisans, actors, mendicants, jugglers and others from oppressing the country.

(ibid. 259)

The Goldsmith should cause the gold and silver work of the citizens and the country people to be carried out by workshop artisans. They should do the work with the time and the [nature of the] work stipulated, without stipulation as to time when there is the excuse of the [nature of the work]. In case the work is done otherwise [than as ordered there shall be] loss of wage and a fine double that [amount]. In case the time limit is exceeded, [he shall receive] a wage reduced by one-quarter and a fine double that [amount]. The [artisans] shall deliver in the same condition as to quality and quantity as they receive the entrusted metal. And even after a lapse of time, [customers] shall receive it in the same condition, except what is lost [in manufacture] and worn away [by time]. The [Goldsmith] should be conversant with every detail in connection with the characteristics and the manufacture of gold and its articles by workshop artisans. In the case of gold and silver ... a loss of one *kakani* in a *suvarna* may be allowed. One *kakani* of iron – twice that in the case of silver – is the insertion for color; one-sixth part of that is the loss [allowed]. In case of diminution of quality to the extent of one *masa* at least, the lowest fine for violence [shall be imposed]; in case of diminution of quantity [to that extent], the middle [fine]; in case of deceit in scales and weights, the highest [fine], also in case of fraud in an article manufactured. For a [person] causing the manufacture [of an article] unseen by the Goldsmith or in some other place, the fine shall be twelve *panas*. For the artisan, [the fine shall be] double, if there is a valid excuse. If there is no excuse, the [person] shall be taken to the magisterial court. And for the artisan, [the punishment shall be] a fine of two hundred *panas* or the cutting off of the fingers of his hand. They shall purchase the scales and weights from the Superintendent of Standardization. Otherwise, [there shall be] a fine of twelve *panas*. ... Fraud in the balance, removal tapping, boxing and embedding are the means of pilfering [by artisans]. ... Gems, silver or gold form the embedding in solid or hollow articles. Of that, heating or breaking is [the test of] purity. Thus the embedding. Therefore, the [Goldsmith] should ascertain the class, appearance, quality, quantity, the ornament made and the characteristics of articles made of diamonds, gems, pearls and corals. In the course of testing articles that are made or in the course of repairs to old articles, four ways of stealing [are practiced]: knocking off, cutting out, scratching out or rubbing off. ... Sudden movement of the hand, the weights, the fire, the wooden anvil, the tool-box, the receptacle, the peacock's feather, the thread, garment, talk, the head, the lap, the fly, attention to one's person, the bellows-skin, the water-platter, and the fire-pan, – these he should know as the means of pilfering. Of silver articles he should know that as fraudulent which smells like raw flesh, easily catches dirt, is rough, very hard or changed in color. In this manner, he should test the new and the old as well as the article that has changed its appearance, and should impose penalties on the [artisans] as prescribed.

(ibid. 116–121)

Kautilya also stipulates similar rules and regulations governing activities of several other groups: artisans, weavers, washermen, metal workers, physicians and actors.

Incentives and penalities

Judging by the large number of incentives and penalties prescribed in *Arthasastra*, it is very likely that Kautilya believed in the role that incentives play in modifying human behavior, especially in so far as they influence economic activity:

> In case of damage to the ploughing or seeds in another's field by the use of a reservoir, channels or a field under water, they shall pay compensation in accordance with the damage. In case of mutual damage to fields under water, parks and embankments, the fine [shall be] double the damage.

> The ownership of a water-work, not in use for five years, shall be lost except in cases of distress. When tanks and embankments are newly constructed, an exemption [from taxes] for five years [should be granted], when those that are ruined and abandoned are renovated, an exemption of four years, when those that are overgrown with weeds are cleared, for three years, when dry land is newly brought under cultivation, for two years.
>
> (ibid. 221)

> If one obstructs a customary water-course in use or makes [a new one] that is not customary, the lowest fine for violence [shall be imposed], also if one constructs in another's land a dam, a well, a holy place, a sanctuary or a temple. If a [person] himself or through others puts to mortgage or sale a charitable water-work, continued since old times, the middle fine for violence [is to be imposed], the highest on witnesses, except when it is in ruins and abandoned.
>
> (ibid. 222)

> For one breaking a dam holding water, drowning in water at the same spot [shall be the punishment], the highest fine for violence if it was without water, the middle if it was in ruins and abandoned.
>
> (ibid. 284)

> The king should do what is agreeable and beneficial to these, when they build dikes that are of benefit to the country or bridges on roads or carry out works beautifying the villages or defenses [of the villages].
>
> (ibid. 226)

> The Superintendent of Yarns should cause trade to be carried out in yarns, armors, cloth and ropes through men expert in the work.... After finding out the amount of yarn, he should favor them with oil and myrobalan unguents. And on festive days, they should be made

54

to work by honoring [them] and making gifts. . . . And when starting mills for the weaving of [cloth] . . . and cotton yarn, he should gratify the [workmen] by gifts or perfumes and flowers and by other means showing goodwill.

(ibid. 146–147)

The Salt Commissioner should collect at the proper time the share of salt as well as the lease-rent, also the price. . . . The purchaser [of salt] shall pay the duty and a protective duty corresponding to the loss sustained by the king's goods; one who purchases at another place [shall pay] a fine of six-hundred *panas* in addition. [A person selling] adulterated salt shall pay the highest fine [for violence], also the person living [by salt-manufacture] without permission, except forest-hermits.

(ibid. 109–110)

And he [the Director of Trade] should fix a profit for them of five per hundred over and above the permitted purchase-price in the case of indigenous commodities, ten [per hundred] in the case of foreign goods. For those who increase the price beyond that or secure [a profit beyond that] during purchase or sale, the fine shall be two hundred *panas* for an [additional profit of] five *panas* in one hundred *panas*. By that is explained the increase in fine in case of increase in price.

(ibid. 261)

Metholodogy

The last section [Section 15] of *Arthasastra* deals with methodology:

The source of the livelihood of men is wealth, in other words, the earth inhabited by men. The science which is the means of the attainment and protection of that earth is the Science of Politics. That contains thirty-two devices of treatment: topic, statement [of contents], employment [of sentences], meaning of words, reason for [establishing] something, mention, explanation, —, reference, application, indication, analogy, implication, doubt, – contrary [corollary], – derivation, – exception, one's own technical term, the *prima facie* view, the correct view, invariable rule, —. Thus this science, expounded with these devices of a science, has been composed for the acquisition and protection of this world and the next. This science brings into being and preserves spiritual good, material well-being and pleasures, and destroys spiritual evil, material loss and hatred.

(ibid. 512–516)

CONCLUSION

A vision underlay the concept of *arthasastra* [i.e. science of wealth], one of the four "sciences" on which the business of government rested, a science closely related to "political science." This vision embraced a predominantly rural, bureaucratic and centralized state, albeit one with a great deal of local autonomy [though less temple-economy than developed later on], with a population whose class structure was based on the four varnas, each of which was almost exclusively responsible for certain economic, political and social functions. Underlying this state was a quite complicated economy resting on both a bureaucracy and private enterprise, much of it under guild rule.

(Spengler 1980: 41)

The economy as described in the *Arthasastra* is completely dominated by the state. Private economic activity other than crop production was only residual and even then subject to strict government regulation and control.

He [the Administrator] should record the number of villages by fixing their boundaries, the number of fields by an enumeration of ploughed and unploughed [fields], dry and wet fields, parks, vegetable gardens, [flower and fruit] enclosures, forests, structures, sanctuaries, temples, water-works, cremation grounds, rest-houses, sheds for drinking water, holy places, pasture lands and roads, [and] in conformity with that he should keep records of the size of boundaries, forests and roads, and of grants, sales, favors and exemptions, concerning village-boundaries and fields, and [keep records] of houses by an enumeration of tax-payers and non-tax-payers.

(Kautilya 1986: 182–183)

There is an implicit assumption that individual behavior could be controlled to a significant degree through economic rewards and penalties. Kautilya looked at economic issues from the perspective of an administrator. But he recognized that regulations must be consistent with human propensities in the economic sphere. He also seemed to be aware that controls must encourage rather than repress desirable economic activity. We must not forget that the primary purpose of Kautilya's *Arthasastra*, as Spengler noted, was "instruction of the king in the business of extending and preserving his dominion, by whatever means, political economic, that seem suitable to his end" (Braibanti and Spengler 1963: 233–234).

We have already noted that the word *Arthasastra* can be, and sometimes has been, translated to mean science [*sastra*] of wealth [*artha*] or economics. In what sense is economics a science? How do economists explain economic phenomena? Insofar as economics attempts to provide systematic explanations supported by empirical data and to provide rigorous, deductive theories of human action, economics can claim to be a science. Can Kautilya's *Arthasastra* lay a claim to be a science in this sense? The answer clearly is an emphatic *no*. Before 1700, there were no economists and there was no science of economics in the sense of providing rigorous, deductive theories of human action.

However, we should note that George Sarton described the *Arthasastra* as "a treatise on government and administration, which is of considerable interest to the historian of science, for it contains information on medicine, mining, census-taking, meteorology, ships, surveying, etc., and affords glimpses into almost every aspect of Hindu life" (Sarton 1959: 147).

It appears that while *Arthasastra* has been mostly neglected by economists other than Spengler, its contribution has been noted by at least one historian of science:

> The *Arthasastra* was partly derived from Vedic sources, that is, from the fourth Veda, the Atharva-veda, dealing with magic and sorcery. The bulk was probably the creation of Kautilya himself, an Indian Machiavelli of considerable experience. Historians of science will consult the book with profit not only to understand government and administration about the beginning of the third century BC but also to obtain information on Indian medicine, mining, census-taking, meteorology, shipping, surveying, and so on, and above all to observe many aspects of Indian life.
>
> (Sarton 1959: 198)

NOTES

1 The author has learned only since the revision of this paper of the following: (1) the publication of Kautulya (1992) *The Arthashastra*, L.N. Rangarajan (ed. and trans.) New Delhi: Penguin Books India (P) Ltd., and (2) the 1990 production of "Chanakya," a television costume epic (in Hindi) in 16 VHS video cassettes, (1990/1993) New Delhi: Kuip, available as (1992) Madison, Wis.: South and Southeast Asia Video Archives, General Library System, University of Wisconsin-Madison.

2 An earlier version of this paper was presented at a session of the annual meeting of the History of Economics Society during June 1994. The author wishes to acknowledge the helpful comments by the discussant, John Adams, at that session as well as the many valuable suggestions for improvement of an earlier draft of this paper made by Omar Hamouda and B.B. Price. The usual caveats apply.

3 The word *Artha* as used by Kautilya has also a more broad interpretation than just wealth or material well-being. As Kautilya says in the last part of his book: "The source of the livelihood of men is wealth, in other words, the earth inhabited by men. The science which is the means of the attainment and protection of that earth is the Science of Politics" (Kautilya 1986: Part II, 512). The difficulty of translating Sanskrit words is probably the reason why *Arthasastra* has been interpreted to mean "Handbook of (the King's) Profit," "A Treatise

on Political Economy," as well as "Principles of Politics" at various places in the fifteenth edition of the *Encyclopaedia Britannica* (1974).

4 The first known published English translation of *Arthasastra* by R. Shama Shastri goes back to 1915. We have relied on R.P. Kangle's version of *Arthasastra*. His work consists of three parts. Part I presents the work in Sanskrit. Part II consists of his English translation of the Sanskrit original. In Part III Kangle presents an introduction to the study of *Arthasastra* as well as an extensive survey of critical studies made of *Arthasastra* and his own commentary. The quotations from *Arthasastra* in this paper are from Kangle's Part II. Kangle's work was first published by the University of Bombay in 1963.

There are controversies and uncertainties about the origin, the date, the scope as well as the author of *Arthasastra*. There is a fairly detailed discussion about these topics in Kangle, Part III. He has concluded that "there is no convincing reason why this work [*Arthasastra*] cannot be regarded as the work of Kautilya, who helped Candragupta to come to power in Magadha" (Kautilya 1986: Part III, 106)

We should also note that there are several prevailing spellings of both the author's name as well as the title of the book. We have chosen the spelling *Arthasastra* for the work and Kautilya for the author just because these happen to be convenient to us. Several other names which appear in this chapter (for example, Candragupta) also have several prevailing spellings. We do not profess our spellings to be more scientific or more popular.

5 Megasthenes was a Greek diplomat and historian who was sent by the Hellenistic king Seleucus I as ambassador to the court of King candragupta. He wrote about life in India in his book the *Indica*. According to *Encyclopaedia Britannica*, "although the original has been lost, extensive quotations from it survive in the works of such later Greek writers as Strabo, Diodorus and Arrian" (1974: Macropedia 9, 350).

6 We believe that it is useful to do this because *Arthasastra* is not widely known among scholars outside India. The title of a session at the annual meeting of the History of Economics Society held during June 1994 was "*Arthasastra*: A Neglected Text from the 4th Century BC"! We should note that while Kautilya's work was not mentioned by Schumpeter in his authoritative *History of Economic Analysis* (Schumpeter 1945), Spengler wrote more than once at length about it (Braibanti and Spengler 1963; Spengler 1971, 1980).

7 The *Upanishads*, which date back to at least 400 BC, form the basis of much of later Hindu philosophy. Durant quotes the German philosopher Schopenhauer as saying: "In the whole world ... there is no study so beneficial and so elevating as that of the *Upanishads*. It has been the solace of my life – it will be the solace of my death" (Durant 1954: 410).

Part II

HEBRAIC ECONOMIC THOUGHT

3

LOOKING FOR OURSELVES IN THE MIRROR OF OUR PAST

With what does economics cope? and the differences in the Jewish and Christian rationales for handling usury

Mark Perlman

WITH WHAT DOES ECONOMICS COPE? THE CULTURAL LEGACY: A "SNAKE" UNDER THE RUG

Part of economists' hang-ups of the late nineteenth and most of the twentieth centuries is their excessive envy for the purported certainties of the "hard" sciences. Being generally secularists, economic thinkers have rejected Natural Law as no more than simple seventeenth and eighteenth century folklore. Instead, they hold that theirs are worlds and minds, both in the nature of the *tabula rasa*. 'Twere only it was so. Ours is not a world starting from a blank slate: Robinson Crusoe was no more than an imaginary device of a clever writer. The difficult problem we must face is how to recognize what has been so indelibly inscribed both in our view of the world, and certainly in the ways that our cognition operates.

The Greek and the Hebraic legacy in broad terms

In years past it was common to write about the differences between two separate elements in our Western cultural tradition, the Hellenistic and the Hebraic. The division is often seen in terms of *the being* contrasted with *the becoming*. The Greek-Hellenistic tradition stressed the centrality of a logical system and accepted without comment its being closed; the Hebraic stressed dynamic quality of an on-going dialogue between man and God and worried little about its openness or indeterminacy. As some would have it, the Greek tradition stressed the perfection, yet with subtle intricacies, of a static system, the Hebraic tradition the essential irrationality (some have preferred to call it the "super-rationality") of a dynamic one. The Greek system was built around logic, a set of rules at the heart of scientifically

61

learned discussion. The Hebraic system was built around hierarchies of learning, some of which could not be understood, even with the aid of keen human rationality.[1] The Greek, or as I have suggested, the scientific, approach offers a neatness, albeit not a simple one; the Hebraic, or as I have suggested, the hierarchical, approach, encourages, through its dependence upon allegory, an imaginativeness, albeit one that is often couched not in objective but in subjective language.

What we, Westerners, currently live with is a merger of the two systems. Of course, the merger is much more of a mixture than it is a compound. As such, our discourses ought invariably to start with a selection of emphases.

An example of derivations from our cultural legacies

It was my practice to point out in one of my opening lectures to students of the history of economic thought that the two traditions could be contrasted in the interpretation of the critical opening challenge in the Book of Genesis. There, we are told that apparently whatever were God's expectations, He became disappointed with Man. Mankind and *particularly Womankind*[2] did not live up to His expectations.[3] In any case, Adam and Eve were informed that they had "fallen" from Grace, and all of us have been made to suffer ever since.

The sin

From our analytical standpoint there are two crucial questions:

1 What was the sin; and,
2 What was the punishment?

The sin seems to have been something combining (1) an inability to follow precise directions; (2) a willingness to be tempted, particularly when one could assert that "one was only doing what everyone else (*sic*) was doing";[4] (3) a greed involving things (something forbidden) and time (instant gratification); (4) an inability to leave well-enough alone; and, (5) an excessive Faustian curiosity. Naturally, as academic intellectuals, we fancy the fifth reason as best, but we fool ourselves if we think that most people find such an excuse tolerable, much less attractive.

Interpreting the punishment

What here interests us directly is the second question, "What was God's punishment for Adam and Eve's vicarious sin, for which all mankind suffers?" Although a distinction has been made between what happened to Man and what happened to Woman (differing sexual roles, with Woman the home-body and Man the outside-worker), the one clear answer, *particu-*

larly as seen by Thomas Aquinas and by most economists ever since, was that mankind has been condemned to live with the paradigm of scarcity of goods and services and with a schedule of appetites and incentives which are, at best, confusing.

In the more modern terms of William Stanley Jevons, ours is a world of considerable readily available pains and only a few pleasures, most of which are costly. In order to consume, we are driven to produce, and production is done mostly by the distasteful sweat of the brows and the tiring strength of the back. The study of economics – of the production, distribution and even the consumption of goods and services – it follows, is the result of the Original Sin. When Thomas Carfare called economics the "Dismal Science", he was, if anything, writing in euphemisms; economics, *per se*, is actually a principal derivative for the Punishment for Sin. The thrust of the foregoing is that scarcity is a necessary part of the fundamental paradigm in most economists' systems. The other necessary part is need or utility. Absent scarcity or absent utility, there is no economic problem.

But it is another line of analysis, perhaps novel to many, which I will put to you. Scarcity, as a necessary part of the paradigm, may not have been the greatest punishment, because scarcity, as such, can usually be overcome. Scarcity simply means that one has to allocate between one's preferences, and the thinking man, it would seem, ought to be able to handle the situation. We use our reasoning power, surely tied up with Free Will, to allocate priorities and thereby overcome the greater disasters of scarcity. Instead of scarcity, what was the greater punishment, indeed the greatest punishment, is more basic. In so far as we are aware, it was identified early on by another Aristotelian, one writing shortly before Aquinas, Moses Maimonides.

Maimonides suggested that God's real punishment was to push man clearly beyond the limits of his reasoning power. Maimonides held that prior to the Fall, Adam and Eve (and presumably mankind generally) knew everything concerning them; after the Fall they only had *opinions*.[5] Requisite to the wise use of power is understanding and full specification. What was lost was any such claim previously held by man to complete knowledge and the full comprehension of his surroundings. In other words, what truly underlies the misery of scarcity is neither hunger nor thirst, but the lack of knowledge of what one's preference schedule will do to one's happiness. For if one had complete knowledge (including foreknowledge), one could compensate accordingly.

If one pursues Maimonides' line of inquiry, it seems that uncertainty (which is based not only on ignorance of what can be known with study or data collection, but also an ignorance tied to the unknowable) is the real punishment, since there is nothing around to mitigate its possible severity.

ECONOMICS: ITS ASSUMPTIONS, PARADIGMS AND COROLLARIES

In recent decades it has become the fashion to formalize the presentation of economics as a series of strong and weak propositions, ancillary corollaries, and testable hypotheses. Even so, the fact is that logical argument rests upon assumptions, some, but clearly not all, of them testable in terms of observation.

The assumption of scarcity

We inherit most directly from Plato and Aristotle knowledge of the underlying economic paradigm of scarcity; it is said that whatever else economics is concerned with, it is concerned with the scarcity of desired goods and services. Without such scarcity, there is no economic problem, from which it has been derived that there would be no economic solution. Given the absence of a problem and the absence of any solution, there is nothing left of the discipline. But generally subsumed in this discussion is that the scarcity refers to the supply of goods and services. As goods and to a certain extent services can be rationed, there is something of a rational basis for overcoming this kind of scarcity.

The assumption of uncertainty

As we have already seen, there is also the paradigm of the invariable scarcity of necessary knowledge; such is the paradigm of uncertainty. This paradigm should be seen to have surfaced early and well in the literature, with the concept of uncertainty thus also at the heart of hearts of the economics discipline. But what is meant by uncertainty? The literature on economic uncertainty has at least nine points of focus.[6] First, let me dispose of some easier aspects at the outset.

Uncertainty is not the same as risk. Risk relates to knowledge of the appropriate probability distribution;[7] uncertainty implies that we do not know whether any such distribution exists, and that in fact it may not exist.[8] As I here employ the concept, however, uncertainty is also not synonymous with indeterminacy; for example, the solution of the Edgeworth Box problem, however difficult, is indeterminate, albeit within a bounded range. Nor should uncertainty be confused with "curable ignorance"; many facts and conventions can be identified through discovery, that is, by one or another form of observation. What we are examining is "true" (totally incalculable or irremediable) uncertainty.

The simplest kind of uncertainty to conceptualize involves games of chance with known probabilities, but requiring some large number of repeated throws for the probability function to surface.[9] A related kind of uncertainty stresses the absence of enough experiences to yield a stable probability function.[10] A more interesting version of the common expression of uncertainty involves the situation in which one assumes that experience, held to reduce the uncertainty, can be had at a cost.[11] Perhaps the most profound kind of uncertainty involves an epistemic (generally read "subjective") rather than an ontological (generally read "objective") approach. Epistemic uncertainty exists in the mind of the thinker and involves the way he perceives the unknown,[12] perceptions then reflecting the differences between optimistic and pessimistic minds.[13]

None the less, on the concept of uncertainty in our inexcusable ignorance we have just failed to realize what was staring us in the face. We saw only what was obvious to us. We failed to perceive that unlike other scarcities, the scarcity of necessary knowledge, particularly knowledge of the future (what one writer, G.L.S. Shackle call unknowledge) is not susceptible to rationing. Scarcity of information could not be solved by a direct system of rationing; it just cannot be said to exist at the moment when it is most needed. Thus, scarcity of knowledge leads to a substitute, opinions; but opinions are a sorry substitute.

The Assumptions of utility and individualism

A more recent, and perhaps lesser, paradigm – perhaps it is no more than a corollary, but one which has come to dominate much of modern economics – involves empirical observation of individual choice, from which has been derived paradigmatic concepts of individualism and utilitarianism.

Here is it necessary to mention a little about the concept of individualism. Individualism is really close to the essence of the Christian tradition, because there the Last Judgement is tied to each individual, not, as in the Jewish tradition, to the Peoplehood. In sum, the Christian unit of account is the individual, the test is the Last Judgement, and good Christians rely on their Salvation through the intercession of Jesus Christ (and perhaps His Mother, if they are of the Roman or Orthodox persuasions). Thus from the concept of individual accountability before God comes the original concept of individualism, a concept not truly part of the Jewish communitarian accounting system.

But what has been difficult to incorporate into the Christian tradition has been the *materialism* inherent in the concept of utilitarianism. There is little need to explain at length why observation tends to focus on material things, but it is important to stress that if observation tends upon the material, somehow the subjective and the spiritual are de-emphasized.

In some major sense empirical observation, this "lesser-paradigm or corollary", has been the cause of much of the secularization not only of modern life, but also modern economics.[14] The empirical method suggested by Hobbes in *Leviathan* (1651; 18), expanded by Mandeville in his *Fable*

65

of the Bees (1714), formalized first by Hume and then applied to economics by Bentham (and later only partly refined by J.S. Mill) is for most of us now canon. Friedrich Hayek served until his death as the most recent Pope of this revelation, because whatever else he may have believed, Hayek put individual choice at the center of his system. We are moderately comfortable arguing that the theory of subjectivism is a related corollary to this particular corollary-or-lesser-paradigm; in his secular view it fits nicely into the paradigm of individualism, although to be sure for many Christian believers the theory of individualism could get, and has gotten, along without it.

The assumptions of verities

There are other paradigms to be considered under the issue of the role of faith in knowledge, an old question with some very old answers.[15] There could be an economics paradigm geared to stable ethical imperatives, sometimes called institutions and other times called revealed and Natural Law verities. This theme, even if it has proved to be difficult to handle, crops up regularly in the literature.

Many of the stable and transitional elements in the institutional paradigms belong essentially to Pareto's contribution. In brief, Pareto established a division between rational societies (wherein the economist was the principal explainer) and non-rational societies (where the sociologist flourished). I would also fit Pareto's ideas into the first although he, himself, decided that the topic was too difficult for unsophisticated economists to handle and assigned it to more worldly sociologists. The topic stands outside of the system, even though a case can be made that it actually could dominate it. Pareto defined residuals as systemic rationalizations of sets of cultural imperatives.[16] Accordingly, there are no rules of logic or order, except as they are culturally imposed. The application of this point, essentially foreign to our analysis, is that regularities (i.e. certainties) in one culture may become uncertainties in other cultures. Whether the reverse is the case or not is too thorny a rose to pluck; one man's uncertainty about the existence of his personal soul may offer him a certain denial of the existence of a personal Heaven, which some other, more conventional believer (one who believes he has a personal soul) might "sweat about every waking hour of the day".

Another paradigm that has achieved superior significance in modern economics relates to the choice of testing method (logic imaginative speculation, objective empiricism, moral or categorical imperatives). This is the paradigmatic body properly called "methodology". It has been argued generally of recent decades that the methodology of logical positivism is dominant. Unfortunately, for those interested in ancient economics, there is a paucity of objective observations which can be used to test all but the most elementary of hypotheses. This is to say, that the changing price of wheat can serve to indicate the matching of market supplies and demands, but it cannot reveal who was at one time included in the market and is excluded at other times. In a world of shifting populations, to say nothing of a world of unstable social hierarchies, changes in prices basically measure only changes in prices – as Marx and countless others have pointed out, those changes may not indicate truly profound changes in social structure. Yet, it is true that this approach of logical positivist methodology represents something of a non-rational revealed truth. How do we know that we observe, how can we verify subjective observations, and how can we convince others of the truth and stability of our observations?

A third paradigm relates directly to theological truths. Perhaps economists generally are reluctant to handle theological treatments of problems. If so, is it because of cowardice or of ignorance? Surely, our mutual Scottish uncle, the Professor from Glasgow, was a believer in Natural Law, and if one grants verities there, one is well on the way to admission of theological arguments. Smith's text did not reveal his Deism and thereby his theology; his use of capital letters in his description of the underlying mechanism (i.e. the Invisible Hand) did.

Withal, however, there is a literature about the topic, and whether the literature describes practice or even, additionally, both rationalizes and justifies it is worth examining. The Jewish and Christian authorities seem to have differed somewhat.

Most Christians perceive God as omnipotent as well as omniscient. The Christian God is all-powerful, yet one who has granted Free Will to let man try to be worthy. Christians see the role of God's religious teachings as having direct economic impact. The two Papal Encyclicals, *Rerum Novarum* (1892) and *Quadragesimo Anno* (1932), may be said to have direct meaning mostly to Roman Catholics (but, in fact, not necessarily to all of them), yet their communitarian message is accepted by many Protestants as furtherance of the principles of Augustine's City of God on earth. Bishop Joseph Butler (1900), writing in the eighteenth century, anticipated much of the thrust of the two encyclicals.

The Jewish perception of God is somewhat more complex, and I cannot do justice to it briefly. However, there is the story in Genesis 32: 24–32, where Jacob wrestled the night and was wounded but not pinned, only in the morning discovering that he had been wrestling with God. From this the rabbis have drawn the lesson that while man cannot pin God, apparently God cannot always pin man. Later in the Babylonian Talmud there is a thought-provoking extension of this theme. In a debate between Rabbi Eliezer and his colleagues, he called up successfully four successful miracles to substantiate his opinion (one actually involved a Voice from Heaven), thereby indicating that Heaven was on his side. His antagonist, Rabbi Joshua, dismissed all of these miracles as irrelevant, because as he said in Deuteronomy 30: 12, it was revealed at Sinai that the law is made on earth, not in Heaven. No miracle has the power to annul that Divine Revelation.[17]

Comments

The foregoing is an effort to show the complexity of the foundations of our thinking. I suggest that, where Marx argues that it is the dominant set of economic (technological) relationships which give shape and meaning to the "superstructure", it is the patristic legacies which are even more basic in interpreting the nature of the economic relationships. They, even more than technology, provide the principal paradigms in our thinking. We do our intelligence no credit when we oversimplify the foundations of our perceptions.

Having made this general statement, I think it useful to give some specifics. I have chosen a difficult topic to illustrate my points. The topic is difficult simply because it puts certain cultural paradigms in conflict with the mechanics of necessary business transactions. Let us examine the question of usury.

SOME OBSERVATIONS ON THE JEWISH AND CHRISTIAN HISTORICAL TREATMENTS OF USURY

Usury is often considered to be an excessively high charge made by the lender to the borrower for the use of money. In the Hebraic tradition it seems to have meant other things as well, principally exploitation of the weak by the strong. For this the Jews introduced the idea of a Jubilee Year (the fiftieth year), when property was to revert to its original owners and slaves were to be manumitted. The Jewish tradition, a tradition based on a Peoplehood even prior to the religious revelation at Sinai,[18] sought seemingly to prevent divisions within its own community. Certain "dirty" tasks were to be done by and to "outsiders," not by members of the group to other members, lest the solidarity wither.

By way of contrast, the Greek tradition held that paying for the use of money was simply wrong because, as Aristotle put it, money was not fungible (it was, itself, sterile and could produce nothing compared to the fertility of land and labor which could be said to yield tangible, organic benefits).

While part of the Christian tradition was to protect the weak from the strong, there was during the Middle Ages[19] a concern that money-lending was itself an evil,[20] irrespective of the comparative strength of the borrower and the lender.

Two levels of analysis: the theoretical and the "practical"

When Raymond de Roover wrote his seminal work on medieval economics he was able to approach the topic from two standpoints – the theory of market performance (involving first the Just Wage and then the Just Price), and the practices of market performance. I think that within probably every cultural tradition a sophisticated scholar should be able to observe the same distinction. Let me use the evolution of the Hebraic treatment of usury as my example.

The Jewish theoretical statements

It comes as no surprise that the biblical Books of Exodus, Leviticus, and Deuteronomy forbad the taking of interest from those within the Peoplehood of Israel:

> If thou lend money to any of My people, even to the poor with thee, thou shalt not be to him as creditor [noshe], neither shall you lay upon him interest.
>
> (Exodus 22: 24)

> And if thy brother be waxen poor and his means fail with thee, thou shalt uphold him. . . . Take thou no interest of him or increase; but fear thy God; that thy brother may live with thee. Thou shalt not give him money upon interest, nor give him any victuals for increase.
>
> (Leviticus 25: 35–37)

But, it is the prohibition in the Book of Deuteronomy which is the most interesting both because of its exceptions and its qualifications:

> Thou shalt not lend upon interest to thy brother; interest of money, interest of victuals, interest of anything that is lent upon interest. Unto a foreigner thou mayest lend upon interest; but unto thy brother thou shalt not lend upon interest; that the Lord thy God may bless thee in all that thou puttest thy hand unto, in the land thou goest in to possess it.
>
> (Deuteronomy 23: 20)

Clearly, the prohibitions applied only to those within the group, but the Deuteronomy directive was interpreted to mean that even the most mild of special interactions between creditor and debtor was to be prohibited. For example, there was a special prohibition of a Jewish debtor when passing in the street nodding first to his Jewish creditor if the reason for this deference was in any sense tied to the debtor–creditor relationship.

In the Five Books of Moses (which are the significant texts because they are the truly inspired ones) the taking of interest was not a commandment (felony); rather, it was a statute on the level of torts. Only later in the Books of the Prophets was it "promoted" to a felonious offence.

The Jewish practical approach

Not withstanding all of this discussion, the history of the Jews suggests clearly that it was realized from early on that the prohibition would bring the economy to a standstill. The interesting question was how to use the mind to bend the restrictions. (There is evidence on fifth century BC papyri that little or no effort was made to evade the prohibition.)

During the period of the Talmud (second century BC until about the fourth century AD) the interpretation worked in both directions. One set of views (called *avak ribbit*, or the "dust of interest") was that nothing vaguely resembling creditor profit could be allowed. For example, the lending of a bushel of wheat at one time to be repaid by a bushel of wheat at a later time fell under the prohibition, since the market (money) price of the two bushels could have in the interim changed.

Yet, during this same period, the need for market interaction clearly dominated both market life and the need to provide a loosening of the interpreted law. While it is true that the creditor could not demand the equivalent number of goods after a period of time, the debtor could voluntarily sell him the same number of goods at a cheaper price at the time of debt-settlement, or the same as the original number of goods but in a state short of completion. Loans in the form of shares in ownership (i.e. partnerships) were also allowed (a procedure in common use in Islamic countries to this day). Justice Cohen of the Israeli Supreme Court notes that,

> One jurist even held that it was permissible to let money on hire, like chattels, against the payment of rent, as distinguished from giving a loan against payment of interest. A vendor may sell goods on credit at a price of 100 units payable at a future date and immediately repurchase the goods at the price of 90 units payable cash down; each of the two contracts of sale would be valid.
>
> (Cohen: 31)

Another form was to use a non-Jewish intermediary; each transaction was interpreted as legal. However, what was most telling was the slackness of enforcement in the religious courts. At the same time that the prohibition of taking interest from non-Jews was being discussed, and there was a tendency to discredit money-lenders as witnesses, the historic fact was that at no time was penalizing the lender in the form of making him sacrifice the full value of his capital suggested.

In the post-Talmudic period most effort went into the further loosening of the anti-interest principle. Typical was the argument that, if the borrower used the loan profitably, the lender was entitled to more than the value of the loan if he paid the borrower something for his skill – as in the case of someone who lent 100 which was used to make (over time) 200 – and the original lender could claim twenty of the additional hundred if he designated two of the twenty as payment to the borrower for his entrepreneurial skill. Rashi, certainly one of the greatest commentators on the Talmud, even held that the use of intermediaries could involve only Jews as agents, since the agents were clearly not the principals and the prohibition applied only to the principals. Even more interesting was the writing into the loan of evidentiary requirements which were clearly impossible of presentation, and in their absence the larger repayment was allowed.

The Christian approach

How does all of this differ from the evasions allowed by the Christian Fathers, particularly Aquinas, who must have been pleased to find his answer in Aristotle? He recognized three:

1 A loan could contain small provisions set up to insure against aggregate losses through non-payment of loans made by him, generally.
2 A lender could require payment for the opportunities to make profit he forwent by the tying up of his money.
3 A lender could expect compensation for the consumption pleasure he forwent while his money was tied up.

Lessons to be drawn

On the whole the differences can be associated not with the ways de Roover reports that evasions were made, but in the way that the actual prohibitory terms were phrased. The taking of interest was seen in the Talmud as a matter of interpersonal relationships – the need to keep equality in the group. The evils of interest-levying, in other words, were tied up with what it did to the fellowship, not what it did to the economic process. Given that definition as it differed from the Christian, the line of reasoning went in somewhat different directions. The Jewish approach wandered from the focus on group solidarity towards the goal of economy preservation; the Christian towards a better focus on just what economic operations were summed when money was borrowed. Both, however, were consequence-oriented – the one to the sociology of intra-group responsibility, the other to the logic of what was personally morally involved.

The most important lessons are ones of similarity. First, both traditions had "theoretical" ethical approaches and practical market approaches. The second lesson is that the practical focus was not on the rightness or wrongness of the theory of the non-fungibility of money, but on the principles of who should not be exploited, and if exploitation was inherent who was to carry the curse of the extortionist. From this second lesson we can easily infer that the market was not to be an impersonal place reflecting merely the practice of transactions. Rather, part of the importance of the market lay in the terms of who was admitted as a participant and the ethics of participation. In the end, the explosive aspect of the usury question was not as the young Bentham so facilely reasoned. Interest was more than the price of money; it was part of the warp which made a social fabric strong and useful.

CONCLUSION

"With What Does Economics Cope?" was the opening question. My answer is that, in addition to coping with the distribution of goods and services, and in addition to coping with such things as incentive systems (as affected by open, and alternatively supervised, markets), it copes with the historical experience of the peoples affected.

It is, as I noted earlier, easy and perhaps attractive to abstract from the cultural baggage which we have to carry when we try to develop economics into a formal science, but it does little credit either to our understanding of the situation or our capacity to look beneath the surface not to face the "snake" that is so major a portion of our history.

NOTES

1 The Decalogue was not a set of rational principles; insofar as rationality was concerned, the Decalogue could be interpreted according to rational principles, but then not always that, either.
2 Much has been made of the failure of women, perhaps that is because men wrote up the history. I should add, in order to avoid a deleterious political correctness (and thereby cut off provocation and discussion), that since Eve was the proximate cause of the Fall, and Eve represents sexual attraction or desire, some (particularly St Paul, whose opinion of womankind was problematic) have considered that sexual attraction was in some way even more responsible for the Fall than anything else. Put crudely, even if economics is not a sexy subject, its origins were sexual.
3 What that says about His omniscience and/or omnipotence is, at the very least, paradoxical.
4 Cf. Genesis 3: 9–12, 16–19:
    [9] But the Lord God called to the man and said to him, "Where are you?" [10] He replied, "I heard the sound as you were walking the garden, and I was afraid because I was naked, and I hid myself." [11] God answered "Who told you that you were naked? Have you eaten from the tree which I forbade you?" [12] The man said, "The woman you gave me for a companion, she gave me fruit from the tree and I ate." [Note: the story, as recalled, suggests that Adam was dependent upon Eve (for what?), and the price of that

dependency was to be agreeable to Eve ("it was really all her fault – I only did what You [God] had laid out for me").

[16] To the woman he said, "I will increase your labor and your groaning, and in labor you shall bear children. You shall feel an urge for your husband, and he shall be your master."

[17] And to the man he said, "Because you have listened to your wife and have eaten from the tree which I forbad you, accursed shall be the ground on your account; with labor you shall win your food from it all the days of your life. [18] It will grow thorns and thistles for you, none but wild plants for you to eat. [19] You shall gain your bread by the sweat of your brow until you return to the ground; for from it you were taken. Dust you are, to dust you shall return."

(Again, for those civil libertarians amongst us, kindly note that God forced Adam to testify against himself. Who says that the Bill of Rights is an inherent aspect of Divine Justice? Far from it; in the Last Judgement, "pleading the Fifth" won't do at all.)

5 This point is to be found through an expansion of the thinking of Maimonides see 1947, Chapter 2). His question is, what was the state of man's knowledge before and after the Fall? The line of his argument is that man did not have any worries before the Fall, because he knew Truth and everything was taken care of. The Fall, coming about only because God had told man to avoid just one thing which man then did not avoid, led to man no longer being taken care of, and man, having become mortal, has to spend his days worrying about the unknown. Where once man could count on a certain future, now man had to worry about the unknown, about which he could only have opinions, i.e. limited expectations. Maimonides (1135–1204), a native of Cordoba, Spain, spent the greatest part of his career in Cairo, where he was the Court physician. Maimonides is one of the great Aristotelians, and although much of his theology was considered questionable by Thomas Aquinas, Aquinas had little trouble with Maimonides' Aristotelianism.

6 These are discussed in a forthcoming paper by Charles R. McCann and myself, "Varieties Of Uncertainty" (forthcoming), as well as in the chapter by the same authors (forthcoming), "Keynesian Economics and the Meaning of Uncertainty", in O.F. Hamouda and B.B. Price (eds) *Keynesianism and the Keynesian Revolution in America*, Cheltenham: Edward Elgar.

7 Risk implies the existence of (and the knowledge of) a definable numerical series, the constituents of which can be identified and discounted. Von Thunen is popularly credited (for most of us, because of passing references in Frank H. Knight's *Risk, Uncertainty, and Profit*) with differentiating risk from uncertainty (Knight 1921: 19, 26).

8 Robert Lucas and the Rational Expectationists; John von Neumann, Osker Morgenstern and the other proponents of Game Theory; and Leonard J. Savage and the subjective utility theorists, all have developed theories of decision-making more properly identified as risk-based, albeit each insists that uncertainty is being treated.

9 Assuming an honest coin, there is good reason to believe that some number of honest tosses will result in an equal number of heads and tails. But, what if there is only one toss? The outcome is then uncertain. Assume as another example that only one in a hundred aspiring cellists makes the grade as a concert artist. How is the father of a child to know whether his is the one or among the ninety-nine? For good reason, this is the kind of uncertainty of which most people are aware.

10 Given sufficient cases, a distribution can usually be found; but just how many cases (how much "experience") is required cannot be known *a priori*.

11 The question then arises, at what point does the cost of procuring an additional case approximate its marginal value? Quality control experiments readily establish the requisite outcomes. Those involving more complex inputs, like agricultural products, can also be worked through. However, the important question is, can there be any role for uncertainty outside of the experimental realm or in the absence of a lengthy empirical series?

12 Two thinkers can perceive the unknown quite differently – each from his own idiosyncratic combination of experiences and imagination.

13 When I asked Kenneth Boulding to review G. L. S. Shackle's *Epistemics and Economics* in the *Journal of Economic Literature*, his reaction was that he could not stomach easily so broad an assumption of uncertainty. When I reviewed later *Imagination and the Nature of Choice* in the same journal, I stressed that empirically uncertainty had had a bias towards kindly outcomes; such outcomes were called technological advance.

14 Being secularist is trendy. Yet, if one looks at the face of the Great Seal of the United States (to be seen on the back of every dollar bill), one finds balancing the phrase, *Novus Ordo Seculorum* (New Secular [nonhierarchical] Order), no less than two items which are revelational in nature, one the Eye (the Masonic symbol for God) over the pyramid, and the other the phrase *Annuit Coeptis* (He has delivered us [as he did the Israelites from a similar tyranny]).

15 The question of the role of faith in knowledge is an old one, with old answers, whether as from Fregisius, a student of Alcuin at the eighth-century court of Charlemagne, who wrote a dissertation on the matter of darkness and nothingness, or George Bishop Berkeley, the most famous of whose questions involved one's faith that a tree falling in a forest, where there was no one to observe the event, still made a noise as the limbs hit the earth.

16 For rationalists the dominance of cultural imperatives need constitute no insuperable problem. Consider, even the hallucinations of madmen are the basis of objective, scientific studies. Such underlies Pareto's marvelous treatment of non-rational societies in his *Trattato di Sociologia Generale*, translated into English as *Mind and Society* (1935).

17 The Talmud goes on to note a legend that when the prophet Elijah was asked how God took this assertion of the independence of human reasoning, "He laughed [with joy] saying ... 'My sons have defeated Me. My sons have defeated Me'" (quoted in *Baba Mezi'a* [or *Baba Metzia*] 1935 edition in English).

18 For Jews the Peoplehood preceded the religion; for Christians it is the other way around. In practice, this difference means that Jews may or may not believe; so long as they don't believe another religion, they remain Jews. To renounce one's Jewishness is to renounce membership in the group; whether one has the faith is another matter – many Jews are agnostics, even atheists; yet they are still Jews. For Christians faith is the simple test; technically one can hardly be a Christian if one has no faith.

19 The dating of the Middle Ages is tricky. Certainly by the fifteenth century the economic and ecclesiastical organization of Christian Western Europe had changed markedly from what it had been in the tenth century. Perhaps it is useful to use the thirteenth century as the watershed. In any event, by 1472 the city of Sienna had established a municipally owned Banco dei Monti Paaschi to capture the trade of the Jews who had been the local money-lenders.

20 Two additions should be noted. At an early point, usury did not refer to money as such, but to all exploitation of the weak by the strong. The concept of the Just

Wage and its derivative, the Just Price, stemmed from this original perception of usury. Also, rules against money-lending originally seem to have applied more to the clergy lending to the laity than to the laity lending to other laity.

4

ANCIENT AND MEDIEVAL RABBINIC ECONOMIC THOUGHT

Definitions, methodology and illustrations[1]

Ephraim Kleiman

INTRODUCTION

"When we recall the period in which the Talmud came into being", wrote Sombart over eighty years ago in a frequently quoted passage, "and compare what it contains in the field of economics with all the economic ideas and conceptions that the ancient and medieval worlds have handed down to us, it seems nothing short of marvelous" (Sombart 1911, 1962: 291). One does not have to share Sombart's highly exaggerated view of the role of Jews in European economic development (or of the economic sagacity of the Talmudic doctors) to realize that the economic ideas of the Talmud must, until quite recent times, have affected the economic thinking of a significant segment of the Western world's business community. Nor is it necessary to search (à la Sombart) for the real or imaginary Jewish ancestry of prominent economists and moral philosophers, to conclude that at least some of these ideas could be expected to have percolated the mainstream of Western intellectual tradition.[2]

Nevertheless, the economic ideas embodied in ancient and medieval Rabbinic literature receive little, if any, attention in works devoted to the history of economics. Most authors ignore ancient Jewish literature altogether, going straight from the economics of ancient Greece to those of the medieval schoolmen.[3] Others, referring only to the Old Testament, dismiss its pronouncements on economic matters as ones of ethics, devoid of any analytical content.[4] Both groups seem unaware of the vast amount of economic discussion in the Talmud, in its commentaries and in the Rabbinic *responsa* relating to them.

Obvious reasons for this neglect are the inaccessibility and sheer size of this literature: written in Hebrew and in the akinned Aramaic, often in a cryptic style fathomable only by the initiated, the Babylonian Talmud alone runs to no less than two million words in the original![5] But even the occasional scholar who surmounts these hurdles, often falters in delineating properly the area of the investigation or in choosing an appropriate research agenda.

WHOSE ECONOMIC THOUGHT?

The variety of Jewish existence means that there is no one definition of what might constitute "Jewish" economic thought. Were we to borrow Sombart's racial approach, we would soon have to face the vexing question of what makes a person a Jew, and how long it takes for it, so to say, to wear off, only to come up with a hodgepodge of views having nothing in common except the accident of their proponents' birth.[6]

The same basic cause also leads us to reject a linguistic criterion, this time, however, because of its narrowness. Medieval *responsa*, as well as theological treatises such as Maimonides', were often written in Arabic, while in latter days, much writing that would by common consent be regarded as quintessentially Jewish, was composed in Yiddish and Ladino, not to mention some less known vernaculars.

But while we, thus, cannot speak of a "Jewish" economic thought in the sense one speaks of, say, a Spanish or French one, we may still define it by a religious criterion, in a way akin to that in which we conceive of Catholic or Protestant economic thought, as that inherent in the attitude of Judaic religious law towards economic matters. This is the definition adopted in most writings on what are loosely, and mistakenly, called Talmudic, and should properly be called Judaic or *Halakhic* economics – *Halakha* being the totality of religious law regulating orthodox Jewish behaviour.

Judaism having long had no supreme religious authority, the currently held law is composed of the opinions and verdicts of Rabbinic scholars since ancient and up to contemporary times. As a rule, writers on *Halakhic* economics regard this agglomeration as an integral whole, treating as one views originating centuries and continents apart.[7] The economic content of currently held religious dogma is, of course, a perfectly legitimate subject of research, as illustrated by the recent arousal of interest in Islamic economics. But its analysis belongs more to the realm of comparative economics than to that of the history of ideas.[8]

To this we may oppose the study of the history of what will be called here, somewhat arbitrarily, Rabbinic economics, meaning the study of the economics of Rabbinic authors considered in the context of their respective time and place. As the terms Talmudic, *Halakhic* and Rabbinic are often used almost synonymously, a brief explanation of them may be called for. Talmud is the great ancient compendium of Judaic legal discourse, of which more below. Because it came to govern so much of Jewish religious law, the *Halakha*, "Talmudic" is the adjective used sometimes to describe mainstream orthodox Judaism. As the formulators, interpreters and teachers of this law were Rabbis, the same is true of "Rabbinic".

Strictly speaking, however, Rabbinic literature is the body of the written works of Rabbis, of which the Talmud is by far the major, but by no means the exclusive one. Because of its pre-eminence, the term Talmudic literature is often extended to cover, in addition to the Talmud proper, all other Rabbinic writings contemporary with it. Not all the dicta of Rabbinic literature, not even of the Talmud itself, necessarily form part of the *Halakha* as it evolved over time, having been rejected outright by more authoritative ones, or put in abeyance, modified or superseded in later times.[9]

WHAT DO WE MEAN BY (ANCIENT) ECONOMIC THOUGHT?

Books on the history of economic thought, if they deal at all with pre-modern authors, tend to reveal an inconsistency of treatment. Treating ancient, patristic and even scholastic literature, they discuss ethical attitudes and, to a lesser extent, the socio-economic background against which these were formed; whereas when they turn to later periods, they concentrate almost exclusively on the analytical content.[10] The latter approach is also followed by those works which ignore the pre-modern world altogether. It is as if the term "history of economics" had a different meaning when applied to different historical periods.

The evolution of ethical standards, value judgements and beliefs forms part of the general history of ideas. Its study belongs to what Haney (1911; 1936: 3) and Schumpeter (1954: 38–41), trying to differentiate between the two, had suggested should be labelled the history of economic thought, as distinct from the history of *economics*.[11] It is probably much more important for the understanding of mankind than the study of the development of the analytical concepts which form the economist's kit of tools. But it should not, and cannot, displace the latter. In so far as ancient economic analysis did exist, it should be capable of being examined in the same way as the current one.

One reason for pre-modern literature being examined for its history of economic ideas, rather than history of economics, content is the oft reiterated argument, that the ancient and medieval worlds could not have yielded any economic analysis in the modern sense of the word: "Man cannot begin to theorize about the economic process as long as this is so simple as to require no special explanation" (Roll 1961: 21). This presumed simplicity of the ancient economy seems to have been inferred from its primitive technology. But the two are not necessarily correlated. It was, for example, precisely the precariousness of ancient seafaring vessels which necessitated the sophisticated risk-sharing schemes of Athenian marine loans echoed in today's Lloyd's syndicate concept, and gave rise to the Rhodian sea law, still reflected in contemporary maritime codes.[12]

Nor was the role of markets, often considered the strongest single stimulus to the development of modern economics, as restricted in people's lives as the prohibitively high transportation costs of the ancient world led some authors to maintain.[13] Given relatively low productivity levels, the share of output passing through the market could have been significant, even if its total volume was small. Certainly the Talmudic literature, described below, is replete with references to (admittedly institutional, not conceptual) markets and market prices.

It is also sometimes argued, that what the ancient and medieval worlds had were "commonplace economics", which "require(s) nothing beyond everyday experience" (Niehans 1990: 15); that they lacked what it needed to transform such observations into economic theory. In the present context in particular, it has been claimed that it was only the Greek attraction towards speculative thought that made it possible for the transition from observation to theory to begin.

Admittedly, the ancients did not theorize about economics in the present-day sense. The Rabbinic authors, for once, failed to formulate their speculations in the abstract. Concretizing these speculations diverted attention from their theoretical aspect. But observing everyday economic phenomena, they couldn't help trying to associate cause and effect. They also often tried to examine the consequences of alternative sets of assumptions. Consequently, their deliberations yielded something beyond "commonplace economics" – the *proto-economics* described by Spengler as the "incomplete visions of imperfectly conceptualized worlds" (Spengler 1980: xii).

TALMUDIC AND POST-TALMUDIC RABBINIC LITERATURE

The ur-source of Rabbinic literature is, of course, the Old Testament. Though many of its precepts had far-reaching economic implications, the Old Testament did not proceed beyond some not very profound "commonplace economics". We know little about the evolution of Judaic law during the period of Babylonian captivity and the earlier part of the Second Commonwealth. But the upheavals wrought upon Middle Eastern society by the conquests of Alexander the Great did not bypass Judea. Sooner or later, the need arose to adapt and expand the relatively simple Mosaic code of Leviticus and Deuteronomy, to contend with the economic conditions and social attitudes of a more complex society.

Taking the form of court decisions and discussions in religious academies, this transformation of Jewish law also marked the beginning of the decline of the priestly class and their supporters, the Sadducees, and the rise of a popular intellectual and religious leadership, the "Scribes and the Pharisees". With the destruction of the Second Temple in AD 70 and the extinction of its cult, it was the rules and traditions established by the latter which became the essence of Jewish religion, remaining so until this very day. Successive generations of post-Destruction scholars, known as the Tannaim, tried to establish the correct version of laws preserved in oral traditions, elucidating many new ones in the process. These were ultimately redacted and committed to writing by Rabbi Judah the Patriarch, the religious and civic head of Palestinian Jewry at the turn of the third century.

Not all of the material available at the time was included in Rabbi Judah's canon, the Mishna. Some alternative variants as well as further rules have reached us either as quotations of extracanonical material (*Baraita*) embedded in later exegesis, or as a collection of addenda compiled at some later date (the *Tosephta*). Together with the Mishna, they form what is known as the Tannaitic literature or tradition.

This tradition was further studied and expounded in the Jewish scholastic academies of Palestine and Mesopotamia. The objective of the later schoolmen, the Amoraim, was no longer the establishment of the correct reading of a tradition, but its interpretation and application to diverse situations. The reports of their deliberations are called the *Gemara*. They survive in two parallel compilations, known as the Jerusalem and the Babylonian Talmuds, redacted about AD 400 and 500, respectively, of which the latter is the more extensive and authoritative one.[14]

In the following centuries, up to the end of the first millennium, the Rabbinic tradition took on two highly distinct forms. One is that of the homiletic literature, the *Midrash* books, which flourished in Palestine in the last three or four centuries before the crusades. Much of it takes the form of fables and legends, far removed from our subject. But the *Midrashim* also occasionally contain allusions to the events and conditions of the day, reflecting the economic understanding of their times.

The other strand is that of the replies of the Mesopotamian academies to queries addressed to them from other parts of the Diaspora, once the Arab conquests made communications easier, and especially after Baghdad became the seat of the Abbasid Caliphs. Collectively known as *Geonica*, after the title bestowed on the heads of these academies, many of these *responsa* survived in individual collections, or embedded in later works.

The decline of the Mesopotamian center, and the growing geographical dispersion of Jewish communities, resulted in the proliferation of Talmudic exegesis and of verdicts and *responsa*, some of which reflect specific local conditions. Because of the difficulty of following the Talmudic discourse, attempts were also made to distill from it its main binding opinions. These activities continued throughout the middle ages, as they continue, in fact, until today, yielding a vast amount of Rabbinic literature of widely differing degrees of acceptance and circulation.

Within this vast literature, a few opera stand out for their practically universal acceptance and lasting influence. One is Rashi's eleventh century commentary on the Talmud. Another is Maimonides' twelfth century codification of Talmudic rules, the *Mishneh Torah*. Finally, with the passing of the Middle Ages, the sixteenth century witnesses the publication of an authoritative, ultimate codex of all rules formed until then, regulating orthodox Jewish behaviour until this very day, the *Shulhan Aruch*.

We thus have the Hebrew Bible at the basis of Rabbinic thought; the Mishna, *Baraita* and *Gemara* of the Talmud proper, which is the great collection of ancient and early medieval Rabbinic thought and the source of *Halakhic* interpretation throughout the ages; and which, together with other contemporaneous material, forms Talmudic literature in the narrow sense of the term; and the vast, still growing and in many respects highly heterogeneous mass of Talmudic exegesis, summary classifications, rulings and responsa of post-Talmudic Rabbinic literature.

THE SCOPE AND THE METHOD OF THE INQUIRY

Given the vastness and variety of Rabbinic literature, the question inevitably arises as to which of the opinions expressed in it can be regarded as representing "Rabbinic thought". In such situations, there is always the temptation of singling out some obscure authors whose utterings strike a chord in the heart of the modern reader, but failed to reach the ears of their contemporaries, not to mention of later generations. There is also the danger of failing to recognize that some currently justly forgotten authors might have had considerable impact on their contemporaries.[15]

To avoid such pitfalls, one should try to distinguish between the economic ideas encountered in what may be regarded as mainstream Rabbinic literature, and those encountered in the rest of it. While the exact boundary between the two cannot easily be delineated, there should be little difficulty in identifying the core of Rabbinic literature. This may be defined as consisting of those works which enjoyed a close to universal acceptance in the Jewish world. With regard to the ancient and the early medieval periods, this core would be represented by the works surveyed in the preceding section, with the possible exception of parts of the homiletic literature and the *responsa*.

The study of the economic thought of this mainstream should be supplemented by that of its periphery, as well as of the schools of thought opposing it. In the case of the Tannaitic literature this would include, first and foremost perhaps, the writings of Josephus and the later Dead Sea scrolls, as well as the New Testament and such early Church figures as Origenes. For the later, Amoraic period, the parallel Patristic literature and, for the early medieval opponents of Rabbinic Judaism, that of the Karaites. Such external sources tended to be completely ignored, so far, by researchers in this field.[16]

But even within the much narrower bounds of mainstream literature, there arises the question of the amount of material which has to be combed for an occasional discussion of economic relationships (as distinguished from the much more often referred to economic phenomena). Few of today's researchers have the encyclopedic knowledge of the Talmud acquirable only in traditional rabbinic seminaries, which was common enough in the past among those whom secularization deflected from their rabbinic vocation and enabled them to treat the Talmud critically.[17] However, we are lucky to have now at our disposal research aids which were unavailable to earlier generations. First and foremost among them is Kasovsky's monumental set of concordances of the Babylonian Talmud and of the Mishna and the *Tosephta*, extended by his sons to cover also some of the *Midrashim* and the Jerusalem Talmud.[18] These list the words appearing there with citations of all the passages in which they occur, greatly facilitating the search for texts with potential economic significance.

As regards medieval sources, Bar-Ilan University's computerized *responsa* project, still in progress, covers by now over 200 printed collections, representing more than half of those extant in print. This is classified not only by author and period but also by subject matter, which, again, makes the task of the researcher much less arduous.

To reconstruct the economic thought reflected in a literary corpus, one would ideally start by deciding on a list of basic concepts, then try to establish how they were treated there. Unfortunately, at the present stage of the investigation, this approach is ruled out by the vastness of the literature concerned and the fragmentary nature of its economic discourse. All we can do, for the time being, is go over the grounds, looking for whatever bits of evidence that come to light and, like archeologists, putting together the broken fragments of ancient statuary, hope that we have them all, and that all we have belongs to the same piece. It is only when enough such piecemeal findings are available, that we may be able to start adducing the general picture.

TANNAITIC AND AMORAIC ECONOMIC CONCEPTS

Needless to say, the Tannaitic and Amoraic sages did not concern themselves with economic theorizing for its own sake. Their interest in economic problems stemmed from the various injunctions of the Mosaic code bearing in one way or another on economic activity. But as the following examples illustrate, this often led to the discussion of economic concepts and of rudimentary economic theory.

Interest, nominal and real, ex-post and ex-ante

Not unnaturally, a problem tended to attract the sage's attention more, the stronger the conflict between these injunctions and the pressures and temptations of everyday life. Perhaps the greatest such gap concerned the proscription of usury. In the smallholders economy of the Judges or of the Davidic kingdom (when the Pentateuch seems to have been redacted), there must have been little scope for borrowing other than for consumption or for seed, when that was lost through disaster or improvidence. Lending was considered there in terms of charity, not of commercial relationships:

[A] And if thy brother be waxen poor, and fallen in decay with thee; then thou shalt relieve him.... Thou shall not give him thy money upon usury, nor lend him thy victuals for increase.

(Leviticus 25: 35, 37)[19]

But a rule which might have been self-evident in simpler days, had to be further specified in the much more commercialized Hellenistic and Roman times. In particular, the need arose of defining more clearly what constituted a loan, what should be considered interest?

The biblical text makes it clear that the ban on usury pertained to both money loans and those in kind. Inflation made us realize that if prices change, the real interest on money loans changes too, as does also the nominal, money rate on loans in kind. But with inflation relatively slow in pre-paper money days, the ancients were probably much more aware of the possibility of a change in the price of a given good, than in the price level as a whole. Consequently, they considered interest in purely nominal terms. The Mishna cites a generally liberal pre-destruction sage, Hillel the Elder, to the effect that

[B] A woman may not lend another a loaf of bread before turning it into money [values], lest the price of wheat rises and they be partaking in usury.

(M BM 5: 9)[20]

Nevertheless, the Tannaim made a clumsy attempt to distinguish between nominal and real interest, associating them with the two separate terms of [A]. Usury was identified with the nominal, explicit rate of interest, the lending of "a Sela [= four denarii] for five denarii, two Seah [measures] of wheat for three" (M BM 5: 1). "Increase", on the other hand, was real, implicit interest, illustrated by the case of wheat contracted for at a given price, but demanded for delivery after its price rose, to be exchanged for another good (ibid.).

The Amoraim clarified the matter further, by constructing cases where positive nominal interest was accompanied by zero real interest and vice versa:

[C] He lent someone one hundred [perutah] for [a repayment of] a hundred and twenty. Initially they were a hundred to a sixth [of a denarius], but ended at a hundred and twenty to a sixth. Usury there is here ... as he takes from him something he did not give him; increase there is not, for he made no gain, a sixth he has lent him and a sixth he took from him.

(TB BM 60b)[21]

[C]'s conclusion depends, of course, on the denarius being the purchasing power standard, which, as implied by [D] below, it indeed was. The above distinction was ultimately rejected by Rava (d. 351), who argued that, looked at in money terms, "usury" and "increase" were identical in that the lender either expected to end, or actually ended up with more of the nominal standard than he lent (ibid.).

But in reaching this conclusion, the *Gemara* clearly distinguished between *ex-ante* and *ex-post* interest, pointing out, with respect to [C], that "if we go by the initial [situation], there is both usury and increase; and if by the final, there is neither" (ibid.). The matter is tested further in a case where the *ex-ante* interest rate is zero:

[D] He lent him a hundred [perutah] for [a repayment of] a hundred. Initially they were a hundred in a sixth [of a dinar], but ended at a hundred in a fifth. Going by the initial [situation], there is neither usury nor increase here; judging by the final – there is both.

(ibid.)

Being bent on ensuring that no contravention of the Mosaic code will occur under any circumstances the Amoraim tried to proscribe all transactions resulting in either *ex-ante* or *ex-post* interest. But their making an exception of the lending at interest of funds held in trust for orphaned minors (TB BM 70a), and already earlier, the Tammaitic sanction of discounting monthly rents when paid in advance in a lump sum (M BM 5: 2), suggests that the Talmud's stand on this question reflects adherence to the law as a religious duty rather than a moral objection to interest taking.

The search for an absolute standard of value

The nominal attitude adopted with respect to usury manifested itself also in the discussion concerning the finalization of commercial transactions. The Tannaitic view was that a transaction comes to an end, so that neither party can renege on it, only with the passage of the goods into the possession of the purchaser, not of the money to the purveyor (M BM 4: 2).[22]

In the multiple currency world of the Roman empire this immediately raised the question of dealings involving the exchange of different types of coins and, more broadly, of what should be regarded as money and what as goods:

> [E] Gold acquires silver, but silver doesn't acquire gold. Copper acquires silver, but silver doesn't acquire copper. Bad coins acquire good ones, but good ones do not acquire bad ones. A token acquires a coin, but a coin does not acquire a token. Movables acquire coin[s], but coin[s] do not acquire movables. This is the rule: all movables acquire one another.
>
> (M BM 4: 1)

The *Gemara* pursued this problem further, asking also whether the definitions of what constituted a good or produce and what constituted money, were absolute or, as [E] might suggest, relative ones. The discussion is a lengthy one, drawing on rules pertaining to a diversity of situations, including, *inter alia*, the redemption of the first-born, the exchange of small denominations for large ones when going on pilgrimage, and the other way round for paying the "second tithe" (TB BM 44b–47b).

The debate almost unavoidably led to a search for an absolute standard of value. Citing a Tannaitic view that, for a certain purpose, "a silver denarius is a twenty-fifth of a golden one" (TB BM 44b), the *Gemara* argues that:

> [F] If you say [of a gold denarius] "it is a coin" – the Tanna [cited] refers to [it as] something [of] constant [value]. But if you say "it is produce" – [you would have] the Tanna referring to something which could appreciate or depreciate, [so that] sometimes the priest has to give him change [from a gold denarius] and sometimes he has to give the priest more.
>
> (ibid.)

This view of money as the standard of value may have been influenced by the existence of certain sacerdotal payments and of fines which had to be paid in fixed silver quantities already stipulated in the Mosaic code, such as, for example, the five silver *Sheqels'* redemption money of a first-born son. For this purpose, the Pentateuchal *Sheqel* was considered to be represented by the Tyrian *Tetradrachm*:

> [G] All fixed [amounts of] money [decreed] in the Torah – Tyrian silver; those [decreed] in their [i.e. the Sages'] rules – the [current] money of the country.
>
> (TB.b Kid. 11b)[23]

The discussion of "money versus produce" led also to a distinction between barter transactions and those involving money, raising the question of the attributes of the latter.[24] As the *Gemara* has it, for currency to be considered money, it has to enjoy wide circulation, i.e. acceptance. This, in turn, requires it to be stamped with a figure or a legend and to be approved by the Ruler. We may also note, passim, that [E] contains also an early formulation of Gresham's law.[25]

Opportunity costs

The Rabbinical ban on interest seems to have been based, first and foremost, on a religious imperative, not on moral condemnation. Attempts to find some legalistic subterfuges circumventing it, which culminated in the seventeenth century generalized transaction permit (*Heter 'Isqa*), are already evident in the Mishna. In particular, there is no trace of the Aristotelian notion that money is "barren". In fact, distinguishing between advance and post-paid interest (both of which it proscribes), the Mishna quotes Rabban Gamliel the Younger (second half of first century) as explaining that

> [H] There is advance interest and there is deferred interest.... He borrowed from another and returned him his coins, and sent him [a gift] saying: [This is] for your coins which have been idling with me that is deferred interest.

> (M BM 5: 10)

The borrower is explicitly shown here to be compensating the lender for the latter having foregone the use of his money while it was on loan, i.e. for the opportunity cost of credit.[26]

Lest it be argued that this is a misinterpretation of [H], it should be pointed out that a similar terminology – "the wage of her idleness" – is also used elsewhere in the Tannaitic literature, to denote recompense for worktime lost (TB.b Kid 16b).

The mere idea of compensation for enforced inactivity, which appears already in the Pentateuch (Exodus 21: 18–19), is commonplace. But the Tannaitic discussion of how it should be estimated seems to go beyond commonplace economics. Thus, in the case of a person recuperating from an injury, the Mishna's view was that

> [I] He is to be regarded as if he were a watchman of cucumber [beds], for he has already been given the value of his hand.

> (M BK 8: 1)

The explanatory clause in [I] was due to the need to justify the decision to estimate compensation for temporary inactivity (coming on top of that for any permanent loss of income suffered) by post-injury, rather than pre-injury alternative wages. A non-canonical, lengthier version, which made this clear, even asked whether or not "justice was impaired thereby?" (Tos. BK 9: 2).[27] Less justifiably, a person returning lost property to its owner was to be compensated for the time this took "as if he were an unemployed labourer" (M. BM 2: 9).

The discussion of the reasons underlying these decisions lies beyond the scope of this paper. But as I have shown elsewhere, the Tannaim's explanations of them clearly reveal their awareness of what constitutes the real opportunity cost in each case (Kleiman 1987b). This is true, as well, of the Amoraic discussion of the subject, which also contains examples of tort cases in which the full opportunity cost had to be paid in compensations. Furthermore, in all these cases, it was the market price that was supposed to provide a measure of the opportunity cost.

A mental experiment – compensating and equivalent variations

The case of injury compensation provides further evidence of the Tannaitic and Amoraic discussion of economic matters going beyond the mere observation of economic facts, i.e. of commonplace economics. This is certainly true of the consideration given in the *Gemara* to the problem of assessing compensation for pain.

By the time of the Mishna, the old *lex talionis* has been substituted by a system of pecuniary compensations for physical injury. For this purpose, the effects of injury were divided into a number of separate components, the compensation for each of which to be assessed independently. The five were injury (i.e. permanent damage), pain, healing (costs of medication), loss of time (when recuperating), and what would go today under the heading of mental anguish – "indignity".[28] For the monetary assessment of "pain", the Tannaim suggested the subjective valuation of: "How much a man like him would be willing to take to suffer as much" (M BK 8: 1).

As the Amoraim, however, were quick to point out later, this raised the question of separating the valuation of pain from that of other injury components. For pain associated with the loss of a limb (where the approach of the last quotations would have been impractical), they resorted to assuming an offender sentenced to a loss of his arm, foregoing the option he has been given of having it done under some sort of anaesthetic (or by pharmaceutical rather than purely surgical means):

> [J] It is estimated how much would a man demand to be paid, to have his arm, which is due to the state, severed [choosing, in favour of the latter] between potion and sword.

> (TB BK 85a)

But as "even in this case one would not take [money] and suffer" (ibid.), the option offered was reversed. This also solved the problem of there being, probably, no bidders for the pain of others, while there might be some suppliers of its prevention:[29]

[K] Instead, it is estimated how much would a man be willing to pay, to have his arm, which is due to the state, severed, [choosing in favour of the latter] between sword and potion

(TB BK 85a)

Or as the blunter, less hair-splitting Jerusalem Talmud has it:

[L] They get hold of a man and ask him: "How much are you willing to give not to have such pain inflicted on you?" And as much as he says they award him [i.e. the injured party].

(TJ BK 8: 1)[30]

Estimating the sum of money for which the individual would be ready to forgo the pain killer, as suggested in [JJ], amounts, of course, to estimating the Hicksian (pain) compensating variation in income (compare Hicks 1946). On the other hand, in [K] and in [L] the pain is valued by the amount of money offered to avoid it, i.e. by means of the Hicksian equivalent variation in income. The awareness of the similarity, but at the same time also of the difference between these two measures suggests a certain degree of speculative, analytical thought, even if disguised in a concrete garb.

The general characteristics of Talmudic economics

My earlier strictures on periodization to the contrary, Tannaitic and Amoraic economics have, at this stage of research, been treated as one. This despite the fact that the former flourished in Roman Palestine, while the latter is mostly the product of the academies of Sassanid Mesopotamia. Also, the Tannaitic material examined for economic content does not as yet include the homiletic *Midrash* literature. In fact, even in the canon covered so far, interest has focused, not unnaturally, on the parts dealing most directly with economic matters, i.e. in the order of *Nezikin* (damages).

With these reservations in mind, what can be said of ancient Rabbinic economic thought? The cases presented in the preceding section demonstrate that it did go beyond the mere observation of obvious economic facts or relationships. Occasionally, as in the case described in the last section, it displayed a surprisingly high degree of sophistication. Nevertheless, and despite the much wider range of topics touched upon, it seems to lack the coherence which would turn it into an economic system similar to that developed by Aristotle in the *Nicomachean Ethics*. Though there is still much economics left to uncover in Talmudic literature, it is doubtful whether it will change the present impression.

The reasons for this are manifold. Though both Roman Palestine and Sassanid Mesopotamia had highly developed markets, they were also predominantly agricultural economies. Unlike in ancient Greece, which had a highly developed shipping and maritime trade sector, domestic supply there, especially in Palestine, was extremely dependent on weather conditions. Fluctuations in supply being thus mostly exogenous to the economic system, served to stunt the development of a richer value theory (Kleiman 1987a). Furthermore, most of the literature considered came into being in the period following the destruction of the Second Temple and, in any case, reflected the views of a social group which had never been saddled with problems of macro-economic governance.

It is typical of this situation, that the Amoraic economic discussion of taxes, though again in certain respects quite advanced, is restricted to problems of distributive justice (Kleiman 1988, Schwartz 1990). Nowhere does it question the efficiency effects of taxation, or the determination of the general tax level. Except for complaining, about them, it does not consider analytically any of the main fiscal instruments of the day. In fact, the only explicit reference to macro-economics in the Talmud, of which much has been made by some authors, is an elegantly worded, but analytically fairly clumsy attempt to distinguish between prosperity and depression as times when prices are high and money (income?) plentiful, and times when prices are low and money is scarce (see, for example, Liebermann 1979).

The possibility should not be ruled out that some macro-economic thinking was done by groups associated with ruling the country in pre-Destruction days. Long-buried scrolls might perhaps one day surface, to reveal to us the economics popular in, say, Herod the Great's court circles, or among the High Priesthood or the Sadducee élite. But as beyond a certain point in history the ideas of these groups cease to be part of the Rabbinic mainstream, they would in any case be only archeological curiosities, having had no role in shaping the minds of the generations that followed them.

POST-TALMUDIC, MEDIEVAL THOUGHT

Little research has been carried out so far on Rabbinic economic thought in the post-Talmudic medieval period. What has been done is mostly embedded in investigations of *Halahkic* economics which do not lend themselves easily to periodization. Nevertheless, some very tentative generalizations will be ventured here, which may have to be reversed once more research has been done in this field.

Of the different forms of expression of Rabbinic thought characterizing this period, one, that of the codification of the obligatory rulings emanating from the Talmudic discussion, displays a certain ossification, as far as the topic at hand is concerned. The *Gemara*, being really stylized stenographic reports of the main Amoraic debates, constitutes a rich lode for researchers to mine. This format, however, made it extremely difficult for the uninitiated to follow, not to mention to deduce from it the precepts of everyday behavior to which they were supposed to adhere. Hence the greatness of Maimonides' *Mishneh Torah*, which extricated from the Talmud all such rules, categorizing them by subject. But because it strove to be a codex, not the proceedings of the underlying discussion, it did not indulge in hair-splitting debates and almost eschewed explanation altogether. It thus fails to provide us with a base for reconstructing Maimonides' own view and understanding of economic phenomena.[31]

Further such collections followed. But in so far as their redactors present notions not encountered in Talmudic literature, it is only rarely possible to establish whether these reflect some since then lost ancient texts, or ideas current in their own times.[32]

The *responsa* literature promises to be more rewarding in this respect. For it deals not with the by then already codified general rules, but in their application to yield rulings on until then unencountered problems, or to old problems arising under until then unencountered conditions. The occasional consideration, in economic literature, of such Rabbinic answers suggests that much can be learnt from them regarding their understanding of imperfect competition and of distributive justice.[33] But systematic research in this field has yet to be done.

POSSIBLE INFLUENCE ON MAINSTREAM ECONOMIC THOUGHT

While the exact place of Jews in European economic history might be a matter for debate, there can be but little doubt that they played a significant role in it. Up to quite recent times most of them would have had some religious education, including, *inter alia*, some familiarity with the main economic notions of Rabbinic literature. It would have been only natural for some of these to pass into general circulation.

This almost certainly didn't happen in relatively recent times. Not only do the general writings on economic subjects of latter-day Jewish authors fail to make any reference to the Rabbinic tradition, but so does also a Hebrew economic textbook of close to a hundred years ago, obviously aiming at a Jewish readership (Hurwitz 1900, Kleiman 1973b). By the time these authors began to write, the accepted corpus of economic analysis was already developed enough for them to feel that the economic notions of Rabbinic literature did not merit serious consideration, and that their mention would only expose them to charges of parochialism. To have had any influence on mainstream economic thought, any transmission of these notions had to take place much earlier.

But we can only speculate on whether, and in which way, ancient and medieval Rabbinic economic concepts may have entered the mainstream of Western economic thought in some earlier times. Our method of tracing intellectual influences relies heavily on the evidence of literary sources. There is little to look for there for our purpose: unlike the Bible, the Talmud – the *Gemara* in particular – remained a closed book as far as the Christian West was concerned. The medieval schoolmen who cited Maimonides' *Guide to the Perplexed* probably never even heard of the *Mishneh Torah*, his codification of the Talmudic law.

A possibility which cannot be completely discounted is that these were rabbinically trained apostates, who might have passed on some Rabbinic economic notions in their contacts with the Gentile world. In Spain in particular, there has been since the fourteenth century a considerable number of converts who figured prominently first in the Synagogue and then in the Church.[34] But given the latter's condemning attitude towards Jewish religious writings other than the Scriptures, and the precarious position of New Christians, especially after the establishment of the Inquisition, they may well have refrained from doing so. Sooner, it would have been the successful Jewish royal treasurers and tax farmers of the Iberian peninsula in pre-expulsion days, which may have fulfilled this role. But there is no evidence that they ever did.

A much broader, though perhaps also less intensive, interface for some such transfer of ideas may have occurred through the innumerable everyday, commercial and other, contacts between Gentiles and Jews, many of whom used to set aside some regular time for studying the religious law. In particular, it was the clergy which, most probably, would have felt it their duty to draw Jews they encountered into a religious debate that could easily branch into economics as well.[35] But such an intellectual osmosis remains, as a rule, undocumented.[36]

TWO VOICES FROM THE RENAISSANCE

Succumbing to the temptation mentioned earlier, of focusing on (at their time) marginal authors and ideas, let us conclude by considering two views from the threshold of the modern era. One belongs to a scholar-banker, the other to a professional scribbler. They both wrote within a span of three-score years centering on the year 1530.

Scion of a long, established Pisan banking family who were friends, or at least clients of the Medicis, Yehiel Nissim da Pisa (1507–1574) served also in the rabbinate of Ferrara, as well as of his own town. Unbeknownst to him, he had also the distinction of some of his writings making the pages of the *American Economic Review* (Marx 1916). An author of some religio-philosophical discourses, he completed in 1559 a monograph on usury entitled *Hayei Olam*, i.e. "The Life Eternal", which was intended to be printed in Ferrara, but survived only in manuscript copies (Rosenthal 1962). The book constitutes one of the best and most exhaustive descriptions of the financial instruments of the time. It outlines the ways in which interest can legally be taken, without offending against the religious law. But like almost all Rabbinic writers over the ages, nowhere does da Pisa question the logic of the proscription itself.

Abraham Farrisol (1451–1525), on the other hand, was a professional writer, whose geography book merited a Latin translation published at Oxford in 1691. Having participated in a religious disputation at the court of the Dukes of Ferrara in about 1490, he put his arguments in writing. The popularity of the resultant work, *Magen Avraham* ("Shield of Abraham") is attested by no less than thirty-four surviving manuscript copies.

Farrisol disdained the traditional Jewish defence on the usury question, that while forbidding it to be taken from a "brother", one of the Pentateuch versions of the ban allows it to be taken from "strangers". Instead, he tackled the whole interest issue head-on. Once the old paradisaic order of things has vanished,

> [M] a new order was required, to assist others in exchange for a remuneration.... And had nature so ordained that one should provide anybody who needs money with a free loan, the same should have applied to houses and horses and all other things.
>
> (Farrisol 1928: 292)

And the reason he gives for this scheme of things is that:

> [N] Had everybody to provide others with everything for free, without remuneration, it would have started great jealousy and quarrels in society, for how would it have been then decided who is to serve, and who is to be served.
>
> (ibid.)

That is why, Farrisol concludes, the custom has spread to "help and serve at agreed prices and wages".

Was Farrisol's vision of prices as allocators his own? Did it influence the thinking of others? We know he was much influenced by the writings of Don Ytzhaq Abarabnel, the philosopher and scholar who served as the last Jewish financier at the court of Castile. The chain of ideas which might thus be established is startling. But research has failed so far to pinpoint the source to Farrisol's view of prices and of interest in any of the erudite Don's writings.[37]

NOTES

1 This is a revised version of a paper originally prepared for a conference on Ancient and Medieval Economic Thought, held at the MIT, 10 June, 1994. I wish to acknowledge my debt to Betsey Price, the co-chairperson of the 1994 MIT conference, and to the late Don Patinkin of the Hebrew University, for

their most detailed, penetrating and helpful comments on an earlier draft. To Patinkin, who first introduced me to economics, I am also greatly indebted for encouraging and abetting my interest in Talmudic and Rabbinic economics.

2 As a matter of fact, there were hardly any Jewish economic theorists until the present century. Of the 232 economists born before 1900 listed in the *Calendar of Economists' Birthdays*, seventeen at most could be regarded as being of Jewish origin. And most of them were probably too far removed of this origin for it to have had any direct bearing on their thinking. See also note 6 below.

3 Thus, for example, the article on the history of economic thought in the *Encyclopedia of the Social Sciences*, goes from the Greeks straight to Rome and Christianity (1931: vol. 7, 346); while the section devoted to economic thought in the ancient period in the *International Encyclopedia of Social Sciences* mentions only Greek and Roman thought, proceeding from them straight to medieval scholasticism (1968: vol. 4, 430–431). The same is also true of most recent textbooks in the field, in so far as they refer at all to pre-modern economics. See, for example Lekachman (1959), Bell (1980) and Ekelund and Herbert (1990). The honorable exception is the late B. Gordon, whose writings on both Judaic economics and economic ethics (1975, 1986, 1989) did much to arouse interest in the subject.

4 Thus, for example, Roll (1961), who devotes more attention to the Old Testament than most writers. See also, for example, Spiegel (1971), whose three (out of a total of eight hundred) pages' survey of Biblical economic thought goes under such headings as "The Sabbath", "Slavery", "Jubilee Year", and speaks of views on the dignity of labor. Haney, though he treads much the same ground and lumps together "the Hebrews and the Hindus", at least raises the question of the understanding, or its absence, of the economic implications of ethical precepts (Haney 1911, 1936: 39–55).

5 Translations of the whole Talmud (as distinguished from single tractates or fragmentary selections) into European languages start appearing only late in the nineteenth century: into Polish (1859–1864), into German (1897–1922). A translation of the Jerusalem Talmud into French appeared in 1871–1889. The first full translation of the Babylonian Talmud into English is Epstein (1935–1952); and of the Palestinian one, Neusner (1982–1994). The Mishna itself fared better, a Latin translation appearing already in 1698. The standard English translation is Danby (1933).

6 Of the great post-biblical ancient authors, Philo Judaeus the Alexandrian (c. 30 BC to AD 45) reflected Stoic ideas and went on to influence the Church Fathers, rather than the Rabbis. In more recent times, the writings of Joseph Penso, the author of *Confusion de Confusiones* (1688; 1957), the first known description of the stock exchange, and of Ricardo, have probably little in common except for both authors having been brokers. The former started his life as a son of a crypto-Jew, the latter ended his as an apostate.

7 The fact that the standard editions of the Talmud carry latter-day commentaries and glosses on the same page with the original text itself, contributes to the confusion of which the following statement is typical: "In the *Babylonian Talmud* [redacted c. AD 500], a medieval commentator, R. Nissim Gerondi (1320–1380) quotes . . ." (Ohrenstein and Gordon 1992: 59).

8 Though in Islamic, as in *Halakhic* economics, the two are often mixed up together. See, however, the clear distinction drawn by Essid (1986: especially 97 ff.) and by Kuran (1986).

9 Orthodox Jews regard the *Halakha* as immutable, although on the face of it, it seems to keep evolving in response to changing conditions, trying to cope

with such problems as whether the use of electricity desecrates the Sabbath, or what is the suitable order of prayers for an Astronaut orbiting the moon. These, however, could be regarded to be but the applications of timeless rules to current conditions. The Talmud proper often cites rules which were found unauthoritative, to clarify the authoritative ruling. See also the section on Talmudic and post-talmudic Rabbinic literature below.

10 See, for example, Bell (1980), Lekachman (1959), and Spiegel (1971). Even Roll (1961), who shows more interest in pre-modern thought than most other authors, emphasizes the ethical and political aspects up to the rise of mercantilism. Theocharis (1961) provides an exception, but his interest is limited to mathematical models.

11 However useful, the Haney–Schumpeter distinction failed to become widely adopted in contemporary literature. To avoid confusion we will continue using here the term "economic thought" in the accepted (in itself confusing) manner, referring to both economic ideas and economic analysis.

12 Thus, for example, Anglo-Saxon law on jettison still reflects the *Lex Rhodia de iactu*, the stance of the Rhodian sea code on the subject. See Carver (1982), paragraph 1346.

13 Speaking of the moment when economics could develop into a science, Finley argues that it "never came in antiquity because ancient society never had an economic system which was an *enormous conglomeration of interdependent markets*" (Finley 1985: 22, emphasis added). But Roll, from whom the emphasized passage is taken (Roll 1961: 371), used it to explain the difference between classical and modern economics. Most probably Roll also had vertical, rather than spatial, market interdependence in mind.

14 The Talmud and the Mishna to which it refers, is known in Judaism as the "oral tradition", or oral law, as distinct from the written one of the Pentateuch.

15 I am grateful to Professor Betsey Price for pointing out this parallel to me.

16 Sperber (1974) made good use of all these, as well as other sources. But his interest lay in the economic history of the Talmudic period, not in its economic thought.

17 Even so, while the late nineteenth and early twentieth centuries witnessed the appearance of works on, for example, Talmudic medicine (Israels 1845, Wunderbar 1859, Preuss 1911, 1978), zoology and botanics (Loew 1891, Loew 1924–1934, 1967), agriculture (Vogelstein 1894), or economic *realia* (Ejges 1930), not to mention law, there was hardly any discussion of its economic theory. For a general discussion of Talmudic *realia* as well as for further references to works referring to them, see Krauss (1910–1912). German used to be the main language of modern Jewish studies as they evolved in the last century, almost up to World War I.

18 It is almost incomprehensible how one man, even in the course of a long and industrious life, could have singlehandedly produced, in pre-computer days, the fifty-odd volumes of Ch. J. Kasovsky (1914, 1967: 4 vols), (1933–1961: 6 vols) and (1954–1980: 41 vols) His work has been continued by B. Kosovsky (1955–1966: 4 vols), (1967–1969: 4 vols) and (1970–1974: 5 vols); and by M. Kosovsky (1980–) in progress, of which 3 volumes have been published so far, in addition to 3 volumes of proper names.

19 This injunction repeats the one in Exodus 22: 24 (22: 25 in the Authorized Version) and is repeated in Deuteronomy 23: 20–21 (23: 19–20 in the Authorized Version). The last-mentioned verse was to assume great importance in later days, in disputations with the medieval Church, as it explicitly permitted lending on interest to "strangers", i.e. Gentiles. The same view of the use of credit is

implied by Ezekiel 18: 8–17, where the taking of interest is condemned along with oppressing the poor and the needy.

20 The accepted reference system to the Mishna is by initials of tractate title, and by chapter and rule numbers. Thus, the present reference is to the third rule in the fifth chapter of the Mishna tractate *Bava Metzia* [or *Baba Mezi'a* (ed.)] (M BM 5: 3), the "Middle Gate" (part) of the order of *Nezikim* (Damages) in the Mishna. The standard translation of the Mishna into English is Danby (1933). But though it comes closest to preserving the flavour of the origin, there is an unavoidable interpretative element even in this translation. I took the liberty of occasionally departing from it, placing the additional words needed for understanding in square brackets. A similar procedure was adopted also with respect to the English translations of the Babylonian and Jerusalem Talmuds, by Epstein (1935–1954) and Neusner (1982) respectively, which hold also the Mishna.

21 The Babylonian Talmud is referred to by initials of tractate, and by number and side of the folio leaf in the *editio princeps* printed in Venice in 1520–1523. Thus, the present reference (TB BM 60b) is to the verso page of leaf 60 in the *Bava Metzic*, the 'Middle Gate' (part) of the order of *Nezikin* (Damages) in the Babylonian Talmud (the divisions of which parallel those of the Mishna on which they center).

22 The rule was intended to provide an incentive for the seller to guard the goods against damage, as long as they were physically in his possession. As an old *Baraita* put it, had the transaction been consummated once money changed hands, the seller could tell the buyer "your wheat burned down in the attic", and not be held responsible for it (TB.b BM 47b).

23 The lower-case "b", following either the BT or TJ (Jerusalem Talmud) designations, denotes a *Beraita* (i.e. Tannaitic material not included in the Mishna) embedded, as the case may be, in either the Babylonian or the Jerusalem Talmud.

24 For an opposite interpretation of the Mishna's view of money as the standard of value, see Neusner (1990, e.g. p. 80).

25 [E] reflects, of course, the bi- or even tri-metallism of the Roman monetary regime in the second century. The *Gemara* for [E] mentions an earlier version, in which "silver purchases gold", which is also the text of the Mishna preserved in the Jerusalem Talmud, suggesting a change in the relative moneyness of the two metals sometime around AD 200. See Kleiman (1973b), Sperber (1974).

26 Although the Mishna doesn't say so, this also is, of course, the reason for what it refers to as "advance" interest, i.e. the borrower sending a gift to the lender at the time the loan is made. Reducing thus the sum actually borrowed, but not that to be repaid, amounts to discounting the repayment.

27 The *Tosephta* (collection of Tannaitic rulings alternative to, or excluded from, the Mishna) is referred to by tractate, chapter and rule in the standard Zuckermandel edition of 1880 (Zuckermandel 1880, 1963).

28 We follow here Danby's (1933) English terminology. The Epstein (1935–1952) edited translation uses "depreciation" for the first and "degradation" for the last of these terms. For a fuller discussion of the subject, see Kleiman (1987b), on which this section draws heavily.

29 Though as watchers of Fellini's *Satyricon* may remember, there seems to have been a demand for having such amputations on sentenced offenders performed in theatricals, presumably for a consideration.

30 The Palestinian, or Jerusalem Talmud, denoted here by TJ, is referred to by initials of tractate and number of chapter and rule.

31 Though Baron (1941) portrays Maimonides as having no economic views beyond those of the Talmud, he must have had some. Beside his interests in philosophy, Jewish theology and *Halakha*, and in the medicine he practiced, Maimonides was also a (sleeping?) partner in his brother's Red Sea pearl trade. For a translation of a holograph letter from the latter to Maimonides, discovered in the Cairo *Genizah*, see Goitein (1974: 207–212).

32 Neusner, in fact, claimed the same to be already true of the Talmud with respect to the Mishna, arguing that "exegetical documents of the Mishna follow the program defined by the Mishna and amplify and refine ideas of the Mishna" (Neusner 1990: 152). But while this might, indeed, be true of the Talmudic agenda in general, it does not seem to apply to the discussion of individual problems. The task of latter-day codifiers having been to extract simple rules from the detailed, lengthy and often convoluted Talmudic discussion, it allowed them much less leeway than the succinctness of the Mishna allowed the Amoraim.

33 See, for example, the various cases quoted by Lieberman (1979) and Tamari (1987).

34 The most prominent names in this context are probably those of Abner of Burgos (1270–1340), later known as Alfonso of Valledolid; Joshua ha'Lorqi (Hieronimo di Santa Fe, d. 1419); and Shlomo ha'Levi (1351–1435) who, as Pablo de Santa Maria, ended up as the bishop of Burgos. For outside influences on Spanish economic thinking, see Grice-Hutchison (1978).

35 The genre of Jewish jokes set in the framework of a priest and a rabbi travelling on a train probably echoes some such episodes. Because populations used to be small, there were few separate Jewish travel conveyances before quite modern times.

36 An example of the tantalizing bits of inconclusive evidence which surface occasionally is the French idiom "entre chien et loup", describing a dusk hour, which I came upon by chance (in an English book review!) while revising this paper. This is practically identical with the "from the time one can distinguish *between wolf and dog*", which the Talmud uses to describe the time at dawn from which the morning prayer can be said, as well as the dusk hour (TB Brachot 9b, emphasis added). But the earliest recorded (i.e. written) use of the French expression is by Mme de Sevigne, in 1675 (see Robert 1989). Such an idiom, however, could have developed independently wherever wolves were common.

37 See D. Ruderman (1974), *Abraham Farrisol: An Historical Study of his Life and Thought in the Context of Jewish Communal Life in Renaissance Italy*, Ph.D. thesis (in Hebrew, with English summary), Jerusalem: the Hebrew University.

Part III

GREEK ECONOMIC THOUGHT

5

REFLECTIONS OF ANCIENT ECONOMIC THOUGHT IN GREEK POETRY

Bertram Schefold

GREEK ECONOMIC THOUGHT AS A PROBLEM OF HISTORICAL DOGMA

Introduction

The interest here is in seeing what kind of understanding of economics, in its connection to politics and society, is manifest in the literary work of Greek antiquity. For example, how long before systematic economic theory was there an understanding of regularities in the economy? Were political-economic necessities felt and if so, expressed? In which form was the image of a good economy, one ordered according to established principles, conceived?

But does it make sense at all to draw literature in as a source in the search for economic thought, as we plan to do here? At first glance, examination of ancient literature seems especially hopeless, because most of the poetry expresses life by mirroring it through myth, and therefore economic analysis in a modern sense is nowhere to be found. It is not our intention to study how, according to aesthetic criteria, literature depicts aspects of the economy – that is the task of the historian of literature. We hope, instead, whether owing to the special insight of the author, to realistic changes of an epoch, or to a reflective attitude which happens to consider both human destiny and the state's economic necessities together, to acquire from the older texts a clear picture of the economic life of earlier cultures, and, beyond antiquarian details, a better understanding of the situation, within which people were trying to resolve the economic problem(s) of their surroundings at the time. We are also interested in seeing how far the literature expresses the constantly changing economic picture of the earliest eras. Lastly, it might be shown that there was in antiquity a collective expression of a certain economic understanding in both the literature and the philosophy.

The following premises seem to suggest the potential for a certain success:

- According to their own viewpoint, the Greeks found myth and poetry, especially with Homer as the teacher, in fact art in general, to be directives in life. Long before literature and science had divided itself into genres and disciplines, they had a basic ability to express the world as it was, which can be viewed by us now much later with respect to, among other things, its economic aspects.

- Greek philosophy at the end of the classical period presented systematic statements about the economy, state, and society, namely in the works of Plato and Aristotle, which, while they do not contain a causal economic analysis in the modern sense, clearly and with great effect express the economic ethics of Greek classical society. In asking here historically what teachings preceded and influenced their works, early Greek poetry, although not the only source of their economic thought, stands as a very substantial one. Allowing for the long transition from the aristocratic period of heroes to the democratic polis during which some of the values underwent shifts, the essential foundations of the economic thought in Greek philosophy can be traced back to Homer.

- The limitations of Plato's and Aristotle's philosophically expressed understanding of economics are obvious not only when compared to modern theories, but also when set within the course of Greek economic history, in which we see more money-economy and capitalistic activities than their traditional teachings about the collective life of the stably provisioned extended autarchic household within a politically and culturally autarchic polis would suggest. For this, however, we can listen to the voices of the Sophists and other pre-Socratic and Socratic philosophers. A certain autonomy of a society's economic processes rings through their work, even their poetic work.

The philosophical economics teachings

The philosophical economics teachings of the Greeks are so well known (and addressed by others in this volume) that a tight summary, which applies primarily to Plato and Aristotle,[1] will suffice here. The starting point with respect to Aristotle is the *Politics*, followed by his thoughts on the art of running a household, which comprises both social leadership and material provisioning. Also included are marriage, the raising of children, and the directing of slaves and paid workers. Slavery[2] was an institution that the Greeks saw as unfortunate but necessary. Slavery required the least justification when the slaves were uneducated barbarians; they would be disposable when the work could be done by automatons. The goal of the household economy was to prepare for free citizens a basis for the "good life" according to philosophical knowledge. Unlimited or desired growth of wealth was not permitted, but neither did Aristotle suggest the asceticism advocated by the Stoics. This position was politically-economically actualized, for example, in the repeatedly issued laws of antiquity and the Middle Ages against what was found to be excessive luxury.

The Greek household is based at its core on agricultural self-sufficiency; this is the "natural art of profit" or "economics". Aristotle based the inclusion of various activities as natural arts of profit on a comparison to their role in the animal world: the abilities of hunters, gatherers, peasants, and even that of thieves are thus legitimized; as we shall see, however, ideas tied to tradition hide behind the Natural Law constructs.

The "unnatural" art of profit consists of the collection of wealth beyond the customary bounds, according to the maxim of "endeavor to live, rather than to live well". This so-called "chrematistics" is based on goal-oriented employment: a shoemaker should think of sandal sewing as he does it, not of the profit that he will make. The inversion of goals is made possible through the twisted use of money. (As we shall see, money as an anonymous, incomprehensible and socially destructive power can be traced back to classical Greek poetry, especially to Sappho and the Archaic period, and most functions of money fall under the category of "unnatural" forms of profit.) Originally intended to serve only the exchange of goods between otherwise independent autarchic households, it can become the object of an abstract profiteering for wealth. Thus, next to the naturally appropriate bounty of the household, there is the unnatural wealth, where money is increased without bound, as happens in trade and usury.

Some occupations, as a result of the inversion of goals, are added to the unnatural list, like doctors when they have their eye on their pay rather than on healing a patient. That trade and the collection of tribute were essential to the economic life of his time was not something about which Aristotle thought. It did not occur to him to advocate bans on tributes or speeches against usury. The good life indirectly required institutions such as slavery and usury, despite the fact that they do not represent an acceptable existence for free citizens. Also detectable are gradations making exploitation of the misery of the poor more contemptible than the activities of bulk-traders. For the practical teaching of this "unnatural" art Aristotle recommends some textbooks that are lost to us. When Heracles, for example, stood before the same crossroads, he sought to attain the good life intelligently and tried at least to avoid the lure of unnatural profit.

It may contradict modern social thought, but the virtues that were most important to Aristotle could not all be followed simultaneously in a successful state.[3] The Stoics were the first to look for a solution that would allow all people to live the good life, in which slavery would be abolished and the post-classical concept of cosmopolitan goals would suppress the emphasis on the polis.[4]

In this philosophical conceptual system, devotion to the carefully made product plays a large role.[5] Plato and other authors emphasize that the idea of division of labor is not to increase production but to improve quality. The concrete product stands so far in the foreground that the Greek language has no word for the general concept of work. Since the division of labor exists only for the beauty and quality of the product, the self-sufficiency of the household cannot mean that production – ideally agricultural – with its political connection to the city produces everything on its own, but rather only, that regulated exchange, which can be protected from the rapidly changing market circumstances, takes place.

In this way, the idea of the just exchange is based on the maintenance of an ordered society. Aristotle does not consider it as an individual economic problem, but rather as an application of his teachings on justice, which besides the ideas of distributive and commutative justice also includes the justice of reciprocity (*antipepontos*). Reciprocal trade and charity (*metadosis*) hold the polis together. Aristotle mentions the practice of building altars to the Charities, the goddesses of poverty, in order that the citizen will bring himself to giving and to thanking the gods.[6] There thus exists a three-way division of the relationships of reciprocity: to violence even unfair violence can respond; to giving, a spontaneous return gift, and finally, the unmediated exchange (*antidosis*). This last, the only one that is in our sense an economic transaction, in order to be just, must obey the principle of appropriateness in such a way that the status and worthiness of all parties are conserved.

While mathematical proportions are used here to illustrate the idea of appropriateness, a closer examination proves that Aristotle neither wants to nor can find a quantitative analysis of the exchange relationship. Further, the equivalence of the exchanged objects must be already determined, so that their relative status will not be altered through the exchange. It must namely hold, that if A and B are people of different status, and a and b are the objects to be exchanged, then the relationships of the people to the objects remains the same despite the exchange, or, symbolically:

$$(A:a):(B:b)=(A:b):(B:a)$$

which means that a=b, or, in other words, equivalence is necessary to maintain the proportional status A:B.

Elsewhere, Aristotle clearly states that the concrete components which define the status of a person change with political circumstances, and are different in democracies from in oligarchies, so the question is not to determine from an equivalence of the persons – as according to labor or utility – an equivalence of objects. Aristotle considers that people vary and is amazed at the possibility of the equivalence of objects, which is a wonderful thing, because it allows everything to be measured against every-thing else. That which seems to be impossible can thus be transacted, and this is facilitated through money. Money steps in as the representative of the need that always precedes the exchange. This need refers back to the necessities of a good life, whose natural worth is equated through exchange; and money is introduced nominally as a simplification of the exchange process. There is here no reference to inflation, which could legitimize interest rates as a part of the inflation.

These are the somewhat tiresome explanations, which historians of eco-nomic thought have wanted, with various tricks, to draw toward a favorite economic theory – whether the possibilities of equating them are with reference to the labor theory of value or to utility theory. Aristotle's text rescues itself, however, from both applications: the requirement of appropriateness rests exactly on the inequality of the people and on the qualitative difference (in appeal) of their hopefully well-made products whose quantitative equivalence presents the problem. An abstract concep-tion of labour is not to be found in Greek philosophy.

For similar reasons we cannot refer to utility, which concept was tested by the ancient Greeks in the form of hedonist philosophy – naturally, still without the Fundamental Equation relations of marginal utility theory. Utility is completely ignored by Plato and Aristotle as an independent principle guiding behavior, because one should strive for the Good (not the Useful). A need for trade is indeed stated, but the intensity of the utility is not mentioned and thus not pulled in as the explanation for supply and demand, to be discussed later.

Some think that Plato began as a hedonist. It is clear that he rejected hedonism in the later dialogues. However, in the more critical than con-structive early dialogue *Protagoras*, we see Socrates experiment with utility theory. He pursues hypothetically, without saying so, the consequences of the assumption that demand determines trade (Plato, *Protagoras* 357B). Plato clearly saw the consequences of hedonism. It led him to a calculation, that could be handled mathematically and that replaced the traditional ordering of life forms according to various dimensions, with a one-dimen-sional measurement.

It is characteristic of Plato to build a hierarchy of forms of existence and to place at the top the Idea of the Good. Ideas as quintessential, whether they be as abstract as the Idea of Circle or as concrete as the Idea of Monarchy, all have some aspect of the Idea of the Good. Out of idealism come peculiar models of thought, which we can understand, although they have little to do with modern economic models. The sense of utility preference arises from the creation of a hierarchy of options which, where there is no indifference, between two alternative pre-defined things can clearly identify the preferred one.[7] Also the universal art of measuring pleasure and pain, presupposed by *Protagoras*, must be subsumed under differentiation. He who, in pursuit of happiness, comes upon unpleasant consequences, has evidently made an error in calculation. Better calculation would take into account the unpleasantness that events might bring about as consequences, so that those who start with a hedonist perspective, in firmer understanding, eventually turn to good. This is the progression of Plato's search in the later dialogue *Philebos*. The decision about the course of life must be pursued out of individual choices according to the technique of utility calculations based on a supra-human ordering of goodness, which, for example, in the dialogue about laws, limits possessions.

One can also find some utility theory elements in Aristotle's work: dealing with hedonism permeates his work. Two things make the comparison possible. First, the happy state of the soul that should, according to Aristotle, be striven for, eudaimony, is apparently like Bentham's "happiness". Second, Aristotle discusses the Useful as a Good, which is not good because of its own qualities but because it is a means to another Good, so that at least verbal analogies to utility theory formulations exist. Is then not the Good here similar to the Useful, and besides that, the Useful itself determinable as a differentiable ordering?

A deeper analysis of this question is not possible here, but if utilitarianism is nothing more than paying attention to goal–means relationships, there is no philosophical direction that is not utilitarian. To check its presence in Aristotle's work, it must be more carefully defined. As H.G. Gadamer (1978: 100ff.) shows, Aristotle does indeed start with a criticism of the Platonic ideas of goodness, which does not directly determine human action, but it is noteworthy that Aristotle holds to the theoretical ideal of life rather than to the life of pleasure or politics. Aristotle's business life was completely forced (*o chrematistes bi aios tis estin*); wealth is not the good to be striven for, rather, it is "there for another [end]". The task set for humankind is to exercise its abilities as best it can, especially the mental ones (Aristotle, *Nicomachean Ethics* iv–viii, especially 1098a18). This is the way to eudaimony; other good things can be helpful in this attempt (Aristotle, *Nicomachean Ethics* 1099b28). From this kind of life, pleasure in all situations is derived, as opposed to the result of hedonism, where pleasure is sought out as the main goal.

In an interesting essay by Kraus (1905: 573–592), the basic ideas of Aristotelian philosophy are psychologically interpreted, so that observations, like that of the rare being especially distinguished, seem to indicate a subjective value theory. Thus, gold is considered more valuable than iron because it is "harder" (presumably, to acquire) (Kraus 1905: 588).[8] This is more of a general formulation of the paradox of value than an Aristotelian utility theory resolution. The originally intended exchange value is conceptually no different from the use value. Further, it remains open whether use possibilities should be determined more by the individual or by the society. The extended connection is that a methodological individualism aimed at a mechanism of trade is far off because economic and political order should be considered with respect to the final goals of the polis. Utilitarianism can only be discussed in the most general terms: that the good life is *also* a pleasant life, that the things in service of the good life are useful, and that to him who seeks only the pleasant life the good life is easily missed (Aristotle, *Nicomachean Ethics* 1099a5–15).

Valuation according to utility was present as a concept in Aristotle, as it was generally in Greek thought; it was not, however, the leading idea in their attempt to understand the process of exchange. There, socially determined distributive justice dominates far more as the regulating principle. In so far as demand is the initiator of exchange, the question is what are its determining factors. The fact that demand starts in the household means that eventually the question ends back at the normative theory of leading the good life. This has, as we shall see in Homer, its roots in the aristocracy.

The economic philosophy of the Greeks understandably did not limit itself to the extensive works of Plato and Aristotle; one of the most important of their contemporaries is Xenophon, who is less important here for the writings attributed to him on the *Income of a State* and on household economics – both, like the *Oeconomia* attributed to Aristotle's school, are more of documentary than theoretical interest – than for his late sixth century *Memories of Socrates*. These show us how the philosopher could share the practical advice which reflected his own basic principles, in conversation with all manner of people from all walks of life. When we hear from Plato that it is the worst form of deception to pretend to be a statesman without the required knowledge, we hear Socrates warn away from politics a young man whose ambition leads him to the speaker's stand without giving him knowledge of state finances, the war-preparedness of Athens, or anything else that could be important in the leading of a state (Xenophon, *Memories of Socrates*, III 6 vi). Socrates gave advice on proper construction, on the care of the blacksmith and of the painter, how co-house dwellers should be sensibly kept busy at work although they are free individuals (not slaves); he even knew how to advise a hetaera (Xenophon, *Memories of Socrates*, III 11 ix).

This book is not, as concerns our issue, in opposition to Plato and Aristotle, but is rather a clarification because it is much more concrete. Further, it is related to pre-Socratic thought, which in spots reveals slightly other directions of thought. In line with pre-Socratic natural philosophy, Xenophon harks back to the tradition of the mother earth in mythology (Diels 1934: vol. 1, 135, Fragment 27). It might be justified, given such a general foundation-like formulation, to think also of the experiences of agriculturally productive people, whose work could be summarized by the saying: the earth is the mother of wealth; work, the father.

From the pre-Socratic period, partially from the same philosophers, comes the great discussion of the question of just laws which we can follow primarily from Solon. From Xenophon, however, who tells us that the Lydians were the first to make coins (Diels 1934: vol. 1, 130, Fragment 4), comes the strange observation that the Greek city of Colophon, Xenophon's hometown, is imitating the Lydian extravagance (ibid. vol. 1, 129ff., Fragment 3). Obviously he is complaining about the effect of conspicuous consumption. It is characteristic of the philosopher that it is not the phenomenon as such that is interesting, but rather its context,[9] in this case the development of the state under the influence of rising wealth.

In Heraclitus' work (c. 500 BC) we find many connections between natural philosophy and economic thought centered on conflict (Diels 1934: vol. 1, 162). In Hesiod also we will see a clear connection between conflict and forms of rivalry (competition) in reference there, however, to the sources of dialectical thought. In his work an even wider association between natural philosophy and the economy is indicated. He comments on a "reflexive turnover" – "Everything for Fire and Fire for Everything, just as goods for gold and gold for goods." (ibid. vol. 1, 171).

Democritus was a contemporary of Socrates, perhaps a bit older. Of all the philosophers before Aristotle, he was "the most multifaceted and learned" (*Paulys Realenzyklopadie* 1903: vol. 9, col. 136). Of his extensive works we have only fragments, almost exclusively transmitted through Aristotle.

Columella tells us that Democritus wrote a book on agriculture and quotes him as saying that "those who wall in their gardens are unwise, because a flimsy wall will not survive the wind and rain, while a stone wall will cost more to build than the wall itself is worth" (Diels 1934: vol. 2, 150). This is at least an early sign of the weighing of (objective) utility and costs. Other passages seem to reveal the attempt at creating space for utility valuation (Diels 1934: vol. 2, 159).

What words we have of Democritus directly with respect to the household show that while he held to the general understanding of the art of household maintenance, he advocated a posture of greater freedom in role fulfillment than had Plato. Even a brief look into the fragments on politics and ethics show that – in comparison with Plato's position – he held to a creed of democracy (Diels 1934: vol. 2, 195, Fragment 251) and liberal thinking (ibid. vol. 2, 194, Fragment 245 and 194ff., Fragment 248). He lets us see not only more tolerance than Plato (ibid. vol. 2, 204, Fragment 284), but he also refers to the job of the rich in democratic politics, to contribute spontaneously to the good of the community. He emphasized the necessity of education for the right use of wealth (ibid. vol. 2, 203, Fragment 297). The family is to lead by example (ibid. vol. 2, 187, Fragment 208). In general, there is more to be achieved through "encouragement and convincing words" than through "law and force". He felt that brute force leads to the concealment of wrongdoing (ibid. vol. 2, 181ff., Fragment 181).

So we learn, as we move closer to it, to recognize differentiations in Greek economic philosophy. We also see that their essential components are found in the comparison of the works of Plato and Aristotle.

One might be of the opinion after reading the philosophical texts that the effort to find philosophical economic teachings is a waste of time. What is the point of concepts of just exchange that give no standard of justice? What is the pertinence of the Charities, the goddesses of poverty, to the exchange economy, when goddesses come more readily to mind in connection with Botticelli's paintings or charity, translated as mercy, with Luther's New Testament translation of Luke I. 30, for example? This sense of uselessness is also not to be fully assuaged by a look at the economic realities in Athens during the height of its influence, for what is the point of faded ideas of the autarchy of the household in the specialized-labour, handicraft-oriented city it was? Why the denunciation of chrematistics, when long-distance trade was essential to the life of the city state of Athens? Are these not just topoi that no longer reflect the reality of the fourth century?[10] And yet I hope to show how often the abstract texts of the Greek philosophers will seem easier to understand if we go nearer into their world of thought through the literature upon which their reflective, and even somewhat systematic, if not causally analytic, thought picture of economic ideas is based.

Reconstruction of the Attic economy

As is reported in other places,[11] there is a conflict between the scholars who subscribe to the line of argument of Rodbertus and Bücher (1893), according to which Greek economics in the Classical period was not far from Aristotle's depiction, to be understood primarily as household economics, and those scholars who place emphasis on a more modern interpretation. According to the latter, trade and factories were significantly developed, comparable with the West European development in the early mercantile period, with differentiated money and banking and an export economy that spread through the Mediterranean lands. Finley (1979), according to the *New Palgrave* the most important ancient historian dealing with economics, re-publicized the controversy between Bücher and his opponents Meyer (1895) and Beloch (1886), and it seems that the opinion of the specialists tends more strongly towards Bücher.[12] Of course, the most modern of them are correct in saying that the stylization that accompanies the concepts of household, *oika*, or latifundian economics may not be taken too literally. However, Bücher is right in that the goal of the citizen remained to go from a well-established estate in the country to the city to take part in its political and cultural life, while the artisanal tasks were extended to the slaves and non-citizens, and paid workers led an unhappy existence on the edge of society, in any case in a standing lower than slaves designated for more important duties, by which they established some claim to freedom.

More than anything else, Meyer (1895) is guilty of choosing modern concepts whose one-sidedness is made notoriously clear when his sources are examined. He claims (Finley 1979: 103) that trade trips were common in the *Odyssey*, although there is little evidence for it, and what there is leads more directly to the conclusion that traders were more the exception than the rule. Or else he points to evidence for the existence of export industries in Xenophon (*Memories of Socrates*, II 7 vi), who says that most of the Megarans made a living by making jackets; thus, that these jackets were exported from Megara. But Xenophon may not necessarily mean the existence of industry in the modern sense any more than the worldwide export of hard cheese from the Alpine flatlands in the Middle Ages was "industry".[13]

We find much more household production in this context: we saw how Socrates shared a type of economics lesson with the leaders of households when he showed how the women in his household, the relatives, sisters, nieces, etc., could be drawn into working, in order to hold themselves above water in bad times (Xenophon, *Memories of Socrates*, II 7). Although businesses were comprised of a few dozen workers, the organization of production is easy to imagine; there was no real book-keeping and no real separation between the consumption expenses of the household and those made for production, and also, the bank and credit systems were not very developed. The existence of regional and even actually quite adventuresome long-distance trading is not completely ruled out by this description. The standard of living remained low and contrasted with the gleam of the cultural achievements.

It may be of special interest to look more closely at the new attempt of Raymond Goldsmith (1987: 16–33), who, as a specialist in the calculation of GNPs, tried to estimate the GNP and the wealth of the people in classical Pericles' Athens. He occasionally uses Athenian institutions in inappropriate ways to calculate his GNP although he stands nearer to Bücher (1893) than Meyer (1895) with respect to the meaning of the state of economic development. The result is that the labor contributions of the householders and slaves are included in the calculation, as far as it can be inferred that they contributed to the production of salable products; however, the work of women is not included because they only produce for the household itself and not for profit. Although this kind of differentiation is hardly supported by Greek thought, we want to offer this result as an illustration of the audacious estimations carried out completely within the mindset of "political arithmetic".

Thereafter the population of Attica was something over 300,000 people, where perhaps a half comprised citizens, a fifth, freemen, and a third, slaves. The natural population growth led to a strong emigration to the colonies and was able to withstand losses due to the plague of 429 BC as well as those due to the almost constant state of war. The differences in income, which were clearly expressed in Solon's division of classes, were disparate, although nowhere near as greatly so as in the Roman Empire. The slight difference in income between various workers is striking; also, the commander of the armies earned only four times as much, and an officer twice as much, as a soldier; in this respect, the differences were significantly greater in Rome or the Middle Ages.

On the income and expenditures side, each worker earned 100 Drachma per head, and this, expressed in gold or wheat, provided for a somewhat higher standard of living than in the Roman Empire.[14] The concentration of wealth is estimated based on the Solonic class division, such that if the highest class possessed about a fifth of the private wealth, the next highest had a quarter, while the lowest class, about a third of the free population, had barely ten percent.

The national wealth is more difficult to estimate.[15] While numbers, although a bit unreliable, exist for such quantities as mint runs or animal holdings, and we know of the most important buildings (occasionally with their cost), land prices represent a critical factor. Total wealth should have amounted to about six times income levels, in a plausible rank order.

An astonishingly high portion – about one-half – of the state's budget was expenditures for religious and political reasons, like common celebrations, state buildings, and for things which can only loosely be called political expenses, such as payment to over a third of the populace for taking part in theater and public meetings, and many other public functions. The rich as well as the poor were recipients of this wealth. Those mentioned and also military expenditures were covered by the income from the silver mines of Laurion and by tolls and a few taxes, like the taxation of dependents and a head tax on slaves. There is conflicting evidence on the existence of an income tax; it is clear, however, that liturgies, or the rich taking over state expenses on an originally voluntary basis, played a significant role. Theater productions as well as the building of warships were financed thus. The high state expenditures of Pericles' Athens can hardly be explained without high liturgies and the considerable contribution from the Attic sea-trade alliance – the tributes.

A credit system had not been fully developed. First came mortgages on land property, but otherwise banks were little more than currency exchangers. For private credit there were generally interest rates of 12–18 percent, but in individual cases where there was a lack of collateral they could reach 36 percent. Here consumer credit was dominant; the only important form of trade credit was related to the financing of ships and trade trips, where interest rates of 15–30 percent seem to have been customary. An actual state credit financing did not exist.

In summary we must make it clear that the attempts which started with Böckh (1817) (and continued by Büchsenschuetz (1869), Meyer (1893), Beloch (1886), and in this century Andreades (1965) and many others) offer many individual details pertinent to Greek economic thought. They come from the analysis of literature, epigraphy, and archeological discoveries. We are able to create a much better image of many institutions, and after centuries of (data) collecting, a Goldsmith (1987) can even attempt to make estimations of state expenditures, GNP, and general income levels.

However, critics like Bücher (1893) have correctly and consistently pointed out the uncertainty of any quantitative reconstruction. Although some have attempted – like Heichelheim – to represent quantitatively the business cycles of ancient times, we will never be able to describe statistically the economic cycles of ancient times and therefore we will never be able to represent the functions of these systems using modern economic methods.

So we will restrict ourselves to conjuring up a representation of the specifics of the Attic economic style on the general basis of a system of production with help from self-employed freemen, slaves, and paid workers, all enabled by the market. The specific aspects of style – like the differences between State and social forms and the economic organization in Athens and in Sparta – were known to the ancient Greeks and were described in Pericles' speeches, the works of historians like Thucydides and of philosophers like Aristotle, and also by Xenophon. And without these subjective findings, results, like the high ratio of State wealth to private wealth or the liturgies as substitute for taxation, would be impossible for us to understand. In fact, how an economic thinking was developed that allowed, in a democracy, for so much public wealth next to so much private poverty (and from which cultural and economic sources it is derived), is one of the questions that stands behind the following literary examination. The concentration of property in the State could be an expression of a repressive, autocratic dictatorship. In the democratic period of Athens, it appears to have been, however, the expression of a unique participation of the citizens, in the tradition of common meals and celebrations, and of reciprocal hospitality and generosity.[16]

History has time and again searched for other methods to clarify the peculiarities of the Attic community. On the basis of a decade of source study, in his eight-volume *Voyages du Jeune Anarchasis*, Barthelemy, a classical historian of the late Ancien Regime, described the classical Greek world minutely in the style of a travel writer through a fictive Scythian who travels through the country. Here, we want to look at the subjective side, by placing the works of Homer in the center because, as Jakob

Burckhardt (1898–1902) writes in the introduction to his history of Greek culture, it is from him one must start.

WEALTH, HANDIWORK, AND EXCHANGE IN THE MYTHICAL WORLD OF HOMER

Homer as a source

At first glance it seems to be pointless to look for depictions of economic events in Homer's work: the human and godly spheres intermingle, and by no means only in the sense of a heavenly joining. More often, Olympus mirrors the human conflicts of the time, and where at one point Zeus with power determines fate, at another Aphrodite can take part in a battle, be wounded in her lovely hand, and flee to Olympus. The Trojan war, set, according to the reconstruction of an implicit chronology in a later legend, at the beginning of the twelfth century BC, played itself out improbably. The *Iliad*, which depicts only the happenings that were connected to Achilles' rage in the last year of the war, has the Greeks only then fortifying themselves in their harbor town – an action that we would have expected at the beginning of the war.

Further, the constructs of Greek myth play such a large role. Over the Olympian gods stands Zeus, over him an unnamed power of destiny, under him all the gods and demigods who populate the lakes, rivers, water sources and landscapes, and then the heroes. Humankind itself can, through godly virtue, be of the highest or lowest form. Limitations, like wealth, education and character, separate the heroes and princes from their people, where there are again freemen and slaves, rich men and beggars. Even the lowest, like the beggar Eumaios, can have godly characteristics, just as the highest often plummet into contemptibility.

The core of Homeric fiction seems to have appeared in the eighth century; however, it is debated to what extent particularly the *Odyssey* was created over time by multiple poetic figures. Many modern philologists accept the thesis that both epics, because of inner artistic unity, stem in essence from *one* Homer (Schefold and Jung 1989: 7–14). In their transmission by the rhapsodes, or poetry performers, the original texts were consistently extended, changed and rewritten. Solon is said to have ordered the performance of all of Homer's works. There were even more changes made to the Homeric text in an edition made under the Attic tyrant (Pesistratos); the only certainty is that finally a classical canonical version existed.

One is forced to admire the never-ending refinement of the poetic fabric without always being able to see the intertwining of the threads. Some oppositions are simple to understand, like the one between the fairy-tale character of the travels of Odysseus to Polyphemus or Circe and his return home to the completely realistic and mortal Ithaca. The amazing breadth of the clearly defined life connections, well beyond the demands of outside life, includes, however, not only the class divisions and values of a past era, but also alludes to the citizen's connection to the later polis. This is made especially clear with Hector, who is shown in the sixth song of the *Iliad* as responsible for the city and his house; he is not, as Achilles, great because of his sufferings but because of his role as leader, mediator, and caretaker. We may therefore take the Homeric epics as a historically grown, in the sense of "fictionalized", synthesis of a long tradition. Because of their multiple levels of meaning it is equally possible to find in them documentary evidence of all kinds of "realities", as it is the poetic expression of modes of thought.

It is a notorious question, how the Greeks even lived before Troy. In *Iliad* VII, 467 we see that there were supplies of wine, brass, and oxen, and the song, Book IX, 72, tells us that Agamemnon received daily supplies of wine from Thrace. When we take into account the adventures of Poseidon, enemy of Odysseus, we find it hard to believe that this regular provisioning was possible. At another point, when the Greeks and Trojans get wood for the cremation of Patroclos, i.e. Hector, the lumberjacks are so clearly depicted at work that one imagines seeing an old forestry play (Homer, *Iliad* XXIII, 115–127; XXIV, 782–784). Of course it is not such antiquarian details that interest us, but rather the bases of economic thought, which are repeated continually in variations throughout the text: details about household economics, work, the representation of values, social order, etc.

Here we feel supported by the ancient tradition, which treats Homer as the educator of Greece. Plato reports that there are people who believe that this poet has educated Greece, that, with respect to State – and war – regiments or even to the training of humanity, one must take Homer in hand and study him, and that one should lead one's own life according to Homer (*Republic* 606E). Socrates cannot agree with this opinion, but he grants Homer the position of a great poet. This honor is – exceptionally – also supported empirically and quantitatively. Among the far more than a thousand literary scrolls found in the sands of Egypt, almost half are copies of Homer's works, while only fragments of the great Attic tragedies have been transmitted to us.[17] Also lost – except for fragments – are many epics of lesser quality from the Homeric period, which addressed the other parts of the Trojan cycle and the rest of the myths of Greece.

The environment of Homeric literature

Patzer (c.1970: 3) suggests, because of the evident emphasis on the aristocracy of the heroes according to birth and ability, their war adventures and battles, their luxurious households with the necessary slaves, and the almost complete exclusion of the cultural and working worlds of the non-noble freemen, that the "art of poetry was limited to an audience that belonged to the war aristocracy and that institutionally glorified itself as a class in this artwork even, as if obliged by its own nobility". The heroes, more so their imitators, and most of all the gods, possessed the virtues of a war aristocrat in the extreme. From the orientation of the epics to their audience, it becomes clear which figures in the legends are most important and which persons or classes are shoved off to the side. The non-aristocratic solo fighter takes part in the military meetings but does not affect the outcome and remains nameless. In front of the background of a mass of simple warriors, the heroes stand out. They also last through a changing relationship: the army or the people of a city honor the front-line fighters and kings through gifts which are appropriate to their rank; in return, they feel the obligation to justify these honors through success in battle. Just as in Plato's "State", the warrior community must protect the city. What count as honors are exceptional portions of war plunder, hospitality gifts, competition awards, and also natural gifts from the people (Patzer c.1970: 11). War deeds are a significant source of earnings for the princes. The nobles, however, when they move around, can count also on receiving gifts according to their rank, as Menelaos, conscious of his prestige, boasts as he invites the young Telemachus for a tour of Argos (Homer, *Odyssey* XV, 79–84)

The large landowners who visit Telemachus, or those that adhere to Odysseus, have many employees and workers. Such people show up only in the wake of the noble freemen; the beggar on the threshold of the celebration hall can become a meaningful figure. Artisans would obviously be brought to the palace according to need (ibid., XVII, 382–385). On the other hand, the discussion does not turn around individual city inhabitants or small farmers, as occurs in Hesiod.

Nonetheless, through the story's action, economic production at the court becomes visible. Odysseus gladly hears a "poor woman" proclaim the end of the freemen (ibid., XX, 107–108). She complains at night, continuing to work alone because she has not yet filled her quota of wheat. Hers is the scant lot of the dependent.

So can the environment of the Homeric epic, despite the multi-dimensionality of the poem, be more accurately identified? The aristocratic life is realized in the houses of the princes, in their visits to one another, in their warfare, in the cultivation of virtues, and in their stewardship of goods. The aristocratic character of this clearly stated ideal had, even in the late Greek age of the polis, a power over the free citizens – although naturally no longer exclusive. So just as the Homeric hero, despite the different fighting strategies in the battle of Marathon, remained an example for the Greek infantry through his heroism, the other virtues – honor, eloquence, and beauty – were also important to the later Greeks.

When Aristotelian politics takes its starting point from the view of the individual household, it stands doubtlessly within this early Greek tradition. It would therefore be appropriate, in pursuing a deeper investigation of Homer, to begin with palace economics. For economists, however, there is also a well-founded tradition of beginning with division of labor, because wealth must first be created before it can be distributed and enjoyed. And it is a perhaps surprising result that the Homeric song, created from travels, festivals, and battles and raised far above the workaday, is indeed rich in detail on production and organization. We will thus proceed on what seems a logical path from work and its social status to the conception of household and wealth, to gift, reciprocity and exchange.

Craft

As Vidal-Naquet (1983) has shown, the craft artisan is the holy hero of Greek economic thought. One would expect this, if one thinks of the artistic height of Greek handiwork, but it can be concluded without much ado, especially from certain philosophical texts, that craft activity was viewed primarily as a little-appreciated form of work, best left to the servants. To be directed to work wholly with the hands was not considered worthy of freemen. The dependence, even mediated by work earnings, was defined as unnatural by Aristotle. In treating the division of labor, however, Plato and others put forth that this division should serve quality and not productivity.

"Margites", a comic poem from the Homeric period of which we only possess fragments (attributed to Homer by Aristotle himself), reflects clearly the attitude that the ability to do everything is therefore no absolute ideal; more important is that every handiwork is learned and sensibly applied (Homer 1911: 156ff., Fragments I–III). Odysseus, full of invention (*polumetis*), is an exception in that he can build a raft to save himself as well as shoot an arrow, is capable in all the arts of war, and is supranaturally intelligent. If Odysseus is therefore considered godly, Margites is the laughable bungler.[18] While Odysseus proceeds according to plan, the unwise Margites does not know how to use his abilities.[19]

In the Homeric hymn, "To Aphrodite", a simple Ur-image of the established artisanship which infuses itself into life and decorates it is attributed to Athena (Homer 1986: 94, ll. 12–15). As a productive act, work holds its dignity. The source of the division of labor lies thus in the various gifts of the gods. The different gifts are in myths clearly embodied in the gods themselves. They represent not only certain forces of life, like love or death, or natural areas, like the sky and seas, but even – I don't know how far this is paralleled in other religions – abilities, and not only basic abilities like the ability to hunt (Artemis), but, in the case of Athena, also craft, which requires planning, and, in the case of Hephaestos, all forms of blacksmithing. Ugly and lame, Hephaestos still makes the most beautiful metalwork and the most splendid armor.[20] The genius of the Greeks can be seen in Hephaestos' power to construct robots for himself (Homer, *Iliad* XVIII, 372–377). His technical inventions are naturally connected, however, to the highest quality of his workmanship – no lance will penetrate his shield – and to representations that lie close to real life, as in the social activities depicted on Achilles' shield.

Through devotion to the product of the work, the products themselves are given certain characteristics. So ore appears "cruel" and Penelope's key is "ivory-like" and "beautiful" (Homer, *Odyssey* XXI, 6–7). The antiquarian detail of whether there were in the twelfth century BC, or only thereafter, keys with ivory handles is not confirmed by this comment on Homer. But these and many other verses support the sense of hand-worked beauty, bound up with admiration for the intelligence of the hand-worked invention (namely the keyed lock) and the exactness of the creation. This sense of reporting represents, according to the words of Jakob Burckhardt ((1898) 1–12) even more a "fact of higher certainty", than technical praise for a key.

The exactness of craft is not only heavily emphasized when the work is described; it is also used as a comparison to other attributes (Homer, *Iliad* XV, 410–413): justice,[21] multiplicity of talents,[22] and honor. Craft is first the concentration on the substantial; the division of labor brings the exceptional and the substantial to the forefront, which then earns praise (ibid. XI, 514). Likewise he who makes himself exceptional earns fame and honor; in the end, the taking back of an honor gift, Agamemnon's demanding back Briseis from Achilles, brought on the rage of the Pelides, and Achilles' bitter complaint about his mistreatment (ibid. IX, 318–320).

Just as it is entirely in keeping with the theory of distributive justice that honor gifts must not be the same and must be appropriate to the rank of both giver and receiver, which in turn rests on earlier gifts, so too is it in harmony with Aristotelian theory, although never suggested, that different forms of work should be remunerated differently, because the value of the work depends first of all on the product. As earlier suggested, however, there was very little differentiation of wages in ancient Greece. There exists an unusual witness to this in the form of bills for construction work on the high-Classical Erechtheon on the Acropolis. "In the single year 408–407 more than 2600 lines of writing on marble tablets were buried and set for eternal accounting" (Gruben 1966, 1976: 203ff.). The name, homeland, work and pay of every individual craft-worker were written there. According to this, everyone from the architect who led the site to the carpenter and stoneworker earned the same pay of one drachma per day. At times one master worked with several sons. In one column there are 350 daily wages, wherein it is especially surprising to see that some of the same master workers, who had worked the ornamentation, were at work on the creation of the weight-bearing girl figures of the entranceway. There was no difference made between the so-called routine work and the creation of a masterful sculpture.[23]

Workers and slaves

So, to whose careful work, about which we know only a little knowledge, can production be attributed? Our own sense of propriety has had us create a deep divide between the work of freemen and slaves, but as we have looked closer at manual work, we see how freemen, even princes, worked side by side with slaves. In the *Odyssey*, for example, Nausika is doing the wash with her slaves, and Odysseus associates with his godly deer, Laertes in the garden. It is also no accident that Odysseus' loyal slaves fought for him upon his return against the traitorous freemen. As Finley has shown, free laborers were looked down upon in the *Odyssey*. In the *Iliad* we note further how such views of the palace and free workers outside it are rare in Homer's works.[24] Free workers who help with the harvest seem to appear, but without clear definition. More obvious are the housebound slaves, who in part enjoyed a certain standard of living, in individual cases oversaw other slaves, and were in any case "paid" through their maintenance. We find the men primarily in the fields and the women in the house.

While in our image of the Roman Empire we see the horrible images of chained slaves, slave revolts and crucifixions, a patriarchal view of house slavery, as Homer brings out, was a longer after-effect. Emperor Julian the Unfaithful, bound to the Greek tradition, suggested that slaves, who converted to Christianity from the heathenism which he had restored, be freed to the punishment of being without supplies, or in other words, that they be thrown out of secure housework and into the destitute world of paid work. The freeing of slaves is not mentioned by Homer.

The loss of freedom of a secure existence must have seemed horrifying. Aristotle, who himself ordered the freedom and support of certain of his slaves, believed, as noted, that an automatized production would, if it existed, make slavery unnecessary. For this he did not hark back to Homer. Nonetheless, what is amazing is that we see this image brought to life already in the god Hephaestos: he possesses homemade, artificial virgins who are just like the living and who support him "with reason in the breast and speaking voices" – although they were probably not completely like living beings (Homer, *Iliad* XVIII, 421).

As the *Iliad* deals with war we find, as compared to the *Odyssey*, fewer freemen working together with the slaves. To be more precise: the men are occupied with their war while the women and their maids pursue their housework. However, slavery counts as one of the great horrors of the shameful war. There is the stirring face of Lykaon, a young son of Priam,

116

who meets Achilles, "longing for murder and violence", in a rage after the death of Patroclos. Lykaon had been taken by Achilles himself while working in the orchard and had been sent to the island of Lemnos to be sold. Lykaon was resold, escaped, and fled to his father's palace, where, after only a few days' freedom, he had to fight in the battle. He implores Achilles to spare his life, and, kneeling, promises a threefold solution, but Achilles still runs him through (Homer, *Iliad* XXI, 35–127).

Hector has sympathy for his wife Andromache, who after his death and the fall of Troy will have to weave or carry water for another (Homer, *Iliad* VI, 458). It is of course understandable that the conquered slave women, like Briseis, could be taken as lovers, and pity the ones who, like a few of Odysseus' women, give themselves to the wrong men. Such a slave is, in the end, less of a person than a freeman (Homer, *Odyssey* XVII, 322–323).

How this contrast between two truths, the lack of freedom and the human closeness to the house slaves, can be maintained is in Homer an expression of his artistic greatness.[25] In the lament for Patroclos we see the ambivalence: Briseis, who, as Achilles' lover is bound to his friends, is truly filled with grief for the fallen, but not the other women, who out of duty take part in the lament.

Working relationships are thus quite mixed up and complex in the close personal connections that form the basis of the prince's court. In reflection, Greek philosophy names the leading of a household as the first political art.

Household and wealth

None of the thoroughly worked out ideas of Greek economic philosophy is as clearly expressed in the Homeric epics as the idea that the good life is had in a well-ordered and rich, but not opulent, house. At the beginning of the *Odyssey* we see the palace on the edge of ruin through the freemen's mishandling, in contrast to the ordered seat of King Nestor in Pylos, and of Menelaos and Helen in Sparta, whom Telemachus visits in the search for his father. In the happy house of the Phaeakes, Odysseus finds his shelter, after he left the grotto of Calypso and survived his ships' sinking at sea. To the great, unforgettable images of the *Iliad* belongs the return of Hector to his wife Andromache in the sixth Book: he who went everywhere for his city, brothers, wife, and his son's nursemaid who was the only one who – as she will attest after his death – was friendly to Helen, shows himself as the god's blessed hero, while in the Greek army there are many – Ajax, Diomedes, Patroclos, Achilles – who are stronger than he. After the horror of the preceding battle we see Hector behave according to Aristotelian precepts as the leader of his household, husband, and father, before he steps renewed before the defended wall, while Andromache returns at ease to her women at their weaving (Homer, *Iliad* VI, 499–501).

Even the heroes take part in the production of the household. In the *Odyssey*, the homeward Odysseus finds his old father shabbily dressed and working with his gardeners. Even the princess of the fairy-tale rich Phaeakes, Nausika, goes with her women to the stream to wash; she eats in the open, plays ball and sings with them.

Limiting needs, so important to later philosophical debate, I have found first expressed in Homer (ibid.). It is made quite clear in the simplicity of the agricultural idyll. The core of the well-being of all the princes – as later that of the land-owning citizens of Athens and finally also of Rome – is land obtained through inheritance, takeover, or rewarded for war actions, which became fluid, through sale and resale in the late ancient period, and also grew, due to concentration, but which, for the first time only in Homeric times, could in sizable amounts be considered a given – otherwise Laertes would not be working in his garden. However, we find everywhere, in clear contradiction to the emphasized modesty of this period, lists of extensive wealth – somewhat like what Agamemnon promises Achilles as atonement: the unbelievable sum of ten talents of gold, tripods, chalices, stallions, women from past and future conquests, and even seven cities, if Achilles took the hand of his daughter (Homer *Iliad* IX, 121–156). How comforting it was to believe that one is safe in secure wealth is expressed in the powerful image of an aristocrat who, at a good omen, widened his influence (ibid. XXIV, 317–320). Such wealth is clearly not earned through production alone, but through conquest and plunder – a part of what Agamemnon promised Achilles consisted of promised future conquests and portions of plunder.

Plunder does not produce wealth, it merely concentrates what survives the torch in the hands of the princes and most distinguished fighters. Even if this process stands outside the polis' ideas of distributive justice, it belongs, paradoxically for us, according to Aristotle, and as opposed to trade, as a natural form of earning wealth. Other forms of natural profit are hunting, fishing, theft, nomadic travel, farming – yes, theft is on the list – not only because these abilities are literally natural (there are animals who live from theft) but also because Aristotle holds theft as one of the first ways to acquire wealth. The first reason cannot be challenged, and the second is difficult to prove in the Greek tradition. Indeed, both Plato and Aristotle are moved, each in his own way, to limit the rights of the stronger – Plato, through the observation that the suffering of injustice is better than the perpetrating of it, and Aristotle, in that he sets man under the law of society because man is by nature a societal creature. However, tradition is still visible, in Aristotle, when he acknowledges theft as a natural activity and preserves some of the old legal structure, although he seeks to set societal peace under the protection of natural rights, while

118

previously, the Sophists, presented by Plato in *Gorgias*, considered the right of the stronger to be a natural right.

For us, distinguishing between communities in Homer, this interpretation stands as a cruel, influential power – even Zeus sets himself against the other gods by drawing his right from his power.[26] While even the heroes sink deep into grief-filled thoughts at the misery of war, it occurs to no one in either epic to question institutions like slavery. Wealth may be stolen only under conditions of war, and during peacetime it should be freely distributed through gifts and return gifts, tributary payment, or, if the expression may be allowed, social support for those who need it.

It is primarily Hector who first complains that Troy, a city famous for her gold and ore, lost her possessions and must therefore sell her jewelry (ibid. XV, 106ff.). Another text of the *Iliad*, XVII, 220–226 is about war taxes that maintain the alliance of cities but exhaust the people. Hector also is most willing to say that he is one of Troy's most impressive heroes, who keeps the population of Troy out of slavery (ibid. XVI, 833–835). He spurs his fighters on by reminding them that they not only lose all fame when they fall but also the livelihood of the wives and children whom they leave behind (ibid. XV, 497ff.) – it is interesting that normal encouragement seems to be based on such a strongly stated reversal of fortune.

There have been many attempts (significantly one by Andreades 1965) to clarify the redistribution of wealth as a system of taxes and state entitlements; no one can find it easy to differentiate between a naive or an ethnologically based interpretation of the distribution in a system based wholly on status-determined gifts and the assumption of a regulated financial system based on legally set claims and obligations.

We should again bother less with an actual reconstruction of relationships of which we have little real information, as in how far the Homeric poets used the real Troy of the twelfth century BC or contemporary observations of the seventh or even sixth centuries BC, and more with an understanding of the modes of thought that appear in this era. And here, obviously, the most important point is that wealth is distributed according to rank among the rich princes, the individual farmers, and the poor freemen, but that it is rarely seen as a means to private pleasure. It is in general seen from the viewpoint of the societal functions of reciprocity of giving, distribution, and so forth – ideas that are foreign to modern economics but not to the science of ethnology.

Exchange, reciprocity, distribution, and trade

If Homer as a poet of the epics summarizing old tradition belongs to the eighth or seventh centuries, his work, and in any case his present time, predates the coin, while the Attic edition of his work is younger than the coin. This historical quirk alone is reason enough to regard Homeric trade situations with caution, especially in that the later writer may not have even understood the old "market processes" – if pre-monetary exchange can be called that.[27] Our analysis must try as early on as possible to lay consistent thought structures out as independent, where the close examination of the ancient writings permit.

A rich example for the valuation of goods can be found in the Homeric reports of prizes for competitions, like the games that took place upon Patroclos' death; there a tripod was worth twelve oxen, or a slave was worth four oxen (Homer, *Iliad* XXIII, 702–705). Once a bull is the second prize and a half talent of gold, the third (ibid. 750ff.); another time the bull serves as a value measure for a chalice. Obviously there is an interest in confirming such expressions of value; however, these expressions and the hierarchies and equivalencies that are bound up with the awarding of the prizes are not always plausible. Because there was no universal measure of value, the affordability of things in a particular area is made understandable primarily through individual description. Precious metals can clearly be measured by weight; it was with pleasure that Odysseus himself weighed out the ten talents of gold for Achilles (ibid. XIX, 247). In the bronze age to which the *Iliad* belongs, a ball of iron was a special wealth (ibid. XXIII, 834), that gave the owner an iron supply for five years. An especially "shiny" silver pitcher has evidently an odyssey of exchanges in behind it. It was bought by Sidoners (ibid. 744–745); they give it away, and then it becomes the selling price of the unhappy son of Priam, Lykaon, until Achilles, the final buyer of Lykaon, finally offers him as a prize in a contest.

So we find nothing in the epics that had a basic monetary function, despite the usage of oxen as measurement of value. The complexity of the exchange processes and the amount of recorded equivalencies help us understand better why Aristotle celebrated money as a practical invention that makes it clearly necessary to measure everything in an exchange – although Aristotle, as we saw, is far from setting up quasi-mechanical rules of the exchange, the charm of the older world, where the values were not so well-known, is threatened.

What we see more clearly than exchange trade are the transactions of reciprocity; giving and returning the favor, as in natural societies, are discovered to be well-developed and to provide a developed system of alliance-forming, as described by Malinowski (1965). Gregory attempted, in *Gifts and Commodities* (1982), to make a systematic comparison of the exchange of gifts and commodities in natural peoples. He could show that gifts are hierarchically structured, that there are also separate spheres where gifts of higher or lower rank circulate, that the obligation to give a gift in return is bound up in part with a large time delay and can often be indirectly fulfilled in that it is passed along to another, and that, especially with regard to dowries between branches of a family, certain relationship rules must be obeyed, which define the equivalencies between the changing debts between the families involved in the exchange of brides and gifts. The complexity of the representative transactions is clarified by Gregory using matrix algebra and the creation of a certain analogy with classical systems of natural prices.

There are no such regularities to be seen in Homer, but there is great variety in the forms of reciprocity. There are many examples of the gifts that hosts and guests exchange, and indeed, it is usually the host who gives the guest a gift, which then makes the guest obliged to entertain the host or his relatives.[28] Hector, after an undecided duel with Ajax, suggests the giving of "glorious gifts", so that everyone could see how they had fought and then afterward, how they reconciled and became good friends. Also, large gifts are often recorded from the bridegroom, which are reminiscent of a bride-prize if the bride does not "earn" the gift because the groom fell in battle (Homer, *Iliad* XI, 243).

That the institutions of giving and returning gifts could be misused is not surprising; we saw how Menelaos invited Telemachus for a visit so that he could collect gifts (Homer, *Odyssey* XV, 79–84). And while it belongs to the idea of giving and returning gifts that equivalence is not based upon the market value of the gifts, they must still be appropriate to each other in that they belong, so to speak, to the same economic value class (which is not described in any more detail by Homer). Such classifications are known from ethnology. The most famous example in the *Iliad* is the oft-quoted example of Glaucos and Diomedes, who recognized each other as allies on the field when they realized that their forefathers were hospitality friends. As a sign of their bond they exchanged armor; thus, Glaucos "enraged" Zeus (Homer, *Iliad* VI, 234) in giving his golden armor against the brass armor of Diomedes without a second thought. Homer makes two major contrasts clear with this example: as armor the gifts are in the same class, but not as pure metal; and hospitality friendships overrule the obligation to fight.

The heroes and princes place special value upon appropriate gifts and shares of plunder if they have achieved military successes or hold prominent positions – their honor is wounded when the division is not made according to honor. What Aristotle says about exchange, that the exchangers should hold the same rank before and after the exchange,[29] fits much better in this context of status relationships and gift exchange than in his context of the exchange of shoes for a house. The conflict about the assignment of the beautiful Briseis between Achilles, whose virtue is that he was the best fighter, and Agamemnon, the leader of the army, is a central motif of the *Iliad*: that Achilles should set aside his claim to his promised gift of honor – who was also his lover – so that a less capable but higher ranking soldier could take her is the cause of his rage and his hesitation to continue the battle, which was nearly fatal to the Greeks.

BERTRAM SCHEFOLD

So the question remains of how material gifts can cause or relieve immaterial obligations. The Trojans keep trying to reconcile with the Greeks over the kidnapping of Helen by offering to pay something like a fine. Paris did something heinous to convince the exemplary Trojans to take his side and not return Helen (Homer, *Iliad* XI, 124), and thus created an even larger blood debt.

Andreades (1965: book 1) tried to reconstruct a Homeric "state economy". The hospitality that princes practice has a public function. In particular they have meals for the distinguished folk who seem to have a right to eat at the kingly table. So even Telemachus cannot throw the feasting masses out of the palace of his absent father, because they are descended from the nobility of Ithaca. It is expressly an exception, however, when the Phaeakes practice such regular hospitality that they escort home every boatless stranger to the sea (Homer, *Odyssey* XIII, 173–174).

In times of war the promise of plunder seems to take the place of payment to the soldiers. How the soldiers earn a living through the exchange of primarily iron, oxen, prisoners – or rather, plunder – is mirrored in the *Iliad* VII, 472–475. Thucydides believes[30] that the Greeks could have conquered Troy faster if there had been fewer thieving trips and plunderings. On the other hand, the courts earn their income from kingly privileges, like Odysseus in Ithaca gets from his lands and herds. One can assume that certain gifts that were expected were really typical taxes or even tolls and that they also included the standard stints of community service.

The inclusion of modern ideas, like taxes for liturgies, can, through a sort of morphing between the old institutions and their modern counterparts, give the impression of a better understanding of their functionality, but this process holds the danger of eliminating the specific differences between the old and the new. If even the expression "gift" is declared a euphemism and replaced with "tax", where it appears that the seemingly freely done work, like the suggested donation of wood, is replaced with a sort of force, there is the advantage of being able to explain easily the existence of the palaces, walls, and ships without having to assume an excessively large number of slaves. But then one basically works with no proof for the changed interpretation of the modes of thought. Unexplained is why the oppression of slaves finds such a vocal expression where the pressure that must weigh upon the tax-obligated freemen finds no voice. Finally, it cannot be explained why the tyrants, with their various forms of pressure, call up such hate from the Greek memory, while the Homeric era with its princes remains the ideal.

Perhaps here the comparison with the philosophical writings gives again the information, in which the openness of voluntary work for the state is considered a requirement for the survival of the State. Even the modern taxpayer hopes that his payment will eventually become a state service that

122

will do him some good, but there is for him a clearly defined obligation to pay his taxes, even when the State does not come through. However, where there is a gift, the return gift must be closely associated with the first gift. This mode of thought, which is ossified between similarly ranked people through inheritance, is carried over to the traffic between lower and higher persons and is reflected – in Homer as in natural societies – in the relationship between man and the gods. Sacrifices are made to the gods that they might give a certain protection; sometimes the prayer is answered (Homer, *Iliad* XV, 378), sometimes not (ibid. VI, 311). Because Hector so faithfully made his sacrifices, he is spared from extensive rot after death when Achilles commits the outrage of not allowing him to be buried.

The image of evening things out is the scale; repeatedly a balance between the forces of war in the *Iliad* is described using the image of a scale. Even as one side is stronger in the fight or luckier in wealth, the other side is favored by the fates. Therefore, scales are used for the measurement of fate, and at the high point of the drama Zeus brings about the decision with their use (ibid. XXII, 209–212). And finally it becomes clear that in this world, where the market had not yet placed an exact monetary equivalent on every product, the idea of balance or imbalance of giving and returning the gift holds such a fascination that balance images come up in the language in a hidden form. So the opposites are defined when Achilles says that he wants to compel a duel (ibid. 261ff.).

Scales are used often as poetic tools to demonstrate an overriding balance right when the opposites are most powerfully defined. In one of the most astounding scenes of the entire work, Priam and Achilles recognize each other simultaneously with their outstanding but completely different characteristics as the old king and the undefeated warrior, when Priam slips into the Greek camp at night to ask his son's murderer for the corpse (ibid. XXIV, 471–691). Also, one could recognize the high point in the fact that it is not clear if it is the drama of the passionate Achilles or the tragedy of Hector and his situation that forms the central theme. An image of the balance that always returns only to be lost again is also the casks of Chronion from which he evenly distributes pain and healing (ibid., 527).

Since the "Essai sur le don" by Marcel Mauss, we know how the code of reciprocity represents a basic principle of the organization of archaic societies. Emile Benveniste showed at the beginning of his *Le vocabulaire des institutions indo-europeennes* that the thought structure of reciprocity is deeply anchored in the old Indo-germanic languages (Beneviste 1969). Laura Slatkin shows how these traditions in Homer not only become clear in the dealings and destinies of the heroes and gods but that they are also means of poetic representation.

We still have to investigate how trade is incorporated in this world of thought: as a natural continuation of the exchange of goods or as some other relation. Some trade certainly exists: the Greek soldiers give the traders, on the provision ships, pieces of plunder in exchange. In the *Odyssey* I, 184, the discussion is of a trip to "incomprehensible peoples" to trade copper for iron. That the trader is seen as an opposite to the warrior is shown by the verses where Euryalos challenged Odysseus by saying that he is not a man who understands the fight (Homer, *Odyssey* VIII, 161–164). The provocation works, Odysseus is outraged and prepares himself for a duel.

Myths tell still more in that they give the protection of trade to the roguish Hermes; he received the honor from Zeus in "On Hermes" (Homer 1986: 516ff.). It is the same Hermes who had personally taught Autolykos, one of Odysseus' forefathers, to hold "thieves' opinions and perjuries" (ibid. XIX, 396).

The text gives us no more. I have found, for example, no traces of hatred for usury. In a pre-monetary economy, loans may exist – even gifts imply a debt of sorts – but someone who grants loans for a living is difficult to imagine before money. Therefore the anger against usurers found in Aristotle is new, at least compared to the Middle Ages. That there is in Homer's time already prejudice against traders is easily understood, for the cool calculation of a profitable goal does not fit in to the hero profile. The word for profit had already in Homer, the unfriendly connotation of an unfair attempt to gain advantage; it characterizes the cunning of Antilochos, who created an advantage for himself by using an unfair trick in the chariot races at the games after Patroclos' death (Homer, *Iliad* XXIII, 515).

Measured against this point of view, Aristotle is not so bad a national economist as many moderns think. On the one hand he does support the popular prejudice in that he counts trade, especially deceitful small trade and usury as consumer credit, as unnatural activities. On the other hand, he looks, to solve this problem, for a fair trade-off that fits in traditional society and has reciprocity. He also never says that one should forbid trade or usury, or even that they should be regulated – this decision belongs to the Church. He wants only to explain why trade tends to lead to the explosion of the "good life" – and that traders, philosophers, and warriors all have different mentalities or ways of life, which is difficult to challenge – as Max Weber says, different economic mindsets.[31]

Aristotle's ordering of violence, gifts, and the exchange of equivalencies in one big idea of reciprocity that sums up our subject seems to me to be very deep: the warriors' attitude, which is correct between two enemy States but incorrect inside of the polis; the giving and counter-giving of gifts which, through voluntary work, holds the polis together with a call to the godly, the grace of the Charities; and finally, the reciprocity in direct exchange which rests on whether or not it maintains the social order. It is important to note that, for Aristotle, the content of justice depends on the historical circumstances – they change somewhat from the monarchy to the democracy – but the general principles of justice remain unchanged.

We can therefore see that our attempt to understand better the philosophical economic teachings of the Greeks confirms that there is no old inheritance that could be used to develop an economic analysis in the sense of the modern causal explanation – naturally we are even further away in the Archaic poetry than even in the Classical philosophy. But how the living relationships of a time naturally strange to us can be determined by an examination of the economic order becomes clearer through such an examination. It also makes the coherence of the Aristotelian system visible, while the economic conditions of Homer's Greece differ, radically, from those of the Classical period – because of the intervening invention of money.

FROM HESIOD TO THE CLASSICS

Hesiod and the world of the peasants

Hesiod belongs historically to the Homeric epoch; he is the first poet about whom we have any personal information. In his *Works and Days* – we will not discuss the *Theogeny* here – he shows us himself, how he became a winner in a singing competition because the muses "blessed him with light song". He shows us "the world of the small farmer who is closely hemmed in by his own existence and who shrinks from the unknown distance of the sea" (Hesiod 1966: 68). The poetry was created for a simpler, non-aristocratic audience; and so the singer also comes forward as belonging to the land.

An inheritance conflict is the outward theme of the poem in which Hesiod seeks to teach his brother about the rules of honest agriculture.[32] Basically, the tiny farmhouse equals the Homeric prince's court. The wife works here as well, at weaving, at least at certain times (Hesiod 1966: 778), although she should also be able to handle the livestock (ibid. 405). The discussion includes a few slaves. At best they are without families, and the women without babies (ibid. 601), and they live very simply, so much so that they have to be advised in the summer to build huts for the winter (ibid. 501ff.). The hardest work comes before the harvest, and afterwards all the slaves wish to stretch their legs and set the oxen free from their yokes (ibid. 607).

The gods demand sweat before they grant relaxation, or in other words (Hesiod 1966: 288), "work is no shame" (ibid. 310), but "shame lives with unhappy poverty" (ibid. 318). The admonitions to work would not be found so often in the poem if Goodness did not mention so often that one can be tempted into wanting to live unemployed for a while.

The household economic teaching, which later philosophy only names

125

without elaboration, is described in some detail here. It has little structure and is mixed with calendric rules, which offer ethnology some insight into the popular beliefs of the people, but which after the Greek enlightenment of philosophical economic teachings sound only like a summons to careful trade.

Order is a basic principle (Hesiod 1966: 470ff.), and care is recommended, whether in plowing or building a wagon. Before all else, order shows itself in the careful division of work according to the season. Wood must be brought from the mountains in winter (ibid. 427), and even the age of people and animals is taken into account in the division of labor – the 40-year-old is the youngest able to dig a straight trench and not just look around (ibid. 442ff.).

While Hesiod admits to having been on a "well-nailed ship" only once in his life, he recommends taking to the sea at the appropriate times to bring home profit for the household. Here the word *kerdos* has a positive connotation (Hesiod 1966: 629ff.). Long-distance trade is not viewed, however, as a widespread means of profit but rather as a support in connection with local production.[33] Each trip is dangerous, only to be dared at the best times of the year, and the entire property of the household should never be risked on a single ship's excursion (ibid. 688ff.).

So the farmer remains bound into a community where neighborliness and friendship are maintained through reciprocity.[34] Rules like "give to him who gives" or "giving is good, theft is bad" follow each other, because the neighborhood alliance would not preserve itself without rules; neighbors will help out the fellow who hasn't worked and is starving twice or three times, but no more than that (Hesiod 1966: 400ff.). Those who sit in the "common hall" because they do not have enough to eat are full of "evil hopes", and the unemployed man (*aergos aner*) often falls into evil (ibid. 497–500). He who gives, enjoys giving (ibid. 356ff.) – but here there is still no attempt to separate the spontaneity of reciprocity from the interest in it (ibid. 721ff.). Punishment follows, however, as the gods take revenge, when the thirst for profit – here again the word *kerdos* is used – confuses the senses and causes one to take wealth with force (ibid. 351).

It is none the less recommended to increase the wealth of the household (Hesiod 1966: 362). So that the wealth is not split, it is better to have only one son to care for (ibid. 372) – that way, one can pay the debts (ibid. 403). It is also better not to put anything unnecessarily off to the next day (ibid. 409) – in short, the complete catalog of middle-class virtues and frugality are listed, but in a historically specific form, which bans the old lust for plunder of the great lords and does not anticipate the possible connection between civic virtue and large trade. The farmer fears theft and war. The goal is not to increase already significant wealth but to guarantee a comfortable standard of living.

It is not a systematic explanation, but rather mythical ideas that order this way of thinking. It is from myths that Hesiod develops his collection of basic precepts of household economic rules.

In a first insight lifted from myth the poet suggests that there is not one Eris, not one goddess of conflict, but two. The first feeds only "evil enmity and ugly discord" and is unpopular. In some respects, trade seems to belong to this evil, fighting Eris (Hesiod 1966: 28ff.).[35] The other wakes mankind to blessings and the weight of work, so that neighbors want the same standard of living (ibid. 25ff.).

One could think that Hesiod is describing competition. Of course he means here rivalry and prize competition, not competition in the strict sense of maximizing profit. In reality the competition of neighbors is not geared toward getting ahead of the neighbors but toward placing the household on a good footing (*oikon t' eu testai*) (Hesiod 1966: 23).

The enjoyment of competitive games, which started with the Greeks, is deeply anchored in the Homeric epic and only finds its most obvious expression in the games; it requires reining in, and this is right according to Hesiod. But before that, disaster and deficiency must be explained.

Prometheus gave, against Zeus' will, fire to mankind – as punishment he sent the mixed gifts of Pandora. She learned from Athena how to spin webs, from Aphrodite she learned grace, but thieving ways were Hermes' gift. And she went and brought humanity many disasters and sicknesses. Afterwards, the trials of humanity are punishments for the hubris that led people to reach for the fire of the gods. Most significantly, Zeus "concealed" the "nourishment" – it must be won through cultivation – and so he made what is today called "scarcity" and thereby the necessity for work (Hesiod 1966: 47ff.).

Hesiod tells yet another myth: that of the different ages of time. In the gold age, human beings lived happily and without care; they became ghosts that traveled the earth and gave out wealth. In the silver age mankind was without moderation and did not honor the gods, in the next one they were warlike and obstinate, and in the fourth there were heroes and demigods who survived the wars of the Greek sagas, especially those over Troy. A final, bad, iron age is the one where hospitality, friendship, even relationships and the respect of children for their parents threaten to disappear; intimidation and other forms of unfairness are everywhere. Human beings are oppressed by cares. There is, however, one comfort: *dike*, or right and law, pursues injustice and is the ordering power (Hesiod 1966: 226–230).

It is in no way the logic of law itself that gives men comfort and peace when they behave rightly, but rather godly power and human insight work together with nature (Hesiod 1966: 233). It is the luck of fathers that women bear them children who are just like them. Evil-doers are punished, however.

Law as the earthly core of this extensive order is given to human beings; Zeus has set the wild animals to eat each other "because there is no law among them" (Hesiod 1966: 277). We are far from the Aristotelian attempt to overcome the conflict between *nomos* and *physis*, between legal right and nature, through a natural law construct. Law is also not systematic, but inherited. The lords who spoke against Hesiod in his inheritance conflict with his brother are slandered in the poem, and the word used is *dorothagoi*, "gift eater". Already in the *Iliad*, the gods punish the false judge (Homer, *Iliad* XVI, 386-387).

And even in Aristotle we find the concept of reciprocity as a part of justice, and not treated as a part of custom, separated from law.

In the aristocratic world of Homer, virtues are individual, destiny, a guiding principle that exceeds the person. In the Aristotelian polis, the images of virtues are formally structured through moral statements and legal concepts in a teleologically ordered system. Only in the "wealth of nations" does it come to the balancing of interests according to a quasi-mechanical rule.

Archaic lyric and educational literature

In Plato's *Protagoras* a fight is used in the analysis of the idea of virtue with emphasis on archaic proverbs. Socrates refers in his explanation to the Spartan mode of educating in life's wisdom; it makes it possible for the Lacedamones to express themselves laconically. They thus became an example for the seven wise men, whose insights live on in temple engravings like "know yourself" and in oral tradition. Indeed we can deduce pre-Socratic philosophy almost exclusively from quotations made by later writers. Lyric and educational literature often stand near each other and make the bridge between feeling and reflection, between religious explanations and those of the inner world. These elements are bound together in Solon's elegies.

Far-reaching societal, political, and also economic changes in the Archaic period separate the spirit of that age from that of the previous Homeric age or the succeeding Classical period; to the Archaic belongs the invention of the coin, beginning in Lydia in the seventh century BC according to the testimony of Herodotus (I, 94). The building of wealth, which is connected to the expanding monetary economy, and the social tensions that develop from it are the cause of a new type of thought. Sohn-Rethel (1970) claims, taking from George Thompson, that the idea of proof, failing in the pre-Socratic era, became mathematics out of the practical art of calculation and surveying, thanks to the schooling in the abstract thought which is connected to the premises for value abstraction in money. Meyer believes that social and economic relationships were changed from the ground up. The entrance into debt destroyed many lives. The sentence *chremat' aner*, "money makes the man" (Sappho and Alcaeus 1971: 324), is said to be the truism of the age (Meyer 1892: 23ff., esp. 110).

As was suggested at the beginning, Bücher – and with him the majority of today's historians – holds Meyer's (1895) assumed expansion of capitalistic transactions in Archaic Greece to be exaggerated. But it is the extent, and not the character, of the phenomenon that is challenged.

The old Spartan praise for noble contests and courageous war actions is to be found in Tyrtaios, whose work is dated around 640 BC; death is better than flight without honour (Tyrtaios 1960: 28). In one of his elegies, Tyrtaios celebrates the constitution of Sparta that was suggested by the Delphic oracle. The rule of the land starts with the kings and the *gerusia*, the council of elders, but the citizens should accept their suggestions; conquering and power should follow the popular will (Tyrtaios 1954: 64).

In the world of Sappho, the greatest of the female poets, we find ourselves in a refined high society. She raised in friendship young girls who learned dancing, harp playing and singing, manners and education in the service of the Muses (Sappho 1954). Unfortunately, this is not the place to discuss her love poetry, but Sappho clearly sets herself apart from the warlike world (Sappho 1954: 35). And love is not esoteric: Helen, who followed her Paris, remains the example of this. There are traces in Sappho's poetry that prove that she did not remain unaffected by the tragedies of the time, namely the conflict between the sinking aristocracy and the start of the rule of the people, which again led to the tyrants. In a fragmentary poem to the daughter of Kleis she wants to give the daughter a piece of fine jewelry, but she unfortunately cannot give such gifts (often seen as an example of opulent wealth), as she knows from Lydia (Sappho 1954: 81).

To the community of art and love, which Sappho establishes for herself, doubtless not only joy belongs, but also a sort of wealth (Sappho 1954: 73). Ancient scholarly versions of her work exist, saying, for example, "that wealth with virtue reigns far and wide" (Sappho and Alcaeus 1971: 139). The fifth pythic ode of Pindar also begins with the connection of "all powerful" wealth and virtue. So it is only wealth, if it has the upper hand without virtue, that damages the household. The problem which emerged, that wealth – differently from the Homeric epics – is made to be problematic, must be brought into connection with the contemporary political confusion, which was doubtless bound up with the rise of a monetary economy.

Alkaios, a contemporary of Sappho's in Mytilene on the isle of Lesbos, lets the passion of the political storms show through in his poetry. In Chios in 600, democracy was already in place; Solon brings it to Athens in 594 BC. Alkaios was clearly more than just a political writer, even in exile (Alkaios 1963: 139). He had had to leave Mytilene on Lesbos, for taking part in a conspiracy against the tyrant Myrsilos, whose failure brought with it his banishment. With the death of Myrsilos he could have returned in triumph (Alkaios 1963: 45). Alkaios was thus then enraged, that the people themselves had called for another dictator – here Pittakos,

"An ignoble son, Pittakos, was set up as the tyrant of our old city! Everyone who bore him ill was seduced by demons, forgot their grudges and cheered loudly for him" (Alkaios 1963: 53)

In exile, Alkaios longs to take part in the democratic process, although he is aware of the faults of his fellow citizens (Alkaios 1963: 21). So, democracy from her birth forward is bound up with the danger of corruption through the bad sense of the citizens; ancient testimonies ascribe the following to Alkaios, "that it is not stone nor wood nor the art of construction that should build the cities, but instead there should be walls and cities there where there are people who know to protect themselves" (Alkaios 1963: 81). This protection is not only a question of military preparedness, says the poet, who since then has been credited throughout the centuries as having said "money makes the man" (Alkaios 1963: 53).

In rare greatness, which suggests a comparison to Dante and Goethe, Solon combines in his time the art of the poet and philosopher with that of the statesman, who opened the path to democracy in Athens in that he secured basic rights for the people. We begin, with his own testimony, which Aristotle quotes in his "Constitution of Athens", and we hear how Solon returned mortgaged land through a land reform and, even more importantly, abolished debt-induced slavery (Solon 1963: 98 and Solon 1954: vol. 1, 148ff.). After that, in principle, only foreign prisoners of war were sold as slaves – in a certain sense, their loss of freedom was a necessary condition for the early development of democracy. Finally, Solon makes the laws reconciling "violence and law" in that he set himself above raw financial interests, as alone as a wolf in the company of dogs. The debt-related decrees, the removal of debt-induced slavery, the division of the populace into four classes for tax purposes, and the contribution to justice and the law cannot, of course, individually be the substance of representations in poetic form; the poem reproduces, however, the sworn mandate to remain loyal to the laws according to the new order in a unique link between religious timidity and revolutionary consciousness. Solon leaves no doubt that only his own ethics stopped him from transforming his prestige into a dictatorship as the tyrants did later. One obeys the right and wrong commands of the ruler (Solon 1954: vol. 1, 154). A city is destroyed by great men, and the people fall into slavery through their ignorance (Solon 1954: vol. 1, 122). Under the title "The Lawgiver", there is a preserved fragment that notes how hubris is produced when too much wealth falls to him whose spirit is not *artios*, "perfect" (Solon 1963: 100 and 1954: vol. 1, 120). So Solon advises the rich to not be greedy and to moderate themselves in their claims (Solon 1954: 142).

Solon himself wished for fame and fortune, as in the prayer to the muses, but the wealth should not be unjust, for he who practices injustice will eventually be horribly punished, and if not he himself, then his children or grandchildren (Solon 1963: 94). Since in this poem Solon pursues the lust for wealth of the men in this poem, with all of their many confused imaginings to which they cling until they collapse, he describes the multiple division of labor. Naturally Solon invokes next, the image of the contrast between the profit-hungry sea trader and the cultivator of land (Solon 1954: vol. 1, 128, verses 43, 44, 47). Finally he describes the craft arts of Athena and of Hephaestos, as well as those of the muses and the seer. It is, however, not a rational economic principle that orders the thoughts on division of labor, but Moira, the goddess of destiny, who brings good and evil to all areas of work (Solon 1954: vol. 1, 130, verses 63–65).

And so this verse follows, one which is regularly quoted: "The goal of wealth [the Greek word also means the finishing post in horse-racing] does not lie clear to mankind" (the Greek for "lie" also means the writing down in lawbooks; the word for "clear" is "the shining-out" which in pre-Socratic philosophy is used when the manifestation of a deeper godly state is intended as the "phenomenon"[36]) (Solon 1954: verse 71, Stobaei 1958: 355 and Solon 1963: 96). The result is that, as in the battle of the Homeric heroes, Ate, the fate of the gods, appears punishing – here in the battle for wealth. Solon does not help with the insight that "many rich folk are bad, but many good folk are poor" (Solon 1954: vol. 1, 132); but he does not want to exchange wealth and virtue, because virtues remain forever, but wealth will in turn always be possessed by someone.

So one must think about the actual standard of living. We find that the conception of the autarchic household, in an Aristotelian sense, is of a household that can fulfill its essential needs, although this end is not expressed. The images are not shown conceptually but visually (Solon 1963: 101).

Solon would not have had to fight for his law making if it was – in his evaluation – not for the expansion of a lust for profit combined with unscrupulous politics. This has found little direct literary expression; even now it is from Bias – like Solon, one of the seven wise men – that the anecdote of the early sixth century BC is quoted, that when Solon was asked which actions men delight in, he answered "making a profit" (Diogenes Laertus I, 87). In a critical form the references are more frequent. From Pittakos of Lesbos, also one of the seven wise men,[37] comes the word of the "unfulfillable lust for profit" (Diels 1934: vol. 1, 64, verses 17ff.); also here is found the earliest usage of the word oikonomia for "household education" (ibid. verse 19). Phokylides of Milet, in the second half of the sixth century BC, is the first to mention economists. In an elegant poem, he compares women to animals: to dogs, bees, wild pigs, and to long-maned mares, to which different characteristics are assigned. Naturally the bee is the best housekeeper (Phokylides 1954: vol. 1, 174), and the poet prays that his friend can lead such a woman to a happy marriage.

In Theogonis, who is believed to have flourished at the end of the sixth century, we have a lyricist whose elegies, in so far as they are not drinking and love poems, contain educational reflections on friendship, and societal and economic destinies. Theogonis is said to come from Attic Megara, where he experiences the fall of the aristocratic rulership, of which he felt a part. So his poetry contains many complaints that the nobility does not count anymore. Most of his poems are written to a friend, Cyrnos (Theogonis 1960: 31, nr. 2 and 1954: vol. 1, 232, verses 27–28). He teaches the morality of nobility, but he also advises fitting in.

The changes apparent in Theogonis' writing include, besides new wealth from trade and simple competition, new property relationships in agriculture, just as Aristotle describes them in his "The State of the Athenians" (Theogonis 1963: 118). Many aristocrats were expelled and lived, like Theogonis, in exile. He who lives in exile has no friends, which is bitterer than the exile itself, he writes (Theogonis 1954: vol. 1, 252, verse 209ff.). His heart became black from the thought that others owned his fields and that his farm animals did not go under the yoke for him (ibid. vol. 1, 376, verses 1199–1201). Corruption and private lust for profit and power lead to civil war, and that, to the tyrant – that is the repeated explanatory model (ibid. vol. 1, 234, verses 43–52). So one should never make friends with corrupt individuals (ibid. vol. 1, 242, verse 113ff.), and he advises Cyrnos that it is better to live with a few good men in piety than to be rich with unjustly held property. Man should live moderately and prudently (Theogonis 1960: 32, nr. 8 and 1954: 246, verse 153ff.).

In many parts of the text quotes from Solon can be found with small modifications, including some on the limitlessness of wealth, which we already know. Scholars differ on how the mixed character of the collection, whose core is attributed to Theogonis, came into existence.[38] Its ironic verses, such as the one which seems to mean "don't ever strive for too much!" (Theogonis 1960: 39, nr. 55), sound authentic (ibid. 37, nr. 40 and 1954: 362, verse 1117ff.). Its aristocratic character is connected to the despising of slaves; these never hold their heads high, rather their necks are bent, and the child of a slave is never free in his mind, even as an onion never gives birth to a rose (Theogonis 1954: 292, verses 535–538; 302, verse 621 and 1960: 42, nr. 76).

Perhaps Theogonis himself lived with the pressure of poverty, tempting him into dishonest trade, although he knew better (Theogonis 1954: 308, verses 649–652). He wanted for himself one thing and prayed for it above all: happiness – *eudaimony* (Theogonis 1954: 308, verse 653ff.). Poverty oppresses the noble more than the average fellow (Theogonis 1960: 37, nr. 41 and 1960: 248, verses 173–178). The famous, often quoted verse comes from him: "Not to have been born is the best for the peasant" (Theogonis 1963: 112 and 1954: 280, verses 425–428).

Alongside the seriousness of the archaic poets, a lighter note was also struck. One happily escapes at a banquet from the forces of the monetary economy, the danger of debt, and the fiery political conflicts, as shown by Anacreon and the Anacreonistic drinking songs (Anacreon 1954: vol. 2, 84, nr. 50, verse 24ff. and 1960: 60ff.). Behind these pious, serious, angry, bitter, sad, friendly, loving, and playful songs, we see, as we look back to our original question, a search for law and order in the call for the old custom and aristocracy, or the hope for a new equality and the confirmation of the claims of the people. The lyrical voices vary from passionate to moral. In their tension, explanations for the changes and guiding lights for the future are sought. Rational analyses are missing. Even the household economics, where rational allocations first appear, changes from moderation and morality on the one hand to greed and waste on the other. In view of this tradition, the task set for philosophers is not to search for causal explanations, where rationality hardly exists, rather it is to find the norms that order the moral attitudes and laws, in order to find a setting for life in which it can unfold also as an economic activity. This theme, only slightly altered, defined the Classical period.

I end this section with a reference to Classical lyrical verse from Pindar. Aristotle claims that "water" is "the best", as proof for the statement that something common could be more valuable than something rare because of its usefulness (Kraus 1905: 588). The poetic confrontation of the first Olympian ode awoke in me first the association of precious, clear fountain water on a hot day in the South, and a Greek piece of gold jewelry that shimmers in the dark. But when Aristotle cites the verse as a proverb it must have become for his contemporaries an expression of the opposites set up between a wealth that, although it is everywhere, belongs to no one, and a "fitting for the great" precious object. Water, however, is good, even the "best" – its usefulness outweighs the other, says Aristotle. In this way the paradox of setting value to things makes itself clear. Pindar searches for a simile for the winning of a competition – being named the "best" – and finds in the following lines one, daylight, that, as free as water and as bright as gold, brings the two images together.[39]

Comments on Classical tragedy and the comedies of Aristophanes

It would be presumptuous to try to portray in this limited space the unbelievable world of Classical tragedy which had so many after-effects – one needs only to think of the many dramas about Electra's fate in ancient and more recent literature. There is also little to say with respect to economic questions, since in the fifth century a specialized literature, at least with respect to household economics, had developed, and, although drama touched upon many questions of existence, archaic drama offers little in the way of new economic points in general. These new ideas are not – as I see it – that much different from the old, while the philosophical literature searched for a systematic way to proceed. The new realism of the comedy in the time of Aristophanes, who in the form of parody brings everyday conflicts to the stage, is, however, full of economic facts which are interesting at least to economic history. How much this results in essential variation in economic thinking remains an open question for me.

Doubtless tragedy leads to a deepening of the appreciation of political conflicts which, for example, become clear in Aeschylus' *Orestia*, the only surviving trilogy. Here common law which saves Orestes from the guilt of becoming his mother's murderer, preserved by Athena, is set triumphantly up against the old mindset of revenge. This conflict is so well reflected that the references to, and variations of, these themes become very meaningful through the following tragedians Sophocles and Euripides: I can hardly feel myself, however, prepared to draw out of the apparent understanding of political development any kind of altered interpretation toward economic thought.[40] The conflict of the classes, which is directly and naively represented by Solon and Theogonis, is mythically represented. Although Homer's spheres of life are so woven together that the depiction of the abstract-godly destiny, a supernatural fairy world, the fights of the heroes and the existence of the simple people mingle together, the form of the economy can none the less be determined from the representation of the simple people and from the supernatural elements, the conceptions of economic ideas. The tragedy, however, moves on such a poetic level that the reconstruction of material details can be undertaken only with difficulty if one is not to be dogmatic. On the other hand, general connections disappear behind the concrete action in Aristophanes. We see how slaves are praised and punished, they seem to us as if they are living people, and thus the actual destiny of slaves is painted, not abstracted like in Homer's works into a few broad strokes.

It would possibly be worth it to a careful observer, to reveal the layers in the Greek plays that I have not noticed – possibly even in the Classical poetry, although I have, with an eye to this topic, re-read Pindar and consistently set him aside (until I was led through Aristotle to the often repeated meaning of the first Ode). For the area of theater I must be satisfied with a few comments on the preserved fragments of Aeschylus, Sophocles' *Antigone*, Euripides' *Electra*, and Aristophanes' *Plutos*.

The god Prometheus, whose existence was updated through Goethe's poetry and drama fragments, appears on stage as the bound one in the first, virtually independent and completely preserved part of Aeschylus' trilogy. He, an old stock Titan, is chained to the rocks by Hephaestos, who acts unwillingly on Zeus' command, because he stole fire from heaven and gave it to mankind. At the same time this Titan took foresight away from humanity and gave it hope instead (Aeschylus 1988: 439, verses 448–451).

Previously humanity had never even believed in the seasons, but then

Prometheus showed it the path of the stars, "number, the highest artifice of mental ability" (ibid. 439, verse 459), writing as the "mother of all of the Muses' works" (ibid. 439, verse 461), the taming of animals, whereby humankind could have breaks from work, and finally, the ability to go to sea. Before all else though, because mankind had become the master of fire, it would discover many arts (ibid. 439, verse 254). Among these are healing, prophesy, and finally the discovery of "what the earth kept hidden" (ibid. 441, verse 501) – the metals, ore, iron, silver, and gold.

Barry Gordon (1975, 1976: 13) interpreted this as a belief in progress, and doubtlessly, in this century more than in the previous centuries, the titanic power of human inventiveness is admired, which inventiveness is led by hope but developed by men who, despite all of their gazing into the future, do not know their true destinies. The evident theme of Aeschylus' drama is a not unreserved but rather shuddering admiration for the Titans who dared to challenge even the great god Zeus and confront the punishment of eternal bondage, and who refused to give up conflict with the ruler of heaven.

The first play of the trilogy ends with Prometheus and his rock sinking into the sea after being struck by lightning. In the second play of the trilogy, Prometheus recognizes his sufferings, in that he is not only bound to the Caucasus but a vulture eats his constantly regenerating liver by rummaging through his living intestines. He wishes for death (Aeschylus 1988: 478, fragment 35, column 23). From legends we know that Heracles frees him. It is believed that the third piece, "Prometheus, the fire-carrier", where Hephaestos could prove himself Prometheus' friend and cousin, brought about the entry of the torchlit parade of the Prometheus cult into Athens. The Titan who stuck to his rights became Prometheus, the wise friend of Hephaestos, and also the god of fire and pottery, who enjoyed great honor; and the mistrusting, cruel tyrant, Zeus, becomes the just and mild ruler of the world (Aeschylus 1988: 750). How the ironic ending is brought about in the piece we do not know; we have to be satisfied with the observation that Athenian piety required it. "Progress" appears as offensive, brought about by the rebellion of the Titan; it must have been, for Aeschylus, bound up with a new world order that is very cult-like.

After this introduction it becomes easier for us to understand the famous chorus song in Sophocles' *Antigone* (Sophocles 1920: 234), reminding us of Hölderlin's translation, "*Ungeheur ist viel*", "The monstrous is abundant". Antigone stands in conflict to the arbitrarily set law of Creon, who evilly forbids the burial of her brother. The chorus makes clear in its song the great and dangerous possibilities of free human actions in conflict with nature. Its solution is to follow the rules of society. Antigone, whom Creon threatens with death for the discovered burial of her brother, calls upon ancient, god-given duty. Through arguments of original divine law, human love, and politics – because the people secretly judge Creon –

attempts are made to effect mercy for Antigone. Finally, the Seer prophesies revenge and civil war. As Creon is prepared to give in, it is too late; his son, whom Antigone loves, has killed himself, and the continuing calamities finally bring Creon – too late – to insight into the error of his arbitrariness. The technical-economical power of the people, reflected in the song of the Chorus, which can lead to good or ill, and which makes it necessary for the Greeks to have each man set himself under his own and god's law, is equivalent to political power, which, through arrogance, revokes fate.

Antigone's Creon does not set himself outside the law on purpose; he calls much more upon Zeus, the ruler; and to his own ruling power, derived from Zeus, it seems to him that greed for personal profit is very dangerous (Sophocles 1950: 20, verses 295–301). He makes clear that this search for profit (*kerdos*) is not denounced with respect to any specific method of earning wealth but to the general hoarding of wealth (Sophocles 1950: 20, verse 312). None the less, we can see in the choice of words the reaction to institutional changes. While in Archaic lyric, as far as I can tell, only general expressions like "gold" and "wealth" can be found, here, the "evil silver money" is named, with an expression which seems to show a nominal understanding of money: *arguros kakon nomisma* (ibid. 20, verses 295–296). Although in context, the particular form of money as coin does not play a role, it is, in fact, an anachronism for Sophocles to give to Creon, of the time of heroes, a familiarity with minted money.

Classical Greek drama repeats the most important themes of economic thought in the Archaic epoch. In the democracy of Periclesian Athens, enlightened thought did not remove the traditional conflict between individual freedom and human determination of what is right, on one side, and the traditional values of community and family, on the other, although the personalities in the plays reveal themselves ever more clearly as individual characters.

In the *Orestia* of Aeschylus, Orestes is the main character throughout, and his sister, Electra, has a far less important role. In *Electra* from Euripides, more complicated in terms of plot, the individual miseries and the unpredictability of fate are dramatically presented. The drama reaches farther than its predecessor with respect to setting and society. Therefore we see, which is interesting, Electra, after having been thrown out of the royal house, entering as the wife of a poor peasant in front of his hut. This situation allows a reflection, which is peripheral to the main action, on the differences between wealth and poverty, between aristocratic and peasant life, between the roles of the sexes. Since the tragic survival, according to the tradition of Greek drama, of the dependents of the hero's family is maintained, this exposition may in itself be a sign of a democratic development. It underlines, freely within the bounds of the tragic style, the sadness and misery of the daughter Electra, who saw her mother

Clytaemnestra, with the help of another man, attack Clytaemnestra's husband Agamemnon on his return home.

Electra performs without complaint, even willingly, the duties attendant on being in a peasant household. The peasant does not touch her, however, out of respect for her nobility. Electra wants to mourn and not to dance in the role of the peasant girl. Thus an internal state of being is made visible to the audience; we see, however, that the lower ranking person, namely the male peasant, is made remarkable through nobility of the mind because he is able to control his passion, while the queen, Clytaemnestra, did evil and was punished for it.

Orestes asks what sets the noble apart from the peasant (Euripides 1948: 22). Wealth and the lack of it both lead equally to evil. Even the lance is no longer guaranteed to the nobility. Not even the old "use by association" makes the nobles unique, no, "those such as he are citizens of rank" (ibid. 23). This is of course the idea of democracy, which is made clear to Orestes through the "misery" and the "poor roof" of the "royal daughter", who must work at the loom and carry water, far from festivals and robbed of her society (ibid. 20).[41]

Democracy, although of a new spirit, calls upon tradition; in this tragedy it again takes up the old values about wealth, where wealth melts the hand of the evildoer. Male superiority in the order of the household is maintained (Euripides 1948: 45); however, the guilt-ridden murderer of her own husband, Clytaemnestra, remonstrates against it angrily, in that she rebukes the murdered Agamemnon for his continuing offenses. Orestes avenges his father when he kills Clytaemnestra. The guilt of murdering his mother, which applies despite the rightness of the revenge, will – this is in Euripides only a promise for the distant future – only be resolved exclusively by the gods.

In the fantasy and parody world of Aristophanes, which is still basically the everyday world of the average fellow, as is often the case in satire, actual conflicts of the time's modern way of thinking are brought directly to the stage, until, after all the developments, the family relationships manage to preserve themselves. An example is the treatment of the usurers in the "Clouds". A peasant, who had to go into debt because of the ambition of his son, seeks help from Socrates, because he wants to learn the sophistic art of speechmaking, so that he can hopefully defeat his creditors before a judge. His "Weep, you usurers!" (Aristophanes 1946: vol. 1, 213, verse 1155) seems to be a parody of Euripides. But the memorized sophisms will not help the peasant, because his son uses them too, to hold his father to the contract between generations, and finally, the general anger turns to Socrates himself, whose house is burnt to the ground.

In *Plutos*, the last work of Aristophanes that has been saved, which, although now considered dramatically weak, was earlier loved, a very human-seeming servant and his good master Mr Chremylos meet Pluto, blinded by wealth. They go about healing him, and the result is that he shares his wealth, now money, fairly, that is among those that are fair and good. Indeed, say the master and servant in turn, "there is satiation in everything, in love and bread, in honor and cakes, in ambition and leavened bread, but not in wealth" (Aristophanes 1946: 98, verse 190ff.). Pluto gave to all who were poor and brought the peasants into comfort. There remains, however, a conflict between being full and being fulfilled, with which the fairy-tale plays.

In a similar way, a very important objection to poverty's being personified is removed. Poverty threatens misfortune, such that everybody would like to drive her out of Greece. She says that general wealth is not possible, because then who would want to work, build ships, sew or tend the fields? (Aristophanes 1946: 114, verse 512ff.). Chremylos tells her that all this work would be taken care of by slaves. "Where would all these slaves come from?" asks Poverty. Chremylos answers: "From Thessalia, from other countries". Since overcoming poverty through general growth is not even thought of here – that is a modern idea – it was truly unavoidable to fall back on imported slaves; this is, however, too ugly a thought to be pursued in the comedy. Poverty turns to another argument: she brings frugality and virtue, with her are decency and morality (ibid. 116, verse 559ff.). Also, it is only the rich speakers, pricked, who conspire against the people and democracy (ibid. 117, verse 567ff.). The familiar, standard state of politics should be carried on in a modest and unassuming manner. Chremylos, who himself is a just man, seems to be at a loss for an answer. The only option left to him, he says, is to not let himself be overruled, even if he is convinced, and with that he pursues Poverty. Poverty curses and claims that they will need her again someday, but her threats do not come true in this happy play.

And so the good, poor people become rich. Others suffer then: an old woman, who had hired a young man to stay with her, must watch as he runs away from her; even the god Hermes seems unhappy because no one sacrifices to him, as no one requires his ambiguous services anymore. But a new cult is raised to worship Pluto, Hermes becomes a judge of war games in exchange for his lost sacrifices, and even the old lady follows in the procession.

Thus we see that Aristophanes recognizes and thematizes the tension between lack and need, between frugality and gratification. Naturally utility is not dealt with as a given for the individual thing, but rather, as derived from Aristotle, according to the circumstances. A weapons dealer wishes therefore that there were battles (Urbain 1939: 191). Such changes in the use of wares are in Aristophanes in many ways connected with the observation of weakening prices; the same phenomenon is also addressed with respect to salaries (ibid. 193). Many aspects betray a clear view of economic circumstances, and hence the suggestion that the use of less valuable copper money – because bad money displaces good – can be brought into play only through a decree that makes this type of money illegal (ibid. 195). Elsewhere there are signs that one may not hope to maintain the restrictions on importing and exporting that come with a state of war, without forgoing price control (ibid. 198).

Urbain pulls the "absence de contradiction dans l'ensemble des idées et faits presentés par l'auteur" (Aristophanes) into the open (Urbain 1939: 199). But this lack of contradiction requires no more than a gift for sharp observation and a reasonable mind, not, however, the explicit, written, or verbally passed down formulation of economic laws as individual hypotheses or as a system. This, in fact, is not claimed by Urbain, who emphasizes the value of Aristophanes to economic history, and not to the history of dogma. In his economically ethical conception he does not step beyond the limits prescribed by Greek philosophy.

CONCLUSIONS

If one wants to measure the achievements of the Platonic and Aristotelian philosophies in the areas of knowledge for which economists are usually responsible, the result, after this overview, must be very different from one ensuing from the modern conception of theory creation.

One could suggest that, even proceeding as we have, we are comparing apples and oranges in our attempt to look in detail at Homer's economic world with notions of craft and division of labor, and exchange and reciprocity, while we have doubtlessly neglected the same themes in Aristophanes, with his peasants and their gardens and agriculture, with their sale of vegetables and usurers. First, the existence of such descriptions in both does not mean that any sort of modern scientific understanding of the economic proceedings can be deduced. Homer could, in order to make a comparison, unforgettably describe the use of a lance: how it is threateningly shaken, how it flies with no intention of doing good, how it, missing its target, sticks into the ground next to the shaken hero and shivers. As the description of this event requires no understanding of ballistics, even Aristophanes would need no more than good observational representational skills to describe suitable war threats.

It is different with respect to the representation of human relationships in connection with a given economic order. Here we see that the narrator of the myth is enlightening in his own way, when he sets the terror of war against the peace of the household, when he lets Odysseus have his beloved Ithaca despite his disastrous fate, and also, when he marches the wonders of artfully completed work before our eyes. The listener learns before all else about the intricacies of the acts of reciprocity in all their complex forms.

Homer prepares the way for what Hesiod with his legends of the gifts of law and what Solon with his proud report of his statesmanship make clear. From unbelievably old ways of thinking, which can even still be found in certain aspects of the language, the concept of good is formed and remains throughout the twisted path of history, bound in a completed order, and made concrete through the writing of laws, without a complete break with religious powers and old traditions.

The first economic problem that was dealt with scientifically – that is, seemingly simply, in a systematic representation of the context – came up in the firming up of "right" relationships of the household and the State. To secure the core of the political context, one sets those economic relationships in the forefront, in which a simple patriarchal family life is secure with respect to subsistence and in which the communications of the community can be included. Thus the "old economics" came to be; its "loss" has since been shown (Egner 1985). As Wagner (1969) confirmed, these economics determined virtually all the economic thought of the ancients, as far as that has been passed down to us, and it was long preserved through Church tradition, housefather literature, and Cameralism.

The Hellenistic and Roman reception, and even more the Church, changed the old economics and limited it dogmatically. Making the simple picture of the old economics a rigid norm, right up to the forbidding of interest, laid the foundation for such occurrences as the fatal limitation of monetary trade to Jews and the hopeless discrepancy between churchly ideals and capitalistic reality which appeared early in the new era.

The development of Greek economic thought was very open – witness Solon's effort of equalization and the general acceptance of democratic ideas. Antiquity itself was proud of its development, which led to the success of the Greek and Roman cultures, whose influence extended far beyond their military expansion (Polybius, VI).

The concepts of order, that go back to Hesiodic times, have been strongly bound into all the succeeding systems. German economics uses a concept, the politics of order, which might clarify this intellectual development. The spreading of order is not designed to lead to a more liberal form of government, but the market is the important catalyst for the mediation of the exchange of products outside of the household in a society with division of labor, that is, inside a city as well as between States. Hierarchical allocation principles lead to the opposite, an eastern theocracy.

On the other hand, the limits of this order are sharply felt – with respect to slavery and the threat of the dangers that come from economically caused changes of power, the rise of trade and monetary economics, etc. These things make the old form of reciprocity obsolete or destroy it outright.

As far as the role of knowledge goes in the attempt to establish "order", the voice of Aristophanes, otherwise so useful to the economists, is only one among many. The high and late Classical time period is when conceptions of order can be found in the voices of the philosophers in the system which – and this is the deciding factor – had the job of bringing the Greek image of humanity, the idea of a good life, and as far as possible, economic forces into harmony.

It is impossible that in antiquity a utility-based theory would have developed, with given preferences as the determining factors in the demand. As we have seen, such a theory would be conceivable, if a Democritus had seen that the truth of one can be replaced with the taste of another, which is completely in line with the modern conception. Utilitarianism, in the form of hedonism against which Plato and Aristotle critically set themselves, derives in the "old economics" from the institutional framework and posing of questions, but it misses the mark, because it is primarily concerned with exchange maxims for the ideally highly self-sufficient household, and not with a preference theory for the disposing of a given market-earned income. As a trade theory, the principle of pleasure is tossed out in Socratic philosophy, although it is discussed by Plato in *Philebos* and is not completely without an echo in poetry, or in the Anacreonistic songs. In the school of Epicurus, on the other hand, hedonism is refined so much that to ensure that human comfort demands equanimity; it fostered control over life-urges and the level of demand. As a consequence, even the image of the good life was limited and not idealized as an unlimited aspiration for wealth. This is not effected in the same way as in the neoClassical household management theory, where namely the preferences of the muses are the opposing force to desires without satiation – work cannot be the limitation of consumption because it is left by the rich to the slaves. Further still, one ought not limit oneself to the earnings of one's own work in the use of wealth to lead a good life. Thus, demand must also be limited by itself, not from the rewarding achievements.

Besides, a large income should not be used to the limits of the modern budget, because there were no savings. Instead – something which newer theory does not predict and which sounds to us more idealistic than is intended – any extra money was shared with friends and the state. Behind the more recent imperative, to lead a distinguished life with respect to one's cultural role, stand the older motives of reciprocity and self-representation through generosity.

In a basic form, utility theory is thinkable and was suggested by the hedonists, as an extension of the topic of individual consumption, and also referred to by the Socratics. An educated form of utility theory in the form of the marginal utility teachings was, however, for conceptual reasons, not possible for the Greeks. The notion of function belongs first to the seventeenth century, and also, it made no sense for the strict thinkers of antiquity to create the fictive concept of marginal utility, which approach utility theorists have replaced today with indifference curves.

Also impossible for the Greek mind to conceive would have been the concept of self-regulation of the market. This requires a conception of mechanical processes, which was first developed in mechanics – one thing which is clear, in any case, is that the invention of the self-regulating clock and the Newtonian mechanics of the stars led to the carry-over of the "invisible hand" as an image in astronomy, into economic events. A decent analogy of the difference between modern science and classical economics can be made through the difference between Aristotle's teachings of nature with its deterministic organic growth and his economic ethics; this analogy shows which economic goals serve, or do not serve, under certain historical conditions, like a monarchy or a democracy.

Between the images of economic activities and forms of transport, which can be found through thoughtful reading in early Greek poetry, on the one hand, and the integration, completed by the Socratic philosophers, of the teachings of the economic institutions, on the other, can be found a remarkable and partially downright secretive connection. Basic ideas like reciprocity and its symbolic or sacred representations through the Charities are present from Homer to Aristotle, although the tradition thins significantly, until the Emperor puts through the claims of the State, after which at last the wealth of the Periclesian democratic State finally made room for public poverty along with private concentration of wealth. On the way there, socially critical concepts become more radical even in the late Classical period. Decadent display no longer belonged there. Of the conceptions of order of the democratic Greek city and community and their economic basis there remain at the end, so to speak, only the images of the enemy; as when Horace's clear contrast between the strong state and weak society is made clear (*Carmina* III, 24). The unlimited and deceptive gains of money, whether from individual fate or the sum of the individual fates, were considered a societal problem in the Archaic and Classical time periods. When ultimately in the Middle Ages, around 1100, the poem about Geizhals by Marbod of Rennes (1974) is written, in which accumulation of wealth is a sin because it is senseless, the trouble-maker of the medieval Church appears as a literary character, more as laughable than dangerous, until the rules of the play change from the bottom up, because of the entrance of more players, especially entrepreneurs and workers.

The historical significance of organizing Greek economic thought within philosophy by means of the Socratics can hardly be contested, and also unchallenged seems to me to be the lesser position, which they assumed, *vis-à-vis* their own forefathers – we have looked at the poets among them – and their descendants up until the Middle Ages. How meaningful other ancient poets were on economic questions that lie perhaps closer to modern liberal formulations cannot be clearly decided. One can, however, believe that if pre-Socratic authors, like Democritus, had suggested alternatives with the same systematic power, at the very least, more references would have been made to them by authors like Cicero.

Should we then say that with Aristotle, to name him alone, the glass is, so to speak, half full, because, although he offers us no economic theories – or very few – he gives us instead a logical economic ethical system? It would be better to speak here of two different glasses. In the economic theory glass of Aristotle, we find only a few drops, while today's glass is overflowing. In the economic ethical glass, we find Aristotle's to be full, while we, as McIntyre so succinctly commented, operate cluelessly with the old concepts of virtue, without even being able to draw the line between "wisdom" and "prudence" – just like someone who has forgotten the physics but still throws around the ideas of elementary particles. Following this comment, the suspicion arises that something has been poured out of the "economic ethics" glass.

However one wants to judge the value of the Greek inheritance for our time and its completely different situation, we see that the economic thought of ancient philosophy is much earlier imprinted in the literature. This conclusion would hold, even if there were fewer clear gradations of Greek economic thought in the literary reflection, than have been found for other areas of Greek life, especially for politics. The connection between the development of economic thought and politics is established through justice. With the transformation of the aristocratic ideals and the building of democracy, extensive wealth is placed under question in the old epics, despite the power of the princely life. In terms of economics, only a few elements appear as new: so that the love of work in Hesiod as opposed to Homer is a criticism on the less-than-virtuous attempts at wealth in the Archaic epoch, or the anxious question in the Classical period about who would rule the forces of progress. Societal constraints that threaten the effectiveness of money have been named since the introduction of the coin, first in early lyric poetry, then in drama. In Aristophanes we find criticism against usurers and a familiarity with the way a money-economy works, which had never before been seen in literature. But as in all changes, the central categories of thought stand firm, including the principle of reciprocity, which can be traced back to the beginning of humanity. Even more remarkable is the impression of continuity, in the constitution of institutions from the Classical era through and beyond Solon into the Homeric period, in contrast to the completely different concepts of order and analysis of those of the modern world.

NOTES

1 A more detailed summary of Aristotle's economic thought can be found in Schefold 1989: 19–55.
2 Slavery in antiquity was actually a differentiated phenomenon and summarily named as one thing only later by us, cf. Schefold 1992: 18, n. 9.
3 Just as, for example, a Christian community could not succeed if all its members

simultaneously followed Paul's example and renounced marriage and children, cf. Schefold 1992: 19, n. 10.

4 Cf. Vorlander (1963), 139–146.

5 Cf. below the discussion of the product in Xenophon.

6 Cf. the poem about the Charities by Theocritus (1949: 96).

7 Elsewhere Plato says that for ideal States, monarchy would be the best form of government, because, or as long as, the king can, as the good shepherd, embody goodness. However, for realizable States, which take human short-comings into account and must consider the possibility of ruthless tyrants, democracy is best. Cf. Aristotle, *Politics* 302 b.

8 Cf. Aristotle, *Rhetoric* I 1364a23.

9 For another example, cf. Aristotle's well-known story in the *Politics* about Thales. Thales, one of the seven wise men, wanted to show that a philosopher could, if necessary, prove his practical abilities. This same Thales, who had made himself look like a fool with his absent-mindedness when he fell into a stream while gazing at the stars, had correctly predicted a rich olive harvest, had therefore rented the olive presses on the island for the right time frame and, since the peasants wanted to make oil, had earned a big profit. He had done this only to show that a philosopher could be practical, when he wanted to be. We can conclude from this anecdote that speculative and monopolistic business practices were so much the norm that they were uninteresting to philosophy.

10 On economic topoi in the Renaissance, cf. Reichert 1992: 91–107.

11 Cf. Schefold 1989: 19–55.

12 Bücher (1893) deserves credit because he set himself ethnologically against Meyer (1895) with respect to the modern comparisons and because he tried to illuminate concepts like reciprocity and exchange or even the characteristics of simple markets by comparison with institutions in African societies. As a result, many more syntheses between modernistic and primitivistic viewpoints have been attempted.

13 Bücher (1893) emphasizes that the supremacy of Athens could never have rested on trade alone, as trade and especially the trade of grain had to be controlled, because the importation of grain was vital to survival and could not be guaranteed in any other way.

14 This level is comparable to the average standard of living of all developed countries in 1960, although less than that of England and Wales in the late seventeenth, or that of the US in the early nineteenth century.

15 There was a large public treasury in India, although it was far outweighed by private wealth.

16 It was originally the expression of the citizenry's far-reaching free will, before, as it were, the organization of production directed since by theocratic methods, which has been correctly or incorrectly attributed to the East. Cf. chapter 8 in this volume by Vivenza.

17 For example, complete pieces like Aeschylus, Sophocles, and Euripides, although in a smaller selection. The names of 150 writers of tragedy are known to us through compilations, engravings, etc. Even in Alexandria only seventy-five of the ninety tragedies of Euripides were extant.

18 These writings are related, says Aristotle, as tragedy to comedy.

19 This failing is emphasized by the philosophers: Plato, *Alc.* II, 147b; Aristotle, *Nicomachean Ethics* 1147a15. Cf. Forderer (1960).

20 It is not for nothing that the *Iliad* names Charis, the goddess of grace and thankfulness, as the wife of Hephaestos.

21 For example, Odysseus' measure in building his bed (Homer, *Odyssey* XXIII, 197).
22 For example, the representation of the multiply artistic works of Hephaestos' weaponry (Homer, *Iliad* XVIII, 410).
23 Cf. Schefold 1992: 44, n. 91 and Kula 1986: 102.
24 Cf. one example, in Book XII, 433–435.
25 In a similar manner, later, in Aristotle's works, the conflict between a lack of justification and economic necessity is addressed by his philosophical honesty.
26 Even Hera, Zeus' wife, is none too pleased to give in to him (Homer, *Iliad* XV, 106ff.).
27 Cf. Benveniste 1969: 66–70.
28 For example, Homer, *Odyssey* XXIV, 265–285.
29 Cf. the earlier discussion of the relationship between equivalence and status-based proportional formula from Aristotle's *Nicomachean Ethics* 1133a8.
30 Cf. Andreades 1965: 15, n. 2.
31 For the meaning of the term "economic mindset" in Weber, cf. Hennis 1987: sections 2 and 3.
32 We are reminded of the verse of the *Iliad* XII, 421–423.
33 Hesiod (1966: 621–622) advises linking the art of shipbuilding with peasant activities.
34 Not to kill the neighbor's cattle is only one of the many precepts that defines neighborliness (Hesiod 1966: 347).
35 In the reading of this quote we need to ask ourselves if the expression of the trade of the "market-place" (*agores*) really – before the coin – meant a market-place and not more so the "discussion" at the "place of judgment" or the "meeting place". Cf. West on verse 125 in Hesiod 1978.
36 For example, in the writing of the pre-Socratic Anaxagoras (Diels 1934: vol. 2, 43).
37 Cf. Alkaios 1963: 66, against him.
38 Cf. Pauly 1894: Vol. 10, Column 1972ff.
39 Hölderlin's free translation with its swinging rhythm suggests the mythical contrast between Helios in the sky and Pluto, the god of the underworld who is, for the Greeks, synonymous with wealth (Holderin 1987: vol. 15). Cf. also Bowra 1935, 1951: 1.
40 Cf. Meier (1988).
41 As Orestes appears to Electra and she wants to invite him, the son of a prince, to dinner, it occurs to the peasant how he can use the situation to his advantage (Euripides 1948: 24). There are things the poor can also do, especially as only the wealthy can become sated.

6

GREEK ECONOMIC THOUGHT

Initiators of a Mediterranean tradition

Louis Baeck

THE TRAJECTORY OF GREEK THOUGHT

About five thousand years ago, the Mediterranean region became the cradle of a number of civilizations. Egypt, Mesopotamia, Syria and Persia figure in the history books as creative incubators of our cultural heritage. Their palace and temple complexes were of an unparalleled grandeur and arouse our awe even today. Their civilizations had relatively developed economies, with surplus production efficiently mobilized and redistributed for the administrative and religious establishment. Their scribal schools produced a great number of manuals with detailed instructions for the running of the complex system. But, in their compact world-view there was no space for the emergence of an autonomous body of political thought and still less for one of economic thought.

Classical Greece made a quantum leap in the humanization of arts and philosophy. Its rationalism came as a challenge to the mythical world-view and to the religious legends and liturgies. Greek thinkers produced an "intellectual" ferment, spinning cloth for the secularization of myths and gods. The Ionic philosopher Democritus even coined a new myth, illustrating the Promethean thrust of man as founder of concepts and as finder and developer of techniques. The progressive differentiation of the compact world-view into separate domains like religion, philosophy, ethics and political science came in the wake of this moral and intellectual revolution. Athens played the role of academic eminence for the Aegean region, and its orators praised its democratic constitution as a model.

The Greek rhetoricians and scholars were also the first to write extensively on problems of practical philosophy like ethics, politics and economics. They opened the economic agenda with the so-called *"peri oikonomias"*. In the post-Socratic demarcation of disciplines, ethics was the study of personal and inter-individual behaviour; politics was the discourse on the ordering of the public sphere; and the term *oikonomia* referred to the material organization of the household and of the estate, and to supplementary discourses on the financial affairs of the city-state

146

administration. Greek economic thought formed an integral but subordinated part of the two major disciplines, ethics and politics. The discourse on the organization of the oikos and the economic ordering of the polis was not conceived to be an independent analytical sphere of thought (Baeck 1994).

In the traditional and Socratic paradigm, the ethical norms of the polis had pride of place over the pragmatic considerations and the hedonistic motivations characteristic of the professionals on the economy. By the founding fathers of the polis (*patrios politeia*), people engaged in commerce and in money matters were held in low esteem. With the development of the money-economy, however, the innovative movement of the Sophists broke the traditional consensus. They were the first intellectuals to confer moral and social respectability on the efficient organization of the oikos and the polis, as well as on the economic agents engaged in business. Well-known orators like Isocrates and Demosthenes, and also the pamphleteer Xenophon picked up this line of thought, although in a tempered way. The Socratic philosophers under Plato's ascetic and idealist leadership, however, orchestrated a theoretical and moral revival of the value judgements embodied by the *patrios politeia*.

Plato's most gifted pupil and later "guest professor", namely Aristotle, who had been associated with him for about twenty years, left the Academy and founded his own Lyceum. Aristotle had a far wider range of scientific interests than his eminent colleagues. He was not only an encyclopedist, he was moreover the founding father of logical positivism. He was also the first scientist to have at his command a multi-disciplinary research team with an impressive staff of assistants. To satisfy his interest in biology he collected and dissected a great number of animals and insects. In order to illustrate his treatise on the *Politics* with empirical evidence, he garnered, classified and systematized no less than 157 constitutions.

In the field of economic analysis Aristotle may be called a pioneer. His two treatises, the *Politics* and *Nicomachean Ethics*, were benchmarks with tradition-building echo-effects. In his economic methodology, he produced a balanced synthesis between an analytical approach based on theoretical concepts as well as human experiences and the state of arts. Educated in the idealistic climate of Plato's Academy, he sensed the tempting danger of Sophism, even in its relatively mild versions – namely the pragmatic school of Isocrates and the management models of Xenophon – as the intellectual advocates of the emerging technocracy. In Aristotle's classification of sciences, the study of ethics, politics, and also economics, belong to "practical" philosophy. In his practical philosophy, he departed from Plato's idealistic paradigm, specifically with the separation of ethics and politics from metaphysics, i.e. from pure theoretical knowledge. To a certain degree, he felt, the problems of practical philosophy cannot be treated with the same precision, since they concern the unpredictable behaviour of man and his society. Thus, with his ethics and politics deeply rooted in practical reason, enriched by human experience and by concrete evidence, Aristotle held an intermediary position between, on the one side, a Sophist connection represented by Isocrates, Demosthenes and Xenophon and, on the other side, Plato's metaphysical idealism.

With the exception of the pan-Hellenist Isocrates and Zeno the Stoic, the Athenian scholars sought to retain "the small is beautiful" ideology of the limited city state. But Alexander's conquests of Syria, Egypt and Persia transformed the Greek *Kleinstaaterei* into a vast multicultural empire. The world entered into a new stage, of Hellenes in intellectual cross-fertilization with the Egyptian, Syrian, and Persian cultures, and their big-scale State organization. This aggregation of peoples over a vast area was linked together by the common Hellenism of the ruling class. The idea of Zeno's universal community of citizens (*oikomene*) and the Stoic stance on the equality of races and cultures strengthened the trend to scale aggrandizement and to universalism. Moreover, Zeno's position on the non-rational dimension of life prepared the way for a reassertion of Oriental religions of salvation.

When the Roman empire took over the reins of power, whole armies stationed in Egypt and Syria became converts of the Hellenized Isis–Osiris cult. History took yet another and unexpected turn, when Emperor Constantine opted for the until then underground movement of the Christians. The cultural synthesis of their evangelical message and the Neoplatonic stream of late antiquity, worked over by a converted Roman rhetorician named Saint Augustine, became the spiritual thrust of the early Middle Ages in the Latin West. In Byzantium the Neoplatonic tradition lived on undiminished for ages. Its exiled Chaldean Christians relayed the Neoplatonic synthesis of Plotinus, Proclus and Porphyry to the Magians of the Persian empire ruled by the Sassanids. They passed it to the invading Muslim ruling class and its intellectual élite. Since the time of late antiquity, successive generations of scholars from different cultures took the Greek heritage of texts as a classical reference. This resulted in an impressive chain of translations into Syrian, Persian, Arabic, Catalan, Latin, and later into a great number of other European languages.

In the Roman empire, a Latinized Stoicism had pride of place with Cicero and Seneca; and even Emperor Marcus Aurelius tried to cure his nostalgia with the writing of a manual on Stoic non-attachment. In the eastern lands of Islam, the Neoplatonic stream prevailed, more particularly in al-Farabi's treatise on the Virtuous City, while, in the western part, the Aristotelian tradition had an eminent proponent, namely the Andalusian Ibn Rushd. His commentaries on Aristotle's *oeuvre* found their way to the Parisian University where they caused a philosophical and theological stir. Two scholastics from the Dominican Order, namely Albertus Magnus and Thomas Aquinas, worked out Latin commentaries of Aristotle's treatises. Their admiration for the Stagirite came near to his canonization. For the medieval scholars of the Islamic lands as well as of the Latin West, the Greek constructs of a natural order arrived at by human reasoning were used as a conceptual underpinning of their theonomic vision of the world. In both cultures, speculative theology endeavoured to work out a scholastic synthesis. From the thirteenth to the seventeenth century, Aristotle was commented upon in an almost unending stream of publications. Although having lost the favour of the modernizing intellectuals with the breakthrough of the Enlightenment, Aristotle's practical philosophy, since the 1970s, is experiencing a new stream of interest in the making.[1]

THE UNFOLDING OF TRADITIONS

The history of ideas informs us that changes in world-views and scientific paradigms are generally the work of a spiritual and intellectual élite who launch a new tradition of thought or who inspire the re-interpretation of an old one. A "tradition" is a historical embodiment of the institutionalized communication of the élite, which in the course of time matures into a classical reference for later generations. In its maturation process, the following stages are important: thematization, textualization, institutionalization, and canonization or canonicity.

Thematization

The first step is the process of *thematization*. This is a condensation of élite communication aroused by changes in the historical perspective, by a rupture in collective experience, by technical improvements, by scientific discoveries, by social disruption, by economic crisis, and/or by environmental and ecological degradation. New thematizations are generally elicited and become manifest in the wake of a crisis mood, generated by shocks in historical consciousness.

In fourth-century Greece, the crisis of the city-state provoked an intense wave of treatise writing, with a notable concentration in Athens. After the catastrophe of the Peloponnesian War, Athens had lost its hegemony as the Aegean Sea power and its masses were pressing for more influence in public affairs and benefits for themselves, i.e. for more democracy and welfare programs. Orators and essayists engaged in petulant debate on a variety of subjects, but they all focused their attention on the problematic drift of events. Establishment writers raised the spectre of sociopolitical hubris or of the emerging tyranny of the masses (*ochlokratia*); the Sophists denounced the conservative *patrios politeia* mentality; Isocrates pleaded for a pan-Hellenist solution; Xenophon published a financial rescue plan for the polis and a blueprint for agrarian development; Plato came up with a philosophical treatise on the ethical prerequisites for a virtuous or ideal republic; and Aristotle wrote his primer on the novel theme of *Gemein-schaft* and *Gesellschaft*. For him, the development of a monetary market economy functioning on commercial exchange between socially unrelated individuals and the emergence of a chrematistic mentality would adversely affect the traditional values of the community and gradually undermine the public spirit of the polis and of its citizenry.

Textualization

The *codification* process is the second step in the unfolding of a tradition; the results of thematization have to be put down in written form. This codification may also be called the process of *textualization*. Lost texts rarely lead to the founding of a tradition. The most important publications of the Sophists were lost. Their ideas are known to us only indirectly, the most important transmitters being the writings of Xenophon and Plato.

The vehicle of language is also important. Greek became the *koine* or *lingua franca* of the Mediterranean in the Hellenistic Empire and in Byzantium. The Roman intelligentsia was Latin-Greek bilingual. Men like Julius Caesar, Cicero and other orators, had been on scholarship trips to several Greek intellectual centers of learning.

Institutionalization

Fundamental themes put down in manuscript, even those written in beautiful prose, like Plato's dialogues, rarely develop into a tradition without the supplementary process of institutionalization. The maturation of texts into classical references is facilitated by the creation of institutions which function as transmission belts. The school of Isocrates, Plato's Academy and Aristotle's Lyceum were examples of the institutionalized propagation of texts. Long after these eminent authors' deaths, disciples kept alive their intellectual heritage and went on editing their texts.

In the early Middle Ages of the Latin West, the monasteries were the institutional vehicles of the Neoplatonic–Augustinian synthesis. From the thirteenth century on, the Sorbonne in Paris became a hotbed for Aristotle's texts and ideas. The student body and also the lecturers of the medieval universities were more multinational than today. This made for the rapid spread of Aristotelian texts from the Sorbonne to the other universities and to the many seminaries of religious orders.

Canonization or canonicity

The process of canonization is the last and also the supreme phase of tradition-building. Canonization is a selective process of text-stabilization and theme-focusing. In the course of this process it happens that the original texts are understood and absorbed in a different way. They may also be re-adapted by the canonizing authorities, most of the time according to their interpretative scheme and/or to the intellectual needs of the time. Ibn Rushd's comments on Aristotle's *Nicomachean Ethics* are not exactly the same as those of Thomas Aquinas, and both deviate from the comments written by notorious commentators of antiquity. This may be due to concept shifts resulting from translation, but in most cases the changed concrete historical context, a new consciousness or awareness of problems and novel perspectives play a role as determinants.

Major strands of economic discourse

As an introduction to the agenda of the different strands of Greek economic thought, it might be interesting to ask why and how the genre of *"peri oikonomias"* came to the fore in the fourth century BC in Athens. Scholarly debate on the economic history of that time has focused our attention upon the rapid and problematic economic development, resulting in a contemporary expansion of trade and money transactions. Although these spurts of development have been ably demonstrated by a considerable mass of research findings, the contextualization does not reduce the basic nexus. Moreover, over-emphasis of the material context would amount to materialist reductionism. The novel creation of an analytical space for economic thought had, in my view, more to do with the intensification of élite communication. This became manifest in the public debates by orators and in the publication syndrome of essayists and philosophers who felt emancipated from the ruling establishment. Indeed, before and after the appearance of the economic thought agenda on the Athenian scene of the fourth century BC, many earlier and later civilizations were witnesses to drastic economic change and intense development. History has recorded many spurts in social and economic development without the appearance of discourses on its fundamentals.

In Athens, the critical mass for polemic debates and for deeper analyses was present.[2] The unfolding of the Athenian democracy, the structural changes in the deep layers of its society and the basic questioning of its moral base set élite communication on the economic register in motion. Academic freedom, coupled to a cultural milieu that cherished public debate, formed the substratum for the intensification of polemic discourse. Polemos the god of war, and also supposedly the Olympic father of Greek "polemic", had endowed man with the intellectual impetuosity to discuss in public and to fight for his ideas. The famous dialectician Heracleitus had, long before the fourth century, proclaimed that the complexity of problems was such that, for a clear understanding, they ought to be analyzed from different vantage points.

Three major strands of economic discourse evolved. First came the essays on efficient, but gentleman-like or honorable estate management, more particularly on the development of the natural economy, with emphasis on agriculture. In this genre Xenophon's *Oikonomikos* figures as a classic.

Second were the treatises on politics, ethics, social justice, economic value, exchange relations, the intermediary function of money, and on the practice of usury. In this fundamental register of issues, different philosophical schools, namely the Socratics, the Cynics, the Epicureans and the Stoics, flowered as prominent streams of thought. But only the Socratics and the Stoics had a major influence in later ages, i.e. on the Roman intelligentsia as well as on Muslim and Christian scholars of the Middle Ages.

In Athens, philosophy was less sequestered from reality than it seems mostly the case today. There, the philosophical discourses on politics and ethics functioned as fundamental directors of élite consciousness in a culture and in a city-state that relished the art of public and polemical debate. With the zest of a new sect, the Athenian orators and philosophers broke open a wide intellectual space and provided the conceptual tools for discourses on economic matters. Yet, the embryonic economic thought did not gain sufficient academic and moral standing to achieve an autonomous status. In the tradition of ancient Greece, the fundamentals of economic thought were integrated as a subordinated and limited part of practical philosophy, i.e. of ethics and politics. Its most elaborate form is in Aristotle's work, with its schematic discourses on:

1 The hierarchization of ends and the instrumental means to obtain them; the supreme good (*eudaimonia*) for the citizen and the city-state.
2 The ideal or harmonious relationship between the public good of the polis and the private sphere, including the household affairs of the citizens.
3 The demarcation of moral frontiers between the natural economy, in its relation to honorable basic needs, and chrematistic mis-development, oriented towards the superfluous. This demarcation proceeded not so much on quantitative criteria but rather on the underlying intentions of the economic agents. All philosophical schools, with the exception of the Sophist and the Epicurean, agreed that material goods and wealth have no intrinsic value; they are only the necessary means to achieve the sociopolitical and moral ends of the polis. In their teleological and organicist world-view, the intentions and motivations of the economic agents were critically evaluated in relation to their political and ethical consequences.

The third strand of economic thought consisted of the public debates and essays on the public economy, fiscal administration, and on the mobilization of human and physical resources for the budgeting of the city-state. Isocrates, Demosthenes and other orators devoted published speeches to this problem, but it is Xenophon's *Poroi* or *Ways and Means* that has been singled out by most historians of thought as a classic in the field. Aristotle briefly discoursed on this problem in the last chapter of Book I of his *Politics*. The pseudo-Aristotelian tract *Economics*, treating the problem more extensively, was most probably written by his disciple and successor at the Lyceum, Theophrastus.

THE MAIN SCHOOLS OF THOUGHT

Since the end of the nineteenth century a vast amount of scholarly research findings and studies have been published on the economic thought of ancient Greece.[3] A certain number of these proceed from a retrospective reading. This questionable method consists in an approach where the conceptual matrix and the norms of today's economics are used as perspectival prisms. My preference goes to the reading of the ancient texts from the standpoint of their own perspective and *Sitz im Leben*.

The genre of pragmatic essays

Socrates was rector of a school founded for the education of youngsters with ambitions to become politicians or public administrators. Socrates was also a fervent proponent of interstate solidarity and an advocate of a pan-Hellenic confederation. His pragmatic view on politics and economics was based on his firm belief in the synergism resulting from common sense mixed with the plurality of public opinion, all this guided by professional expertise. One of his many pamphlets, namely *Trapeziticus*, treated in detail the concrete situation of the Athenian economy and its financial and monetary problems. His non-dogmatic approach was in line with mainstream thinking and as such more representative of the *Zeitgeist* than the élitist asceticism of his Socratic rivals. His thesis that Greek thought was destined to become the teacher of the world rode the crest of the Hellenistic commonwealth brought together by Alexander.

Xenophon, a former disciple of Socrates, had in his mature age come under the influence of Socratic pragmatism and worked out a well-balanced synthesis between the two strands of thought. In a number of didactic treatises he sketched several archetypes of *kalokagathia*, i.e. honourable and virtuous behaviour, coupled with professional efficiency: for military commanders, for city-state administrators and for managers of rural estates. His essay on the estate manager is a superbly written primer. Xenophon's *Oikonomikos* (1971) is more concerned with the basic aspects and strategies of professional management than with agronomic techniques and operational skills. Although he spells out in minute detail how the wife of the master should educate the children and handle with care the personnel of the estate, his greatest attention is given to strategic planning. An optimal match of strategy with its target requires that the various elements of the agribusiness firm work together as a coherent and harmonious whole "to swell the surplus". Xenophon held a plea for balanced growth between the production capacity of the estates in the countryside and the expansion of towns, so that the rural exodus and the pernicious consequences of overcrowding in the polis could be kept in check.

The *Oikonomikos* was the first published handbook on the efficient planning of the human and material resources of estates, inspired by sound business ethics. The author seems not to be morally affected by profit-making, the only condition being that business growth be implemented by a knowledgeable *kalokagathos* or by a gentleman with acumen. The "swelling of the surplus" comes as a reward for his professional skill and strategic foresight (Baeck 1994: III. ii. 3). The *Oikonomikos* became a best-seller for generations of landowners of the Hellenistic commonwealth and the Roman empire. It was avidly read by all *latifundaria* until the end of the Renaissance. His blueprint, however, for the economic development of the Athenian polis and the city's financial administration aroused mixed feelings already at the time of its writing. It did not evolve into a classic in later times.

The philosophic strands of thought

Plato's asceticism

The major stimulus of the Socratic tradition unfolded in reaction to the Sophist movement with its pronounced theses on relativistic morals and its penchant for technocratic devices and professional management. In this counter-movement, the school of Isocrates, and also Xenophon's ideas, came under heavy attack. The first and most fundamental blast came in Plato's *Republic*, the Academy's blueprint on the ideal or virtuous State. Plato's views on the ideal state were heavily influenced by his metaphysics. The supreme good is knowledge, and ethical norms, especially the virtue of justice, stem from pure reason, i.e. from theoretical speculation.

Although he was the most anti-economic master of the Academy, Plato wrote an original and penetrating chapter on the genesis of the State, with a clear emphasis on the material base of society (*Republic*, 369b–371e). Man is a sociopolitical being but in his material needs he is not self-sufficient; society is the response to the premise of mutual need (*emetera chreia*). Plato the aristocrat, however, became the ascetic proponent of a frugal state. In the primeval stage of development, he saw no fount for acquisitive vices; people cooperate by necessity, on the basis of a rudimentary division of labour and an innate sense of reciprocity. They proceed to a limited exchange of each other's surplus in a spirit of social solidarity. In the incisive continuing dialogue, Glaucon, upon entering the scene,

154

disdainfully labels the frugal condition "a state of pigs" (*Republic*, 372d). He profiles himself as a demiurge of development in true Xenophontean style. Against the frugal state, Glaucon holds up a plea for more comfort, more and better manufactured goods and for specialized services, like music, and the arts and sciences. All this requires more production and trade so that markets can develop, with shopkeepers in retail and entrepreneurs in long-distance and maritime trade.

For Plato, this developmentism would end up not only in a luxuriant, but also in a "feverish" state, a state in which the acquisitive desire is let loose and in which avidity and cupidity become the driving forces. Indeed, the drive for more comfort and opulence corrupts the mind and disrupts social harmony. When the entrepreneurial spirit, stimulated by insatiable desire, takes hold of the citizens and pulls the lever of accumulation, civil virtue ebbs away from the traditional mould. The uneven growth of wealth creation produces a widening gap between the citizens. The lust for wealth sows the seeds of conflict, more specifically between the poor and the rich. The appalling material inequality elicits social strife, ripping the moral links of society apart. In this *diastasis*, the polis breaks down into two parts, plotting against one another. In the works of his mature age, like the *Statesman and Laws*, Plato had grown more nuanced in his analysis and somewhat milder in his value judgments. These publications are especially attentive to the practical problems of administration, elaborating also on the function of money.

Plato was disgusted with the din of party politics and with the moral corruption stemming from the luxuriant, feverish state. In his eyes the feverish mentality stimulated, instead of satisfying, the acquisitive desire and lust for wealth. Plato became a very harsh critic when, with aristocratic prejudice, he indulged in lambasting commercial people, who truck and barter for a living. In Plato's idealistic view of the polis, people engaged in profitable businesses – the *chrematistai* – the traders, craftsmen, bankers and money-changers, are located in the lowest echelon of society. They are driven by desire and by the acquisitive mentality; as such, they form the occupational link with the feverish and luxuriant State. The guardians of a just and virtuous State had to watch these busy do-it-alls; the ideal solution was a philosopher as supreme ruler. In the medieval monasteries this call was heard, and in their spiritual endeavor to approach the divine, the monks lived the sober, contemplative life cherished by Plato and his Neoplatonic disciples.

Aristotle's analytical breakthrough

Aristotle's *Politics* forms a synthesis of his research findings and lecture notes on the political regimes of the Aegean. The first chapters of Book One open with a discussion of the basic hierarchical and other differences between the superior art of politics and *oikonomike*, the more instrumental art of household management. Chapters 8–11 offer a penetrating discourse on the stages of transition from the natural and familial practice of the household economy, governed by traditional social motivations, toward a market economy in which unrelated individuals seek profit through commercial exchange. The driving force of this monetarized mode of wealth acquisition (*chrematistike ktetike*) is the evolving dominance of the profit motive. Mis-development consists in the ruling of a misguided desire by which commercial exchange looses its function of natural wealth-getting and degenerates into commercial and speculative money-making (*chrematistike kapelike*). These passages are a striking reminder of Plato's juxtaposition between the frugal community, and the luxuriant state, with the expansion of commercial exchange inducing people to profit, and money-making as a corrupter of the polis and its citizens.[4]

Aristotle analyzes with remarkable subtlety the operational and motivational changes of economic agents in the course of the transformation from barter exchanges, to satisfy natural needs, to the exchanges of a society in commerce for profit. In the analysis the Stagirite is guided by an interpretative scheme frequently used in his studies on physics and biology, namely the unfolding of all forms of life from their potentiality (*dynamis*) to their actuality (*energeia*). In the transition to a chrematistic stage of development, money plays a key role. Originally, money was a mere conventional intermediary or instrument of commercial exchange (*ploutos organou*), but in the chrematistic stage, it changes nature and becomes the proper end of wealth acquisition (*ploutos nomismatos*).

In Chapter 10 of Book I, Aristotle introduces the form of trade and money-making most viciously contrary to nature, namely the trade in money itself on the basis of interest-taking. The literal meaning of interest is *tokos*, or offspring. Interest is money born from money: *tokos ginetai nomisma ek nomismatos* (*Politics*, 1258b 7–8). In Aristotle's view money is sterile, since it is a mere intermediary of exchange; it cannot beget offspring in the form of interest. The philosopher's categorical stand against *tokismos* is a striking reaction against the more lenient position of influential orators, like Isocrates in his *Trapeziticum* and Demosthenes in his oration *Against Aphobus*. These two leading rhetoricians defended interest-taking as a prerequisite of commercial development, on the condition that business be regulated by law to prevent usurious practices (Cohen 1992). Aristotle's paradigm on the sterility of money experienced a theoretical revival in the treatises of the Muslim and Christian scholastics. In their scriptures the Stagirite's stern position flowered into a canon.

Aristotle not only initiated the conceptual scheme of change from the potential *dynamis* of the original socio-economic archetype (*Gemeinschaft*) to the actualized *energeia* of the blooming socio-economic archetype (*Gesellschaft*), he was also a practical philosopher with a keen interest in just behavior or ethics. In *Nicomachean Ethics*, Book V, chapter 5, he expounded his celebrated theorem on justice in exchange relations where law has left a free hand. The thematization opens with the basic principle that in the social bond (*koinonia*) of the polis, originally constituted to meet the material necessity of natural need (*chreia*), the leading form of justice consists in proportional reciprocity. The bond on which the polis is built can only function properly and be maintained in an orderly or just way if the exchange relations are conceived and realized, not on the basis of equality (*kat' isoteta*) but on the basis of proportional reciprocity (*kat' analogian*) (1132b 34–35).

On account of the differences in value of goods and services, and the unequal quality of producers who deserve dissimilar rates of reward (an hour of a doctor's services is worth more than one hour of a shoemaker's), the theoretical challenge consists in finding a comparable standard in order to solve the problem of commensurability. In his search for a common standard of measure, Aristotle muddles through three interwoven passages which have caused headaches for commentators up to the present day. In the conceptual world of the polis theoretician, it is common need (*chreia*) which had logical priority in the search for equitable or just exchanges.[5] But, with reference to his discourse on economic development in the *Politics*, Aristotle brusquely introduces money, as a conventional middle term (*meson*) and measure (*metron*) in the process of exchange equalization. In the evolving commercialization and monetarization of the economy, money emerged as the conventional standard measure of all things.

In the next step Aristotle opens a new perspective on the nature and the function of money; in due time it becomes the "representative" of *chreia*. Money serves as an acceptable surrogate of the intrinsic or basic value measure: "*hupallagma tes chreias*" (*Nicomachean Ethics* 1133a 29–30). In his view, money is not only a medium; it became in due time also a value measure in exchange relations. Money serves moreover as a stock of purchasing power for future transactions. Since money is only a conventional instrument based on common agreement, its value is liable to fluctuations.

Aristotle's chapter on justice in exchange relations (*Nicomachean Ethics* V. 5) proved to be fundamental. In the scholastic economics of the Latin West, variations on this theme were repeated as a refrain. The complexity of the Stagirite's thought and the subtlety of his arguments left some leeway to later commentators to interpret his texts from their own intellectual or their society's ideological needs. In the Middle Ages, the Aristotelian tradition of economics ramified like a river flowing into several cultural beds.

The contribution of the Stoics

Zeno was born in Citium on the island of Cyprus in the year 336 BC, and reached Athens in 314 where he started teaching under the painted porch (*stoa*) on the north side of the agora; hence he and his followers were called Stoics. He was a superb teacher and his ethics spread to the newly founded "cosmo-poleis" of the Hellenistic commonwealth: Alexandria, Apamea, Pergamon and Antioch. Zeno owed a considerable debt to Heracleitus and to Socrates, but he established his own emphases. His doctrine of resignation before circumstances, of self-discipline (*encratia*) and of the basic equality of men as actors in the divine drama, bloomed in the multicultural commonwealth into a firm tradition. Against the patriotic chauvinism of the then defunct Plato and Aristotle, his universalism responded to the new situation. His later disciples, Cleanthes, but especially Panaetius and his disciple Poseidonius, brought new developments. Their "Middle Stoa" ethical stance had a more modern ring. Panaetius opened new vistas on to the conflict between pure ethics and the impact of practical efficiency. He kept his own feet firmly on the ground, with the result that the Stoics moved nearer to the real world and its historical compromises than Plato and Aristotle ever had. Panaetius declared that the material conditions of the individual (including private property and wealth) are reconcilable with the needs of society.

But the man who relayed the ethics of the "Middle Stoa" and its matter-of-fact economics to the Middle Ages was a Roman rhetorician, namely Cicero. After study stays in various Greek intellectual centres, he elaborated his own synthesis. Although he was a busy tribune and political activist, he regularly retreated to his country house at Tusculum where he wrote in limpid Latin on the highest virtue (*humanitas*) and on practical matters like *oeconomica*. At the age of 20 he translated Xenophon's *Oikonomikos*, and this pragmatic connection would stay with him for the rest of his life (Nicolet 1988). In several of his works he ventured into the more fundamental issues of ethics, where he proved to be familiar with the theoretical approach of the Greek Peripatetic School. Cicero's ethics, however, had a firmer footing in the real world.

Cicero's ideal state was never to be only a mental construction, but a governable republic, suited to men as they actually are (Wood 1988). Being an accomplished popularizer of complex and abstract ideas, he devoted considerable attention to the details of governmental economic policy: public credit, taxation, relief programs for the poor, land reform and agrarian colonization. As a cultural urbanite and man of means he showed no particular moral qualms with the accumulation of properties and with the accruing financial surplus of his investment ventures.

Plato and Aristotle had discoursed with more than usual emphasis on the acquisitive motives of economic agents, where production and consumption are pulled by the desire of the superfluous. For Cicero, this categorical distinction was not pertinent since notions like basic need and the superfluous are relative notions; they are relative to time, place and the social status of the person. By the notion "time" the Roman rhetorician meant the historical phase of development. A developed urban economy like Rome could not thus be compared with a backward situation at the periphery of the empire. What is superfluous in some places would mean a sober life seen from Roman standards. For a senator, a yearly income of 100,000 sesterces permits only *parsimonia* or relatively sober living, while, for a local official in the periphery, it would mean *luxuria*. On the practical relevance of Aristotle's exchange theorem Cicero was more reserved still.

Except for Xenophon's pragmatic approach, Cicero had only a limited interest in the theoretical schemes of Plato and Aristotle. With mild irony he remarked in *De Officiis*, Book II, section 87 (1913): "This whole subject matter of making and investing money and spending it as well, is more appropriate for discussion by the worthy gentlemen who congregate around the Middle Janus, than by any philosopher, whatever school he may belong to."[6] In the Middle Ages Cicero's economics, characterized by earthly pragmatism, were absorbed by the civil-law schools and even by some theologians. In the fourteenth century Cicero's Stoic texts were fertile germs for the Italian humanism and its glorification of the *homo faber*.

THE CONTRIBUTION OF ISLAM

From 750 to 1250 the Islamic civilization was hegemonic in the Mediterranean, culturally as well as materially. The revealed *shari\a*, or the divine law, was the binding element of the community of believers. Islam literally means submission to God's Law. Consequently, the study and the application of law to the changing circumstances became the master science of the Muslim world. The *shari\a* prescribes in great detail how believers should conduct their lives, how to submit to God, how to deal with their neighbors, how they ought to sell and buy in the market-place, etc. The jurisprudential commentaries and the literature on commercial legislation (*hisbah*) offer a mine of information on the normative constraints to the Islamic economy. Their value resides not so much in the slender analysis they offer than in the empirical information they contain.

The same is true of the other source of Islamic economic thought, namely *kalam* or scholastic theology. Since the origin of Islamic laws is divine revelation, it is only the interpretation by scholars that can be characterized as economic thinking in Islam. The most celebrated authors who offered valuable interpretative schemes in this field are: Zaid bin Ali (699–738), Abu Ysuf (731–798), al-Shaibani (750–804), al-Ghazali (1055–1111), Ibn Taimiyya (1263–1328), and Ibn al-Quayyim (1292–1350).

The genre of "Mirror of the Prince" literature and the work of the historians Ibn Khaldun (1332–1404) and al-Maqrizi (1364–1441) are even more specific. Ibn Khaldun was without doubt the greatest social scientist of the Islamic world. He was more than any other medieval author attentive to the proper laws of the society at large and to its economic dimension.

The first Hellenizing philosopher of fame was al-Farabi (873–950), a scholar of Turkish origin. With his comments on Plato's *Republic* and on Aristotle's ethical works, he initiated in eastern Islam the Greek tradition of practical philosophy based on human reason. His discourses on ethics, politics, and economics, elaborated independently from the norms of revelation, aroused the outrage of the devout *ulema* and of the orthodox scholars. His major work was a treatise on the Virtuous City (*al-madina fadila*). This was in fact an Islamic version of Plato's ideal state, with a plea that the caliphate should be headed by a philosopher king. In the practical field of economics, this treatise of the isolated and contemplative intellectual professed an other-worldliness without enduring impact on Islam's social ethics. His influence on the mystic movements of eastern Islam was far greater.

The Andalusian scholar Ibn Rushd (1126–1198) became Islam's most brilliant commentator of Aristotle's philosophy. During his lifetime the political and military conflicts between the rulers of Berber and Arab origin came into the open. The Almohad dynasty headed a reform movement based, with the assistance of open-minded scholars, on a politico-religious doctrine of unity. Ibn Rushd joined the chorus, but in his endeavor to harmonize reason with faith, the religious establishment forced him to lower the flags. In keeping with his own theoretical focus and conditioned by the Islamic context, the Andalusian sowed the seeds of a medieval tradition in Aristotelian economics. In the Muslim world he found no audience, but some leading scholastics of the Latin West were influenced by what came to be called Averroism.

In the field of practical philosophy Ibn Rushd wrote commentaries on Plato's *Republic* and on Aristotle's *Nicomachean Ethics* (the text of the *Politics* was not in his possession). In his work on Plato's *Republic*, Ibn Rushd analyzes in some detail the conflict of interest between the classes engaged in politics and those engaged in money-making. In his view, the development and outcome of the power struggle between the sociopolitical and economic constituencies of the state are a determining factor for the different types of political regimes. Under a democratic rule the money-making groups are more controlled and subdued; when they gain more power, the regime may end up in a tyranny. In his commentary, the Andalusian master proves to be more in sympathy with democratic rule than Plato.

The reading and the interpretation of Ibn Rushd's commentary on the *Nicomachean Ethics* presents a problem, since the original Arab text is lost. Only the Latin text (Averroes 1562) and a Hebrew version (Averroes 1981) are available. A comparative reading of Aristotle's work in Greek and the Latin version of the commentary reveals that the Andalusian scholar exposes Aristotle's discourse on ethics rather faithfully, but in a more synthetic way than the original. The Stagirite had not expressed his complex arguments in a compact text. In the effort of systematizing Aristotle, Ibn Rushd was a notable marker, followed in this by his disciples among the Latin Scholastics. In some important parts of the discourse on the terms of exchange and on money (NE: V,5), the glosses of the Cordoban interpreter part company with Aristotle's original text.

In the passage (*Nicomachean Ethics* 1133b 18) where Aristotle, on metaphysical grounds, admits "the impossibility for products so different to be rendered commensurable in the strict sense", Ibn Rushd elucidated the problem somewhat by an interpolation of his own. In his *Metaphysics* (1975) (1052b 20) the Greek philosopher had also stated that each object to be measured "should be measured by a unit of the same species". The Arab philosopher inserted an important interpolation; his line reads: "by the smallest unit of its kind" (*sui generis minimo*) (Langholm 1992: 184). In the analysis of the exchange relations, where the pegging toward equivalence around a mean value may lead to a bargaining process of plus and minus, the perspective of measurement in terms of "the smallest unit" could have opened the door to an original formulation of marginal calculus. But, the Islamic world, as a highly developed commercial society, had long since accepted the intermediary function of money, and the Andalusian didn't elaborate any further on barter marginalism in real terms, although he provided the clue to it.

In the Stagirite's discourse, money had only a footing in the exchange relations as a convenient but artificial medium. It was considered to be no more than a surrogate of *chreia* (in Greek: *hupallagma*). The Andalusian scholar, who lived in a civilization where the monetarization of exchange relations had become an accepted and evident practice, had not the same moral apprehensions against the development of commerce and its mediation by money, as had had the Greek philosophers. In a clear style, the three functions of money are described (Baeck 1994: IV. V.2) money is a medium of exchange (*instrumentum conegociandi*); it is a standard measure of commensurability between different things (*cognitio coequalitatis inter res diversas*); and it is also a reserve of purchasing power for the future (*tanquam fide jussor supplendi necessitatem futuram*). While the Greek philosopher professed a monetary nominalism based on pure convention, the Arab scholar recognizes the mediating function of money in exchange relations as a legitimate and acceptable practice.

The German historian of monetary thought, C. Miller, was to my knowledge the first to discover Ibn Rushd's omission of Aristotle's line (*Nicomachean Ethics* 1133b 17) "that the money standard itself is fluctuating like other commodities, since its purchasing power varies at different times" (Miller 1925: 70). Aristotle's line is in fact an ambiguous statement, for in that context he perceives money as a "commodity" with changeable worth. How can a commodity with fluctuating value be a standard measure of commensurability? The Arabian scholar lifts the ambiguity by his option for an immutable standard. Instead of the Aristotelian locus on the fluctuating nature of money, Ibn Rushd's paraphrase simply states that with the Greeks, money was liable to change according to convention and law; we quote "Et quum ista inveniatur in denario expone ut sit nomen *legis apud grecos denominative sumptum a positione, nominatus est denarius in lingua* greca nomine denominate sumpto a lege" (Averroes 1542: V, E: 241). The Arab scholar, living in a commercial civilization where the stability of the medium of exchange was an absolute prerequisite for its intrinsic quality of being money (*thamaniyah* or moneyness) could neither subscribe to the Stagirite's hint of fluctuating commodity-money nor to his monetary nominalism. As a judge in the Maliki tradition he was in favour of absolute stability for all measures, including monetary standards.

From a metaphysical point of view a fluctuating or changeable standard cannot serve as a measure to make things commensurable, because the exchange relations would end up in arbitrariness and indetermination. Aristotle may have realized this well enough, and this was probably the reason why he degraded money to a surrogate medium. In Ibn Rushd's world money figured as a full-fledged medium. The rulers, however, did not always live up to this lofty principle. From the twelfth century onward, the princes of the Muslim world and of the West indulged more and more in the practice of debasement. This fraudulent practice elicited a whole cycle of essay-writing on the subject, which resulted in a deepening of monetary theory.

In the fourteenth century the Maghrebi historian and socio-economist Ibn Khaldun wrote a masterly introduction to his *Kitab al-ibar*. In this prolegomena or *Muqaddimah* he rejected the extreme idealism of al-Farabi's Virtuous City and also Ibn Rushd's rationalism. Ibn Khaldun had been a political activist in his early career and felt as such in better intellectual company with Cicero's matter-of-fact Stoicism. Ibn Khaldun's treatise was a masterpiece on the cycle of the rise, blooming, and decline of political regimes and societies. It was a genre, initiated by Polybius, a Greek historian living in the second century BC. On account of its comprehensiveness and in-depth analysis Ibn Khaldun's development theory (*ilm al-umran*) surpassed by far the Greek concepts of the historical cycle of regimes (*anakyklosis politeion*). In fact, his *Muqaddimah* (1969) was the first well-documented treatise on the non-sustainability of development (Baeck 1994).

THE IMPACT ON THE LATIN WEST

In the first quarter of the third century, emperor Constantine's cultural reform gave a new historical footing to the ascending oriental religion of Christianity. Its social ethic, based on altruistic love (*agape*), preached the constant, patient search for the well-being of the "neighbour" conceived as brother. During its formative period, the originally Jewish sect absorbed Neoplatonism and Stoicism with appropriate emendations from the Christian perspective. In the Latin part of the empire, a former Roman rhetorician, later to become Saint Augustine, relayed this tradition, together with his own emphases, to the West. His *Civitas Dei* would have a greater impact on the development of dogma and on religious sentiment than any other text, except the Gospel (Augustine 1955). In God's kingdom on earth, *contemptus mundi* was the rule; there was no room for economic thought. The ideal was the contemplative life, historically realized in the monasteries. There the abbot reigned supreme as a religiously inspired philosopher-ruler.

In the eleventh century, the Latin West after an age-long rural slumber, became witness to an urban and economic revival. The Roman legists, who had rediscovered Emperor Justinian's Code, responded to this take-off in development with a novel legal tradition. The flowering of a secular law tradition was concomitant with the emergence of new problems in the social and economic fields. Great legists, like Azo and Accursius, adapted the Justinian Code to the new problems of the age. The canon lawyers of the Church followed suit with detailed codices regulating the expansion of money-lending, interest taking, commercial dealings in the market, together with doctrines of the "just price". The civil jurists and the canonists laid down the binding rules of conduct, but it was left to the more "speculative" theologians to work out in a more substantial way the theoretical argumentation.

In the twelfth century the legacy of Greek science, already worked over by Islamic scholars, was translated into Latin from Arabic. This transfer caused in the West a sudden passion for the systematization of knowledge. In this effort the new, scholastic genre of theology, based on the synergy between faith and reason, entered the scene. Important figures were: Hugh of St. Victor, William of Conches, Domenicus Gundisalvi and John of Salisbury.[7] In the faculties of arts and theology, the old interpretative themes of ethics, politics and economics were passionately reworked on the models offered by the Roman rhetoricians and the Arab scholars. Practical philosophy and moral theology of the twelfth century continued to lean heavily on the Platonic–Augustinian tradition. They received, however, a new methodological impetus from the study of Cicero's treatises, more particularly his *De Officiis*. Cicero's influence would keep the scholarly work of the twelfth century on politics, ethics and the economy in practical bounds, with only an inkling of theoretical analysis along the lines initiated by the Islamic sources, most particularly al-Farabi.

In the thirteenth century, study of practical philosophy and of moral theology took a radical turn towards a more theoretical foundation with the invasion of Aristotle's *Ethics*. The work of the Greek master reached the Latin West in the company of Ibn Rushd's theoretical re-workings. Its intellectual impact provoked a break in the Augustinian tradition. The study of practical philosophy and moral theology was suddenly enriched by a method and an intellectual focus of unparalleled philosophical depth. This new scholastic approach became the glory of the Paris university.

When the two towering figures, Dominicans Albertus Magnus and Thomas Aquinas, arrived in the intellectual forum of the thirteenth century, the study of Aristotle's corpus moved into high gear. The times were ripe for a paradigmatic change from the spiritual idealism represented by Augustine's, Neoplatonism to a new intelligibility of reality and of natural ethics in particular, after the direct translations from Greek to Latin had become available. An intellectual crisis was impending, in which Albertus and his disciple Thomas played a crucial role. In the year 1247 Robert Grosseteste presented his *Translatio Lincolniensis* with the complete text of Aristotle's *Ethics* and a series of comments by early Greek exegetes. In the beginning of the 1260s William of Moerbeke achieved the translation of the Stagirite's complete works, with the *Politics* (up to 1270a30) included.

Before we proceed to discuss Albertus' reading of the new material, a short reference to Moerbeke's renderings (1961) of some of the crucial Aristotelian terms seems necessary, for they influenced Albertus' interpretative scheme of commercial activities and usury (Langholm 1992:c). In Aristotle's original Greek text on the transition of a natural economy to a chrematistic mis-development, the key reference reads as follows: "*poristentos oun ede nomismatos*" (*Politics* (1967) 1257b 1–2). In Moerbeke's first version, this line is translated as "*determinato igitur numismate iam ex necessaria commutatione altera species crimatistice facta est campsoria*". In his second version, Moerbeke offers a slightly different wording: "*facto igitur iam numismate ex necessaria commutatione altera species pecuniativae facta est campsoria*". Plainly formulated, in its development course, the natural exchange of the oikos was overshadowed by another species, namely the monetarized trade for gain, labelled by Moerbeke as *campsor* and in other places *campsoria*. The use of the word *campsor* or *campsoria* for commercial and monetary deals inspired by the profit motive shows that Moerbeke reduced Aristotle's moral disapproval to the money-changer's activity alone. Albertus picked up the line and gave the trading community free rein as long as commercial activities respond to the needs of orderly community life and in so far as merchants did not unduly profit from monopoly or scarcity situations. The *campsoria*, or the business of money-changers and commerce for pure gain *"ex cupiditate"*, on the contrary, was sharply disapproved.

In his early writings like *De Bono* and in his comment on Peter Lombard's textbook *Super IV Sententiarium*, some brief references to the issue of justice in exchange are exposed in Ciceronian rhetorist fashion; but Albertus' trend-setting work in this field came in his two commentaries on Aristotle's *Ethica Nicomachea*. The first version, *Super Ethica*, was written after his return from the Paris university to Cologne (1250–1252) (1968); the second commentary was ready by 1263 (1890–9). Albertus had a fair knowledge of al-Farabi's and Ibn Rushd's exegesis and felt free to depart from the original text in order to adapt it to his own context and outlook. This new technique of paraphrasing, *ex sensu supplevi*, was also applied in his treatment of Book V, 5 of *Ethics* on justice in exchange.

Notwithstanding Aristotle's sometimes confusing analysis on the terms of exchange, somewhat clarified by the Arabian predecessor Ibn Rushd, Albertus' analysis emerged as a well-balanced discourse with new openings. According to Langholm, who published the first extensive study of Albertus' commentary on exchange, the Dominican's main contribution consisted in rejecting "the *status interpretation* and the *intrinsic value interpretation*". Both have been "attributed to the medieval scholastics, without much real basis in the texts". Those on which Albertus "set foot are the *demand interpretation* and the *labour interpretation*" (Langholm 1992: 183). This first full exegesis of Aristotle's exchange relation theorem by a Latin scholar became a historical benchmark in speculative, moral theology on economic matters.

In order to arrive at a just compensation in exchange for both sides, the equality should not be a quantitative but a proportional one (*secundum equalitatem proportionis*). In a further development, proportional equivalence in exchange is specified as the value of one packet of commodities against the value of another: *"secundum proportionem valoris rei unius ad valorem rei alterius"* and in a second line *"res in rem commutatur secundu m valorem"*. Up to this point Albertus stayed solidly in the crux of Aristotelian orthodoxy. When it came to specifying the source of value, however, he parted company with his Greek model. Indeed, for the reason of justice the exchangers should offer to each other an equivalent value *"in pretio secundum proportionem operis ad opus"*. In the first commentary, value does not stem from the status of the exchangers but from the worth of the products. The following lines leave no doubt that the norm for our Latin scholar is based on labour value, or more generally on the cost of the inputs, since he repetitiously uses terms such as *"in laboribus et expensis"* and *"differentia secundum labores et expensas"*. This is illustrated in Aristotelian fashion, by a clear example: "As the farmer is to the shoemaker in labor and expenses, thus the product of the shoemaker is to the farmer's product" (Albertus 1968: 345). But he ended up by adding that the norm of labor and material cost is not an absolute criterion of value. In order that exchange take place, the exchanged products should respond to a need of the exchangers for each other's supply and demand: *"opus diximus esse usum vel utilitatem vel indigentiam"*.

In his second commentary (1890–9), Albertus' reworking of Aristotle's concept of *chreia* comes out still more clearly. It refers not only to reciprocal need (*indigentia*) but also to *necessitas* and even to the more subjective notion of *utilitas*. Albertus did not elaborate on the value-paradox inherent in this dualism. When he arrived at the difficult question of commensurability, he was perfectly aware of the problem raised by measurement to achieve equality between the things exchanged, as Aristotle himself had been: *"Equalitas autem esse non potest sine commensuratione"*. Commenting on Aristotle's *Metaphysics* X, 1, the Arab scholar Ibn Rushd before Albertus had inserted the interpolation that an object's measuring rod had to be the *smallest* unit of its own kind. Albertus, a keen reader of the Andalusian philosopher, picked up the line: *"quia sic unumquodque mensuratus sui generis minimo"*, but he didn't expand on this hint of marginalism. A few decades later the nominalist philosophers, with a greater sensibility for methodological individualism than the holistic Albertus, would break open the horizon.

In the discourse on the functions and the value of money, Albertus comes very near to Ibn Rushd's metaphysical absolutism for measures. In its function of *mensura* or regula, the monetary medium serves as a valuation standard of different commodities and services as they are estimated *in the economic scale of values*. In the ideal situation, money should live up to the quality of stability (*moneta certa*). A fluctuating *"mensura"* entails uncertainty and indetermination in exchange relations. This defect also diminishes the value of money as a stock of future purchasing power. In fact, money with a fluctuating value is an unreliable stock: *"non est fide jussor certus"*. But his feudal context induces him to a more political stand. With some hesitation Albertus resignedly accepts the power of the prince to alter its course, according to the feudal concept of *valor impositus*. The Aristotelian thesis on the sterility of money is emphasized with a biological metaphor *"pecunia non parit"*, money cannot beget money.

Albertus' *Super Ethica* (1968) betokened a take-off in the philosophical foundation of moral theology. His promotion of Aristotle's conceptual rationalism to the status of a privileged authority – etymologically *auctoritas* stems from the Greek *authentes*, or what can be trusted – sowed the seeds of a more radical wave, namely Latin Averroism. The canonization of the Stagirite led to the de-colonization of practical philosophy from the paternalism of theology, i.e. towards its scientific autonomy (Wieland 1981, De Libera 1990). While Ibn Rushd had been unable to consolidate a rationalist tradition in the scholarly world of Islam, Albertus was followed by generations of Latin disciples in the peripatetic tradition, beginning with his disciple Thomas Aquinas who evolved as a celebrity in this field.

Space limits do not permit a detailed treatment of all the new currents that emerged. As time wheeled on, the commentators gradually dressed Aristotle's economic theorems in medieval scholastic suits, by taking into account the differential value of skilled labour in exchange equalization and by the new perception of money as "capital". All this led to an embryo of marginal analysis and to the emergence of new views on money. The Franciscan scholar Petrus Olivi, who quite generally didn't like Aristotle's concepts, was one of the first scholastics to break with the sterility principle. In some commercial transactions, the nature of money changes and turns into capital.

As a conclusion, we briefly refer to Buridan's and Oresme's Aristotelian cursus. John Buridan was a moderate follower of Ockham and became an enthusiast of empirical verification tests in his scientific research. He was moreover a notorious philosopher of the arts faculty in Paris, where he was elected rector of the university. The scriptures of interest for historians of economic thought are: *Questiones Johannis Buridani super decem libros Ethicorum Aristotelis ad Nicomachum* (1513[1]) and *Questiones Johannis Buridani super octo libros Politicorum Aristotelis* (1513[2]), both edited in Paris in the same year. Buridan's treatment of Aristotle's *Politics* is an amalgam of traditional views, enriched by novel overtures on commercial development and its monetary implications. In his more original comments on *Ethics*, he comes out as a benchmarker of marginalist calculus.

In *Ethics* (1513[1]), *questio* 16 and *questio* 17, Buridan refers to Aristotle's passage on exchange relations but goes definitely his own way on the definition of money and the quantification of individual needs. Following the Greek philosopher, Buridan states that *indigentia* is the basic factor in exchange relations. In the search for equivalence between the things exchanged, however, his emphasis on the quantification of the subjective, inter-individual valuations of the exchangers betokens a theoretical departure from Aristotle's metaphysic and holistic approach. According to Buridan's methodological individualism, not the total but only the satisfaction deriving from "the last" units of exchanged commodities play a role in the measurement of needs. On this basis the author's mathematical analysis of proportionality developed into a clear formulation of inter-individual valuation based on marginal calculus.

With the insertion of the metaphysical "smallest unit" notion in the exchange chapter of his *Ethics* commentary (1542), Ibn Rushd had already opened the door to a latent form of marginalism. But in the holistic vision of the Arab philosopher and of the great Dominicans, Albertus and Thomas, this shift in emphasis was left unexploited. Olivi's discussion on the hierarchical graduation of needs, according to different scales of intensity, was a first try toward a more explicit formulation of marginalism. This had moreover been exemplified in the Olivian theory on wage determination, where the differential quality of labour was introduced in a discussion on the just hierarchy of wages. Olivi's writings disappeared out of sight for ages, while Buridan's quantitative approach immediately bloomed into a tradition. The affinity with the *Ethics* commentary of Gerald Odonis (*c.* 1290–1349) is striking (Langholm 1983, Buridan 1988, Dupuy 1989). Buridan was also at odds with Aristotle's monetary nominalism. As an advocate of commodity-money, he took a different tack. In fact Buridan was the first to introduce the metallist tradition in the philosophical constituency of the Latin West. His theoretical pioneer work inspired his contemporary Oresme to write a comprehensive treatise on money.

Oresme's French translation of Aristotle's works was not the first in the field. Around 1305 a certain Pierre de Paris had rendered the *Politics* in the vernacular. Just as Cicero had brought the Greek philosophical legacy into Latin at a time when Rome became hegemonic, just as Dante and Petrarca in Italy had introduced the local language into literature, the French humanists felt the need to render the scriptures of antiquity in the nascent language of the mounting middle classes. The *"translatio studii"* from Latin, which had functioned as a trans-national language of clerics and scholars for ages, into the language of the common people, went hand in hand with the ambition of nation building deployed by the French kings. *"Translater telz livres en francois"*, explained Oresme, facilitated not only the transfer of ideas; it had moreover seminal effects on the native language. On the basis of recent philological research it seems that Oresme's translation enriched the upcoming intellectual idiom with a thousand new words. Like Moerbeke in his time, Oresme on several occasions was unable to find the correct word and proceeded to literal transliteration. Most of the time, however, his imaginative mind was alert enough to spawn new words and expressions. The reading of Oresme's medieval and charming French is an intellectual spell in itself.

For his translations of Aristotle's work Oresme, not knowing Greek, relied on Moerbeke's translation with the well-known moral ban on *campsoria*. The term was rendered in the French text as *changeresse*. Moerbeke's version of the acquisitive spirit *"omnis eorum vita circa acquisitionem pecuniarum est"* becomes *"adonques touz telz mettent leur cure vers acquisition de pecunes"*. Accordingly, the counterfeiting of money by princes was compared to the usurious practice of money-changers. Indeed, the *changeresse* profited greatly from the monetary instability on account of the higher transaction costs of the financial and commercial dealings.

It should be noted that the royal adviser's *"Sitz im Leben"* was very different from the Greek philosopher's. Moreover, Oresme's and Buridan's comments on Aristotle derived from another philosophical mindset than those of the thirteenth century. In fourteenth-century France, the corporate interests of the bourgeoisie had evolved into a social force to be seriously reckoned with in the political field. As a keen observer of the brooding conflict between the royal privilege of seigniorage and the sectional interests of the people, Oresme gives the *marchanderie* a solid footing in his texts (Menjot 1988, Lapidus 1993).

At the end of the fourteenth century the commentaries on Aristotle's theorems had passed their peak. In the Muslim world Ibn Khaldun criticized Aristotle as an armchair philosopher who in his conceptual framework had idealized man and the polis. The humanists of the Italian *Il quattrocento* also read the Athenian philosopher from a new historical perspective. In the literature of that period the humanists Leonardo Bruni, Matteo Palmeri, Leon Battista Alberti, Giannozzo Manetti, and Lorenzo Valla questioned the moral restraint of the Aristotelian and scholastic world-views. They argued that the material and bodily needs of man should be given more leeway. Their discourses on the practical philosophy of the Stagirite were in contrast to the thirteenth century comments; not only written in pure, classical Latin, they also presented a hermeneutic adaptation to their cultural milieu, or a de-Socratization of Aristotle's political views. In their discourses, the ascetic overtones of Aristotelian ethics paled and were coloured by the "civic" rhetoric of Cicero and the individualism of Democritus. In Alberti's *Della Famiglia* also, the Xenophontean dialogue of household management was streamlined to the cultural and business climate of fifteenth century Florence.

With a manifest Epicurean preference, Lorenzo Valla proclaimed that human virtue ought not put too hard a brake on human aspirations for worldly pleasure. In his view the supreme achievements of man are not restricted to the cultural and intellectual domains, they are moreover embodied in the entrepreneurial libido of the *homo faber* manifesting itself in economic life. This humanist proponent of pleasure, on the motto *"voluptatem esse summum bonum"*, comes out clearly as an advocate of hedonism.[8]

With the Italian humanists, a new impetus in the direction of Atlantic economics became apparent. Since antiquity, a long line of scholars had kept its latent seeds in bounds. In Classical Greece, the first try of the Sophists was met by the Socratic counter-movement. The opening of a pragmatic view on the economy by the Roman legists of the twelfth century was kept in low key by the canonists and to a certain degree also by speculative theologians. The Italian humanists acted again as an intellectual transmission belt to novel views. With the advent of the modern age, mercantilists and natural philosophers would gradually turn the basic premises of Mediterranean economic thought upside-down. In the emerging Atlantic tradition, the optimizing of material welfare became the embodiment of the supreme good for the individual. The *"zoon poli-*

tikon" conditioned by a community-oriented ethos was pushed into the background by assertive theses on the "*homo economicus*".

NOTES

1 For the United States, we mention the political scientist J. Rawls and the economist A. Sen. In Europe the movement is headed by a pleiad of scholars: the Germans Gadamer and Apel, the Frenchmen Ricoeur and Pellegrin, and on the Italian side, Volpi, Natali and Berti are leading figures. In a recent collection of studies, a group of philosophers, social scientists and economists published their view on a reborn form of rationality along Aristotelian lines (Berti 1989a, 1989b). In an earlier German study the mounting interest in Aristotle's practical philosophy was titled with the strong label "*Rehabilitierung*" (Riedel 1972, 1974).

   The growing number of economists who advocate the ethical dimension of economics will find a philosophical footing for their thesis in this rehabilitation literature. For economists who are dissatisfied with today's mainstream economics, characterized by formal abstractions, by exaggerated mathematization as well as by an almost exclusive focus on strategies of resource allocation and the neglect of value judgments on ends, Berti's reader brings a refreshing intellectual U-turn to the question of "sense", not only as "fact", and to the notion of "value", not only as "neutral allocative mechanisms". The Aristotelian concept of *phronesis*, representing a balanced symbiosis of practical reason and opinion enriched by public debate, offers a richer promise than the deterministic and mechanistic models of instrumental rationality. Mathematical deduction is but one sort of logic, namely the one of theoretical necessity.

   With the excessive instrumentalization of reason on the model of the natural sciences, the gap between formal economics and the world of decision-making in a historico-concrete context, has become almost unbridgeable. In today's welfare states where between 35 to 45 percent of national income is taxed away and redistributed on the basis of sociopolitical arbitrage and bickering, the separation of politics and ethics from economic analysis reduces a great deal of its theses to armchair lore sequestered from the dynamics of real life. In the crisis of modernity, the actual rehabilitation of practical philosophy forms an encouraging and revitalizing stream of thought.

2 In the compact world-view of the preceding Egyptian, Mesopotamian, Syrian and Persian civilizations, the scribal élite in the service of the establishment bowed respectfully to the ruling authorities. The wisdom literature advised to keep the "hotness of the mouth" in bounds, and scribes shied away from disagreeing in public; there was no cultural or political space for polemics, nor for independent thematization.

3 Among the most recent studies we refer to Baloglou and Constantinidis (1993), Burgin (1993), Karayiannis (1990), Natali (1988), Lowry (1987), Klever (1986), Vandevelde (1986), Ruggiu (1982) and Berthoud (1981).

4 The philological studies and textual criticism of Pellegrin (1982) and Natali (1990) are very illuminating for a better understanding of the basic Aristotelian concept of *chrematistike*.

5 The term *chreia* covered a complex family of realities and concepts which, according to the context, may be translated as common or mutual need, use, utility, necessity, exigency, indigence, want, and/or desire. In the secularizing philosophy of Democritus and the Sophists, *chreia* stood for the human need, want, and desire functioning as a leverage to invent the social and technical skills

that led to development. In Plato's *Republic, chreia* was the original motor for community formation. In Aristotle's economic passages the term was pivotal: first it was used to explain the origin of barter, then for the genesis of money, and finally he designated *chreia* as the basic reference for the equalization of the exchange relation. In his commentaries, Cicero translated the term in Latin by *usus, utilitas* and *consuetudo*, specifying that in a development context, the term *necessitatis inventa* would fit better. Modern translations sometimes render *chreia* by "demand". Since Aristotle was looking for a basic nexus for commensurability in the terms of trade, and was not at all elaborating a demand and supply or marketing mechanism, "demand" in his context is a questionable modernism. For the etymological roots and the various meanings of *chreia*, see Hollerbach (1964).

6 In Rome, the Middle Janus was the market-place for exchange; note also the reference to the "worthy gentlemen".

7 For a comprehensive exposition of the Aristotelian tradition we refer the reader to Langholm's *opus magnum* (Langholm 1992) and to Spicciani's penetrating analyses (1977 and 1990).

8 In 1431 Valla published his dialogue "On Pleasure" (De voluptate), retitled in a later version *De vero bono*.

7

THE ECONOMY OF HELLENISTIC EGYPT AND SYRIA

An archeological perspective[1]

Murray C. McClellan

The ancient Greeks have played a seminal role in the development of Western civilization and have served both as a source of inspiration in the development of economic theory and as a subject for scholarly inquiry by economic historians.[2] This chapter presents a survey of scholarship on the economies of Hellenistic (336–31 BC) Egypt and Syria and suggests how a study of Hellenistic Egyptian and Syrian archeology may lead us to view the economies of these later Greek societies as more dynamic than currently envisioned.

ANCIENT ECONOMIES AND ECONOMIC THOUGHT IN GREEK ANTIQUITY

Modern scholarship on economic activities and economic thought in ancient Greece has been transformed by Sir Moses Finley's epochal studies of ancient Greek and Roman economies.[3] Finley's *oeuvre* marked the culmination of a long, and ultimately fruitless, debate between "primativists" and "modernists", a debate which itself was a reflection of the equally sterile formalist/substantivist schism in economic anthropology.[4] Following the argument, which stretches back through Hasebroek to Weber, that ancient economies were embedded within social and cultural constraints, Finley maintained that Classical Greeks had no concept of the economy and that ancient Greek economic activities were conditioned by concerns for political or social status (Finley 1970: 3–25). According to Finley's model, Greek *poleis* did not establish discrete economic policies, though such politically motivated policies as the Athenian control of the Black Sea grain trade did have an economic effect on citizen and non-citizen alike. Individual Greeks sought to obtain wealth, though not as an end in itself, but rather to be able to own land and thus become free from the social stigma of having to work for another.

In recent years, the dialectics of scholarship have sought to modify, if not to overturn, some aspects of Finley's model of the ancient economy. Some economic historians have emphasized that elements of what can be described as economic theory lay behind the political and ethical writings of Plato, Aristotle, Xenophon, and other Classical Greek authors.[5] Alan Samuel has suggested that modern interpreters of ancient economic thought have been misled by an anachronistic conception that economic analysis should be directed toward the goal of increasing rates of production (Samuel 1983). Samuel argues that, to the contrary, Classical Greek political economists sought to maintain stability in the economic activities of the polis. Thus, while the *Poroi* of Xenophon or the *Politics* of Aristotle do contain isolated discussions of such theoretical subjects as supply and demand or diminishing profit, for Samuel the "failure" of Classical Greek thinkers to create what Schumpeter (1954) has called a superstructure of economic analysis represents not a theoretical shortcoming but rather reflects a non-modern rejection of economic growth in favor of political stability.

Other aspects of the model of the ancient Greek and Roman economy formulated by Finley and his predecessor at Cambridge, A.H.M. Jones, have come under attack by Classical historians and archeologists. Keith Hopkins[6] has suggested that the Jones/Finley model needs to be modified in certain key aspects. Rather than postulating a static economy dominated by the local exchange of agricultural produce in which trade and manufacture played a minimal role and in which the state exercised little influence, Hopkins believes that the last few centuries before and the first two centuries after the common era was a period which witnessed an increase in both agricultural and non-agricultural production. Hopkins sees this increase as resulting from an intensification of exploitation spurred on, in part, by the monetary and taxation policies of the Roman Empire.

Archeologists[7] would tend to agree with Hopkins' suggested modifications, though they are still struggling to obtain the degree of statistical rigor that Finley called for thirty-three years ago:

> It is hardly necessary to say that so far the archeological materials have been studied systematically only for art history, chronology and, to a lesser extent, technology. The potential contribution to economic history is incalculable, provided the conceptual base is radically reconsidered and far greater attention is paid to completeness and to quantitative studies.
>
> (Finley 1965: 35)

This paper will address the contributions that archeological evidence can provide in the reconstruction of economic activities and economic thought within the Hellenistic kingdoms of the Ptolemies and Seleucids. A number of serious issues must be confronted at the outset of such a study. We have already alluded to the problems of interpreting the ancient economy in terms of modern economic structures. Moreover, it should be recognized that the categories of evidence for past economic activities and economic concepts – literary and historical texts, papyri and other epigraphical documents, and the preserved ancient material record – are in many respects incommensurable. The assumption that the audience to whom ancient writers directed their works was the same as the producers and consumers of material products must be avoided. Furthermore, any analysis of the archeological record must first confront the numerous problems involved in the creation of that record before attempting to tackle the thorny, if not intractable, issue of assessing intentionality from material remains.[8] In using the material record to reconstruct the economic life of any ancient society, one must demonstrate that a given set of archeologically recovered artifacts are indeed representative of real economic activities; only once such a demonstration is made can one attempt to ascertain the degree to which individual or institutional policies lay behind the creation of the observed patterns. To undertake such an analysis for the complicated archeological record of Egypt and Syria in the three centuries following the conquests of Alexander the Great is a Herculean task and the present paper can offer only a prolegomenon to such a study.

ARCHEOLOGY AND THE ECONOMY OF HELLENISTIC EGYPT

Hellenistic historiography has received a great deal of attention in recent years and only a few general points need be made here. A century of scholarship following the appearance of Johann Gustav Droysen's *Geschichte des Hellenismus*, published between 1836 and 1843, viewed the Hellenistic world as a monolithic entity in which the cultural fusion (*Verschmelzung*) of Greek and Oriental elements laid the foundations for the rise of Christianity. The colonialist and Eurocentric attitudes implicit in interpreting Hellenistic culture as a triumph of Greek rational, progressive government over Oriental despotism have been repudiated by modern scholars.[9] The current paradigm, itself reflecting the resurgence of modern nationalism and a late-twentieth century disenchantment with the military and advanced capitalistic structures, would characterize the Hellenistic age as a period of cultural separatism, with Greek-speaking settlers and administrators economically exploiting the non-Greek indigenous peoples.[10]

The massive corpus of Greek and Demotic papyri from Ptolemaic Egypt has naturally loomed large in reconstructions of the economy of the Hellenistic world, from the great syntheses of Prèaux (1939; 1978) and

Rostovtzeff (1922; 1951), to the current generation of researchers.[11] It is unfortunate that the archeological record of Egypt in the Hellenistic period is relatively poorly understood and so figures little in these reconstructions of the ancient economy (Bowman n.d.: 240–243).[12] For obvious reasons, the main thrust of archeological research in the Nile valley has been directed to uncovering architectural monuments and funerary remains of the Pharoanic periods. To be sure, several temple complexes in Upper Egypt erected in traditional Egyptian style during the Hellenistic period have been extensively documented.[13] Only a few Hellenistic settlements in the Nile Delta and the Fayum have been subject to scientific excavation. Alexandria, the seat of Ptolemaic control, has been continually occupied since the third century BC and consequently has yielded a very limited amount of archeological material dating to the Hellenistic period.[14] It is especially regretful that almost no systematic regional surveys have been conducted in Egypt. As Susan Alcock noted in her recent synthetic study of Hellenistic surveys, the diachronic approach and emphasis on land use inherent in the survey technique allows surveys to produce evidence which "escapes the Hellenocentric, colonialist and élite bias of the documentary sources and of the majority of archeological excavations and art-historical studies" (Alcock 1994: n. 12, 175).

In addition to the dearth of archeological evidence for the Hellenistic period in Egypt, an analysis of patterns present in the Ptolemaic material record is further hampered by our incomplete knowledge of Egypt during the Late Period (664–323 BC). In order to ascertain the degree to which new economic practices were introduced into the country by the Greek-speaking Ptolemaic administration, one needs to establish the nature of the Egyptian economy prior to the conquests of Alexander.

While the economy of Late Period Egypt certainly continued to be based on irrigated agriculture, there is some indication that the traditional redistributive system of Pharonic Egypt was beginning to be supplanted by a market economy, albeit one in which money played a minimum role (Lloyd 1983: 279–348). The Greek trading settlement established by Psammetichus I in the late seventh century BC at Naucratis increasingly became a focus for the exchange of Egyptian and east Mediterranean goods (Moller 1990). A stele erected by Nectanebo (379–362 BC) at Naucratis lists the imposition of taxes on timber, gold, silver, and items of worked wood (Gunn 1943: 55–59). Archeological evidence demonstrates that Naucratis also provided Egypt with east Mediterranean olive oil and iron technology (Salles 1991: 207–236; Austin 1970).

The pressure to supply an annual tribute of 700 talents during the periods of Persian domination (525–404 BC and 341–332 BC) no doubt accelerated the development of Egyptian surplus production for markets. Moreover, the Greek and Carian mercenary soldiers who served in Late Period Egypt would have been expected to be paid in gold or silver.

Nonetheless, the argument that the Saite pharaohs or the Persian kings consciously sought to integrate Egypt into a larger east Mediterranean or Persian trading network does not stand up to close scrutiny.[15] It seems that such policies as existed were motivated by military or propagandistic concerns and were not designed to increase trade *per se*, as Tulpin, for instance, has demonstrated was the case with Darius' construction of a Suez canal (Tulpin 1991: n. 23, 237–283).

When the Macedonian army replaced the Persians in Egypt, they came as colonists as much as overlords. Within a half century of its foundation, Alexandria was the largest city in the Mediterranean and Greek-speaking settlers had established themselves throughout the Nile valley. There is no doubt that Egypt was fundamentally altered under Ptolemaic rule, though the degree to which Egyptian and Greek cultures affected one another and the exact nature of the economic structures and policies (if any) in Ptolemaic Egypt remains problematic.

According to Michael Rostovtzeff (1951: n. 14),[16] the Ptolemies erected an elaborate, centrally planned state economy directed towards the accumulation of capital and the creation of prosperity for a bourgeoise class through an increase in agricultural productivity via the adoption of non-Egyptian technical developments. Rostovtzeff's model was rooted in his masterful control of the papyrological evidence, which he supplemented with an admirable number of illustrations from the material record of Ptolemaic Egypt. As Reinhold has noted, Rostovtzeff's experiences in Bolsheveik Russia, his antipathy to the emerging contemporary Soviet planned economy, and his admiration for the mechanisms of capitalism can now be seen to have influenced the categories of inquiry he employed in his interpretation of Ptolemaic Egypt and the approbation with which he viewed the supposed proto-capitalistic Ptolemaic economy (Reinhold 1946: 361–391).

In the half-century of scholarly research since the publication of *The Social and Economic History of the Hellenistic World*, Rostovtzeff's model has been thoroughly dismantled. Claire Prèaux has suggested that almost no real technological improvements were developed in Ptolemaic Egypt (Prèaux 1966: 235–250; 1978: n. 14). Alan Samuel has demonstrated that social (and economic) stability rather than an increase of production was the *desirata* of Ptolemaic policy and that the "public/private" conceptionalization of land-ownership does not adequately account for the complicated realities of land tenure in Ptolemaic Egypt, where supposed "public" lands held in *doreai* or *cleruchies* were in fact subject to inheritance or alienation (Samuel 1989: n. 6, n. 12, 57–59). Jean Bingen has shown that the regulations for tax collecting and banking contained in Philadelphus' Revenue Laws represent an application of traditional Greek tax-farming policies to Egyptian conditions and that they were designed to maintain predictable levels of royal revenue rather than to impose a progressive, rational economic plan on the country (Bingen 1978). Sir Eric Turner has argued that Egypt during the reigns of Ptolemy II Philadelphus and Ptolemy III Euergetes (281–221 BC) was far from being the booming kingdom envisioned by Rostovtzeff, but in fact was increasingly under stress from the bankrupting military adventures of its kings (Turner 1984: n. 15).

The concerted rejection of Rostovtzeff's model, however, has not been followed with uniform agreement on the nature of economic life in Hellenistic Egypt. Samuel has suggested that

> administration under Philadelphus was not the rationally planned structure into which we have been trying to fit what are in reality unfittable and disparate pieces of an arrangement put together largely *ad hoc*, created not just by the central authority but also developed on the land by officials who were pursuing their own interests at the same time as they worked to meet the crown's demand for revenue. If a strain was imposed on the population by this structure, I suggest that it might have been created by the nature of the burgeoning bureaucracy itself, rather than primarily because of the needs of the king himself.
>
> (Samuel 1989: n. 12, 59–60)

Samuel has also argued that within this set of *ad hoc* regulatory mechanisms, money continued to play a relatively insignificant role in the life of the Egyptian peasantry (Samuel 1984: 187–206).

In contrast, Turner has postulated two coeval models of economic obligations in Ptolemaic Egypt that imply a more rigidly controlled and monetarized economy than that envisioned by Samuel (Turner 1984: n. 15, 149–159). In Turner's Model I, farmers of royal land (*basilikoi georgoi*) work in partnership with the crown in the production of grain, receiving seeds from royal officials and sharing the harvest. Model II applies to all other agricultural products and manufactured goods, which were subject to a tax:

> To pay the tax the primary producer had first to sell his crop. The state bought it off him at prices fixed by itself. Additionally the state retained the right to process the crop so acquired (whether as tax revenue or by state purchase) into manufactured goods (oil from oil-seeds or olives, beer from barley, linen from flax, etc.). The manufactures were processed in state-owned and state-supervised factories. Finally, the state licensed firms of capitalists to sell the goods either wholesale or retail at prices fixed by itself.
>
> (Turner 1984: n. 15, 151)

It would be desirable to use numismatic evidence to ascertain the role that money played in Ptolemaic Egypt, but we lack a sufficient number of careful studies of coins from hoards and controlled excavations to be able to make any definitive statements.[17] The introduction and apparent widespread use of Ptolemaic copper coins at the end of the third century do indicate that coins were used in day-to-day transactions (Reekmans 1951: 61–120). All one can say at this point is that, from the period of Persian domination into the period of Roman domination, there seems to have been a continual increase in the degree to which the Egyptian economy was monetarized.

One focus of scholarly inquiry into the social and economic life of Ptolemaic Egypt has been the interactions among Greeks and native Egyptians. Much attention has been directed towards the problematic identification of ethnic groups in Ptolemaic Egypt and the functioning of the dual Greek/Egyptian legal systems (Lewis 1986, Goudriaan 1988, Bagnall 1988b). There is some scholarly consensus that Greek-speakers and native Egyptians maintained a strict religious and cultural separation and that the class of bilingual, Hellenizing Egyptians was relatively small.[18] While most scholars have assumed that this separation can be explained by the colonial Ptolemaic economic exploitation of native Egyptians, Bingen has argued that the manner in which the Ptolemies organized wheat production – the thrust of the Ptolemaic economy – left most of the prime farming land in Egyptian hands and relegated the Greek immigrants to marginal positions in business or the bureaucracy (Bingen 1984: 920–940).

In this regard, it would be extremely helpful if one could point to a set of archeological traits characteristic of Greek or Egyptian ethnicity. However, both the problems inherent in ascertaining cultural identity from the material record and the meagerness of our information on settlement archeology in Hellenistic Egypt make this an extremely difficult task.[19] Nonetheless, it is probably significant that one can see little trace of ethnic divisions in the limited archeological evidence we do possess. Excavations in the Fayum, for instance, have revealed several Ptolemaic period houses whose ground plans follow both traditional Greek and traditional Egyptian designs. West House No. 1 and West House No. 2, uncovered by Caton-Thompson and Gardner along an irrigation canal to the north of Karanis (Kom Aushim) have rooms opening onto a central courtyard, much like houses at Olynthus, Priene, and other fourth and third century BC Greek settlements (Caton-Thompson and Gardner 1934: 145–148). On the other hand, in nearby Karanis, houses of the Ptolemaic E level consist of square structures subdivided into a number of rooms or of a series of rooms aligned along narrow passages, much like those from Late Period Nebesheh (Husselman 1979: Map 5, Petrie 1888: plate XVII). It is impossible to determine from the assemblages of artifacts recovered from these Fayum settlements whether a given structure or village was occupied by Greeks or Egyptians or, for that matter, the problematic *Perses tes epigones*. In other words, from a strictly material point of view, there seems to have been a great deal of cultural "fusion" in the households of Hellenistic Egypt.

Another major focus of Ptolemaic studies has been directed to cult. The economic importance of the conservative Egyptian priesthood, which controlled large tracts of temple land, has long been recognized (Quaegebeur 1979: 708–729). Samuel has cogently argued against any notion of religious syncretism in Ptolemaic Egypt or of a special royal policy of promoting the cult of Serapis as a unifying national deity (Samuel 1989: n. 6, 75–101). Nevertheless, it should be noted that support of cults favored by the Greek-speaking population of Egypt was part of Ptolemaic policy and that, as elsewhere in the Hellenistic world, these cults served significant economic roles as repositories of dedications and distribution centers for meat.[20] It is certainly true that major public and religious structures continued to be erected along more or less traditional Greek or Egyptian lines and that instances of mixed architectural or sculptural styles are rare and in part can be explained by independent Egyptian or Greek artistic developments.[21] The material record of major public structures in Ptolemaic Egypt, then, would tend to support the notion of cultural separatism.

While some elements of native and Greek cultures existed separately in Egypt under the Ptolemies, it is probably an overstatement to claim that "the Greeks maintained their culture in Egypt in almost complete separation from the surrounding milieu" (Samuel 1989: n. 12, 45). The Ptolemaic dynasts were certainly adept at manipulating traditional ideology through their support of temple construction at Dendera, Esna, Edfu, Kom Ombo, and Philae, the local economic importance of which programs would not have been lost on either native Egyptian or Lagidae. On an individual level, it would seem that the Greek was more affected by living in Egypt than was the Egyptian by sharing his land with the Greeks. In the *chora*, the Greek farmer faced conditions utterly unlike those faced in the hilly, rain-irrigated countryside of the southern Balkans and quickly adopted indigenous agricultural technology.[22] In the Greek urban center of Alexandria, Egyptian and idealized Egyptianizing motifs were increasingly utilized in the decoration of house and tomb (Brown 1957).[23]

We can also see some evidence of cross-fertilization between Egyptian and Greek technological traditions in the production of vitreous materials. The traditional Egyptian expertise in faience may have influenced the Alexandrian production of the so-called royal *oinochoai* – faience wine jars with depictions of Ptolemaic queens sacrificing at an altar (Thompson 1973). However, faience technology had been long known in the Greek world and the Ptolemaic production of faience may have in fact little to do with earlier Egyptian faience technology (Webb 1978). The production of luxury mosaic glass, formed in molds from sections of multi-colored glass canes, seems to be a clearer example of Greek–Egyptian technological interaction. Mosaic glass vessels, which were first produced in the late third century BC, occur in purely Greek shapes – hemispherical bowls, shallow dishes, jars (Grose 1989: 189–197). On the other hand, the Egyptian tradition of using glass cane sections in inlay work stretches unbroken from the New Kingdom into the Persian period. It is thus not unreasonable to suggest that the development of Hellenistic mosaic glass occurred in or around Alexandria, a city that was to become renown for its glass-making in the Roman period.

Archeological evidence lacks the chronological precision to be able to shed light on specific Ptolemaic policies, such as the detailed list of agricultural and manufacturing instructions sent to an *oikonomikos*, which Turner has associated with an economic and social crisis early in the reign of Euergetes I (*P. Teb. 703*).[24] None the less, some general patterns associated with royal policy can be traced in the archeological record. The Ptolemaic fostering of an intensive exploitation of the Fayum, amply documented in the papyrological corpus, is well represented by the 26 km of canals and tunnels recorded in Caton-Thompson and Gardner's 1927 survey (Caton-Thompson and Gardner 1934).[25] The importance of grain to the Ptolemaic economy can be seen at Marea along Lake Mariotis, where recovered sherds suggest that the excavated late Roman port facilities overlay Hellenistic predecessors.[26] It is likely that the massive Hellenistic warehouse recovered at Tell el-Maskhuta (Holladay 1982: n. 25) and, perhaps, the enigmatic warehouse/fortress supposedly uncovered by Petrie at Naucratis,[27] formed a part of the network of Ptolemaic control of grain production and distribution.

The clearest archeological evidence for Ptolemaic economic policy comes from a recent survey in the eastern desert conducted by the University of Michigan and the University of Asiut.[28] This survey has traced a series of Early and Middle Hellenistic forts and way-stations that led from Edfu to the gold mines at Barramiyyah and a second, partially represented, route from the fort at Bir Samut leading toward the port of Berenice. The amount of energy expended on these forts and stations and the uniformity of their spacing (at about 24 kilometre intervals) and construction (using a standard unit of about 4.5 metre) all bespeak a carefully planned campaign on the part of the Ptolemies to control access to the mineral wealth of the eastern desert and the southern Red Sea trade. It is notable that the Michigan/Asiut survey recovered no trace of a northern route from Coptos to the Leukas Limen port in the Ptolemaic period, though this trade route was extensively utilized in the Roman period.[29]

While archeological data are not particularly helpful in illustrating specific bureaucratic mechanisms involved in the production and exchange of goods in Ptolemaic Egypt, they can provide some evidence of general trends not apparent in the papyri. For instance, the large number of transport amphoras recovered from Alexandria testify to the vitality of the exchange networks that existed between Egypt and the Aegean and belie the impression, derived in part from the regulation requiring foreign gold and silver currency to be reminted, that trade with the extra-Ptolemaic world was somehow restricted.[30] The inordinately large percentage of Rhodian amphoras found at Alexandria is markedly different from the pattern observed in Hellenistic Athens.[31] The explanation for this difference is unclear, though the pattern is probably not a result of a specific royal policy. Rather, it most likely reflects the cumulative result of a number of individual entrepreneurs operating more or less independently of the economic system established by royal decree.

Indeed, an independent network of production and exchange, taxed but not organized by the Ptolemaic bureaucracy, may well be responsible for much of what we can observe in the archeological record of Hellenistic Egypt. Such a network surely was involved in the distribution of the so-called *Hadra hydriae*. These vessels were frequently used as cinerary urns in Alexandrian cemeteries, and at least some of them were produced on Crete for the Egyptian market.[32] We might also suspect that the economic decision-making involved in the production of other materials within Egypt, such as glass, faience, or the pottery *lagynoi* produced in the second half of the second century BC near Naucratis (Coulson and Wilkie 1986: 61–73), was undertaken by a set of individuals seeking to maximize their profits within the limits imposed by the state.

The archeological record of Hellenistic Egypt, then, supplies some tentative evidence to suggest that economic transactions under the Ptolemies were not as rigidly controlled as Turner's model would entail and that the Ptolemies were not completely successful in surpressing growth of production.

ARCHEOLOGY AND THE ECONOMY OF SELEUCID SYRIA

The Seleucid world differed from the Ptolemaic in a number of crucial aspects. While the Ptolemaic empire at various times included Cyprus, Cyrenaica, the southern Levant, and some of the Aegean, the base of Ptolemaic power from its very beginning was Egypt, with its generally homogenous indigenous culture. On the other hand, at its height, the Seleucid empire stretched from Turkmenistan to the western coast of Anatolia and encompassed a wide variety of different, dynamic cultural groups. The political, social, and economic mechanisms, by which the Seleucids maintained control of their empire, were thus much more complicated and diverse than the institutions the Ptolemies developed in Egypt. From the time that Seleucus I gained control of it after the battle of Ipsus in 301 BC, Syria – the region from the northern Levantine coast to the Euphrates –

did form the core territory of the Seleucid kingdom, but it was neither culturally unified nor as overwhelmingly productive as was the Nile valley.

Information on the pre-Hellenistic, Achaemenid presence in Syria is as limited as it is for Egypt.[33] The sources on Hellenistic Syria are more plentiful, but quite different from those for Ptolemaic Egypt. Epigraphy plays a relatively small part in the reconstruction of Seleucid history, though important insights into the empire are to be had from a few passages concerning the Syro-Palestinian region preserved in Egyptian papyri, from the limited, but growing, number of Greek and Aramaic inscriptions, and from the important corpus of Hellenistic Babylonian cuneiform tablets. While there is no preserved, continuous, historical narrative of either the Ptolemaic or the Seleucid empires, one area of the Seleucid world – Seleucid Judaea – is extensively treated by Josephus and the author(s) of I and II *Maccabees*. Another significant difference in the sources of information for Seleucid Syria and Ptolemaic Egypt lies in the much more extensive archeological record we possess for Hellenistic Syria. A number of regional surveys have been conducted throughout Syria and several important settlements have been excavated (Sartre 1989: n. 68, 31–44; Alcock 1994: n. 12). However, in Syria as well as in Egypt, the main thrust of archeological research has been directed toward much earlier epochs and the Hellenistic period is comparatively understudied and under-reported.

Scholarship on Seleucid Syria has been dominated by the question of "Hellenization" – that is, the degree to which the indigenous peoples of Syria absorbed Greek cultural patterns. The traditional interpretation of the Seleucid dynasts saw them as imposing superior Greek political and economic structures upon a soporific Orient organized by the timeless "Asiatic mode of production". In Rostovtzeff's opinion, the Seleucids failed in their attempt to effect a cultural change among their eastern subjects, though they did serve as an important intermediary, transmitting cultural values that were adopted in the East during the Roman and late Roman periods.[34]

As in the case of Ptolemaic Egypt, the colonialist attitudes implicit in this traditional interpretation have been rejected by modern researchers, though there is little unanimity in alternative explanations of how the Seleucid economy functioned or the extent to which Greek settlers imposed their culture on Syria.[35] Briant maintains that the enclaves of Greek settlements in Hellenistic Syria had little effect on the traditional, Achaemenid patterns of economic organization, which, he holds, were characterized by a diverse set of land-ownership relations (Briant 1982c: 351–372). Briant further sees the Achaemenid and Seleucid "tributary method of production" as fostering economic growth and an intensification of land exploitation (Briant 1982b: 405–430). Musti, on the other hand, posits a distinction between "a zone 'outside' the Seleucid foundations, where relations of production remained constant, and one "inside", where there was a development of private property" (Musti 1984: n. 15, 200, fn. 42). Millar, however, has stressed the dynamic nature and regionalism of both Achaemenid and Hellenistic Syria (Millar 1983: n. 68). He cautions against assuming that Syria was ever organized solely by dependent labor, and cites the Wadi Dâliyeh papyrus of 335 BC for proof that slavery existed in pre-Hellenistic Syria. Sherwin-White and Kuhrt also reject as a "red herring" the notion that the Seleucids introduced a slave-based economy into the east, observing that "it was not the Greeks who "awakened the east" with the introduction of a "commercial spirit", encapsulated (so it was thought) by the market economy of a Greek polis" (Sherwin-White and Khurt 1993: n. 12, 69).

A similar appreciation for the dynamic set of cultural processes that lie behind Greek and Syrian interactions throughout the first millennium BC has been emerging in recent scholarship. Millar believes that the sedentariz-ation of nomadic desert groups was to a large degree responsible for "the visible manifestations of a number of mixed cultures emerging first outside the areas of Seleucid, or Roman, control, and then spreading inwards" (Millar 1983: n. 68, 128). In his examination of monumental architecture, Colledge emphasizes the continuity of Greek artistic influences on the east from the Achaemenid period into first century BC, at which time he sees a true hybrid artistic style emerging (Colledge 1987: n. 68, 134–162).

The scope of this paper, again, allows for only the most preliminary comments on how archeology can contribute to the issues outlined above. It should be stressed that the archeological record of Hellenistic Syria, albeit much greater than the extremely sparse record of Ptolemaic Egypt, none the less still lacks basic statistical information needed to undertake the careful quantitative studies Finley called for over three decades ago. Moreover, the problems created by the chronological inexactitude of the archeological record and the difficulty in determining archeological corre-lates of ethnic groups are as operative in the case of Seleucid Syria as they were for Ptolemaic Egypt.

One area where an intentional policy of the Seleucid kings can be traced is in the creation of new urban centers laid out on Greek lines, especially the Dekapolis – the ten cities – founded by Seleucus I (Seyrig 1968: 53–63; Will 1989: n. 68, 223–250; Grainger 1990). Millar observed that one finds smaller settlements with Greek or Macedonian names only in north Syria, around Antioch, Apamea, Seleucia and Laodicea, suggesting that the trans-formation of local property relations as a result of the creation of new urban centers was an extremely limited phenomenon in Hellenistic Syria (Millar 1983: n. 68, 114). That the foundation of new settlements did have some economic impact on their environs is indisputable, though the nature and extent of that impact and the degree to which the Seleucids intention-ally sought it as part of a rational economic policy is difficult to determine.

Sherwin-White and Kuhrt maintain that it was Seleucid policy to promote trade and commerce and that the Seleucid settlements at Ai Khanoum in Afghanistan and Failaka in the Persian Gulf were designed to control trade routes to the east, as well as to increase the agrarian base in these regions (Sherwin-White and Kuhrt 1993: n. 12, 65–71).[36] On the other hand, Grainger observed that, where discernible, every city founded by Seleucus I contains a dominating acropolis accessible independently of its city (Grainger 1990: n. 79, 87). This topographical fact emphasizes the underlying political and, especially, the military role Seleucid cities were designed to play.

In his examination of the archeological and literary evidence for settlement patterns in Hellenistic Syria, Grainger concluded that there was an increase in the number of settlements and thus a rise in population and a concomitant need for an increase in food production (Grainger 1990: n. 79, 118). In her more stringent review of archeological surveys, Alcock also tentatively postulates an increase in the level of urbanization and agricultural intensification in Seleucid Syria (Alcock 1994: n. 12). However, the large number of substantial storage bins encountered at Persian period sites, such as at Tell Kazel or Tell el Hesi, suggests that the process of agricultural intensification had already begun under the Achaemenids (Badre 1991 734–735, Bennett and Blakely 1989). Palaeo-botanical remains from Tell Rifa'at in northwest Syria provides some indication that the Hellenistic period marked a shift in the mode of production of agricultural goods rather than a mere intensification of production: it appears barley was the primary crop grown by the pre-Hellenistic inhabitants of Tell Rifa'at, while in the Hellenistic period market-oriented commodities such as vetches and vines were cultivated (Hillman 1981: 508–510).

Whether or not the tentative evidence from Tell Rifa'at for a shift in the mode of agricultural production during the Hellenistic period is borne out by future palaeo-ethnobotanical studies, there is little reason to doubt that there was an intensification of settlement and agriculture in Seleucid Syria. It does not necessarily follow, however, that this intensification created a general increase in economic prosperity. Briant maintained that, for the inhabitants of rural Asia Minor, "la conquête macédonienne s'est certainement soldée par une dégradation de leur situation sociale et économique" (Briant 1982a: n. 73, 95–135). Sherwin-White and Kuhrt, and Alcock agree with this assessment and would rather see the intensification of land-use in Hellenistic Syria as resulting from the imperialist policies of the Seleucids rather than from the imposition of a Greek market system (Sherwin-White and Kuhrt 1993: n. 12, 70–71; Alcock 1994: n. 12). Be that as it may, it should be noted that there is virtually no evidence for the actual conditions under which the rural population in Hellenistic Syria lived and worked. To maintain the pessimistic view that Seleucid strategies led to a degradation in the social and economic lives of these people may be as much a reflection of the current anti-imperialist, post-colonial *Zeitgeist* as it is an accurate portrayal of past realities.

The coastal cities of North Syria and Phoencia provide a very different perspective on the nature of the impact of the Macedonian conquest of the east. These cities had been participating in an international trading network for many centuries prior to their incorporation into the Ptolemaic and Seleucid empires, during which centuries a wide variety of eastern Mediterranean and Levantine commodities, technologies, and cultural traits had been exchanged.[37] While claims that the North Syrian sites of Al-Mina and Tell Sukas contained colonies of Greek or Cypriot traders may be based on an overly simplistic equation of pottery with ethnic groups,[38] it is clear that the Hellenistic dynasts encountered in these cities a mixed population already well acquainted with Greek material culture and political/economic institutions (Millar 1983: 55–71, Grainger 1991). The monetarized market economies these cities evidently had in the Hellenistic period are thus best seen as continuing a practice begun in pre-Hellenistic centuries.

Taken as a whole, we can see a general pattern of increasing homogeneity in the material culture of Seleucid Syria. Mediterranean goods, such as amphoras and coins, are found in some quantities both on the coast as well as at inland sites.[39] Local pottery is produced in standardized forms throughout the region.[40] We can hypothesize the same level of individual entrepreneurship operating at a level below royal supervision in Seleucid Syria as we have for Ptolemaic Egypt.

In the investigation of the ancient economies of Hellenistic Egypt and Syria, the real value of archeology lies in its potential to provide insights into what the Annales school has termed the *conjonctures* and *mentalités* – environmental, social, and economic constraints that operate on an extended time-scale.[41] In this regard, we can place the Ptolemaic and Seleucid dominations of these regions within a continuum of growth in the production and trade of material goods. In both Egypt and Syria, elements of urbanizism and market economies can be found in Persian and earlier periods. Under their Macedonian dynasts, Egypt and Syria became increasingly tied to a developing eastern Mediterranean trading network that involved at least some significant amount of non-agricultural production and exchange. Under the Romans, this network expanded into a pan-Mediterranean one. This materialist-based perspective obviously suggests that the static Jones/Finley model should be modified.

To the degree to which there were any rational economic policies on the part of the Ptolemies and Seleucids, such policies were mostly *ad hoc* measures designed to maintain a steady supply of revenues to be spent on political and military uses and were not designed to increase levels of production. To assume, however, that the attitudes of the political élite in Hellenistic Egypt and Syria were universally held is yet another example of the centuries-long tendency to idealize the ancient Greek world as being peopled by ethereal agents unconcerned with the mundane. The archeological record of Hellenistic Egypt and Syria – fragmented and limited though it may be – suggests that it was peopled by energetic individuals who engaged in a wide variety of economic activities, with a clear eye towards maximizing their gains. The level of sophistication in the economic thought of these individuals cannot be determined from the scraps of historical texts or bureaucratic documents that have come down to us.

NOTES

1 I wish to thank Professor Betsey Price for her invitation to submit a paper to appear in this present volume. This paper grew out of discussions which took place at the History of Economic Society Conference held at the Massachusetts Institute of Technology on 10 June, 1994 and is in part based on a seminar, "The Economy and Society of the Hellenistic East," which I offered for the Department of Archeology at Boston University in the Fall of 1994. I am indebted to the students of that seminar, Ms Brenda Cullen, Ms Amy Fisher, Mr Mark Greco, Mr Alexander Ingle, Mr Alan Kaiser, Ms Melissa Moore, Mr Yannick Muller, Mr Eric Parks, and Ms Carol Stein, for the high quality of the research and discussions they undertook on this topic. I am particularly grateful for the on-going dialogue I am engaged in with Alex Ingle on matters pertaining to ancient economies. References to papyri as (P . . .) follow J.F. Oates, et al., *Checklist of Editions of Greek Papyri and Ostraca, Bulletin of the American Society of Papyrologists*, Supplement 4 (1985). Errors of fact or omission and other shortcomings in this paper are of course to be laid at my doorstep.
2 Cf., for example, the papers by Bertram Schefold and Louis Baeck in this volume.
3 For an overview of Finley's work, see Finley (1973; 1981).
4 For a bibliography on this debate, cf. Will (1954); Shaw and Saller 1981: n. 2, ix–xxvi; Cartledge 1983: 1–15. For the bibliography of the formalist/substantivist debate in economic anthropology, see Isaac 1993: 213–233.
5 This view has been championed by Klever (1986) and Lowry (1987). Now see also Baeck (1995).
6 Cf. Hopkins 1980: 101–125 and 1983: n. 3, ix–xxv.
7 For example, Greene (1986).
8 For example, Shanks and Tilley (1992); Hodder (1995).
9 Following the general approach of Said (now cf. Said 1993) a number of scholars have pointed out the Hellenocentric bias of traditional interpretations of the Hellenistic world: Will 1985: 273–301; Samuel (1989); Sherwin-White and Kuhrt 1993, Alcock 1994, 171–190.
10 This interpretation informs, for instance, the best general overview of the Hellenistic world now available in English: Green (1990).
11 For instance, Turner 1984: 118–174, Rathbone 1989: 159–176.
12 See also remarks on Bowman by Bagnall 1988a: 197–202.
13 Cf. Lange and Hirmer 1968: 517–534, Grenier 1980.
14 The best survey of Ptolemaic Alexandrian archeology is still the one presented in Fraser 1972: 3–37.
15 As suggested by Holladay (1982) and Lloyd 1983: n. 20.

16 Cf. also Wallace 1941: 147–161.
17 Cf. Christiansen (1991).
18 For example, Samuel 1989: n. 12, 35–49.
19 Some of the issues involved in assigning cultural identities to archeological assemblages are discussed in Shennan (1989). For the meagerness of the archeological evidence on settlements, see Bowman n.d.: 240–243 and n. 12 above.
20 Cf. the papers in Linders and Alroth (1992). For a demonstration of the close connection of cult and trade at Delos, see Rauh (1993).
21 For a general overview of Ptolemaic fine arts, see Noshy (1937); the independence of the two artistic traditions is stressed by Bianchi, for example, 1978, 95–102.
22 Cf. *P. Lille 1* in Oates (1985).
23 Indeed, Egyptianizing artistic motives were popular throughout the Hellenistic world; cf. Pollitt (1986).
24 Cf. Turner 1984: n. 15, 158.
25 Cf. also Butzer 1980: 5–36.
26 Cf. el-Fakharani 1983, 175–186. I also wish to thank one of the excavators of the site, Professor Creighton Gabel of Boston University, for making some of the unpublished material from this site available to me.
27 For the controversy, see Coulson and Leonard, Jr. 1982: 361–380.
28 Several reports on this survey are available on the World Wide Web at: http:// rome.classics. umich.edu/projects/coptos/desert.html. The most recent is Wright and Herbert (1993).
29 The Michigan/Asiut survey discovered Roman way-stations leading to Leucos Limen; cf. also Whitcomb and Johnson (1982).
30 See Rostovtzeff's interpretation of *P Cair. Zen 59021*, 1951: n. 14, 402.
31 80,000 Rhodian amphoras were reported from Alexandria in 1972, compared to only 6,860 Cnidian; cf. Fraser 1972: n. 18, 165.
32 Cf. Cook 1983–1984: 795–798.
33 Cf. Eph'al 1969: 139–164, Millar 1987: 110–133, Sartre 1989: 9–18.
34 For example, M. Rostovtzeff 1928: 155–195.
35 For example, Sherwin-White and Kuhrt 1993: n. 12.
36 For Ai Khanoum, cf. also Bernard 1982: 148–159. For Failaka, cf. also Salles, 1993: n. 68, 75–109.
37 For cultural exchanges, cf. Morris (1992), Burkert (1992).
38 For the excavations at Al Mina, cf. Woolley 1938: 1–30, 133–170. Since the publication of the substantial quantity of Greek pottery found at Tyre, Woolley's interpretation that Al Mina had a Greek population has come under attack: cf. Elayi 1987: 249–266; for a defense of the traditional view, cf. Boardman 1990: 169–190. The presence of Greek and Cypriot pottery, and a single spindle whorl made of local clay and bearing a Greek inscription, has similarly been taken as sufficient evidence that Tall Sukas had both Greek and Cypriot inhabitants: Lund 1986, 190.
39 For example, from Tall Sukas: Lund 1986: n. 91, to Tel Anafa: Herbert (1994).
40 Cf. Christiansen (1991).
41 Cf. Sherratt 1992: 135–42.

Part IV

ROMAN ECONOMIC THOUGHT

8

THE CLASSICAL ROOTS OF BENEVOLENCE IN ECONOMIC THOUGHT

Gloria Vivenza

This chapter is the result of work begun a few years ago,[1] starting from the intention to retrace the intellectual and historical background of a particular use of the term "benevolence" in economic contexts. I was surprised, in fact, by the parallelism between the famous "it is not from the benevolence of the butcher, the brewer, or the baker, that we expect our dinner, but from their regard to their own interest" (Smith 1976: I.ii.2), and a sentence of the Latin philosopher Seneca who, in *De beneficiis* (1982), states that a merchant who sells his corn produces no benefit, although he really saves the life of a man or of a whole city. None of the persons helped by his act is in debt towards him because he did not think to comfort them, but only to look after his own interests (Seneca, *De beneficiis* VI, 14, 3–4).[2] Another passage from the same work has a vaguely Smithian flavour, as it explains that whatever is done for the sake of gain is not a benefit: *ad alienum commodum pro suo veniunt* ("they [merchants] give advantage to others in order to have their own") (Seneca, *De beneficiis* IV, 13, 3). They produce a positive outcome without having this purpose in mind as a sort of "unintended consequence" with which the ancient world, too, was acquainted in its own way.

The Greek and Roman roots of the concept of benevolence are important, I think, for their implications for moral, economic and political problems; but my "modern" starting point compels me to make clear some particular points. What I would like to trace back is the history of that "benevolence" which influenced medieval and Renaissance thought and became a multifaceted concept whose main characteristic was a double "paradigm" with hierarchical aspects on the one hand, and egalitarian on the other (Vivenza 1995: 511–515). All other connections (for example, with charitable or philanthropic activities, or with God's benevolence towards humanity) must be left aside because they could be confusing. They are out of place in this short treatment, although they will be recalled, when necessary to explain the evolution of the concept.

191

The main point to stress, tracing back the origins of "economic benevolence", is that its beginning is more rightly attributed to early notions of beneficence than to benevolence. Even so, a warning is necessary about the "Christian" usages which are out of place in classical antiquity. It is important to emphasise that Christian ethics, which heavily stressed intention, led in most cases to an almost synonymous use of benevolence and beneficence;[3] to a possible connection between benevolence/beneficence and charity; and to a "providential" concept of benevolence. The latter, being now the virtue *par excellence* of God, surpassed by far every human effort, and moreover could not have a return: men can love God but cannot be "beneficent" towards Him, says St Thomas (*Summa* IIa IIae, Q. 31, A.1, 1).

The Classical approach to beneficence took into consideration the (beneficent) fact, put it in relation with some sort of return (even if only of gratitude), and did not usually consider the benefits charitable actions. This chapter's title is thus dedicated to an abstract noun, which is in fact not primary but derivative, coming from both an adverb (*eu/bene*) and a verb (*ergazomai/facere* [sic *velle*]). Etymological dictionaries start from the Indo-European root of *bonus* originating the adverb *bene* which, coupled with verbs like *facere* or *velle*, gave rise in Latin to compound words that are frequently translations of Greek compounds with *eu*. From these came later the substantive (i.e. *beneficium*), and lastly the abstract noun *beneficentia*.[4] Since the initial stress is on action and fact, a proper approach to the notion of benevolence could perhaps also have been from the term *euergesia/beneficium*.

The main topic of this chapter relates thus both to *euergesia/beneficium* (*beneficentia*), and to *eunoia/benevolentia*, i.e. to a fact and to an intention. The results of both are of the beneficial type, and they gave origin to a great exercise of dialectics. I must apologise, therefore, for some imprecision in my English terminology; it is connected mainly with the difficulty of concentrating the subject into a short space.

THE GREEK BENEFACTORS

In the Greek world, *euergesia* (good deed or *beneficium*) is a very important concept, which has received much attention, especially in the anthropological interpretation of ancient history. Most Greek texts, both literary and epigraphic, have generally been interpreted in a context of "reciprocity". Relating to *euergesiai*, an interpretation in this sense can be explained by the fact that on the one side there was a "benefit" or "gift" in substance and on the other, a duty of return (which might well be represented by an honorary inscription, witnessing the "gratitude" of the city towards the *euergetes*).

The famous "primitivist-modernisers" and "substantivist-formalist" debates cannot be resumed here, but we reiterate, nonetheless, their point about the market economy's being a historical phenomenon and not a paradigm by which to measure all other (pre-industrial) economies (Natali 1979: 345–348), for it is a fruitful initial approach for understanding ancient economics, which were certainly less "primitive" than those of certain periods of the Middle Ages. On the other hand, the numerous analyses of ancient history grounded ultimately on the Polanyian categories, however adopted (and adapted)[5], have proved useful to clarify many problems and to raise interesting discussions.

Lastly by way of introduction to the subject of *euergesiai*, I think it indispensable to refer to the well-known, although controversial, work of Paul Veyne,[6] who pointed out the differences between Greek and Roman euergetism. Moreover, I think it worthwhile to quote Veyne's definition of the main character of the "decision-makers" in ancient economics: "Dans les sociétés anciennes, moins différenciés que les nôtres, toutes les supériorités étaient dans les mêmes mains" (that is to say, the landowner was rich and the only one to invest, as well as being a political authority and entrepreneur). "Il était, comme on le voit, peu spécialisé. Du coup, il était peu rationalisé: *il était trop de choses à la fois.*"[7]

Let us now begin through Greek thought to explain why the Roman Seneca would later speak of benefit, of gratitude, and of the fact that a merchant can save whole cities. In the ancient world, the victualling of towns was of primary importance, at least for big towns (namely Athens, Rome and a few others), about which a lot of evidence has survived. In ancient Greece, there were many different initiatives aiming to avoid the risk of a famine. The term *euergetes* is frequently found on inscriptions testifying to the gratitude of the city towards the person who removed the danger of hunger.[8] The "benefactors" intervened mainly through particular kinds of loans, or other measures: for example, they provided corn for credit, or anticipated the fund for a reserve; sometimes they participated in public subscriptions, consented to the restitution's being delayed, or gave up their interests – to a true gift, however, or a donation, there is seldom testimony (Migeotte 1984: 361).[9] In these kinds of transactions, the presence of traders was not absolutely necessary: some benefactors were landlords, or at least, owners of great quantities of corn. Surely, however, there were also rich merchants who wished to put themselves on the level of the city's upper ranks.

The merchant-benefactor could draw from his action the most valued rewards for a trader (a profession scarcely appreciated in ancient society): the right to own land, exemption from taxes, or other such advantages (Austin and Vidal Naquet 1982: 349–350, Garnsey 1989: 71, Migeotte 1984: 129–130). In my opinion, here is the original connection between the concept of benefit and the action which allows escape from a famine.

Although the good deeds or *euergesiai* of the beneficent were, it is well known, by no means directed only towards food supply – they could be displayed by offering feasts and games, or sumptuous public buildings; educational programmes were also carried out through the aid of benefactors (Marrou 1965: 175 and 437, Hands 1968: 116–130 and 194–202) – now, however, we are interested in stressing the conceptual connection between a commercial business (although subject to peculiar public interventions) and the "benefit" of having the corn available. This connection is clearly expressed in a passage of Polybius' history (1954: IV, 38, 10). Describing the trade from Byzantium, he does not hesitate to define the Pontic city as the "benefactor" (*euergetes*) of all Greece, which in turn ought to pay gratitude to Byzantium. Gratitude is the typical response to the beneficial action.[10]

The victualling of the city was thus not a form of public assistance, but rather a measure of civic administration, which involved, almost on equal ground, the politicians, the merchants and the landowners having corn reserves. Interactions between political authorities, merchants and benefactors are recorded (Garnsey 1989: part II, 5).[11] Although price was not formed through what today would be called free-market competition and even if the ancient corn trade was never completely free, the mechanism of supply and demand could yet have some relevance (Montgomery 1986: 47). Of course, the possibility of disposing of corn depended in good measure on traders; accepting to keep the price controlled they acquired the favour of the city – let us say, the gratitude. The city preserved, however, its role and authority: from the content of a Greek inscription, for instance, we can perceive that although the city was in the hands of its benefactor, it maintained its superiority over him, who simply behaved as was expected of a good citizen.[12]

A connection has been noticed between *proxenia* (a public hospitality or patronage, frequently representing the interests of a foreign community) and *euergesiai* (Foucart 1888: 162–169; Wilhelm 1942: 11–86; Meiggs and Lewis 1969: 201–203, 248–250, 275–277).[13] It is not always easy to distinguish between a rich man who benefits a city while exercising a magistrature and a private citizen who acts out of personal generosity. At least during the fifth century BC many benefactors were strangers.

With the fourth century BC came, in any case, the period in which the *euergesiai* of citizens began to prevail, as indicated by a coincidence between literary and epigraphic texts. The explanation of E. Levy (1976) is that, after the defeat of 404, Athenian citizens could no longer identify themselves with an ideology of power and political participation. Therefore, they shifted their ideology towards "service" rendered to the city. The important source of Attic civil orations shows that one of the *formulae* used to describe this devotion was "to serve the city with one's own body and riches" (Aristotle, *The Athenian polis* XXIX, 5).[14] This attitude put on the same ground the defense of the polis and the *euergesia*, i.e. bravery and generosity.

A new "ideology" of moderation and *homonoia* existed, in which wealth, no longer considered a mark of superiority, had to provide for the needs of the city. This perspective had the singular characteristic of presenting the compulsory duties of rich citizens (*eisphorai* and *leitourgiai*) as gifts spontaneously accorded to the polis. The gratitude of the city was usually represented by leniency in trials (Levy 1976: 238–252).[15]

DIFFERENT TYPES OF BENEFITS

Thus by the fourth century, an additional important feature of the virtue of *euergesia* was emerging: the rich man had to benefit both his city and his friends, the city being considered like a friend to be benefited.[16] Here we enter into the field of the concept of *philia*, also relevant in ancient economic thought. Aristotle treated the various types of *philia* in Books VIII and IX of the *Nicomachean Ethics* (1934; 1975), whose influence on subsequent thought could hardly be overrated. On this subject, one of his first sentences is that the rich and powerful man needs friends, *philoi*, to be able to exercise his *euergesia* (Aristotle, *Nicomachean Ethics* 1155a 6–9). If nobody needs his generosity, how would he show it? This assertion runs against the well-known principle that a man of virtue ought to be self-sufficient, as Aristotle himself emphasised (ibid. 1169b 3–10).

Here "euergetic" *philia* ("friendship") is stressed as representing a bilateral relationship between a powerful benefactor and a needy antagonist, so to speak. This situation develops into a conceptualised hierarchical relationship, also involving the concept of authority (Aristotle's examples are "a king and the ruled" and "a father and sons", *Nicomachean Ethics* (1934; 1975) 1161a 10–12 and 20–21).[17] The benefactor is always in a position of superiority in relation to the benefited (also noticed by Thucydides, (1965–69) II, 40, 4). The needy can and does have a personal relationship with his benefactor, although from a position of inferiority.

Since "euergetic" *philia* occurs between unequal persons, it is connected with utility (ibid. (1934; 1975) 1155b 19–21; 1168a 9–14). The most striking inequality is between kings and the ruled; the "friendship" of a king for his subjects shows itself in a superiority of *euergesiai* (ibid. 1161a 11–12). Let us remember, however, that by the same token the rich and powerful, such as the kings, are really in *need* of friends, just to have somebody to benefit. Thus, the relationship, although unequal, is utilitarian on both sides. Examples of utilitarian friendship are those between the rich and the poor, but also between the learned and the ignorant (ibid. 1159b 13–15).

This concept of *philia* is related to the main difference between benevolence and beneficence: the good will and the good action. In ancient thought, these two aspects are connected, but in a particular way, for while "euergetic" and thus directed to action (as Aristotle points out it must be, *Nicomachean Ethics* (1934; 1975) 1168a 6–12 and 23–24), the concept of *philia* (and *philanthropia*, too) was fundamentally connected to a sentiment. Thus Aristotle calls *philia* one of the sentiments prompting beneficial actions. Just as real beneficence ought to be spontaneous, although possibly calculated (in any case, not forced), so too the first characteristic of benevolence is to be voluntary, or voluntarily accepted (for reasons of prestige, politics, or ambition): it also cannot be forced. Therefore, it may have been a very subtle "psychological" reasoning which led wealthy Athenian citizens to claim as *euergesia* towards their city their having had to spend money on liturgies, etc. Perhaps, at this time, the only way wealthy Athenians could maintain their sense of social and political superiority was to attribute their forced generosity to their own free will.

Plato, although talking about good deeds outside the context of friendship, underlines the fact that *euergesiai* are fourfold: they can be exercised by means of money, body, knowledge or speech (Diogenes Laertes 1981: III, 95–96). The *euergesiai* exercised with body and riches have been briefly mentioned above, among the services rendered to the city. Including help given in the form of particular abilities – by means of knowledge and speech – enlarged the field of possible benefits to the services of teachers, doctors, lawyers, etc. The services of the "liberal" professions were reputed in the ancient world to be "benefits" which expected a "return", not a payment or fee (Finley 1985: 50–57).

The "beneficial" or utilitarian friendship had undoubtedly complex rules for returns, especially when the connection was through family or hospitality. In this kind of relationship, it was considered good that "an exact balance cannot be struck: a guarantee that the association will continue" (Millett 1990: 184).

It might be noted that there are also instances of different uses of the concept of *euergesia*, with no (direct) tie to economic activities. From the second century BC the Romans are frequently called *euergetai* in Greek inscriptions. They are considered the benefactors of Greece, and of all humanity, having freed peoples from enemies (*barbaroi*). Another, more peaceful, benefactor, is the mythical inventor of arts and of technical knowledge, the *protos euretes* who redeemed humanity from barbarism and roughness (Wolkmann 1954: 467–470);[18] here, the concept of *euergesia* overlaps that of *philanthropia*.

The non-economic *euergesiai* have a different character from those defined above as services to the city, or between friends. The superiority of the benefactor who addresses his action to a whole population, or to entire humanity, has no longer the character of a really bilateral (almost contractual) relationship, nor is it a personal tie between two persons of different social weight, a tie with certain rules to be respected by both parties. The much greater, and usually non-material, benefit of the mythical "liberator" from fear and barbarism cannot be returned or reciprocated. It is like the gift of a god; and in fact, as we shall read in Cicero, the greatest benefit given by the gods to men is reason: a non-economic good (*De natura deorum* (1951: II, 34); *De officiis* (1931: I, 1, 1).

Here we enter into a subject whose importance for the subsequent "beneficial" theory is crucial. The greatest benefactor is God in Christian thought; but this topos is not completely lacking in pre-Christian sources. In fact, the epithet *euergetes*, alone or coupled with *soter*, has been applied to pagan gods together with other "human" adjectives as just, wise or good. *Euergetes* really pertains to the human sphere; but its use is willingly extended to extraordinary, almost superhuman, performances. Plutarch witnesses a widespread attitude of rulers and generals who, trying to put themselves on the same level as Alexander the Great, called themselves *soteres*, great, victorious, *euergetai*. This custom spread also in Roman times (Plutarch, *de Alexandri Magni forti et virtuosi* (1575): II, 338C).[19] It shows an eagerness, so to speak, to be considered a "benefactor", because this implied an almost supernatural personality.

In the Hellenistic period the worship of *euergetai* is widespread. We are informed that Athenian *ephebes* and their magistrates used to offer sacrifices to the gods and to the *euergetai* in the period between the end of the second and the beginning of the first century BC (Robert 1926: 499–500). A strong tie was thus established between gods and benefactors. Moreover, in some instances the gods themselves are described as benefactors (Nock 1972: 725–726). The relationship of identity between a god and a man exercising his *euergesia* towards other men is further illustrated by sentences, both in Greek and in Latin, which say more or less, "For a man, to benefit others is a way to be divine" (Bolkestein 1979: 173–174).

Thus far, we can summarise the main characteristics of the virtue of *euergesia* in the Greek world. There is, first of all, an emphasis on facts. *Euergesiai* are concrete benefits: corn, other food, buildings or water provisions. Obviously, they give an essential role to the rich, whether landowner or merchant. I find significant that not only traders, but also a commercial centre like Byzantium, deserved this name, implying that, despite the prevailing role of landed wealth, the importance of commercial connections was fully realised. Further, it underlines the main character of the ancient Greek economy. With *euergesia* in connection with *philia*, a peculiar bilateral, and personal, relationship between benefactor and benefited, with its "reciprocative" aspects and its basically unequal relationship, was maintained.

This relationship between benefactor and beneficiary is usually studied in connection with an anthropological pattern of primitive/archaic societies. There is now a literature on exchange relations between donor and receiver, grounded ultimately on Mauss' work on gift and on Polanyi's reciprocity (1983), which has been much elaborated and developed. This sheds light on the origin of particular types of economic relations, for example, the gift exchange that in the long run took the character of a postponed exchange or of a loan (Millett 1990: 181–84, 1991: 36–44 and *passim*). Besides the material benefit, it is, however, possible to single out another kind of advantage, which contributed to a shift in the meaning of the word *euergesia* towards a more abstract sense. The superhuman benefactor, so to speak, comes to the fore. He may be a great general, a great politician, a mythical inventor, and so on. He is a man, but his "gifts" are so great that they cannot be reciprocated, and therefore he is considered almost a god. Here the relationship is no longer between two persons, but on a different level; there is on the one hand the benefactor, on the other, a whole people. Further, it is not the same relation as that existing between city and benefactor. The city, although being a community, is treated "as a friend", or, the benefited partner of the euergetic relationship between two individuals.

THE ROMAN APPROACH

Classical authors' use of the Latin language reflects a very clear preference for *benignitas* instead of *benevolentia/beneficentia*. According to an authoritative opinion, *beneficentia* was created by Cicero himself (Bolkestein 1979: 313). In fact, Cicero is the main user of it (and of *benevolentia*), with Seneca, Val. Maximus and the panegyrists.

Cicero, as is well known, was imbued with Greek philosophy and was very familiar with Greek culture; but we cannot forget that he also had the greatest concern for Roman traditions. One of these traditions was the relationship between patron and client, a peculiarly Roman institution, a "private" connection which, however, is not to be considered completely private, given the political relevance of the personal ties.

The patron–client relationship has important relevance to our subject: it belongs to the patron to give a *beneficium*, and to the client to give, in return, *officium* or *gratia*. The same terminology was also proved applicable to political and inter-state relations.[20]

It has been stressed that the character of this relationship was a "vertical" one, i.e. between unequal parties, and on a voluntary basis (Hellegouarc'h 1963: 163–169, 149–150).[21] Perhaps its most important feature for our subject is that the Roman politician acquires very early the character of a "benefactor".[22] It is difficult indeed to distinguish between public and private in this field (Braund 1989: 142). Moreover, we have to link the patron–client relationship (or at least its terminology) with political ties relating to different levels. The terminology did not change if the *patronus* was a magistrate giving his *beneficia* to the whole population subject to his jurisdiction, or the emperor bestowing important responsibilities and offices on his friends, or gifts on his subjects in general.[23]

198

On the "horizontal" side of social relations, however, a growing awareness of the generalised human capability of collaboration was becoming
incorporated into political and philosophical reasoning. Reading Cicero's
De officiis (1931), we find many references to this natural sociality of men.
Cooperation (and interdependence) among men leads to the gathering and
exchange of products, while the establishment of law and order encourages
the activities providing for the needs and commodities of human life (*De
officiis* II, 11–15).[24] These subjects were philosophically related to the
concept of utility, just as their practical enforcement was aimed at the well-
being of people from, among others, a material point of view. The magistrates charged with the *annona* provided a "benefit" to the body of citizens
(Veyne 1976: 447–451, Giardina 1989: 290). And Cicero placed their activity
(which appears with the character of a good administration), although
prompted by ambition rather than by altruism or carefulness, only in the
category of benefits. Besides the *cura annonae*, this activity involves
the task of increasing the State's resources. Unfortunately, Cicero says
nothing about the ways in which the magistrates carried out this duty (*De
officiis* II, 74; 52–58; 85).[25]

Now, Rome had a political structure very different from Greek and even
Hellenistic cities; moreover, it adopted from the beginning a different
strategy for supplying corn: the military conquest of the corn-producing
districts and the collection of provincial taxes directly in kind (Polanyi
1983: 310, Garnsey 1983: 118–128, 1989: 196–197). Therefore, private "beneficence" towards cities was replaced by state provisioning for the people.
It is of great interest, also for subsequent political thought, that many
enterprises devoted to public utility were categorised as *beneficia* or as the
similar, although not identical, *largitiones*. The donations were not always
inspired only by the principle of donor prestige, although this frequently
happened. Evidence from Cicero shows a minimum of rationality in the
preference of shipyards, harbours, aqueducts, city walls and other useful
buildings as donations over theatres, temples and arcades. It reveals, moreover, that the topic was discussed in these terms even in Cicero's Greek
sources (*De officiis* (1931) II, 60).[26] The modern topos of the "benevolence"
of the statesman has its origin here.

Apart from "public" benefits, there was also a wide range of private
good offices deriving from the favoured term, *benignitas/liberalitas*. In *De
officiis* II, 55, Cicero (1931) defines as *liberates* those who, among other
things, *aut aes alienum suscipiunt amicorum ... aut opitulantur vel in re
quaerenda vel augenda*. It has been noticed that the last independent
clause, while showing a participation in some sort of economic business,
is characteristically placed by Cicero into a "code" of mutual aid, instead
of a context of economic or juridical character. In Rome, as in Greece,
there was an important network of loans which covered a great deal of
social intercourse. Since such loans were considered duties of friendship,

they were kept outside the sphere of interest and of commerce (Nicolet 1982: 930–931).

PHILOSOPHICAL INTERPRETATIONS

In the mean time, Roman interest in ethics deepened research in certain fields, like in the conflict between interest and civic spirit or solidarity. A very famous example from Cicero reports the case of a merchant carrying corn from Alexandria to Rhodes in times of famine, who observes other vessels doing the same thing. Should he reveal this fact at his arrival, or can he keep silent? Cicero, a good moralist, favours total disclosure (*De officiis* (1931) III, 50–53)[27] – his discourse, it must be said, deals with the (supposed) opposition between the useful and the honest.

It is interesting to notice that the matter of ethical commercial behaviour was already discussed by Cicero's Greek sources, the Stoic philosophers Diogenes of Babylon and his pupil Antipater, both firm in opposing positions. However, Seneca deals with the subject from yet another point of view: his merchant does not take conscience into account. Seneca does not tell us if he is working in competition with others, nor does he discuss the general idea of exchange along with its moral implications. The only thing strongly underlined is that nothing is owed to a seller. The fact that Seneca insists[28] on gratitude as *not* being due to the merchant suggests that a long time has passed since the merchant, although selling his corn (even if at a controlled price), was considered a benefactor and received gratitude for it (as well as, it must be remembered, concrete rewards). Over time, the payment received by the merchant rid the purchaser of the corn (and, with it, of life) of the duty of gratitude: good has been done, but for interest.

In fact, we can record a shifting of the beneficial perspective towards a specification of the difference between an economic transaction with euergetic character and a normal contract, which usually puts the contracting parts on the same level and has an impersonal character. This difference is somewhat perceptible between two Roman treatises: one by Cicero, *De officiis* and one by Seneca, *De beneficiis*.

Cicero's *De officiis* (1931) devotes lengthy passages (in Book I, 42–60 and Book II, 32, 52–85) to *benevolentia/beneficentia*, sometimes also defined as *bonitas, benignitas, liberalitas*. The general definition is the well-known statement in *De officiis* I, 20, where the virtues constitutive of society are justice and *beneficentia*, whose other names are precisely *benignitas* or *liberalitas*.

After a "genetic" analysis of the benevolent/beneficent impulse, to which we shall return later, Cicero speaks of various concrete *beneficia*, divided into two main categories. The virtue of *beneficentia/liberalitas* can be acted out in *opera* (labour, but in the sense of a "profession" like that of the *iuris peritus*), or with *pecunia*. Cicero says that the first is *lautior ac splendidior ac viro forti claroque dignior*, but the second is *facilior* (*De officiis* (1931) II, 52). In any case, both can be practised towards the state, as well as towards private citizens. We could, perhaps, recognise here an echo of the Greek *euergesia* towards the city and the friends.

Although Cicero distinguishes only two ways of expressing *beneficia*, the Platonic fourfold division of expressions, money, body, knowledge or speech is not entirely forgotten. In fact, speaking of the benefit by competence (*opera*) given by the ancient interpreters of civil law, their superior knowledge is reckoned by Cicero in the field of *scientia* (ibid. 65). Further, he found it superfluous to recall the great benefits that a good orator can bestow on the state (ibid. 66).

The most instructive passage on public or political beneficence is *De officiis* II, 72–85. Cicero (1931) starts from the well-known principle that the State exists just for safeguarding private property and cannot withdraw from this task. So the *beneficia* of a political ruler are to be against agrarian laws and excessive corn distributions, remissions of debts and corruption. I do not insist on the peculiarity of these conservative Ciceronian positions, which have been much studied in relation to the political history of the late Roman Republic and the character of Cicero himself. What I would like to stress is the fact that these political positions are included in the category of *beneficia*; and that a consideration of benevolence/beneficence in political decisions (and in a ruler's attitude) stood firmly, from this moment onwards, in European political thought (Vivenza 1995: 510).

As for "private" beneficence, Cicero follows traditional euergetic positions, connected with the patron–client relationship. A vaguely ironical observation in *De officiis* (1931) II, 69 informs us that people having a high consideration of themselves refused to recognise the obligation deriving from receiving a benefit. They preferred to die rather than to be called *clientes* and to admit that they received *patrocinium*. The reason is easy (for us) to understand, and it is the same given by Thucydides (1965–69): the person who gives is in a higher position. Therefore, the receiver is humbler; some, it seems, did not like to be in this situation. It is better, concludes Cicero, to benefit a really poor and honest man: at least he is sincerely grateful.

About a century after Cicero, Seneca wrote a treatise intentionally devoted to benefits. Both Cicero and Seneca had political responsibilities, but they were also philosophers trying to reconcile thought and action (Nicolet 1982: 921). In comparison with other writers, they could therefore point out the connections between moral, political and economic considerations with a more complete outlook. Their influence on subsequent economic thought is perhaps greater than has been suspected until now (no need to recall the well-known circumstance that in most textbooks of the history of economic thought the character of originality is usually given to Greek philosophy, while Roman thought is generally dismissed as derivative and unimportant).

As Seneca's *De beneficiis* (1982) is focused just on benefits, the subject is treated with more care and depth than in Cicero's work, which addressed the topic on occasion. We cannot, however, thoroughly analyse it here, so we limit our comments to a few points.

First, there is, generally speaking, a stronger emphasis by Seneca on intention, expressed through words like *voluntas*, but also *mens, animus,* etc.[29] This means not only that the benefit must be voluntarily (i.e. freely) given, but also that, if the good intention cannot be followed by facts (for some inconvenience of which the would-be benefactor is not responsible), a certain consideration must be afforded to the intention itself. We can only briefly hint at the importance of intention subsequently in Christian Biblical ethics: the good (as well as the sin) that you have sincerely wished for in your heart is really done.[30] This means, in a certain way, that reality is not so much a matter of concrete facts, as a spiritual dimension in which the material relations tend to be differently envisaged.

Second, Seneca stresses very frequently a difference between a benefit and an economic transaction, namely usury in most cases. This is a very interesting topic, generally starting from the traditional balance of giving-and-returning, typical of beneficial relations. If one is, however, *too much* attentive to return (whether to receive or to give it), Seneca says, this is the attitude of contracting parties.[31] Here, in Seneca, the connection to friendship comes to the fore. Seneca (1982) emphasises the fact that, in the "contractual" relationship, the payment is liberating: *si reddidi, solutus sum ac fiber*. True friendship, however, does not allow this: the relationship must continue, and begin again after every "gift" and "countergift" (*De beneficiis* II, 18, 5).[32] The latter is simply the beneficial relationship.

What is interesting is that Seneca arrived at a comparison between the two, realising that the economic transaction has an "exact" balance, which the beneficial relationship cannot have, although involving economic interests. The exact balance, in fact, rules out the elements of discretion, and also that of the inequality of the parties. Its neutral or impersonal character, moreover, prevents the traditional elements of benevolence and gratitude from being taken into consideration. This awareness brings Seneca to distinguish between the beneficial and the economic aspects of certain actions: for example, how to evaluate the gift given at the right moment, with future good consequences (*De beneficiis* (1982) III, 8, 3); or how to give the right value to the services of a teacher or of a doctor (where the problem is solved through friendship: *quia ex medico praeceptore in amicum transeunt et nos non arte, quam vendunt, obligant, sed benigna et familiari voluntate* – *De beneficiis* VI, 15, 2; 16, 1).

Third, the traditional dualism between the superiority of the giver and the inferiority of the receiver begins to fade. Seneca asks if a slave can benefit his master and gives a positive answer, although revealing that the subject is controversial (*De beneficiis* (1982) III, 18–28). Something similar can be said of the possibility for a son to benefit his father (*De beneficiis* III, 29–38). To sum up, the "natural" relationship of authority, which could not allow the benefit to go in the opposite direction of authority itself, begins to have fading borders.

I think that this is due to Seneca's stronger emphasis on those benefits which are difficult or impossible to return.[33] This breaks, in a certain way, the bilateral, although unequal, relationship, in the sense that the inferiority of the receiver is so heavily stressed, that whatever he can do to reciprocate will never be enough, that is to say, proportioned to the received benefit. On the other hand, Seneca (1982) repeats the old dictum *qui dat beneficia, deos imitator* (*De beneficiis* III, 15, 4): a superiority further stressed by the fact that God gives also to ungrateful people (ibid. IV, 28, 1–4). This is a more subtle way to alter the traditional relationship. By lowering the importance of the grateful return, the higher status of the giver is clear; all are equal under his rule.

This idea was not completely absent in Cicero's work. In *De natura deorum* (1951) we see that the "beneficence" of the gods towards men is usually defined as *gratia* or *caritas* (man has to return *pietas* rather than gratitude) (Cicero, *De natura deorum* I, 116, 121–122, 124. There is at least one equating of *gratia* with *bonitas* and *beneficentia* (ibid. 121), the virtues of the "person" who is *praestans*, or in highest standing. Whatever brings great *utilitas* to mankind cannot happen without the *bonitas* of the gods towards men (ibid. II, 60); we said above that among the greatest *beneficia* granted from the gods to men was reason. This has to do with deities, but during the later Roman empire, the sovereign will have, as his own character, that of a benevolent/benefactor (Veyne 1976: 621–632; Nutton 1978: 209–221; Nock 1972: 720–735).

CONCLUDING REMARKS

This is by no means a complete picture of the classical concept of benevolence/beneficence, only an outline of the main topics related to this concept.

The most striking feature of traditional beneficence/benevolence is its binding character. The benefit, actually given, must be reciprocated. The anthropological paradigm of gift and countergift relation fits well in this picture, but it is not the only possible one. If it was impossible to do otherwise, in classical antiquity, the simple acknowledgement of being in debt was sufficient to show one's gratitude towards the donor. Furthermore, there were many different ways to reciprocate: from the noted honorary inscriptions to the votes of the Roman *clientes*.

This relationship has a political dimension, deriving ultimately from the ancestral tradition of personal obligations typical of the classical polis. This tradition was already in crisis in the final period of the Roman Republic (Lepore 1954: 343–344); but the political terminology of the ancient world proved to be very lasting (Ignatieff 1986: 126–127).

Many economic and political measures were included in the class of benefits, or beneficial actions, and therefore ascribed to the benevolent, generous, liberal inclination of the person who had the means to do such things. The benefit ought to arise spontaneously from the citizen's civic spirit without any constraint,[34] apart from a moral duty, such as "noblesse oblige". This kind of benefit came from "high quarters": the rich benefactor, the statesman or the emperor. The merchant could be part of this privileged category, provided he was rich enough and well integrated into the ruling society.

With regard to trade, instead of repeating the argument of ethical and social discrimination, let us point out the other side of the coin: even in the ancient world trade was regulated by ethical principles and law. The same Ciceronian passage which reports the opposite opinions of Diogenes and Antipater informs us that civil law compelled the seller to state the imperfections of his wares, and to avoid fraud. This may be one of the roots of the modern rehabilitation of commerce, represented as an activity compelling men to entertain relations characterised by correctness and honesty. In general, however, civic organisation in the ancient world gave first place to non-economic relations, even in the case of commercial enterprises connected to the political-administrative sphere. This gave rise to a sort of personal relationship between authorities and citizens, due to a "civic sense" in the Greek polis, to ambition and patronage in the Roman Republic, and finally, in the Roman Empire, to the "benevolence/beneficence" of the emperors, who, whatever they did, were called benefactors.

The virtue which was considered to prompt the beneficial attitude is ambition, love of glory, care for one's own reputation, rather than (or together with) benevolence. Sometimes benevolentia comes from the other side of the relationship: a generous man exercising liberalitas is surrounded by the benevolentia of a lot of people (Cicero (1931) De finibus II, 84). And in De officiis II, 32, Cicero states that voluntate benefica benevolentia movetur: it is good to have the renown of being generous to gain the favour of the multitude.

It is necessary, at this point, to elaborate on a concept which has been too much sacrificed in this discussion: the concept of utilitas, linked from ancient times to another economically relevant concept, "need". It is part of utilitas to rescue men from a condition of necessitas, and the final result is the beneficium. This may happen both on the political level and on the private one, where the relevance of the concept of philia has been pointed out above. In the Aristotelian text, the philia between unequals is grounded on utility. As was said before, a certain self-interested attitude was not limited to the receiver, but it was shared by the giver.

The treatment of *philia* does not belong to this chapter; although it is necessary to point out that in the books of the *Nicomachean Ethics* devoted to this virtue, there is a connection between a traditional aspect of *euergesia* and an aspect of *philia* as "reciprocity", according to which friendship, the bilateral relationship involves a refined balance of giving and receiving (Aristotle *Nicomachean Ethics* 1164b 8–1165a 14).[35] Moreover, in the text of Aristotle, an important distinction is also drawn between *philia* and *eunoia*. The virtue corresponding to *eunoia* (usually translated into English as "goodwill") is a general feeling directed towards all men; it is not reciprocal and may be unknown to its object (ibid. 1155b 32–1156a 5, 1166b 30–1167a 21). Goodwill may be the beginning of friendship, but it is "inoperative", i.e. not aimed at action.

In Cicero's *De amicitia*, where some Aristotelian concepts are recognisable, the Greek *eunoia* is translated quite rightly with *benevolentia*.[36] Now, this *benevolentia* has a different character from the *amicitia* relationship; it is something very near to the primary social link between all men, namely the *societas* and *coniunctio hominum*. This primary social impulse has been called sociability and has gained in importance in modern political thought (Hont 1987). In classical philosophy it was formulated differently by different philosophers, but was connected to the topic of *eunoia/benevolentia*; the human congregation begins in benevolence. This *benevolentia* was placed by Cicero at the opening of his discussion of *beneficentia/liberalitas* (*De officiis* I, 50) where he identifies this different sort of *benevolentia*. It is the goodwill that prompts men to come together and collaborate, following a natural instinct which begins with the human couple and its children, extending itself to brothers, cousins, friends and the *res publica* (Cicero, *De officiis* I, 53–58).[37]

This *benevolentia* has a different character from the euergetic relationship; or, to be more precise, it is one of its preconditions. Although its root is probably the same, or very close, it is different from the euergetic *beneficentia/liberalitas* to which Cicero gives his most complete treatment in Book II of *De officiis*. In Cicero, as well as in other authors, we can find references to both concepts. The name of *benevolentia/beneficentia* is given mainly by him to *liberalitas*, generosity, or also to what we call today, good offices, indicating a wide range of actions. Described by Cicero with a terminology less frequently connected with that of benevolence (*De officiis* I, 11–12; II, 11–15; *De finibus* III, 62–66), this kind of "benevolence" is included in the general study of human nature.

Since Book II of *De officiis* is devoted to *utilitas*, we find in Cicero's discussion material of a utilitarian character instead of the praise of unselfish generosity;[38] he depicts the inclination of man to a *societas vitae* with other human beings as a natural instinct with utilitarian aims.[39] The results of this *benevolentia* (like those of *beneficentia*, friendship, etc.) were of the beneficial type, for here is a type of *utilitas* or *commoditas* arising from this kind of benevolence. The "utilitarian" aspect of the relationship is the result of the natural social propensity (expressed in the form of benefits bestowed on the beloved persons). No house or city could exist, nor cultivation of the soil, and so on, if one were to take away the *ex rerum natura benevolentiae coniunctiorem* (Cicero, *De amicitia* VI, 23).

The kind of utilitarianism resulting from the joint action of a community is, however, of a different sort from that deriving from the benefit bestowed from an important and powerful man. The former is not an unequal relationship, like that of *beneficentia*. There is no rich/powerful party on the one hand, and poor/needy one on the other; the need is shared by all human beings. It is grounded on a different basis: the "necessity" is of all men, and society has an interest in organising itself for co-operation. For this reason, Nature has endowed men with a suitable instinct. Now the element of gratitude leaves the stage, as it is no more a question of benefits (coming from a high level) bestowed by a powerful man on needy people, but of a generalised situation, common to all mankind.

The philosophical interpretations of Cicero and Seneca are mainly directed to energetic benevolence. Cicero emphasises more than Seneca the political prestige given by *liberalitas*. The private side of the Ciceronian beneficence is summarised by the sentence: *summi cuiusque bonitas commune perfugium est omnium* (Cicero, *De officiis* II, 63). It is preceded by a series of advice about giving to the right person, to a deserving man, etc. This casuistry is widely enlarged by Seneca, who illustrates the various ways of giving and receiving. Seneca seems more inclined to stress the private side of this virtue, and not only because the *beneficentia* of Nero could be somewhat difficult to demonstrate. The fact is that Seneca also perceived the distinction between the traditional *euergesia* and an economic transaction in a more subtle way.

It would be out of place to summarise here the ancients' opinions about economic intercourse, such as the well-known Aristotelian censure of usury or of trade beyond the limits of a city's self-sufficiency, but I would like to stress their differentiation between the "beneficial ideology" and an economic transaction. The "exact balance" of a contractual relationship has been expressed by Seneca in opposition to *amicitia*: when I have payed my due, our relationship is finished, and I am free. This sort of "independence" could not have been easily accepted in the ancient world. Moses Finley wrote a famous passage on the fact that the services of the most celebrated Roman lawyer were gratuitous (Finley 1985: 57);[40] but in fact all "benefits" had to be reciprocated: in politics, with loyalty, in private life – according to circumstances and to *status* – possibly only with gratitude. Gratitude is, in a certain manner, the clue to the relationship between the rich/powerful man who gives the benefit, and the person who cannot reciprocate with a material equivalent.

The Latin-Christian rhetorician Lactantius specified that the necessary qualification of *beneficentia* was the need of the receiver, *beneficentia enim nulla est ubicumque necessitas non est* (Lactantius *Institutiones divinae* VI, 11, 26), which is to say that the goodwill of the giver was not enough. It was considered necessary that the receiver had not the possibility to return adequately at the moment, and hence would remain in debt. The impossibility to return with an exact equivalent maintains the obligation of the beneficiary.

I wish to add to this fundamental characteristic that in the beneficial relationship some noblemen's qualities are involved: generosity, magnanimity and liberality on the one hand; gratitude, loyalty and devotion on the other. While the economic aspects of the relationship are not concealed, most important is the social bond which maintains the traditional character of the superiority of the rich and of the (grateful) inferiority of the lower ranks. It is not by chance that this ideology is sometimes tied with that of *homonoia* or *concordia* (Levy 1976: 238, 254–255).[41]

The balance, really, is not even "exact" in commercial relations, according to ancient thought. A well-known (and long-survived) sentence of Aristotle states that commercial transactions involve the profit of one party at the expense of another (Aristotle, *Politics* 1258b 1–2). Both the merchant and the usurer are prompted by avidity and fraud; moreover, they draw a surplus of money from their transactions: this surplus is completely "unnatural" according to Aristotle. It derives from money itself,[42] and not from the virtue of men.

Modern economic thought has devoted a great deal of reasoning to the contrast between benevolence and self-interest. Perhaps, as a final concluding point, it might be useful to keep in mind some Aristotelian and Ciceronian formulations. In the relationship of friendship, the benevolence which extends to others reflects that which we have for ourselves; or, in other words, self-love is the basis for loving others (Aristotle, *Nicomachean Ethics* 1166a 30–1166b 1, 1168b 5–7; Cicero, *De amicitia* XXI, 80). In the Renaissance revival of the Aristotelian "practical" sciences (ethics, economics, politics), Books VIII and IX of the *Nicomachean Ethics* were frequently edited, with the Aristotelian *eunoia* duly translated as *benevolentia*. Book IX is full of pertinent references, and Chapters 2, 5, 6 and 7 are entitled respectively: *singulis pro dignitate beneficia esse rependenda*; *de benevolentia; de concordia; de beneficentia*. Chapter 8 is entitled *De amore sui* (Aristotle's *philautia*, or self-love). I think it is difficult to overrate the importance of the close contact of these two virtues (benevolence/beneficence, and self-love) for the subsequent ethical and economic thought.[43]

NOTES

1 After a first, unrealised project to present a paper on this subject at the nineteenth annual Meeting of the History of Economics Society in 1992, a short paper was written in Italian, cf. Vivenza (1995). This was followed by a seminar given at the Bologna–Cambridge–Harvard Senior Research Seminar Network (proceedings forthcoming). The present chapter is an enlarged version of the "classical" side of the previous paper.

2 Cf. Nicolet 1982: 918.

3 In Thomas Aquinas' definition, *beneficentia et benevolentia non differunt nisi sicut actus exterior et interior, quia beneficentia est executio benevolentiae* (*Summa*, IIa IIae, Q.31, A.4). Cf. also Augustine of Hippo's expressions which link together *benevolentia* and *beneficentia* in *De civitate dei* 18, 51; 8, 25.

4 Cf., for example, Ernout-Meillet (n.d.) on *bonus*.

5 Many of the papers presented at the conference *Economic Thought and Economic Reality in Ancient Greece*, Delphi, 23–26 September 1994 (proceedings forthcoming), show that the "ghost of Polanyi" is still quite alive, with its derivative offspring. Cf. a critical summary of Polanyi's theories in Millett 1990: 169–171.

6 Cf. in general Veyne (1969). On the famous Veyne (1976), cf. Andreau, Schmitt and Schnapp 1978: 307–325. Cf. also Gauthier 1985: 7–10 and Forbis 1993: 485.

7 Debate on anthropological history in *Annales ESC* 1974: 1379; author's italics. Veyne speaks on the authority of R. Dahl.

8 Examples in Migeotte 1984: 41–44, 128–130, 210–212. Cf. also Gauthier 1985: 35, 69–73. Maybe sometimes it was a question of rising prices and lack of distribution, cf. Garnsey 1989: 38 and Rathbone 1983: 48–49.

9 The famous Moschion (on whose liberalities, cf. also Veyne 1976: 223 and 233–234), did intervene three times in the victualling problems of Priene, but only once did he provide the corn for free.

10 Plato, in *Laws* 918B, considers the merchant a benefactor because "he renders even and symmetrical the distribution of any kind of goods". Cf. also Xenophon, *Poroi*, III, 4.

11 In regard to Athenian evidence in the fourth century, cf. especially Garnsey 1989: 154–164.

12 SIG³, n. 495, on which cf. Veyne 1976: 235–236.

13 Also J. Oehler on *euergetes* in Pauly, Wissowa and Kroll (1909), VI: 978–981.

14 Cf. Levy 1976: 250 and Vannier 1988: 106–114.

15 Levy recognises that the character of the source of evidence for this assertion – judicial orations – might distort the relevance of the theme of gratitude. Nonetheless, he asserts that all relations between citizens and polis seem by the fourth century to have been grounded on the dialectics benefit/gratitude. In disagreement with Levy's interpretation, cf. Vannier 1988: 117–125.

16 Cf. Levy 1976: 240.

17 Its importance in medieval thought must be stressed, although I will not be dealing with it here.

18 Cf. also Ferrary 1988: 117–132 (relating only to political "benefactors").

19 Cf. Scott 1929: 124 and Nock 1972: 726ff. Probably Plutarch alludes to Ptolemy VIII Euergetes. The *soter* could have been Ptolemy IX, while the other two epithets can be connected with Antiochus III and Seleucus II. The Roman path to this military (and later on, imperial) propaganda stresses the virtue of *clementia*, related to *benevolentia* (cf. Liegle 1935: 93–94).

20 There is a connection to the concept of (political) *amicitia*, cf. Badian 1958:

152, Brunt 1965: 1–20, Witstrand 1972: 16–17, Saller 1982: 11–23 and Rich 1989: 123–129.

21 As regards the singular topic of patronage, cf. Wallace-Hadrill 1989: 3–4, Johnson and Dandeker 1989: 219–241, Garnsey and Woolf 1989: 157–158.

22 SIG³, n. 618, of the early second century BC, on which cf. Veyne 1989: 401. Cf. also Wolkmann 1954: 475.

23 Cf. Saller 1982: 41–58, 70–73; Johnson and Dandeker 1989: 238.

24 Cf. Cicero, De republica I, 39. Cf also Bianchini 1976: 4–5.

25 Cf. Long 1995: 225–229.

26 A fuller treatment of the subject, which Cicero in De republica notes having written, is unfortunately lost.

27 Cf. Giardina 1989: 278–280.

28 The context is treating "interested" benefits, done with an intention to obtain one's own advantage. In De beneficiis VI, 13, 3, Seneca explains that the benefit is directed to the person, while the sale is a "mercenary benefit", because the main concern is for the price. In Cicero, the "utilitarian" friendship is called mercatura (De natura deorum I, 121).

29 Cf., for example, Seneca, De beneficiis I, 1, 8; I, 5, 2; I, 7, 1; II, 19, 1; II, 31, 1; V, 4, 2; VI, 8, 3–4; VI, 9, 3 and passim.

30 Cf., for example, Math. V, 28.

31 Cf. Seneca, De beneficiis I, 1, 9; I, 2, 3; III, 15, 1–3; VII, 14, 5.

32 Cf. Seaford 1994: 204–205.

33 Cf., for example, Seneca, De beneficiis II, 29–30; III, 14, 4; IV, 3–9 and 26–28; VI, 21.

34 I mentioned above the exceptions constituted by the Greek leitourgiai and eisphorai in the fourth century BC. It is impossible to give here any bibliography on these subjects.

35 Cf. short bibliography on philia in Hutter 1978: 91, n. 1; useful remarks on the socio-economic character of this virtue in Millett 1991: 109–126, 148–159 and passim. Cf. also the forthcoming proceedings of a conference on ancient reciprocity, held at Exeter University in 1993, including an article by D. Konstans on philia.

36 Cf. Cicero, De amicitia V, 19–20; VII, 23; VIII, 26; XIV, 50. There are bilingual epigraphic texts demonstrating the correspondence between eunoia and benevolentia, and euergesia and beneficium. Only as instances, and limited to the Roman Republican period, I give Corpus inscriptionum latinarum (1863) VI, 372 and 374 (= Inscriptiones latinae selectae [1892–1916] 31 and 33); Inscriptiones latinae liberae republicae (1965) n. 363.

37 The Ciceronian "benevolent" sociality is opposed to utilitarian-contractual theories, characteristic of the Epicurean, cf. Lotito 1981: 118–119.

38 This was noticed by Testard in his commentary on De officiis, 1970: II, 43, n. 1.

39 Cf. Inwood 1995: 241–244 and passim and Ferrary 1995: 71. The approach of Stevenson (1992) tends to put family relations (basis of human society) also on the level of "reciprocity". I think that this is a hierarchical interpretation of society, grounded on authority relations, which was a very important aspect of ancient thought, with relevant consequences. I am, however, here stressing the general appetitus societatis pertaining to all mankind. It does not signify a basic equality of men as such, but only that they share a general need to be together and to exploit in common their different abilities (cf., for example, Cicero, De officiis I, 22). I am therefore in a position somewhat different from that of Lotito (cf. n. 37 above). Although sharing his basic argument, I do not perceive a strong opposition between the contractual and the "benevolent"

theories, but rather a possibility of coexistence between utilitarian and social reasons. Anyway, I have not yet thoroughly developed this particular topic.

40 Cf. Finley 1985: 50–57.

41 Also cf. the closeness of Aristotle's paragraphs on benevolence, *concord* and beneficence, quoted at the end of this chapter.

42 The "unnatural" character of usury is demonstrated by the very term indicating interest in Greek: *tokos* = offspring (cf. Aristotle, *Politics* 1258b 5–8). In regard to the commercial transactions going beyond *autharcheia*, it has been frequently noticed that, in Aristotle's thought, the immoral character of the usurious commercial exchange was that the two extremities of the process were constituted by money, not by commodities: M-C-M instead of C-M-C (with money as a medium). Cf. Vegetti 1982: 598, Ruggiu 1982: 91–93, Meikle 1991: 163–167, Natali 1990: 311–315 and White, S.A. 1992: 207.

43 *Nicomachean Ethics* had 25 editions in the sixteenth century, which spread especially over Northern Europe where the *curricula studiorum* were centred on the humanities, while Italy was mainly devoted to scientific thought in that period (Schmitt 1983: 38).

9

ASSUMPTIONS, ECONOMICS, AND THE ORIGINS OF EUROPE

Alan E. Samuel

In her American Historical Association presidential address of 1987, Katherine Fischer Drew (1987: 803–812) complained of a tendency of historians to concentrate on detail at the expense of the larger view of events affecting the broad scope of history in the Western world. In succeeding years, however, the impulse to achieve that breadth has generated a number of excellent books dealing with the sweep of events carrying the Mediterranean world from Roman into medieval times. For the Late Empire as well, in books treating different aspects of history and society during the years AD 400 to 800, historians return again and again to that important change from ancient to medieval society in Western Europe. The reasons for this change have been discussed frequently in the sixty years since Henri Pirenne proposed that it was the isolation imposed by the Arab conquest of much of the Mediterranean littoral which led to the great shift from Romanism to medieval society, and there have been divergent approaches to the issue. While few today accept the details of Pirenne's thesis, the approach he took to the problem has been at the heart of much of the discussion of the centuries during which the Germanic monarchies dominated the West, and many writers have made their interpretations in economic terms.

Recently, however, historians have been more willing to consider that ideas, rather than material conditions, play a role in the evolutions and revolutions in human experience. A fundamental work like Judith Herrin's, a notable study of the Mediterranean civilizations as they evolved over the centuries during which the Pirenne thesis proposes its explanation for events, very deliberately focuses on ideas, in the form of faith, and argues for, among other factors, a divergence in the view of unity, or lack thereof, in leadership of the Christian *oikoumene* (Herrin 1987: 7).[1] To Herrin, Byzantium played the essential role during this period. But it was not only the theological evolution to which the Greeks of the East were so essential; in secular terms the emperors at Constantinople not only provided the

211

"check" to Islamic expansion that created the possibility for the existence of the medieval West, but the weakness of Constantinople was essential to the ultimate division of the Mediterranean into the three zones which came as a result of the Arab conquests. Another approach to the period prefers to emphasize evolution over a long period, rather than focus on breaks and interruptions, and Averil Cameron's recent survey of late Rome sees political events as "stages in a much longer evolution, at the end of which the emphasis shifted toward northern Europe" (Cameron 1983: 193).

I may, therefore, risk running against the tide if I treat this discussion in terms of the categories of Pirenne's arguments, and if I focus on the question in the terms Pirenne saw it: what was the phenomenon which made life in Western Europe different after the Roman patterns were no longer in effect? However evolutionary the change may have been, and however much one may prefer to see a multiplicity of factors at work, in the history of that period, as of all periods, there was something qualitatively different from life in the former Roman Gaul – different both from earlier times and from the contemporary Roman and Islamic East. It is that difference, and its causation, which still can bear discussion, it seems to me. It is true that ideas were fundamental to the changes that took place, but many of those ideas can be traced in the economy, and we can, therefore, pursue some of the specific issues of economic activity, and with the benefit of an enormous amount of valuable work that has transformed our understanding of the ancient economy since Pirenne wrote. "Ideas *or* economics" does not, therefore, seem to me to be a very suitable set of alternatives and exclusions, while even "ideas *and* economics" draws too sharp a line between concepts and their results, which may, in fact, feed upon one another. The strategies adopted by the leaders of society during the difficult years 400 to 800 were dictated to a significant extent by the underlying ideas about society and its material needs, pushed by the recurring political and economic upheavals which were felt most strongly in the western part of the empire.

To a historian used to the almost negligible data available for the fifth century BC in Greece – or even Ptolemaic Egypt – the comparatively plentiful intellectual and material sources of the Late Empire suggest that it may be possible to see how ideas, or, more acccurately, mental assumptions, played their part in generating economic and political decisions which ultimately remade the world of the Western Roman Empire. It is this "remaking" which created a society fundamentally different from what had gone before, and created a break which attracted the attention of historians long before Pirenne. From Pirenne's time on, a great deal of debate has focused on the timing of economic changes, on the growth of prosperity, coinage, urban life, and development of rural units of self-sufficiency, with the idea that a kind of causal relation can be inferred from temporal association. The evidence is still ambiguous, however, with the result that one can still find a range of proposals for the point at which once would place the shift from "ancient" styles to "medieval," and a number of explanations for the reason the shift took place. Did, for example, ancient civilization pass as a result of a decline in prosperity which can be traced in its beginnings as far back as even the halcyon years of the second century? Or did a good deal of ancient economic activity persist for a while into the Merovingian period – even if not as late as Pirenne saw – prolonging Romanism into the German monarchies? Was it the Vikings, Magyars and Arabs, bringing economic disruption, who were eventually responsible for the destruction of ancient society? Was it the sixth century plague? Because so much of our answer – as we have been expressing it – depends on our understanding of the extent of trade in Merovingian and Carolingian times, there is still a great deal of debate about the meaning of the evidence: coin hoards, remarks about goods and traders by Gregory of Tours and others, references to economic activity in legislation and charters, evidence from excavation and archeological surveying. Do these items of evidence attest genuine mercantile trading, as some say, or are they equally attributable to piracy, pillage, gift-exchange, diplomacy, or partial or full combinations of all of these, as other students variously claim? And, to what extent did ideas about trade and the economy influence the decisions that ultimately produced the society we call medieval?

While even the most casual observer would readily acknowledge that the world of Francia in 900 was dramatically different from the Gaul of 400, the issue of change and its causation calls for more specificity. What, precisely, are the characteristics of society which are so changed as to justify the view that a different order of life obtains? In some measure, the conviction of change in Western Europe rests on the relative continuity in the other areas to which Roman organization had extended. The "Byzantine Empire", for all its religious schisms and losses of territory to Persians and Arabs, was an exercise in continuity. Whatever remained to the emperors at Constantinople, secular or theological, built on the Greek culture, religions and history of the Eastern Mediterranean, as they had evolved under Roman control. Most important, the patterns of urban life which marked, to Greeks, the characteristics of human society – with Aristotle's definition of the human being as a "polis animal" – continued in the areas controlled from Constantinople, although there were, of course, ups and downs and regional variations in the nature of urban life. While there was change from "Roman" styles and evolution in city organization and planning, many eastern cities prospered in Byzantine times and often show evidence of a good deal of construction and activity. Even in the heavily urbanized area of Italy, urban patterns persisted while they did not in Gaul.

This has long been known. Furthermore, recently investigations in the areas which came briefly under Persian and then permanently under Arab control, have demonstrated quite conclusively, where the archeological record permits conclusions, smooth evolution from the Byzantine into the Umayyad period. The whole period, and the entire area into which Islam initially expanded, can be represented by a statement about the history of Skythopolis into the eighth century: "the crucial years 636–40 did not leave any visible signs in Bet Shean. We cannot point to a single abrupt change which may be related to the change of regime" (Tsafrir and Foerster 1994: 111).[2] It seems to me to be clear that the continuity in religious and intellectual life which Glen Bowersock has tracked into the Islamic period[3] finds a parallel in continuity in urban agglomerations.

We do not find this kind of continuity in Northwestern Europe, and it is precisely the inability to establish a smooth transition from the fifth to the eighth century that prompts the assertion of "change", and inspired Pirenne to locate it in Carolingian times. The issues are more "when?" and "why?", so that a good deal of the discussion of Pirenne's thesis has focused on evaluating his view that the great change in European history took place around the time of Charlemagne, as the emperor and his successors were forced to make a new foundation for society with the Mediterranean closed to the commerce which had been the underpinning of Merovingian prosperity. There have been very worthy additions to the discussion, such as Robert Lopez' demonstration (1943: 24–27) that the Arab conquest did not terminate trade in so important an item as papyrus or other "regalian" items, or the imaginative proposal of Sture Bolin (1953: 5–39) that in the early years of the Califate, the exploitation of large silver deposits in the East produced a flow of silver into Europe, specifically, into the Frankish empire which acted as intermediary for the transfer to Arab buyers of slaves and North European furs, but that with Scandinavian expansion into Eastern Europe, the trade routes shifted to the river routes in Russia and the Carolingian economy ceased to profit from this activity.[4] A more negative interpretation of the evidence, however, by Philip Grierson (1959: 123–140), holds that the dissemination of "foreign" goods and coinage is better explained by such transactions as ransoms, protection, gift-exchange and the like, rather than by genuine trade. Archeological investigations have emphasized the importance to Carolingian Europe of the trading centers of Dorestad in Frisia and Hedeby in Jutland, both of which are fitted into an interpretation of economic activity which stresses the importance of the Baltic Sea area to European commerce in the seventh century and after. The state of the question has been given a full-dress review by Hodges and Whitehouse (1984). At the same time, there has been a useful examination of the economic relevance of trade and exchange in the first place, with some archeologists arguing that exchange served the goals of prestige and rank more than production or economic utility.[5]

In considering this aspect of the question, I believe that scepticism about the extent of trade is the more reasonable attitude toward the evidence, particularly since virtually all of the reconstructions of economic activity and the purposes behind them ignore some fundamental questions: if the supposed trading existed on the large scale proposed, and if there was a trade-generated inflow of silver to Western Europe in Merovingian and early Carolingian times, who carried it on, and who got the money? If, as Grierson's argument implies, the interest of the Crown in economic matters was more analogous to the treasure-collecting of the kings of Beowulf, then a serious economic rationale can hardly be assumed as the basis for any of the activities attested by Norse archeology, Arabic geographers, or parallelisms between Frankish coin-weights and Arab gold-silver ratios that Sture Bolin adduces. Furthermore, if genuine coinage exchange was involved in only a part of the activity of the populace earlier in Roman times in the first instance, as I believe it was, and that even then, in the undivided Mediterranean, long-range trade offered only limited possibilities for profit, the presence or absence of such exchange and trade in Merovingian and Carolingian times is a little less critical to an explanation of the development of Western European history from the fifth century on. We should not expect to find economic purposes behind events.

I have presented my views elsewhere about the nature of exchange for Ptolemaic Egypt, arguing that despite the minting associated with the Macedonian conquest, coinage was not in extensive use among the peasants of the countryside. There, for the major component of wealth, agricultural produce, currency was not the major means of exchange, which was carried on more by barter and non-coinage forms of money (Samuel 1984: 187–206). These conclusions can be extended in time and place. In Egypt, the situation I have described for the Hellenistic period persisted through Roman and Byzantine times, for those periods show characteristics similar to those I adduced for pre-Roman Egypt. The same high valuations of clothing as against land and house prices, for example, which I found for the Ptolemaic period can be found in Hobson's comparisons between prices for houses and camels (1985: 227–228), Bagnall's price lists for the fourth century (1985: 61–72), and the lists Johnson and West offer for the Byzantine period (1949: 175–214).[6] Furthermore, although from Ptolemaic times on a number of taxes were payable in coinage, at no time did currency take over the whole system of remittances, and many taxes and charges remained payable in kind even through the Byzantine period.

In the Roman period, the major burden of land taxes were in kind so far as field lands were concerned, although the land of specialty crops like orchards and vineyards were subject to money taxes. This situation persisted into the Byzantine period, although a money tax was added to the tax in kind on arable land. There were taxes in land on other products, while the poll tax, so long as it persisted in the Roman period, was payable in money. There was also a wide variety of miscellaneous taxes and charges, some payable in kind, some in coin. Since by far the larger part of the imperial revenue from Egypt came from the land tax and the rents paid on lands, it is clear that for the most part, the peasant's liability to government could be satisfied by payment of part of his produce, even if the system allowed for and attests commutation of these liabilities in currency.

Even though the Roman economy seems to have been substantially monetized, at least in cities, as a recent important paper (Howgego 1992: 1–31) argues, the segment of economic activity accounted for by the goods exchanged for money remains small as a percentage of overall volume and value.[7] It is an important aspect of economic activity only in Greek and Roman urban areas. Nevertheless, the fact that monetization had advanced is an essential part of the complex interaction of town and agricultural life which promoted the very existence of the kinds of cities which we know in the classical Mediterranean. The peasants could only exist if the greater part of their obligations could be satisfied with the produce of the land. So too were the cities stimulated by the activity generated by the quest for small sums of currency.

If the evidence shows clearly that a great part of remittances to the government were made outside of the currency system, there is greater ambiguity in the matter of private exchange. From Ptolemaic times on, the manifold sales attested by the papyri are carried on in most instances in terms of currency. Archives like those of Petaus and Aurelius Isidorus show a great deal of activity in currency terms. Sales of goods, animals, land and produce expressed in terms of silver, and loans of coin which abound in the ten centuries of Greek and Roman rule in Egypt, have been used to demonstrate what is called the extensive monetization of the countryside. But the writers of our papyri were for the most part, as has often been noted, from the upper economic level of village and town residents, and their business affairs are not representative of the mass of the peasants.

Even among members of the upper class, coinage did not completely carry the day. We commonly see transactions carried on in kind for a millenium or more after the introduction of coinage into Egypt. Leases, for example, while sometimes providing for payment wholly or in part in currency, more often state the payment as produce.[8] While this might be expected, the same phenomenon occurs in sales in less natural circumstances. A document like *P. Lond. 1686*, a sale in 565 of three arouras to a monastery in return for the monastery's paying, not cash to the seller, but certain of the seller's taxes, is particularly suggestive of the manner in which the peasant could operate without coin.

Also significant is the evidence for the limited availablity of gold and silver, not only as coinage but even as bullion, and for the nature and use of the copper coinage in which most transactions were expressed. As

216

Bowman (1980: 23–40) has shown for the fourth century, most individuals had little in the way of gold or silver. Even if the nomes were required to produce bullion for compulsory sale to the government, no great availability of such coin is implied. Diocletian's reform of the coinage had little effect on circulation of precious metal. Bronze remained the metal of the currency used in most instances.

The nature of the bronze and copper coins used in later Egypt is instructive. Bagnall (1985: 51–53) has cited the evidence for the extensive importation and even private creation of copper coins in the fourth century, precisely the phenomenon which pertained in the barter-dominated society of rural France a century ago, to seek a parallel for which we have good evidence.[9] On the other hand, the analysis of the papyri dealing with the estate of Heroninos at Theadelphia in the Fayum, which for a long time had been taken to show that on this estate, which was to a great extent vineyard, money was in most instances wine rather than coin, has recently been revised by a re-examination of the archive showing that the estate genuinely used coin (Rathbone 1991). Most important, the fact that the use of coinage was "unsophisticated," and that the élite neither depended on the banking system, nor used either coin or negotiable paper to transfer funds, means that "money", either in coin or in coinage-based paper, did not play the important part in the economy which the transactions of the élite would represent (Howgego 1992: 28–30). It is, in fact, the relative unimportance of currency overall which prompted Bagnall (1985: 54) to remark of the fourth century currency inflation in Egypt that few will have been adversely affected.

So much for exchange. Except at the upper levels of economic activity where transactions were in coin in urban areas or conducted perhaps in bullion or non-coinage transfers by the very wealthy, exchange was largely in kind, and currency did not assume a very great importance. As to wealth, we can now turn to the question of who had it and how it was acquired. By the end of the fourth century, church institutions had supplanted the temples of religious precincts as assemblers of lands and wealth, but church administrators were still far behind imperial bureaucrats in terms of the revenues they controlled. The emperor, his household and officials still disposed of a very large portion of the annual revenue of the empire.

Private wealth still depended on land, as it had in Mediterranean civilizations for centuries, and the great imperial bureaucracy notwithstanding, it was land which was still the great determinant and creator of wealth.[10] As time went on, in fact, more and more land was under the control of fewer and fewer absentee owners to whom it was investment, a phenomenon which had spread extensively into Gaul by the fourth century. In Gaul, too, real wealth came from the land, on which economic life was based, as Lot (1967: 309) remarked, and, despite such fascinating depictions of

commercial activity as that on the Igel column near Trier, trade and manufacturing did not create great fortunes – unless profits thus made founded
a fortune with the purchase of land. The kind of wealth assembled in land
in the Late Empire is near-legendary. A few examples make the point.

The Melania who retired from the world in 404 had, with her husband,
estates in Britain, Spain, Italy and North Africa which brought an income
amounting annually to some 1,600 Roman pounds in gold,[11] a figure which,
even allowing for the possible exaggeration by her admiring biographers,
must be compared with figures ranging between 700 and 6,667 lb for the
gold obtained from all of Egypt by forced sale at the beginning, of
the fourth century. Melania and Petronius' Trimalchio are often cited in
discussions of private wealth in the Empire, but the phenomenon of large
landowning is well attested in the East and West. The fifth/sixth century
estates of the Apion family around Oxyrhynchus are familiar to papyrologists. There were large private estates in Africa, Sicily and Gaul, and it is
in lands that the leisured class saw its wealth. Ausonius' "little inheritance"
that provided him his livelihood was made up of 125 acres of field crops,
about 630 in vineyards, 30 in pasture land, and over 400 in woodland
(Ausonius 3.1).

All this is well known, and the Gallo-Roman upper class is a particularly
well-studied example of provincial prosperity, but it is important to emphasize the overwhelming importance of land and its exploitation as a source
of wealth, in view of the increasing tendency to focus on evidence for
commercial activity. It is important that land was the sign and source of
wealth, and commerce, industry and trade generally was not. There is more
than tradition or even regulation to the rejection of trade by the landowning upper class; they gained no great advantage by involving
themselves in it. We have heard almost *ad nauseum* of the great clothing
empire illustrated on the Igel monument, but nothing of an attempt to put
the Secundinii in economic perspective. Just how wealthy were they, along
with the owners of the grave monuments portraying almost innumerable
forms of manufacturing, trade and commerce?

I have no doubt that many people made good, prosperous livings out
of commerce, even a modicum of wealth, but how many of them really
did graduate from earning wealth to the ranks of the really rich landowners,
the phenomenon Rostovtzeff (1957: 1. 150–191) claims in his enthusiastic
appreciation of commercial activity in the second century? None of these
characters were the Gettys, Carnegies, Rockefellers or Warburgs of the
Roman Empire. A high post in the imperial administration was a much
more likely route to great fortune. By the fourth century, certainly, when
the Gallic wealthy were retiring to their country properties, and the towns
and cities were dropping in size,[12] there was even less potential for a
commercial class to enjoy great prosperity. The influential wealthy were
adopting strategies based on long-standing assumptions about wealth and

its creation: wealth was based on increased accumulation, rather than growth in production, and the increases in accumulation were most stable when based on the land.

Most of what commercial and manufacturing activity did exist was entirely local. Even Rostovtzeff (1957: 1, 159–162), anxious to emphasize the extent of commerce in the Mediterranean basin, was forced to admit that the majority of long-distance transport activity was limited to the shipment of the imperial annona.[13] A few categories of manufacture, glassware, Arretine ware from Italy, and pottery from La Graufesenque and Lezoux in Gaul travelled afield, but the very fact that these are the manufactures always cited to demonstrate inter-city trade shows the scarcity of evidence for this kind of activity.[14] Finley (1985: 134–135, 195) is right that trade in manufactured goods was at an extremely low level in antiquity, and Hendy (1989: 1–23), that the same situation persisted in Byzantine times. For Byzantine Egypt, which by all accounts was one of the most commercially active areas of the Mediterranean from the fourth to seventh centuries, with its economic activity the best documented, the mention of connections with the West are stunningly rare.

Byzantine Egyptian literary sources attest only about a dozen trips to Greece, the Adriatic and Sicily, and three to Rome or Italy in the fourth century; in the seventh century there are reports of three to Gaul, one to Spain and one to Britain (Johnson and West 1949: 141–142).[15] Commercial imports attested in Egyptian papyri are equally scarce. Over the fifth to seventh centuries, four documents mention tin, olive oil or mercury from Spain; three texts note copper, cadmia, wormwood and soap from Gaul; one text, the Life of St Ioan. (para. 10), mentions tin from Britain; *P. Holm* mentions Etrurian wax from Italy (Col. 4.31);[16] scarcely a half-dozen texts (Johnson and West 1949: 146–149)[17] show the shipment from different parts of Greece of honey, kermesberry, misy, copper, stone, Chian earth, shoes, garments, Samian earth, cadmus, wine, salt, marble, racehorses and chrysocalla; while a few texts do mention slaves from Gaul and Mauretania, or use the terms Sarmatian and Gothic in connection with slaves. The same picture emerges for voyages and imports connecting Egypt with further-east locales, but as I am interested primarily in East–West activity, I will not lengthen my text unnecessarily.

The importance of this list is not so much its illustration of the slenderness of evidence for long-range trade, a phenomenon which in other contexts Finley noted and used as a silentium which is significant as an argument for the absence of such trade. It is, rather, that when we do have any evidence at all for such activity, manufactured items play a small part in it. Of the some two dozen items indicated as imported to Egypt, only two, shoes and items of clothing, are manufactures. The same pattern obtains for items imported to Egypt from areas other than the West or for items the origin of which is unknown (Johnson and West 1949: 147–151).

Finally, my own search, a reasonably diligent one, for items from the West mentioned in documents published after 1949, the date of Johnson and West's list, has not been crowned with any success.

The idea of the generation of wealth by commerce in manufactured items across the seas of the later Roman Empire should be abandoned. That helps to explain why later rulers in Europe saw no urgency to provide the urban environments and infrastructure which made commerce convenient. For the most part, historians now see clearly that land was the basis of wealth, and that markets, trade and monetization remained at a low level, even after centuries of Hellenic and Roman culture, organization, and urbanization in the Mediterranean. By insisting on this, I am not denying the existence of a prosperous group of urban residents in the towns and cities of the Empire, people whom Rostovtzeff chooses to describe by the term "bourgeoisie." They existed, not only in the wonderful years of the second century, but through the third and then on into the fifth, sixth, and seventh centuries, at least in the East.

Prosperous urban residents were not international traders or manufacturers. Much of their wealth, as almost always in antiquity, still came from land, and those who represented themselves by their portrayal of manufactures were local worthies, not men of "world class" wealth, if I may use that expression. These local notables, the upper level of the cities, towns and villages of the Empire, made up the class on which the Empire as we know it was based. They provided not only the revenues in taxes in kind and money from the lands and enterprises which they owned, but they also accomplished much of the work of collection and administration which maintained the urbanism of the world-state. While the vicissitudes of war and disruption, as in the third century, might curtail the civic activity of these people in some cities, elsewhere, at the same time, their activity showed prosperity, building, and less of the economic difficulties faced by some of the city and town councils.

In the East, they persisted in some major cities, although imperial and ecclesiastical patronage replaced them to some extent. Beyond the cities, in smaller settlements, some of the characteristics of earlier times are preserved in the epigraphic contributions of more important men. In the West, north of Italy, however, people of this group for the most part were no longer active when those provinces came under the control of the Germanic kings. Indeed, many have argued for the deterioration in their importance throughout the Mediterranean world well before the breakup of the western empire, and the decline of the late Roman state has been variously attributed to their excessive consumption (Jones 1964), or their exploitation and oppression of the peasantry (de Ste Croix 1981). The absence of the urban curiales and potentes in the cities, and the centers in which they thrived in the late Empire, is one of the phenomena which mark the shift from the society of Provincial Gaul to that of Merovingian and Carolingian France.

This provides us the opportunity to shift our attention to Francia and Germania of the fifth, sixth and seventh centuries. When we look at economic activity there, we are forced to agree that in many respects, Pirenne was right that Merovingian times did not diverge from late Roman, even if the similarities which we note are not those which attracted Pirenne's comment. The first of these involves the matter of exchange, and the observation that the Western Europe of the German kingdoms steadily moved toward an increasing use of local self-sufficiency, and, when outside goods were needed, an increase in recourse to the common practice of barter rather than purchase with coin.

In this, let us begin with the coinage itself. The first thing any observer of Merovingian coinage notices is the near-complete diversification of mintage, with the vast majority of the gold *solidi* and *triens* pieces coming from local mints. A cartographic representation of Merovingian moneying looks like a map of France riddled with buckshot, showing a system of moneying which Hendy describes as "bizarrely devolved" (Hendy 1988: 65).[18] There is also no centrally directed pattern of representation of kings or nomenclature. Although most of the gold types show heads or busts, the representations are, I would say, often completely unidentifiable: no king could be seen to be represented. Nor could the kings be denoted by inscriptions, since the coins for the most part carry only identification of places or moneyers. Grierson (1959: 123–140, esp. 126) has argued that the assumption that this gold currency served the purpose of trade primarily is erroneous, and that the transition from gold to silver in the latter part of the seventh century is evidence of the emergence of local markets – which were not the province of long-range trade or of the professional *mercatores*.

Whatever its purpose, gift-exchange, payment of mercenaries, fines and payments required under German law – or trade – this coinage would not have pertained to the realm of activity which we see attested in Egypt at the time. It was exclusively gold until the seventh century, and could hardly have been used for everyday commercial transactions. Everything about this currency confirms the view that the transactions with which it was involved were part of economically non-generative activity.[19] There is, in fact, an almost total absence of the day-to-day low level activity of Roman and Byzantine cities, and in Merovingian France, evidence for the use of coins pertains almost exclusively to the upper class.[20] Internally, commerce in Gaul functioned at the level which an excellent recent book on peasant life in France as late as the nineteenth century should lead us to expect for medieval times: little use of cash, payments largely in kind, rare travel on roads, which were primitive or mere tracks, through dense woods in which wolves and other large predators roamed, constant threat or reality of scarcity and hunger, isolation in hovels, tiny hamlets, and practically no contact region to region (Weber 1976: 3–4). The isolating effects of high transportation costs, which Cipolla (1956: 52–57) has emphasized, would not only discourage low-level commerce, the deterioration in town life would tend to eliminate even that activity which characterized ancient civilization. The only commercial exchange left was that in prestige and valuable items which could bear the costs of transportation: the only kind of coinage needed was high denomination gold useful for such items, a coin which was handy for hoarding and filled the role of royal prestige and display as well.[21]

Even then, coins were not always used when exchange of high-value items or high quantities was involved. If barter, rather than currency, effected exchange at the local level, it could equally do so in affairs of greater moment. What we call barter Grierson (1959) might insist was gift-exchange, citing the work of Marcel Mauss, but in either case it was not commerce. There are some instances of transactions in the works of Gregory of Tours which show how exchange might be effected without coins. Soldiers of King Childebert II, returning from an unsuccessful campaign in Italy, were forced by need to trade weapons and clothing for food (Gregory of Tours, *Historia Francorum* 10.3); a fish miraculously caught was traded for wine (Gregory of Tours, *Vitae martyrorum*, 2.16).

Coinage came into play during a famine (585), when merchants sold a *modius* of grain or a half *modius* of wine for a gold triens (Gregory of Tours, *Historia Francorum* 7.45). On the other hand, in the instance of famine earlier, during the reign of Clovis (470), the senator Ecdicius, a relative of Sidonius Apollinaris, collected over 4,000 of the starving and brought them to his estate, where he fed them until food was available. There was no mention of purchase. Grierson's account of the acquisition of lead for church roofs in Charlemagne's time (1959: 128–129) illustrates how even such an item was obtained in non-commercial ways. And if our sources by their nature might not be expected to give us precise information about how exchange was effected, there is more potential than is generally acknowledged. Among the moral tales which make up a good part of the so-called *Life of Charlemagne* are many in which acquisition, avarice, collection or hoarding is at the heart of the narrative, but almost none of it even in terms of commercial activity relates to coinage and exchange.[22]

Of foreign items we find practically no mention in Gregory. There are wine, dates, olives, oil, roots and papyrus from the East, as well as a few specialty items of building materials. Booty, gifts and relics provide some carpets, communion vessels, and some gold coins sent by the Emperor Tiberius to King Chilperic. There is mastic from Chios, cotton, asphalt, sulphur and amber from Palestine, and incense imported from somewhere unspecified. That is all a careful examination of Gregory's various works can provide.[23]

Looking at East–West trade from the other end of the Mediterranean gives the same picture as that obtainable from contemporary Egypt. Although "there is much evidence of contact even with the Eastern Mediterranean in the centuries following the fall of the Western Roman Empire" (Randsborg 1991: 123), contact, even a great deal of contact, is not necessarily trade, and certainly not trade of a level high enough to have a significant role in the development of society. Some trade existed and continued into the Arab period, in what Lopez designates as "regalian" items like ceremonial fabrics and in the significant product of papyrus.[24] In Merovingian times, however, just like in the late Empire, long-range trade in specialty products, let alone manufactures, was very limited, while the northern route through the Baltic and Russia, argued by Hodges and Whitehouse (1984) as the source of silver in Charlemagne's time, had not yet developed – if it ever did. Even if that commerce was so carefully organized by the Franks, Scandinavians, Russians and Arabs, and the later evidence of inter-State activity cannot be explained at least in part by Grierson's gift exchange so loved by German courts, the fifth, sixth and seventh centuries did not have the benefit of it.

The actual evidence for long-range trade in Carolingian times is not so different from that of the earlier period. The strongest, but not very satisfactory, case for a major Carolingian thrust in long-distance trade is made by Bolin and some who have followed his idea that the great increase of silver production in the Arab world encouraged Charlemagne to promote that trade to obtain the silver he wanted to finance his activities.[25] The more extensive silver coinage of Charlemagne and his successors is taken as support for that idea, but even then, the silver becomes analogous to the regalian gold of the Merovingians, and would not be so applicable to the generation of commercial wealth based on trade. To the very scanty evidence in European sources, allegedly not very interested in that kind of information, of such trade in the time of Charlemagne and after, this hypothesis adds a collection of references to northern trade in Arab sources, often while neglecting to observe how much and many of the goods for which the Arabs are supposed to depend on Northern Europe were in fact supplied also from other sources.[26] Often cited is the now-famous passage of Ibn Khurdadhbih about the Radanite Jews who travel back and forth, east and west, carrying slaves, eunuchs, brocade and skins from the West, spices and other products from the Orient. But the description of this trade suggests much more the occasional trade of opportunity in luxury goods than an organized commerce on which reliable exchange relations can be built.[27]

In the work of Gregory of Tours we have some clue to the trading role of the Jews in Merovingian times – not great or encountered frequently[28] – and there is no indication in the Arab sources that this caravan trade later grew so great as to influence the economy of Europe. As well as the

Jewish traders there are the Rus, Scandinavian traders based in the Slavic realms. Their activity, according to Ibn Khurdadhbih, included voyages from France and Spain to Tangiers and Africa (Ibn Khurradadhbih 1949. 23–25), but the trade is that same caravan trade of specialty items, in their case, also furs and swords. The Slavic connection is repeated by the tenth century traveler Ibn Hauqal (1964: 2. 382), writing that the beaver furs in the Spanish market originated in Slavic rivers, while slaves came from France and (presumably via France) from Slavic areas.[29] These remarks, like almost all the Arab information about trade items, aim at informing either about the origin of certain goods,[30] or about the nature of the products of certain areas. The description of the commerce involved hardly implies the extensive carrying of goods, primarily food items, which we associate with Mediterranean shipping in antiquity, and even that, as I argued earlier, cannot be supposed to have been a major source of accumulation of wealth. And the extent of communication may be judged by Al-Masudi's dependence on a ninth-century account of Frankish history sent to Cairo from Aragon by Godmar, bishop of Gerona. While Al-Masudi's information about the Franks is scanty, he has a survey of their history, against virtually nothing about the Lombards. Demonstrating how little documentation about the West was available, his knowledge depended on a chance find in Fustat.[31]

Finally, it is possible to find resources for the expansion of Carolingian power in at least two aspects of activity not affected by extra-European trade. First, as Murray (1978: 35) observed, the annual mobilization of Charlemagne's army, 25 percent of which was mounted, was based on an agricultural surplus which derived from significant advances in agricultural technology,[32] a phenomenon which would help reinforce the ancient assumption that it was land to which one would look for the generation of wealth. Second, a recent study by Timothy Reuter (1985: 75–94) shows how large sums of treasure, including precious metal and currency, flowed into Carolingian hands. The reports of the annals and other sources make quite clear that the fruit of military activity in the eighth century and after was a great deal of plunder and tribute. Plunder itself probably went to the ravaging troops, for the most part, although the kings had their share of that as well. Formal tribute went directly into royal coffers. The sums involved could be very large indeed, and plunder and tribute played a large part in the financing of Frankish armies – enough to lead Reuter to suggest that the open border in the east provided the wherewithal for the East Frankish kingdom to develop greater political strength after the division of Verdun, despite greater economic development in the western kingdom. In light of this very extensive evidence for inflow of valuables into the Carolingian kingdom, there is less need to posit complex and far-flung trading networks as the source of financing for Carolingian military strength.

The thrust of my argument so far has been to show that great wealth cannot be attributable to trade, either in late antiquity or Frankish Europe, and that any economic planning could not have aimed at commercial rewards. Even the relatively plentiful references in Arab sources to the trade through the Caucasus to the Slavic areas does not suggest a trade so intensive or genuinely commercial as to have damaged any existing Western European economy by its shift east.[33] While some local wealth may have rested on commerce and manufacture, there was no source other than land from which the enormously rich could take their fortunes, just as land was probably the basis for most of the smaller civic fortunes on which the prosperity of the towns of the Empire depended. In other words, the fundamental generator of wealth did not change from Roman to Merovingian or Frankish times. Manufacturing, trade and commerce, its presence or absence, cannot, therefore, be sought as an explanation for the great changes which overtook Western Europe from 500 to 900. Even though one of the great changes which took place was that which Hendy saw for coinage, the shifting of its use as a fiscal instrument in Roman and Byzantine societies to its Carolingian role in private exchange, "whether it actually was convenient and widespread is doubtful" (Hendy 1988: 30). The overall patterns of individual economic activity which characterized Roman and Byzantine civilizations pertain also to that of Merovingian and Carolingian cultures.

If that is the case, we will want to know how economic affairs and ideas do relate to the changes in society and culture which emerged in Frankish Gaul. One of the most significant of these was the diminishing of town life, a phenomenon of capital importance since it was on the urbanism of cities and towns that the structure of Greek, Roman and Byzantine societies depended. We all know that this urbanism based on civic institutions and facilities extended far beyond great centers like Rome, Constantinople, Alexandria, and Antioch, or in Gaul, Trier, Lyons and Marseille. Smaller communities replicated the institutions of the greater all through the Mediterranean area controlled by Rome, from Spain to Egypt and Syria. And the urbanism went beyond affording the facilities of culture and religion, like gymnasia, schools, professors, theaters, festivals and temples – later churches. The whole financial and administrative structure of the Empire depended on the towns, for around them terrain was organized for taxation, and the taxes moved through the hands of the urban owners of the land, many of whom were not only taxpayers themselves but were responsible for the remittance of all the dues of the area. The towns and cities were also the residences of all the notables of the Empire, families of provincial or even greater significance whose sons, after a suitable education, took positions in the imperial administration, or later, the Church, and sometimes rose to make their family names even greater.

All this too is well known and often repeated. However, what might not seem so obvious is the effect this role of the cities played in creating or maintaining the attitudes which determined the nature and pursuits of public and private life. The *polites*, "citizen", was part of an organic whole, taking value from the society of which he was a part, and pursuing for the most part those activities which were deemed valuable in the context of that society. That might be war and aggression in fifth century BC Athens, or service to the Church in Italy or the hermit life in Egypt. For a long time, what we call the State had been an abstract, that entity for which the *nomoi* so venerated by Socrates served to hold the population in unity. The relation of the member of the populace to the polis and then to that institution which we call the "Empire" was very different from the very direct and interpersonal relationship which characterized the mutual commitments in the societies which evolved into the Frankish kingdoms.

The chance survivals of some records of council meetings in the minor town of Oxyrhynchus in Roman Egypt show not only how fundamental the civic institutions were to the workings of imperial government, but also how the use of the institutions was unquestioned even when they posed serious difficulties for those expected to fulfill responsibilities under them. Civic orations, from the time of Pericles to the age of Libanius, all concur not only on the responsibility of the members of the group to contribute to the group effort, but also on the legitimacy of gauging the city's wealth, fame, and beauty as a measure of communal success. The city was the focus of attention, not only in the age of true civic power in Greece in the fifth and fourth centuries BC, but over the many centuries during which kings and emperors maintained a supra-city structure of power and organization. And as time wore on, the utility of the cities to the maintainance of the apparatus of government meant that cities were also the focus of attention for the rulers. From at least the time of Pericles, the ornamentation of the city had been accepted as a suitable and expected application of funds, and at least as much as civic worthies lavished on the cities later came from public sources, once wealth concentrated in the treasuries of kings and emperors.

The acts of kings, from 300 BC on, as benefactors, builders, and even "saviors" of cities are commonplaces. Augustus reported his benefactions to the city of Rome, and his successors looked after repair, assistance and new construction in cities all over the Empire. A careful study of urban patronage in Italy shows how the support of secular activities and buildings on the part of the civil officials tapered off after the third century, as financial stringencies and the reduction in real authority for the town officials prompted avoidance, rather than pursuit of the honor of spending, and secular spending such as there was, was undertaken by officials or emperors (Ward-Perkins 1984). By the Late Empire and Byzantine times, the restoration of cities was a major theme in panegyric, and it was often from the imperial treasury directly, as well as through the indirect expendi-

226

tures of imperial officials and soldiers, that cities maintained some measure of prosperity even in the most trying times, and so carried on the patterns of life and attitudes which characterized urbanism. Despite the frequently prevailing conditions of adversity, there was enough imperial patronage to ensure that the physical environment and security of at least some cities remained satisfactory, when local notables no longer would or could provide the necessary resources. The activity of Julian in the fourth century, for example, served to bolster civic administration and structures, and helped to preserve them from some of the tendencies which had led to deterioration.

This assessment of urbanism in late antiquity is not a new one, but in view of recent discussions, it may require some defense. Michael Hendy has asserted that

> few – if indeed any – serious scholars would now deny that the antique city, with its basically aristocratic-consumer orientation, its degree of statutory self-governance, and the public and planned nature of its monumentality (even if that had been paid for out of first private and later state funds) effectively disappeared in the course of the seventh century and that, whatever the formal legal position, when urban growth in the form of building and population once more becomes generally detectable in the ninth century it is on the basis of a very much diminished scale and a very different nature. The city had thus meanwhile ceased to be a predominantly public entity and had become to an equal degree a private one, a progression noted in a number of other aspects of contemporary life: it was no longer a classical but a recognizably medieval institution.
>
> (Hendy 1989: 13)

Hendy regards the post-seventh century as showing "relatively small and simplified urban sites that antique cities had become by the medieval period" (Hendy 1989: 16), but there was urbanization significant enough to support the Balkan magnates who made up, in Hendy's own words, a "city-based class" (ibid. 18), in a situation different from that of Anatolia. And there was, of course, always Constantinople, an urban agglomeration the size of which in Hendy's "guesstimate" (ibid. 19) of 200,000 awed twelfth-century visitors from the West, as Hendy points out, suggesting, in fact, that the "huge and essentially parasitical city" (ibid. 42) (like an ancient city) was one of the great strains under which the empire suffered. Finally, Hendy's analysis of the weaknesses in place before the fall of Constantinople to the crusaders in 1203/1204 retains a sense of the continuity from antiquity, in general terms if not specifically urban:

> The situation therefore has to be seen rather as one in which the basic structures inherited from late antiquity, having proved suf-

227

ficiently strong to bring the empire through the massive political and
military crises involving economic repression that had marked the
seventh to ninth centuries, nevertheless then – and despite superstruc-
tural adjustments – proved insufficiently flexible to be able to cope
with the long-term economic expansion that to an equal degree
characterized the eleventh and twelfth.

(Hendy 1989: 48)

Another view of the urban situation in the late empire also focuses on the
importance of Constantinople, but sees a general "decline of urban life
with all its traditions of curial control and local resources."[34] If, however,
we consider the evidence of archeology and not just the position of the
curiales, we see a very uneven picture. While MacAdam, considering Philadelphia in Central Jordan, can see a "general impoverishment... in the
Byzantine East in the century or two before Islam" (MacAdam 1994: 121),
Tsafrir and Foerster find that in another area "the Byzantine period brought
the settlements and population to their peak" (Tsafrir and Foerster 1994:
108). Gerasa was "a large and prosperous centre in the Byzantine period",
so that Zeyadeh can assert that it is "widely accepted that the Byzantine
period in this area was a prosperous and flourishing time" (Zeyadeh 1994:
121, 130). And Judith Herrin, acknowledging this evidence of prosperity
in Palestine and Syria, sums up a similar situation elsewhere: "it is now
clear that the cities of North Africa were in a surprisingly flourishing
condition in the fourth century" (Herrin 1987: 123). The general pattern
in the East seems to extend to Sassanid Persia, where, for the period of
the Late Empire, Lee asserts: "No other state or people with whom the
Romans had dealings in this period achieved anything like a comparable
degree of urban development or governmental organization" (Lee 1993:
123). However, "in the Northwestern Empire towns were drastically
reduced and then almost ceased to exist in Late Antiquity" (Randsborg
1991: 174).

What the evidence suggests quite strongly is that, however the organiz-
ational structures of the cities and towns might have evolved in late
antiquity, in Italy, North Africa and the East, at least, the traditional pattern
of living in agglomerations persisted, even when some of the entertainments
and civic activities characteristic of earlier time fell out of use. In many
cities, during the third century or later, the practice of living densely
continued. Many of the Greeks in the empire ruled from Constantinople
continued living in that manner, as did many of those who came to be ruled
by the Arabs, who themselves perpetuated urban life. The characteristic of
density alone is one of the fundamental factors in maintaining the role
of cities as creative centers, as Jane Jacobs (1984) has pointed out, and, as
the density available made the normally difficult job of administration and
tax collection a little easier, the maintenance of old patterns was encour-

aged. In the East, late antiquity saw the continuance of city-foundations by emperors, following the patterns of Hellenistic and earlier Roman rulers (Demandt 1989: 400). To cultured and upper-class Greeks, many of the cities they knew were of very great antiquity, and were themselves a physical aspect of the culture which had the respect of Christians and pagans alike.[35]

The difference between the Sassanid East and German West shows strikingly in the physical remains in North Europe, where the settlements outside the Roman realm were nothing like what we have seen in the East and South – even if deteriorated. There, on the other side of the frontier, the "typical unit of settlement was the village, comprising a virtually random configuration of huts or 'long-houses,' and, on the admittedly limited available archeological evidence, generally covering an area of less than 10 hectares," with the "absence of any central urban settlement which might have been designated a capital."[36] In the area considered Roman, the towns, however patterned on those in the older parts of the empire, played a smaller role in provincial life[37] and were much reduced in size in later antiquity. An interesting case is that of Marseille. Despite a clear expansion of vitality in the fifth and sixth centuries, probably due to the emergence of the city as a gateway on the route north into Gaul, there is an "archeological hiatus" from the seventh to tenth centuries, as in the rest of Provence (Loseby 1992: 165–185). At the same time that Marseille experienced her resurgence, Vienne had declined from about 200 hectares in area to about 20, and Lyons from about 160 to 20. Reims and Metz were 60 to 70, while only fortress cities, like Cologne and Trier, could boast large scopes, perhaps 100 and 300 hectares respectively (Randsborg 1991: 91–92). But even these should be contrasted with the many cities across the empire whose sizes were double or triple that, with Rome in the third century perhaps 1,000 hectares, and Constantinople in the fifth about the same, while Antioch could claim 2,000 (Randsborg 1991: 92). When the German tribes molted across the border, in their initial raids and later invasions, the cities they encountered offered little or nothing to their social structure,[38] or, in the later period, were simply not there at all.

Finally, in reviewing the contrast between the European world and the Mediterranean littoral south and east, the earlier experience of eastern populations is an important factor in determining their maintenance of urban density. Further, the merchant orientation of the Arabs helped encourage and continue the dense settlements of urbanism, and the cities saw a focus on and promotion of commerce which was not only greater than what the centers of antiquity had known, but which produced a very different form of urban landscape.[39] As Hugh Kennedy points out, both Islamic law and the need for space to accommodate the multifarious shops of the souks led to encroachment on the open spaces characteristic of

Classical cities. The concept of what was important about a city shows in Arab texts:

> When Muslim geographers describe a city they mention the mosque and the markets, their extent, prosperity and the different sorts of goods for sale. For them it is the commerce of the city rather than its monumental buildings which are the chief source of interest.
>
> (Kennedy 1985: 25)

But the change in design and purpose does not mean the centers were any less urban or concentrated. Anyone who has visited Fez, still functioning along ninth century patterns within its walls, is aware that the early Islamic city is intensely urban and functioned as a venue for the concentrated interrelations of a very dense population. Although collective expression is found most commonly in the courtyards of the mosques, and the ornamentation of the city focused on the mosques and medersas, the needs and advantages of urban life called for, and obtained, the protection and support of the powerful.

The Frankish kings did not see towns in the same way, nor did they achieve any of their self-image or projection through urban benefactions. In this, they were very different from the Ostrogoths of Italy, who in building as in other areas of government attempted to replicate the traditions of earlier Roman emperors, and thus created a revivification of many cities that helped to preserve urbanism in Italy (Ward-Perkins 1984: 69, 105–107, 158–165). If the *Res Gestae* of Augustus could be seen as a paradigm text for setting the standard of Roman imperial behavior, the largesse and gift-giving by the chiefs in Beowulf are indicative of the patterns followed by Clovis and his successors, although there is some evidence of Chilperic adopting a few imperial expressions of largesse. The Frankish leaders were not hostile to the cities and towns as institutions, but they did not in any way fulfill themselves through them,[40] and royal inattention turned out to be a neglect of which the effects were not so benign. The cessation of public construction brought an end to the infusions of cash for materials and labor which represented an important source of income for urban dwellers in an economy which did not generate much money from town industry and commerce. The progressing disintegration of the centralized tax system also redounded to the disadvantage of the towns, however much it may have ultimately benefitted some of the landowners, for it reduced economic activity in the cities. As the need to have available small amounts of coinage for payment to the central administration passed away with the taxes themselves,[41] so decreased the need to have recourse to the towns for the commerce that would provide them.[42] Furthermore, because economic assumptions and objectives did not depend upon the kind of market and trade activity characterized by cities, no purpose could be found in expenditures to maintain them.

There are, no doubt, many factors which played a part in the decline of the Western cities, but these I have mentioned relate to the structures of society. Hodges and Whitehouse have adduced reasons for the vicissitudes suffered by a big center, like Carthage, and a minor town, like Luni, in arguing not only for the reduction in size and quality of towns but also a general depopulation in the West.[43] There may well have been a depopulation. This may well have been one of the factors responsible for the end of urbanism in Gaul – indeed in Lombard Italy and Visigothic Spain as well.[44] However, I am suggesting that we can find adequate causation in the different social and governmental structures that came along with the establishment of the Germanic kingdoms.

If, however, the two features I have already identified – the lack of interest in urban monuments and the slippage of taxation – are not enough of an explanation, there is another change which took place in Gaul as much or more than in other provinces, and one which would have had its greatest effects in the perimeter areas where the Franks settled most heavily. That is the cessation of pay to Roman troops, pay which, spent where the troops were stationed, would have produced a positive cash flow into those areas for a very long period. While only the tiniest tip has survived from the mountain of pay receipts and pay records which the army issued, there are available two or three clear records which contain evidence to show the issuance and spending of the cash salaries of the soldiers.[45] And the appreciable sums brought in through the soldiers themselves would have been swollen by official expenditures, which were necessary from time to time despite the military requisitions and imposed payments for which the system provided. When there was no longer an Aetius, a Stilicho, to round up and pay armies, and Frankish soldiers took their support from landholdings in some way,[46] the flow of cash from the interior of the Empire to the troubled provinces stopped, and the towns in those areas no longer had an inflow of cash which helped defray their expenses.

Even more fundamental to the decline or advance of urban centers are tacit ideas of economic benefit. In the vitality of the centers of the East we see testimony to concepts of value in the expenditure of money. From the sense of value which urban aristocracies and central government officials brought to the construction of monuments we move to the economic motivations for a heavy infilling in late Byzantine and Islamic times. The shift from the regularity and openness of the classical city to the crowded and irregular pattern of the Islamic city[47] seems to have begun in late Byzantine times, so that it is not specifically Islamic (Kennedy 1985: 12–15). There is no way to explain the practice, however, apart from an understanding that there was a perceived value in spending the resources needed for the building itself, and a reward for the economic rewards obtainable from the use of urban land. From a society which, as I have emphasized repeatedly, saw land and agriculture as the prime generator of

231

wealth, and cities as the repositories of that wealth and the vehicles for the demonstration of the nobility such wealth provided, we see a move to economic assumptions which assess urban, non-agricultural activity at a sufficiently high level to make a significant impact on the physical urban scene.

The absence of these assumptions of economic benefit in the West meant that the towns died when their traditional resources dried up, and their death was a major contribution to the social and political changes we associate with the beginning of "medieval" society. The particularly urban characteristic of Roman civilization was due not to the generation of great fortunes by commercial entrepreneurs, but rather the particular ethos which made conspicuous town expenditure part of the identifier and prestige of wealth, along with the economic and administrative roles which the towns played in maintaining the government structure. The towns were not generators of wealth, they were users. They did not play a productive economic role, and they could have been dispensed with for the most part, in the bulk of trade which involved shipment of foodstuffs, metals and mineral and other natural resources. They did, however, serve ideological and administrative functions, which allowed them to collect the cash they needed. Where those functions ended and the other major source of revenue, army payments, was also lacking, absent perceptions of economic benefit to be gained from urban activity, the towns had no economic viability, and they virtually disappeared, taking with them their social and cultural activities.

The cultural activity we associate with ancient society depended on the existence of urban agglomerations and the availability of surplus, often cash surplus, to be spent in commercially and agriculturally non-productive ways. This is Bowersock's "high culture" rather than the pervasive and flexible "Greekism" which could penetrate villages and farms, and permeate cultures to become part of the medium of expression (Bowersock 1990). It existed in the cities, where theaters and stadia had to be built, where someone had to pay the actors, patronize the poets, and afford salaries or income to the teachers and philosophers. The land and its owners, and then the State, in part, defrayed these costs, injecting the necessary cash into the cities. But the cities themselves did not produce the surplus; commerce in itself could not provide the needed surplus, and so, when cash dried up, so too did the cities, and with them, culture. It would be a new world when urban activity began to be productive enough to support urbanism.

NOTES

1 Cf. Herrin (1987) as a whole for her argument.
2 The same continuity is emphasized by contributors other than Tsafrir and

Foerster to King and Cameron (1994), presenting "a substantial amount of continuity between the Byzantine and the Islamic period" in Zeyadeh 1994: 130, and "continuity of occupation into the Umayyad age... the once-traditional image of serious disruption and social dislocation at the time of the Islamic conquest no longer obtains," MacAdam 1994: 91.

3 Cf. Reuter 1985: 75–94.

4 Cf. pp. 225–227, for my reservations.

5 Theoretical considerations by Renfew 1982: 1–8, with extensive citations. The brief papers in this volume which deal with our period are more suggestive than conclusive; cf. also note 13 below.

6 I may add to this list others that I have noted, none of them outside the expected range: *P. Vatic. Aphrod.* 4, house sale, Aphrodito, V1 3 1/2 sol.; *P. Vatic. Aphrod.* 6, house sale, Aphrodito, Vl, 1 1/2 sol.

7 For examples, even Howgego, arguing for the monetization of the economy, notes "the substantial use in payments in kind for rents" (Howgego 1992: 25), and in connection with the use of payments in coin for wages, "wage labour consisted of a relatively small part of a workforce embracing free independent workers, slaves, and other forms of dependent labour" (ibid. 26–27).

8 This is clear from a survey of the texts listed by Johnson and West (1949: 80–93).

9 Cf. Finley 1985: 134–139, 195.

10 This was true for church wealth as well, as is clear from the resources discussed by Wipszycka (1972). It is emphasized, with a review of the major items of evidence, by Hendy 1988: 33.

11 Calculated by Finley 1985: 102.

12 For a discussion of the wealthy Gallic landowners, and an examination of the patterns of relationships in the society suggesting continuity from pre-Roman to post-imperial days, cf. Wightman 1978: 97–128.

13 Rostovtzeff (1957) expands the role "of the great merchants and the rich transporters" by involving them in transport of foodstuffs for the cities of the empire; how much did they carry of manufacturing goods?

14 As Herrin has recently shown (1987: 123); although she acknowledges that the extent to which exchange attests trade is not clear.

15 It is true that literature shows evidence of familiarity with distant lands, but how that familiarity was obtained is anybody's guess.

16 Cf. also Col. 3.4–4, mentioning that tin was coming from Spain; Col. 16.16, dyeing of Sicilian purple; but the collection of chemical recipes may not prove the use of the products in Egypt.

17 The chemical and metallurgical texts of *P. Holm.* and *P. Leid.* X account for most of the individual attestations.

18 Hendy points out (and his map of Spanish moneying supports his view) that Merovingian moneying was not unique, just more extreme in its scattering, than Visigothic (Hendy 1988: 54).

19 As, for example, the observations of Lopez 1943: 16–18, 28–34, that the gold currency with the ruler's effigy pertain more to the prestige of the central power, and relate to international politics as much as international trade; the nature of the gateway communities like Dorestad attest attitudes toward exchange on the part of rulers who use exchange for acquisition of prestige items, and are therefore to be increased. (Cf. the remarks of Hodges and Whitehouse 1984: 91–101; and also, of Hodges 1982a: 117–123, who discusses the nature of gateway communities more fully in Hodges 1982b: 47–86.) There are many examples of this currency at the gateway ports of Domberg and

Dorestad, while Carolingian coins appear with greater frequency; cf. the summary of the evidence in Jankuhn 1963: 33–42.

20 This is very clear from the citations of Dopsch 1937: 376–377, although not every instance of evidence for gold and silver is really coin; the gold and silver acquired by the fortune-teller mentioned in Gregory of Tours, *Historia Francorum*. 7.44 is surely the vast amount of jewelry which that passage reports her wearing.

21 It is worth noting that virtually all the instances which are cited by Dopsch 1937: 373–383 to demonstrate the existence of a money (i.e. coinage) economy relate to this coinage, and that Dopsch himself sees the currency as a large sum valuation, relief from which may be obtained by alternate means of payment.

22 There is, for example, the story of the bishop who feared he could not meet Charlemagne's request for special cheese, but no suggestion that the arduously collected cheeses were acquired by purchase ([Einhard] *De Carolo Magno* 2.15). Elsewhere, the credulous and acquisitive bishop who was cheated in the purchase of a stuffed mouse negotiated for ridiculous sums of silver by weight, the rare instance of actual purchase in these tales ([Einhard] *De Carolo Magno* I.16). It is also this work that is cited to show "international trade" as Charlemagne sends gifts of cloth to Harun al-Raschid, and other goods go to and from the emperor as gifts.

23 From M. Weidemann 1982: 2. 350.

24 Lopez 1943: esp. 18–20, 35–37 for the fabrics.

25 If, in fact, this idea of commerce at that time is not largely a fantasy; the weaknesses in Bolin's thesis are effectively shown, with alternative explanation of the Frankish coinage: Arab gold/silver ratio, by Morrison 1963: 403–432, esp. 414–426.

26 As, for example, in the ninth century, when the occupation of Spain made convenient enough to move from Europe into the Maghrib, commerce in fact brought the Saharan caravan trade into increasing, importance in the Arab world; cf. Laroui 1977: 111–126.

27 I quote, without retranslation from the French, most of the extract in Hadj-Sadok:

Ces marchands parlent l'arabe, le persan, le romain [grec et latin], le franc, l'espagnol, le slave et voyagent d'Orient en Occident et vice-versa, par terre et par mer. Ils rapportent d'Occident des esclaves des deux sexes, des eunuques, du brocart, des peaux de castor, des pelisses de martre et autres fourrures, et des satires. Ils s'embarquent du pays de Firanja [France], sur la Mer de l'Ouest, se rendent à al-Faramâ [an Egyptian port]; de là, ils transportent leurs marchandises à dos de chameau jusqu'à al-Qulzum, à vingt-cinq parasangs. Ils s'embarquent sur la Mer Orientale pour se rendre d'al-Qulzum à al-Jâr, le port de Médine, puis à Judda [Jidda], ensuite s'en vont au Sind, au Hind [India] et en Chine. Ils rapportent de Chine du muse, du bois d'aloès, du camphre, de la canelle et autres produits de ces pays. Ils reviennent à al-Qulzum, puis transportent leurs marchandises à al-Faramâ et s'embarquent sur la Mer Occidentale. Quelquefois ils se rendent à Constantinople pour vendre aux Rûm [the Byzantines] leurs produits.

(Ibn Khurradadhbih 1949: 21–23)

28 For references to Priscus at the court of Chilperic and Armentarius the moneylender, as well as a few other references to Jews and Syrians, and the dozen or so references to foreign traders, cf. Weidemann 1982: 347–349.

29 Un article d'exportation bien connu consiste dans les esclaves, garçons et

filles, qui ont été enlevés en France et dans la Galice, ainsi que les eunuques Slaves. Tous les eunuques Slaves qui se trouvent sur la surface de la terre proviennent d'Espagne.

(Ibn Hauqal 1964: 1.109)

30 It is worth noting the comment of Al-Masudi (1962: vol. 1, 9), who explains the title of his geographic self-epitome, "Meadows of Gold and Mines of Gems", as "à cause de la haute valeur et de l'importance des [matières] qu'il renferme".

31 So he reports in *Prairies d'Or* (Al-Masudi 1962: § 914, vol. 2, 344): he happened to find the book in a.h. 336 (AD 947); it had been dedicated to the heir apparent to the Muslim sovereign of Andalusia in a.h. 328, so it was very recently in Cairo when Al-Masudi came across it. In his lists of sources, §§ 8–14, he notes no Western text, and his sections on the Greek world, while evincing some knowledge about Greek writers, could all depend on second-hand Arabic material.

32 Cf. also details of the agricultural revolution in White 1962.

33 The dispassionate account of the activities of the Rus and the Kingdom of Kiev, aimed at explicating the history of the Scandinavian element in the area, by Jones 1984: 241–268, suggests very strongly that during the earlier part of the period, when the Scandinavian element in the area remained vital (*c.* 800–1050), "trade" was intermixed with raiding and pillage in the best Viking tradition. Jones refers to many Arab allusions to the Rus trading area, but the items involved in the trade were those luxury items suitable to the caravan trade:

Arabian silver, Persian glass, Chinese silk, narrow-necked bronze bottles from east of the Caspian, exotic purses from India, spices and wines, all these found their way to Novgorod, Gotland and the houses and graces of Swedish Uppland, in exchange for slaves, weapons, honey and wax, and an odorous plenitude of furs.

(Jones 1984: 253)

As we have seen, there is little evidence that much of this penetrated to the West in the form of trade, and Ibn Rustah's description of the Rus in the tenth century hardly suggests that the trade provided them great prosperity or an accumulation of wealth:

They have no cultivated land but depend for their living on that they can obtain from Saqalibah's (Slavic) land.... They have no estates, villages or fields: their only business is dealing in sables, squirrel and other furs, and the money they acquire from these transactions they keep in their belts.

(Jones 1984: 255)

What we do not have in the Arab sources is any notion of how the trade in the furs started, once the animals gave up their skins; the Russian Primary Chronicle, in the entry for 6367 (AD 859), give us one point of departure: squirrel and beaver skins were not traded in the first instance, but were a tribute imposed on households by the Khazars. There is another mention of source in "The Tale of Ihor's Campaign" (in Andrusyschen and Kirkconnel 1963: 11) where squirrel skins are tribute to the Polovtsians after the battle (in 1185).

34 Herrin continues:

In making the necessary adjustments to a village and castle based society the empire witnessed a tremendous upheaval, in which the central administration experienced extreme strains. In place of local autonomy and initiative in self-preservation, Constantinople had to provide for defense throughout the empire.

(Herrin 1987: 317)

35 For the importance of the tradition of culture, and differences between East and West, it is worth noting, a "wealth of classical resources [which] created a living link back to the ancients, which determined much of the East's political direction", while the Western use of ancient resources "created something quite different" (Herrin 1987: 444).

36 Lee adds: "Indeed, the general lack of cities or towns is significant, for urbanization is usually (though not always) a concomitant of state formation" (Lee 1993: 27–28). Cf. pp. 159–61 for a survey of sites.

37 Although urbanized under Rome, the Gallic area did not attain the urban wealth or social eminence of other areas (King 1990: 68–88).

38 Those on the Roman side, in northern Gaul, were quite small in terms of the areas enclosed by the stalls, at least to the extent of excavation (Brulet 1990: 79–99).

39 In the view of Randsborg, the differences between East and West are reflected in the inability of the state to finance the cities in late antiquity while the Islamic cities "were strongly marked by craft and trading interests and less influenced by any aristocracy or state that made its presence felt through the erection of monuments" (Randsborg 1991: 174).

40 Chilperic's circuses at Soissons and Paris were not the subject of the praises customary in Roman times, but rather called pretentious by Gregory of Tours, *Historia Francorum* 5.17, 6.30.

41 This is the case whether or not Goffart (1980) is correct in his conclusion that the hospitalitas of the German settlers merely represented a sharing out of taxes which were no longer payable to the Empire; the Roman tax structure was very quickly dismantled with the advent of the German kingships.

42 The effects of course were gradual; the Merovingians initially attempted to maintain some sort of taxing system. Gregory of Tours (*Historia Francorum* 9.30) reports King Childebert II (died 595) sending out high officials to prepare new tax lists and to require payment. The manner in which the crown lost the taxes is indicated by the same account: when the officers came to Tours, Gregory admitted that the town had been taxed in the time of Lothar (died 561), but insisted that in the reign of Charibert (561–567), the king promised not to change the tax laws to the town's detriment; then a dispute over assessment resulted in the lists being destroyed and Charibert promising that public taxation should be ended for Tours. The untaxed status continued through the reign of Sigibert I (to 575), Gregory asserted, and on through the first 14 years of Childebert's reign. In the end, as a result of the bishop's claim, the King issued a letter of immunity to Tours, as a mark of respect for St Martin.

43 Hodges and Whitehouse (1984: 20–53) suggest that the role the plague of the sixth century played was rendered more long-lasting by the disruption of the social and economic systems which was occurring in the same period.

44 In particular, grand theories of population decrease, as that propounded by Russell (1958), assuming that economic and social interaction in the population was great enough to be seriously affected by numbers, and historical explanations based on population have been challenged even by demographic studies; cf. Salmon 1974 177–79. For Lombard Italy, it is worth noting that the urban construction favored by Theodoric and the Ostrogoths was not, for the most part, carried on by the Lombards (Ward-Perkins 1984).

45 *P. Gen. Lat. 1*, recto, 1; P. Berol. 6866 *P. Aberd.* 133.

46 For the argument that this was done by allocation of tax-liabilities, cf. Goffart 1980.

47 There is an apocryphal story that two architects were sent by UNESCO to Fez, to develop a city map of this heritage city. They disappeared into the Medina, only to be found some months later, driven to hashish to escape the bafflement of trying to fit into cartography streets that wound back on themselves, crossed over and under and through houses, or simply disappeared and reappeared from place to place.

BIBLIOGRAPHY

N.B. Classical authors are quoted with the usual abbreviations.

[Aeschylus] Aischylos (1959) *Tragodien und Fragmente* [in Greek and German], Oskar Werner (ed. and trans.), Munich: E. Heimeran.

Albertus Magnus (1890–9) *Ethicorum, Libri X*, J. Borgnet (ed.), vol. 7 Paris: Vives.

—— (1968) *Super Ethica commentum et Quaestiones I–V*, Institutum Alberti Magni Coloniense (ed.), Munster i Westfalen: Aschendorff.

Alcock, Susan (1994) "Breaking Up the Hellenistic World: Survey and Society," in Ian Morris (ed.), *Classical Greece: Ancient Histories and Modern Archeologies*, Cambridge: Cambridge University Press.

[Alcaeus] Alkaios (2nd edn., 1963) *Alkaios* (in Greek and German), Max Treu (ed.), Munich: E. Heimeran.

—— [and Sappho] (1971) *Fragmenta*, E.M. Voight (ed.), Amsterdam: Athenaeum-Polak and Van Grenrep.

Al-Masudi (1962) *Les Prairies d'Or*, B. de Meynard and P. de Courteille (trans.), C. Pellat (rev. and corr.), Paris: Sociéte Asiatique, Collection d'ouvrages orientaux, 16: vol. I.

—— (1989) *The Meadows of Gold*, P. Lunde and C. Stone (trans.), London/New York: Kegan Paul International

Altekar, A. S. (1941) "The Position of Smritis as a Source of Dharma," in S. M. Katre and P. K. Gode (eds), *A Volume of Studies in Indology Presented to Professor P. V. Kane*, Poona: Oriental Book Agency.

—— (1958) "Vedic Society," in *The Cultural Heritage of India*, Belur Math, Calcutta: Sri Ramakrishna Mutt, vol. I.

[Anakreon] (1954) in *Elegy and Iambus*, J. M. Edmonds (ed. and trans.), vol. 2, Cambridge, Mass.: Havard University Press.

—— (1960) in *Griechische Lyrik*, Eduard Morike (transcript.), Uvo Holscher (ed.) Frankfurt am Main: Insel-Verlag.

Andreades, Andreas Michael (1965) *Geschichte der griechischen Staatswirtschaft: von der Heroenzeit bis zur Schlacht bei Chaironeia*, Hildesheim: G. Olms.

Andreau, J., Schmitt, P., and Schnapp A. (1978) "Paul Veyne et l'énérgétisme," *Annales ESC*, XXXIII: 307–325.

Andrusyschen, C. H. and Kirkconnell, W. (eds) (1963) *The Ukranian Poets*, Toronto.

Aquinas, Thomas (1964–) *Summa theologica* [Latin and English], Cambridge, UK: Blackfriars/New York: McGraw Hill.

Arawi, Abd Allah (1970) *L'histoire du Maghreb: un essai de synthese*, Paris: F. Maspero.

239

—— (1977) *The History of the Maghrib: An Interpretive Essay*, R. Manheim (trans.), Princeton: Princeton University Press.

Aristophanes (3rd ed, 1946) *Aristophanes*, Victor Toulon (ed.) and Hilaire van Daele (trans.), Paris: Les Belles Lettres.

Aristotle (1934; 1975) *Nichomachean Ethics*, H. Rackham (trans.), Cambridge, Mass.: Harvard University Press.

—— (1947) *Politics*, W. D. Ross (trans.), in Richard McKeon (ed.), *Introduction to Aristotle*, New York: The Modern Library.

—— (1967) *Politics* [Greek and English], H. Rackham (trans.), London: Heinemann/Cambridge, Mass.: Harvard University Press.

—— (1992) *The Athenian Constitution*, H. Rackham (ed.), Cambridge, Mass.: Harvard University Press.

—— (1955) *The Ethics of Aristotle*, J. A. K. Thomson (trans. and ed.), Harmondsworth: Penguin Books.

—— (1975) *The Metaphysics* [Greek and English], Hugh Tredennick (trans.), Cambridge, Mass.: Harvard University Press.

—— (2nd edn., 1992) *Eudemian Ethics*, Books I, II, VIII, Michael Woods (trans.), Oxford: Clarendon Press.

Augustine of Hippo (1955) *De civitate dei*, Turnholt: Brepols Corpus Christianorum, Series latina, 47.

Ausonius, Decimus Magnus (1932, 1980) *Decimi Magni Ausonii Mosella*, Walther John (trans. and com.), Trier: Paulinus Druckerei.

Austin, M. M. (1970) *Greece and Egypt in the Archaic Age*, Proceedings of the Cambridge Philological Society, Supplement no. 2, Cambridge.

Austin, M. and Vidal Naquet, P. (1982) *Economie e societa nella Grecia antica*, Torino: Boringhieri.

Averroes (1542) *Aristotelis Stagyrite libri Metaphysicae XII. Averroeq[ue] evis fideliss interprete* in [Aristotle] *Aristotelis Opera cum Averrois Commentariis*, Venice: Junctas.

—— (1542) *In Moralia Nicomachia Expositio* in [Aristotle] *Aristotelis Opera cum Averrois Commentariis*, vol. III, Venice: Junctas.

—— (1981) *ha-Nusahim ha-Ivriyim shel ha-maamar ha-revii shel ha-beur ha-emtsai shel Ibn Roshd le-Sefer ha-midot al-shem Nikomakhus la-Aristo*, Eliezer Zeev Berman (ed.), Jerusalem: ha-Akademyah ha-leumit ha-Yisreelit le-madaim.

Baba Mezi\a (1935, English edn.) London: Soncino Press series: The Babylonian Talmud.

Badian, E. (1958) *Foreign clientelae*, Oxford: Clarendon Press.

Badre, Leila (1991) "Archeology in Syria: Kazel," *American Journal of Archeology*, 95: 734–735.

Baeck, Louis (1991) "The Economic Thought of Classical Islam," in W. Barber (ed.), *Perspectives on the History of Economic Thought*, Brookfield: Vermont, published for the History of Economics Society by E. Elgar, Gower Pub. Co., vol. V.

—— (1994) *The Mediterranean Tradition in Economic Thought*, London: Routledge.

Bagnall, Roger S. (1985) "Currency and Inflation in Fourth Century Egypt," *Bulletin of the American Society of Papyrologists*, Supplement 5, Chico: California Scholars Press.

—— (1988a) "Archeology and Papyrology," *Journal of Roman Archeology*, I: 197–202.

—— (1988b) "Greeks and Egyptians: Ethnicity, Status, and Culture," in Robert S.

BIBLIOGRAPHY

Bianchi (ed.), *Cleopatra's Egypt: Age of the Ptolemies*, Brooklyn, New York: Brooklyn Museum, 21–27.

Bal Krishna, "Economics in Ancient India," *Indian Journal of Economics*, vol. II.

Baloglou, C. and Constantinidis, C. (1993) *Die Wirtschaft in der Gedankenwelt der alten Griechen*, Frankfurt: P. Lang.

Baron, S. W. (1941) "The Economic Views of Maimonides," in S. W. Baron (ed.), *Essays on Maimonides*, New York: Columbia University Press.

Bell, J. F. (1980) *A History of Economic Thought*, New York: Robert E. Kriege.

Beloch, Julius (1886) *Die Bevölkerung der griechisch-römischen Welt*, Leipzig: Duncker und Humblot.

Bennett, W. J. and Blakely, Jeffrey A. (1989) *Tell el-Hesi. The Persian Period* (Stratum V), Winona Lake, Indiana: Eisenbrauns.

Benveniste, Emile (1969) *Le vocabulaire des institutions indo-européenes*, Paris: Editions de Minuit.

Berman, L. (1978) "Ibn Rushd's Middle Commentary on the *Nicomachean Ethics* in Medieval Literature," in Jean Jolivet (ed.), *Multiple Averroes*, Paris: Belles Lettres.

Bernard, P. (1982) "An Ancient Greek City in Central Asia," *Scientific American* 246: 148–159.

Berthoud, A (1981) *Aristote et l'argent*, Paris: F. Maspero.

Berti, E. (ed.) (1989a) *La Razionalita Pratica: Modelli e Problemi*, Genova: Marietti.

— — (1988) *Tradizione e Attualita della Filosofia Pratica*, Genova: Marietti.

Bhagwan Das (3rd edn., 1924) *The Science of Emotions*, Adyar: Theosophical Library.

Bianchi, Robert (1978) "The Striding Draped Male Figure of Ptolemaic Egypt," in H. Maehler and V. M. Strocka (eds), *Das Ptolemaysche Aegypten: Akten der internationale Symposions, 27–29. September 1976 in Berlin*, Mainz am Rhein: von Zabern, 95–102.

Bianchini, M. (1976) "Elementi di economia nel pensiero politico di Cicerone," *Nuova Rivista Storica*.

Bingen, Jean (1978) *La papyrus Revenue Laws: Tradition Grecque et Adaptation Hellénistique*, Rhenisch-Westfälisch Akademie der Wissenschaften, Vorträge G 231, Opladen: Westdeutscher Verlag.

— — (1984) "Tensions Structurelles de la Société Ptolémaïque," *Atti del XVII congresso internazionale de Papirologia*, vol. III, Naples: Centro internazionale per lo studio dei papiri ercolanesi, 920–940.

Boardman, John (1990) "Al Mina and History," *Oxford Journal of Archeology*, 9 (2): 169–190.

Böckh, A. (1817; 3rd edn., 1886) *Die Staatshaushaltung der Athener*, Max Fränkel (ed.), Berlin: G. Reimer, 2 vols.

Bolin, Sture (1953) "Mohammed, Charlemagne and Ruric," *Scandinavian Economic Review*, 1: 5–39.

Bolkestein, H. (1979) *Wohltätigkeit und Armenpflege in Vorchristlichen Altertum*, New York: Arno Press.

Bonacasa, Nicola and Di Vita, Antonino (eds) (1983–84) *Alessandria e il Mondo Ellenistico-Romano: Studi in Onore di Achille Adriani*, Roma: L'Erma' di Bretschneider.

Bonar, James (3rd edn., 1922) *Philosophy and Political Economy in Some of Their Historical Relations*, London: George Allen & Unwin.

Bowersock, G. W. (1990) *Hellenism in Late Antiquity*, Ann Arbor: University of Michigan Press.

BIBLIOGRAPHY

Bowman, Alan K. (1996) *Egypt after the Pharaohs. 332 BC–AD 642 from Alexander to the Arab Conquest*, Berkeley, Calif.: University of California Press.

— — (1980) "The Economy of Egypt in the Latter Fourth Century," in C. E. King (ed.), *Imperial Revenue, Expenditure and Monetary Policy in the Fourth Century AD: The Fifth Oxford Symposium on Coinage and Monetary History*, Oxford: BAR International Series 76: 23–40.

Bowra, C. M. (ed.) (1935) *Pindar: Carmina, cum fragmentis*, Oxford: Clarendon Press.

Braibanti, Ralph and Spengler, Joseph J. (eds) (1963) *Administration and Economic Development in India*, Durham, N.C.: Duke University Press.

Braund, D. (1989) "Function and Disfunction: Personal Patronage in Roman Imperialism" in A. Wallace-Hadrill (ed.), *Patronage in ancient society*, London/New York: Routledge.

Briant, Pierre (1982) *Rois, Tributs et Paysans: Études sur les Formations Tributaires du Moyen-Orient ancien*, Paris: Les Belles Lettres series: Annales littéraires de l'Université de Besançon 269, Centre de Recherches d'Historie Ancienne, 43.

— — (1982a) "Remarques sur 'laoi' et Esclaves Ruraux en Asie Mineure Hellénistique," in P. Briant, *Rois, Tributs et Paysans: Études sur les Formations Tributaires du Moyen-Orient ancien*, Paris: Les Belles Lettres series, 95–135 (originally published in *Actes du Colloque 1971 sur l'esclavage, Annales littéraires de l'Université de Besançon*, Centre de Recherches d'Histoire Ancienne, 6, 93–133).

— — (1982b) "Communautés Rurales, Forces Productives et Mode de Production Tributaire," in P. Briant, *Rois, Tributs et Paysans: Études sur les Formations Tributaires du Moyen-Orient ancien*, Paris: Les Belles Lettres series, 405–430 (originally published in *Zamân* 1980: 76–100).

— — (1982c) "Produktivkräfte, Staat und tributäre Produktionsweisse im Achämenidenreic," in J. Herrmann and I. Sellnow (eds), *Produktivkräfte und Gesellschaftsformationen in vorkapitalistischer Zeit*, Berlin: Akademie-Verlag, 351–372.

Brams, J. and Vanhamel, W. (1989) *Guillaume de Moerbeke*, Leuven: Leuven University Press.

Brown, Blanche R. (1957) *Ptolemaic Paintings and Mosaics and the Alexandrian Style*, Cambridge, Mass.: Archeological Institute of America.

Brulet, R. (1990) "La Gaule Septentrionale au Bas-Empire, Occupation du Sol et Defense du Territoire dans l'Arrière-pays aux IVe et Ve Siècles," *Trierer Zeitschrift*, Trier, Beiheft, 11: 79–99.

Brunt, P. (1965) *Amicitia in the late Roman Republic*, Proceedings of the Cambridge Philological Society, Cambridge: Cambridge Philological Society.

Bucher, K. (1893; 5th edn. 1904) *Die Entstehung der Volkswirtschaft: Vortrage und Aufsatze*, Tubingen: Laupp.

Buchsenschutz, B. (1869; 1962) *Besitz und Erwerb im grieschen Altenthume* [Halle]/Aalen: Scientia Verlag.

Burckhardt, Jacob (2nd edn., 1898–1902) *Griechishe Kulturgeschichte*, Jacob Oeri (ed.), Berlin: W. Spemann.

Burgin, A. (1993) *Zur Soziogenese der Politischen Okonomie*, Marburg: Metropolis-Verlag.

Buridan, John (1513) *Questiones Johannis Buridani super decem libros Ethicorum Aristotelis ad Nicomachum*, Paris: I. Petit.

— — (1513) *Questiones Johannis Buridani super octo libros Politicorum Aristotelis*, G. Baterel (ed.), Paris: I. Petit.

Buridan, Jean (1988) *De Ethiek [Quaestiones super librum Ethicorum]* [Dutch] Henri Krop (ed.), Baam: Ambo.

Burkert, Walter (1992) *The Orientalizing Revolution: Near Eastern Influence on Greek Culture in the Early Archaic Age*, Walter Burkert and Margaret E. Pinder (trans.), Cambridge, Mass.: Harvard University Press.

Butler, Joseph (1900) *The Works of Bishop Butler*, London/New York: Macmillan.

Butzer, Karl W. (1980) "Remarks on the Geography of Settlement in the Nile Valley During Hellenistic Times," *Bulletin de la Société de Géographie d'Egypte*, 33: 5–36.

Calendar of Economists' Birthdays (1978), Chicago: University of Chicago Press.

Cameron, Averil (1993) *The Later Roman Empire: AD 284–430*, London: Fontana.

Cartledge, Paul (1983) " 'Trade and Politics' Revisited: Archaic Greece," in Peter Garnsey, Keith Hopkins and C. R. Whittaker (eds), *Trade in the Ancient Economy*, Berkeley/Los Angeles: University of California Press.

Carver, Thomas Gilbert (1885; 13th edn., 1982) *A treatise on the law relating to the Carriage of Goods by Sea*, Raoul P. Colinvaux (ed.), London: Stevens and Sons.

Caton-Thompson, G. and Gardner, E. W. (1934) *The Desert Fayum*, London: The Royal Anthropological Institute of Great Britain and Ireland.

Chakravarti, Appaswami (1969) "Jainism: Its Philosophy and Ethics" in *The Cultural Heritage of India*, Calcutta: Sri Ramakrishna Mission, Institute of Culture.

Chandra Banerji, Sures (1962) *Dharma Sutras: A Study in their Origin and Development*, Calcutta: Punthi Pusthak.

Chattopadhyaya, Debiprasad (6th edn., 1985) *Lokayata: A Study in Ancient Indian Materialism*, New Delhi: People's Publishing House.

Christiansen, E. (1991) *Coins of Alexandria and the Nomes: A Supplement to the British Museum Catalogue*, London: Department of Coins and Medals, British Museum.

Christensen, Aristea Papanicolaou and Johansen, Charlotte Friis (1971) *Hama: Fouilles et Recherches de la fondation Carlsberg, 1931–1938, III:2, Les Potteries Héllenistiques et les Terres Sigillées Orientales*, Copenhagen: Nationalmuseet Foundation Carlsberg.

Cicero, (1931) *De officiis* [Latin and English], Walter Miller (trans.), London: W. Heinemann/New York: Macmillan.

— — (1951) *De natura deorum* [Latin and English], H Rackham (trans.), London: Heinemann.

— — (1951) *De finibus bonorum et malorum* [Latin and English], H. Rackham (trans.), Cambridge, Mass.: Harvard University Press.

— — (1966) *De republica* [Latin and English], Clinton Walker Keyes (trans.), Cambridge, Mass.: Harvard University Press.

Cipolla, C. M. (1956) *Money, Prices, and Civilization in the Mediterranean World, Fifth to Seventeenth Century*, Princeton: Princeton University Press.

Cohen, E. (1992) *Athenian Economy and Society: A Banking Perspective*, Princeton: Princeton University Press.

Cohen, H. H. (1901–1906; rpt. 1964) "Usury" in C. Adler *et al.* (eds), *Jewish Encyclopedia*, New York: Ktav Publishing House, vol. 11: 27–34.

Colish, M. (1985) *The Stoic Tradition from Antiquity to the Early Middle Ages*, Leiden: E. J. Brill

Colledge, Malcolm (1987) "Greek and Non-Greek Interaction in the Art and Architecture of the Hellenistic East," in Amélie Kuhrt and Susan Sherwin-White (eds), *Hellenism in the East: The Interaction of Greek and Non-Greek Civilizations from Syria to Central Asia after Alexander*, Berkeley: University of California Press.

BIBLIOGRAPHY

—— (1974) [De Officiis] Les devoirs [French and Latin] Maurice Testard (ed. and trans.), Paris: Les Belles Lettres.

Cook, Brian F. (1983–1984) "Some Groups of Hadra Vases," in Nicola Bonacasa and Antonino Di Vita (eds), Alessandria e il Mondo Ellenistico-Romano: Studi in Onore di Achille Adriani, Rome: L'Erma' di Bretschneider.

Copleston, F. C. (1955) Aquinas, Harmondsworth: Penguin Books.

Corbier, M. (1984) "De Volsinii a Sestinum: Cura Aquae et Evergetisme Municipal de l'eau en Italie," Revue des études latines, 62: 236–274.

Corpus Inscriptionum Latinarum (1893–) Consilium et Autoritate Academiae Litterarum Borussicae Editum, Berlin: G. Reimer.

Coulson, William D. E. and Leonard, Albert, Jr (1982) "Investigations at Naukratis and Environs 1980 and 1981," American Journal of Archeology, 86: 361–380.

Coulson, William D. E. and Wilkie, Nancy (1986) "Ptolemaic and Roman Kilns in the Western Nile Delta," Bulletin of the American Schools of Oriental Research, 263: 61–73.

Criscuolo, L. and Geraci, G. (eds) (1987) Egitto e Storia Antica dall'Ellenismo all'età Araba: Bilancia di un Confronto, Atti del colloquio internazionale, Bologna, 31 agosto–2 settembre 1987, Bologna: CLUEB.

Danby, H. (1933) The Mishna, [English], London: Oxford University Press.

Dasgupta, Surendranath (1922) A History of Indian Philosophy, Cambridge: Cambridge University Press.

Dayanand Bhargava (1968) Jaina Ethics, Delhi: Motilal Banarsidass.

De Libera, A. (1990) Albert le Grand et la Philosophie, Paris: J. Vrin.

Demandt, Alexander (1989) Die Spätantike: Romanische Geschichte von Diocletian bis Justinian, 284–565 n. Chr., Munich: C. H. Beck.

Dentzer, Jean-Marie and Orthmann, Winfried (eds) (1989) Archéologie et Histoire de la Syrie II. La Syrie de l'époque Achéménide à l'Avenement de l'Islam, Saarbrück: Saarbrücker Druckerei und Verlag.

de Ste Croix, G. E. M. (1981) The Class Struggle in the Ancient Greek World, London: Duckworth.

Diels, Hermann (5th edn., 1934) Die Fragmente der Vorsokratiker [Greek and German], 2 vols., Berlin: Weidmann.

Diogenes Laertius (1981) De vitis, dogmatis et apophthegmatis clarorum philosophorum libri decem [Latin and Greek], Henricus Gustavus Hübnerus (ed.), Hildesheim/New York: G. Olms.

Dopsch, Alfons (1937) The Economic and Social Foundations of European Civilization [trans. (1918–1920) Wirtschaftliche und soziale Grundlagen der europaischen Kulturentwicklung], New York: Harcourt, Brace and Co., London: K. Paul, Trench, Trubner and Co., Ltd.

Drakopoulos, S. A. (1991) Values and Economic Theory: The Case of Hedonism, Aldershot: Avebury.

Drew, Katherine Fischer (1987) "Another Look at the Origins of the Middle Ages: A Reassessment of the Role of the Germanic Kingdoms," Speculum 62: 803–812.

Dupuy, C. (ed.) (1989) Traité des monnaies (Nicholas Oresme) et autres ecrits monetaires du XIVᵉ siècle (Jean Buridan, Bartole de Sassoferrato) [French] F. Chartrain (trans.), Lyons: La Manufacture.

Durant, Will (1954) The Story of Civilization: Part I. Our Oriental Heritage, New York: Simon and Schuster.

Eadie, John W. and Ober, Josiah (eds) (1985) The Craft of the Ancient Historian, Essays in Honor of Chester G Starr, Lanham, MD: University Press of America.

Egner, Erich (1985) Der Verlust der alten Okonomik, Berlin: Duncker and Humbolt.

Ejges, S. (1930) *Das Geld im Talmud*, Wilna: Garber.

[Einhard] (1969; 1981) *Two Lives of Charlemagne [De Carlo Magno]* [English] L. Thorpe (trans.), Harmondsworth, England: Penguin.

Ekelund, R. B. and Hebert, R. F. (3rd edn., 1990) *A History of Economic Theory and Method*, New York: McGrawHill.

Elayi, J. (1987) "Al-Mina sur l'Oronte à l'époque Perse," in Edward Lipinski (ed.), *Studia Phoenicia V. Phoenicia and the East Mediterranean in the First Millennium* BC.

Encyclopaedia Britannica (15th edn., 1974) New York: Henry G. Allen and Co.

Encyclopedia of the Social Sciences (1931) New York: Macmillan.

Eph'al, I. (2nd edn., 1951–1971) "Syria-Palestine under Achaemenid Rule," *Cambridge Ancient History IV, The Persian Empire and the West*, New York: Cambridge University Press.

Epstein, I. (1935–1952) *The Babylonian Talmud* [English], London: Soncino Press.

Ernout A. and Meillet A. (4th edn., 1985) *Dictionnaire Etymologique de la Langue Latine*, Paris: Klincksieck.

Essid, Y. M. (1986) "Islamic Economic Thought," in S. T. Lowry (ed.), *Pre-Classical Economic Thought: From the Greeks to the Scottish Enlightment*, Boston: Kluwer.

Euripides (1948) *Elektra*, Ernst Buschor (transcript), Munchen: C. H. Beck.

el-Fakharani, F. (1983) "Recent Excavations at Marea in Egypt," in G. Grimm, H. Heinen and E. Winter (eds), *Das Römisch-Byzantinische Ägypten, Akten des Internationalen Symposions 26–30 September 1978 in Trier*, Aegyptiaca Treverensia 2, Mainz am Rhein: P. von Zabern.

Farrisol, Abraham (1928) *Magen Avraham*, in D. S. Levinger, "Selections from Abraham Farrisol's 'David's Shield'," *Hazofeh = ha'Tsofe le'Hochmat Israel*, Budapest, 12: 277–297.

Ferrary, J. L. (1988) *Philhellenisme et imperialisme*, Rome: Ecole Française de Rome.

— — (1995) "Statesman and Law in Cicero's Political Philosophy," in A. Laks and M. Schofield (eds), *Justice and generosity*, Cambridge: Cambridge University Press.

Finley, M. I. (1965) "Classical Greece," *Deuxième Conférence Internationale d'Histoire Économique, Aix-en-Provence 1962. I. Trade and Politics in the Ancient World*, Paris: La Haye Mouton.

— — (1969) *The Ancient Empires and the Economy. Third International Conference of Economic History, Munich 1965*, Paris: Mouton & Co.

— — (1970) "Aristotle and Economic Analysis," *Past and Present*, 47: 3–25.

— — (1973) *The Ancient Economy*, Berkeley: University of California Press.

— — (ed.) (1979) *The Bucher-Meyer Controversy*, New York: Arno Press.

— — (1981) *Economy and Society in Ancient Greece*, Brent D. Shaw and Richard P. Saller (eds), London: Chatto & Windus Ltd.

— — (2nd edn., 1985) *The Ancient Economy*, London/Berkeley: University of California Press.

Forbis, E. P. (1993) "Liberalitas and Largitio: Terms for Private Munificence in Italian Honorary Inscriptions," *Athenaeum*, 81.

Forderer, M. (1960) *Zum homerischen Margites*, Amsterdam: A. M. Hakkert.

Foucart, P. (1888) "Décrets atheniens du IVe siècle," *Bulletin de Correspondance Hellenique*, XII: 153–179.

Fraser, P. M. (1972) *Ptolemaic Alexandria*, Oxford: Clarendon Press.

Gadamer, Hans-Georg (1978) *Die Idee des Guten Zwischen Plato und Aristoteles*, Heidelberg: Winter.

Garnsey, Peter (1983) "Grain for Rome," in Peter Garnsey, Keith Hopkins, and C. R. Whittaker (eds), *Trade in the Ancient Economy*, Berkeley/Los Angeles: University of California Press.

—— (1989) *Famine and Food Supply in the Graeco-Roman World*, Cambridge: Cambridge University Press.

Garnsey, Peter, Hopkins, Keith, and Whittaker, C. R. (eds) (1983) *Trade in the Ancient Economy*, Berkeley/Los Angeles: University of California Press.

Garnsey, Peter and Woolf, G. (1989) "Patronage of the Rural Poor in the Roman World," in A. Wallace-Hadrill (ed.), *Patronage in Ancient Society*, London/New York: Routledge.

Gauthier, P. (1985) *Les Cités Grecques et leurs Bienfaiteurs*, Athens: Ecole Française d'Athènes/Paris: Diffusion de Boccard.

Ghoshal, U. N. (1954) "Social Conditions," in R. C. Majumdar and A.D. Pusalkar and A.K. Majumdar (eds), *The History and Culture of the Indian People: The Classical Age*, Bombay: Bharatiya Vidya Bhavan.

—— (1959) *A History of Indian Political Ideas: The Ancient Period and The Period of Transition to The Middle Ages*, London: Oxford University Press.

Giardina, A. (1989) "Il Mercante," in A. Giardina (ed.), *L'Uomo Romano*, Roma: Laterzà.

Gillard, L. (1990) "Nicole Oresme: Economiste" in *Revue Historique*, 279, 3–39.

Goffart, Walter (1980) *Barbarians and Romans, AD 418–585*, Princeton: Princeton University Press.

Goitein, S. D. (1974) *Letters of Medieval Jewish Traders*, Princeton: Princeton University Press.

Goldsmith, Raymond W. (1987) *Premodern Financial Systems*, Cambridge: Cambridge University Press.

Gopalan, S. (1979) *Hindu Social Philosophy*, New Delhi: Wiley Eastern Limited.

Gordon, Barry (1963) "Aristotle and Hesiod: The Economic Problem in Greek Thought," *Review of Social Economy*, XXI, 2, September.

—— (1975; re-edn. 1976) *Economic Analysis Before Adam Smith: Hesiod to Lessius*, London: Macmillan.

—— (1987) "Biblical and Early Judeo-Christian Thought: Genesis to Augustine," in S. T. Lowry (ed.), *Pre-Classical Economic Thought: From the Greeks to the Scottish Enlightenment*, Boston: Kluwer.

—— (1989) *The Economic Problem in Biblical and Patristic Thought*, Leiden: E. J. Brill.

Goudriaan, K. (1988) *Ethnicity in Ptolemaic Egypt*, Amsterdam: J. C. Gieben.

Grainger, John D. (1990) *The Cities of Seleukid Syria*, Oxford: Clarendon Press.

—— (1991) *Hellenistic Phoenicia*, Oxford: Clarendon Press.

Green, Peter (1990) *Alexander to Actium: The Historical Evolution of the Hellenistic Age*, Berkeley: University of California Press.

Greene, K. (1986) *The Archeology of the Roman Economy*, London: Batsford.

Gregory, C. A. (1982) *Gifts and Commodities*, London/New York: Academic Press.

Gregory of Tours (1937–1951) *Historiarum Francorum libri decem*, Bruno Krusch and Wilhelm Levison (eds), Hanover: Impensis Bibliopolis Hahniani: series Monumenta Germaniae historica, tome 1, pars. 1.

—— *Glory of the Martyrs*, [*Vitae martyrorum*], Raymond van Dam (trans.), Liverpool: Liverpool University Press.

Grenier, J. C. (1980) *Temples Ptolémaïques et Romains: Répertoire Bibliographique*. Cairo: Institut français d'archéologie oriental du Caire; series Bibliothéque d'étude, tome 75.

Grice-Hutchison, M. (1952) *The School of Salamanca*, Oxford: Oxford University Press.

— — (1978) *Early Economic Thought in Spain*, London: George Allen & Unwin.

Grierson, Philip (1959) "Commerce in the Dark Ages: A Critique of the Evidence," *Transactions of the Royal Historical Society*, Cairo: Institut français d'archéologie orientale du Caire. Ser. 5 (9): 123–140.

Grimm, G., Heinen, H., and Winter, E. (eds) (1983) *Das Römisch-Byzantinische Ägypten, Akten des Internationalen Symposions 26–30 September 1978 in Trier*, Aegyptiaca Treverensia 2, Mainz am Rhein: P. von Zabern.

Grose, David F. (1989) *Early Ancient Glass: Core-Formed, Rod-Formed, and Cast Vessels and Objects from the Late Bronze Age to the Early Roman Empire, 1600 BC to AD 50*, New York: Hudson Hills Press and Toledo Museum of Art.

Gruben, Gottfried (1966; 2nd edn., 1976) *Die Tempel der Griechen*, Munich: Hirmer.

Gunn, B. (1943) "Notes on the Naukratis Stela," *Journal of Egyptian Archeology*, 29: 55–59.

Guthrie, W. K. C. (1981) *A History of Greek Philosophy*, Vol. VI, Cambridge: Cambridge University Press.

— — (1988) *The Sophists*, Cambridge: Cambridge University Press.

Hands, A. R. (1968) *Charities and Social Aid in Greece and Rome*, London: Thames and Hudson.

Haney, L. H. (1911; 3rd edn., 1936) *History of Economic Thought*, New York: Macmillan Co.

Hauqal, Ibn (1964) *Configuration de la Terre (Kitab Surat al-Ard)*, J. H. Kramers and G. Wiet (trans.), Paris: G. P. Maisonneuve and Larose.

Havelock, Eric A. (1957) *The Liberal Temper in Greek Politics*, New Haven: Yale University Press.

Hellegouarc'h, J. (1963) *Le Vocabulaire Latin des relations et des Partis Politiques sous la République*, Paris: Les Belles Lettres.

Hendy, M. (1988) "From Public to Private: The Western Barbarian Coinages as a Mirror of the Disintegration of Late Roman State Structures," *Viator* 18.

— — (1989) "Economy and State in Late Rome and Early Byzantium: An Introduction," *The Economy, Fiscal Administration and Coinage of Byzantium*, Northampton: Variorum Reprints, 1–23.

Hennis, W. (1987) *Max Weber's Fragestellung*, Tubingen: J. C. B. Mohr.

Herbert, Sharon C. (1994) *Tel Anafa I: ii. Final Report on Ten Years of Excavation at a Hellenistic and Roman Settlement in Northern Israel*, Journal of Roman Archeology Supplementary Series 10, Ann Arbor: Kelsey Museum.

Herrin, Judith (1987) *The Formation of Christendom*, Oxford: Basil Blackwell.

Herrmann, J. and Sellnow, I (eds) (1982) *Produktivkräfte und Gesellschaftsformationen in Vorkapitalistischer Zeit*, Berlin: Akademie-Verlag.

Hesiod (1966; special re-edn., 1985) *Theogonie; Werke und Tage* [Greek and German], Albert von Schirnding (ed.), Munich: Artemis and Winckler.

— — (1978) *Works and Days*, M. L. West (ed. and comment.), Oxford: Clarendon Press.

Hicks, J. R. (2nd edn., 1946) *Value and Capital*, London: Oxford University Press.

Hillman, G. (1981) "The Barleys from Iron Age Rifa'at" in John Matthers (ed.), *The River Qoueiq, Northern Syria and its Catchment: Studies Arising from the Tell Rifa'at Survey 1977–79*, Oxford: B.A.R., part 508–510.

Hobson, Deborah W. (1985) "House and Household in Roman Egypt," *Yale Classical Studies*, 28.

Hobbes, Thomas (1651; 1991) *Leviathan*, Richard Tuck (ed.), Cambridge/New York: Cambridge University Press.

Hodder, I. (ed.) (1995) *Interpreting Archeology: Finding Meaning in the Past*, London: Routledge.

Hodges, Richard (1982a) *Dark Age Economics, The Origins of Towns and Trade AD 600–100*, London: Duckworth.

—— (1982b) "The Evolution of Gateway Communities" in C. Renfrew and S. Shennan (eds.), *Ranking, Resource and Exchange: Aspects of the Archeology of Earthly European Society*, Cambridge/New York: Cambridge University Press.

Hodges, Richard and Whitehouse, David (1983) *Mohammed, Charlemagne and the Origins of Europe: Archeology and the Pirenne Thesis*, London: Duckworth.

Hölderlin, F. (1975) *Sämtliche Werke*, D. E. Sattler (ed.), Frankfurt am Main: Verlag Roter Stern.

Holladay, J. S. (1981–1982) *Cities of the Delta, Part III: Tell el-Maskhuta*. Malibu, California: Undend Publications American Research Center in Egypt, vol. 4–6.

Hollerbach, H. (1964) *Zur Bedeutung des Wortes Chreia*, unpublished Ph.D thesis, Cologne.

Homer (1911) *Opera*, David B. Monro and T. W. Allen (ed.), *Hymni, Cyclus, Fragmenta*, Oxford: Clarendon Press.

—— (1961) *Homerische Hymnen* [Greek and German], A. Weiher (ed.), Munich: Ernst Heimeran.

—— (1976–1978) *Iliad*, A. T. Murray (ed.), Cambridge, Mass.: Harvard University Press, series Loeb Classical Library

—— (1992) *Odyssey*, William Cowper (trans.), Peter Levi (ed.), London: J. M. Dent/Rutland, Vt.: Tuttle.

Hont, I. (1987) "The Language of Sociability and Commerce: Samuel Pufendorf and the Theoretical Foundations of the 'Four-Stages Theory'," in A. Pagden (ed.), *The Languages of Political Theory in Early-Modern Europe*, Cambridge: Cambridge University Press.

Hopkins, Keith (1980) "Taxes and Trade in the Roman Empire," *Journal of Roman Studies*, 70: 101–125.

—— (1983) "Introduction," in Peter Garnsey, Keith Hopkins, and C. R. Whittaker (eds), *Trade in the Ancient Economy*, Berkeley/Los Angeles: University of California Press.

Horace (4th edn., 1940) *Die Gedichte des Horaz* [Latin and German], F. Burger (ed.), Munich: Ernst Heimeran.

Howgego, C. (1992) "The Supply and Use of Money in the Roman World, 200 BC to AD 300," *Journal of Roman Studies*, 82: 1–31.

Huan-Chang, Chen (1911) *The Economic Principles of Confucius and His School*, New York: Columbia University Press.

Hurwitz, Ch. D. (1900) *ha'Mamon*, Warsaw: Tushya.

Husselman, Elinor M. (ed.) (1979) *Karanis Excavations of the University of Michigan in Egypt 1928–1935. Topography and Architecture. A Summary of the Reports of the Director, Enoch E. Peterson*, The University of Michigan Kelsey Museum of Archeology Studies 5, Ann Arbor: University of Michigan Press.

Hutter, H. (1978) *Politics as Friendship: The Origins of Classical Notions of Politics in the Theory and Practice of Friendship*: Waterloo, Ontario: Wilfrid Laurier University Press.

Ibn Hauqal (1964) *Configuration de la Terre* [*Kitab Sural al-Ard*], J. H. Kramers and G. Wiet (trans.), Paris: G. P. Maisonneuve and Larose, 2 vols.

BIBLIOGRAPHY

Ibn Khaldun (1969) *Ibn Khaldun: the Muquaddimah*, F. Rosenthal (ed.), Princeton: Princeton University Press, 3 vols.

Ibn Khurradadhbih, Ubayd Aliah ibn Abd Allah (1949) *Description du maghreb et de Europe au IIIe-IXe siècle: Extraits du Kitab al-Masalik wa'l-Mamalik, du Kitab al-Buldan et du Kitab al-A'laq an-nafisa*, M. Hadj-Sadok (ed. and trans.), Algiers: Carbonel, series Bibliothèque Arabe-Française, 6.

Ibn Rushd, see Arerroes.

Ignatieff, M. (1984) *The needs of strangers*, New York: Viking.

— — (1986) *I bisogni degli altri*, Bologna.

International Encyclopedia of Social Sciences (1968) New York: Macmillan and the Free Press.

Inscriptiones Latinae Liberae Reipublicae (1954) Atilius Degrassi (ed.), Firenze: Edizioni Fuzzi, Casa Editrice Sanson.

Inscriptiones Latinae Selectae (1892–1916, re-edn., 1954–1955) H. Dessau (ed.), Berolini: Berlin: Weidmann.

Inwood, B. (1995) " 'Politics and Paradox' in Seneca's *de Beneficiis*," in Andre Laks and Malcolm Schofield (eds), *Justice and generosity*, Cambridge: Cambridge University Press.

Irwin, Terence (1989) *Classical Thought*, Oxford: Oxford University Press.

Isaac, Barry I. (1993) "Retrospective on the Formalist-Substantivist Debate," *Research in Economic Anthropology*, 14: 213–233.

Israels, A. H. (1845) *Dissertatio Historico-Medica Exhibens Gynealogica Collectana ex Talmude Babylonio*, Groningen P. Van Zweeden:.

Jacobs, Jane (1984; 1985) *Cities and the Wealth of Nations: Principles of Economic Life*, New York: Vintage Books.

Jacques, F. (1981) "Volontariat et Competition dans les Carrières Municipales durant le Haut-Empire," *Ktema* VI.

Jankuhn, Herbert (4th edn., 1963) *Haithabu: Ein Handelsplatz der Wikingerzeit*, Neumunster: K. Wachholtz.

Johnson, Allan Chester and West, Louis C. (1949) *Byzantine Egypt: Economic Studies*, Princeton: Princeton University Press.

Johnson, T. and Dandeker, C. (1989) *Patronage: Relation and System*, in A. Wallace-Hadrill (ed.), *Patronage in Ancient Society*, London/New York: Routledge.

Jones, A. H. M. (1964) *The Later Roman Empire 284–602: a social economic and administrative survey*, Oxford: Blackwell.

Jones, Glyan (2nd edn., 1984), *A History of the Vikings*, Oxford/New York: Oxford University Press.

Kane, P. V. (2nd edn., 1968–1977) *A History of Dharmasastra (Ancient and Medieval Religious and Civil Law in India)*, Poona: Bhandarkar Oriental Research Institute.

Karayiannis, Anastassios D. (1988) "Democritus on Ethics and Economics," *Revista Internazionale di Scienze Economiche e Commerciale*, 4–5.

— — (1990) "The platonic ethico-economic structure of society," *Guaderni di Storia dell'Economia Politiea* No. 1.

— — (1992) "Entrepreneurship in Classical Greek Literature," *South African Journal of Economics*, vol. 1.

— — (1994) "The Eastern Christian Fathers (AD 350–400) on the Re-distribution of wealth," *History of Political Economy*, 26, (1), Spring.

Kasovsky, Ch. J. (1914) *Otzar Leshon ha'Mishnah*, (Thesaurus Mishnae), 2 vols., Jerusalem, Ramberg (2nd edn., 1967), M. Kasovsky (ed.), 4 vols., Tel-Aviv: Massada.

— — (1933–1961) *Otzar Leshon ha'Tosaphta*, 6 vols., Jerusalem: ha'Ivri Press.

— — (1954–1980) *Otzar Leshon ha'Talmud* (Thesaurus Talmudis), 41 vols., Jerusalem, Ministry of Education and Jewish Theological Seminary.

Katre, S. M. and Gode, P. K. (eds) (1941) *A Volume of Studies in Indology Presented to Professor P. V. Kane*, Poona: Oriental Book Agency.

[Kautilya] (2nd edn., 1972) *The Kautiliya Arthasastra* [Sanskrit and English], K.P. Kangle (ed. and trans.), Bombay: University of Bombay/(3rd edn., 1986), R. P. Kangle (ed. and trans.), Delhi: Motilal Banarsidass.

Kennedy, Hugh (1985) "From Polis to Madina: Urban Change in Late Antique and Early Islamic Syria," *Past and Present* 106.

Kenny, Anthony (1992) *Aristotle on the Perfect Life*, Oxford: Clarendon Press.

King, Anthony (1990) *Roman Gaul and Germany*, London: British Museum.

King, G. R. D. and Cameron, A. (eds) (1994) *The Byzantine and Early Islamic Near East II, Land Use and Settlement Patterns*, Princeton: Darwin Press.

Kleiman, E. (1973a) "An Early Modern Hebrew Textbook of Economics," *History of Political Economy*, 5 (2): 339–358.

— — (1973b) "Bi-metallism in Rabbi's Time: Two Variants of the Mishna 'Gold Acquires Silver'," *Zion 38*, 1–4, 48–61 (in Hebrew).

— — (1987a) "Just Price in Talmudic Literature," *History of Political Economy*, 19 (1): 23–45.

— — (1987b) "Opportunity Costs, Human Capital, and some Related Economic Concepts in Talmudic Literature," *History of Political Economy*, 19 (2): 261–287.

— — (1988) "Public Finance Criteria in the Talmud," Department of Economics, Working Paper No. 192, Jerusalem: the Hebrew University.

Klimar Mastra, Sushil (1925) *The Ethics of the Hindus*, Calcutta: Calcutta University.

Klever, W. N. A. (1986) *Archeologie van de Economie: De economische Theorie in de griekse Oudheid*, Nijmegen: Markant.

Knapp, A. B. (ed.) (1992) *Archeology, Annales, and Ethnohistory*, Cambridge: Cambridge University Press.

Knight, Frank H. (1921) *Risk, Uncertainty, and Profit*, New York: Houghton Mifflir Company.

Kosambi, D. D. (1977) *The Culture and Civilization of Ancient India in Historical Outline*, New Delhi: Vikas Publishing House.

Kosovsky, B. (1955–1966) *Otzar Leshon ha' Tanaim. Mekhilta d'Rabi Yshmael* 4 vols., New York: Jewish Theological Seminary.

— — (1967–1969) *Otzr Leshon ha'Tanaim. Torat Kohanim*, 4 vols., New York: Jewish Theological Seminary.

— — (1970–1974) *Otzar Leshon ha'Tanaim. "Sifrei" (Numbers and Deuteronomy)*, 5 vols., Jerusalem: Jewish Theological Seminary.

Kosovsky, M. (1980–) *Otzar Leshon ha'Tanaim Talmud Yerushalmi*, Jerusalem: Israel Academy of Sciences and Humanities and Jewish Theological Seminary.

Kraus, Oskar (1905) "Die aristotelische Werttheorie in ihren Beziehungen zu den Lehren der modernen Psychologenschule," *Zeitschrift fur die gesamte Staatswissenschaft*, 61: 573–592.

Krauss, S. (1910–1912) *Talmudische Archäologie*, Leipzig: G. Fock.

Kuhrt, Amélie and Sherwin-White, Susan (eds) (1987) *Hellenism in the East: The Interaction of Greek and Non-Greek Civilizations from Syria to Central Asia after Alexander*, Berkeley: University of California Press.

Kula, Witold (1986) *Measures and Men*, Princeton: Princeton University Press.

Kunhan Raja, C. (1969) "Vedic Culture," in *The Cultural Heritage of India*, Calcutta: Sri Ramakrishna Mission: Vol. I.

Kuran, T. (1986) "Continuity and Change in Islamic Economic Thought," in S. T.

Lowry (ed.), *Pre-Classical Economic Thought: From the Greeks to the Scottish Enlightment*, Boston: Kluwer.

Lactantius, L. Caelus Firmianus (1994) *Epitome divinarum institutionum [Institutionies divinae]* Eberhard Heck and Antonie Wlosok (eds.), Stuttgart: Teubner.

Lange, Kurt and Hirmer, Max (1968) *Egypt: Architecture, Sculpture, Painting in Three Thousand Years*, London: Phaidon Press.

Langholm, O. (1983) *Wealth and Money in the Aristotelian Tradition*, Bergen: Universitetsforlaget.

— — (1992) *Economics in the Medieval Schools*, Leyden: E. J. Brill.

Lapidus, A. (1993) "Metal Money and the Prince: John Buridan and Nicolas Oresme after Thomas Aquinas," paper presented at the 20th meeting of the *History of Economic Society*, Philadelphia, pp. 1–29.

Laws of Manu, The (1991) Wendy Doniger (trans.), New Delhi: Penguin Books.

Lee, A. D. (1993) *Information and Frontiers: Roman Frontier Relations in Late Antiquity*, Cambridge: Cambridge University Press.

Lekachman, R. (1959) *A History of Economic Ideas*, New York: Harper and Row.

Leo XIII, Pope (1892; 1983) *Rerum Novarum* Encyclical Letter of Pope Leo XIII on the condition of the working classes, London: Catholic Truth Society.

Lepore, E. (1954) *Il princeps ciceroniano e gli ideali politici della tarda Repubblica*, Napoli: Instituto Italiano per gli studi storici.

Levinger, D. S. (1928) "Selections from Abraham Farrisol's 'David's Shield'," *Hazofeh = ha"Tsofe le'Hochmat Israel*, Budapest, 12: 277–297.

Levy, E. (1976) *Athenes devant la defaite de 404. Histoire d'une crise ideologique*, Athens: Ecole française d'Athènes/Paris: Depositaire, Diffusion de Boccard.

Lewis, Naphtali (1986) *Greeks in Ptolemaic Egypt: Case Studies in the Social History of the Hellenistic World*, Oxford: Clarendon Press.

Lieberman, J. (1979) "Elements in Talmudic monetary thought," *History of Political Economy*, 11 (2): 254–270.

Lieberman, J. (1989) *Business Competition in Jewish Law* [Hebrew], Ramat Gam: Bar-Ilan University.

Liegle, J. (1935) "Pietas," *Zeitschrift fur Numismatik*, Berlin: Weidmann.

Linders, Tullia and Alroth, Brita (eds) (1992) *Economics of Cult in the Ancient Greek World: Proceedings of the Uppsala Symposium 1990*, Uppsala: Almqvist and Wiskell.

Lipinski, Edward (ed.) (1979) *State and Temple Economy in the Ancient Near East: Proceedings of the International Conference Organized by the Katholieke Universiteit Leuven from the 10th to the 14th of April, 1978*, Leuven: Departement Orientalistiek.

— — (ed.) (1987) *Studia Phoenicia V. Phoenicia and the East Mediterranean in the First Millennium bc*, Orientalia Lovaniensia Analecta 22, Leuven: Uitgeverij Peeters.

Lloyd, A. B. (1983) "The Late Period, 664–323 bc," in B. G. Trigger, B. J. Kemp, D. O'Connor, and A. B. Lloyd, *Ancient Egypt. A Social History*, Cambridge: Cambridge University Press.

Loew, A. (2nd edn., 1891) *Thierschutz im Judenthume nach Bibel und Talmud*, Budapest: F. Buschman.

Loew, I. (1924–1934, 1967) *Die Flora die Juden*, Vienna: R. Lowit.

Long, A. A. (1995) " 'Cicero's politics in *de officiis*," in Andre Laks and Malcolm Schofield (eds) *Justice and generosity*, Cambridge: Cambridge University Press.

Lopez, Robert (1943) "Mohammed and Charlemagne: A Revision," *Speculum* 18: 16–34.

Loseby, S. T. (1992) "Marseille: A Late Antique Success Story?," *Journal of Roman Studies*, 82: 165–183.

Lot, Ferdinand (1967) *La Gaule*, P. M. Duval (ed.), Verviers: Marabout.

Lotito, G. (1981) "Modelli Etici e Base Economica Nelle Opere Filosofiche di Cicerone," in A. Giardina and A. Schiavone (eds) *Societa romana e produzione schiavistica*, Bari: Laterza, 3 vols.

Lowry, S. Todd (ed.) (1987a) *Pre-Classical Economic Thought: From the Greeks to the Scottish Enlightment*, Boston: Kluwer-Nijhoff.

—— (1987b) *The Archeology of Economic Ideas: The Classical Greek Tradition*, Durham, NC: Duke University Press.

Lund, John (1986) *Sukas VIII: The Habitation Quarters*, Publications of the Carlsberg Expedition to Phoenicia 10, Copenhagen: The Royal Danish Academy of Sciences and Letters (Historisk-filosofishke Skrifter 12).

MacAdam, H. I. (1994) "Settlements and Settlement Patterns in Northern and Central Transjordania, *c.* 550–*c.* 750," G. R. D. King and A. Cameron (eds), *The Byzantine and Early Islamic Near East II, Land Use and Settlement Patterns*, Princeton: Darwin Press.

McCann, Charles R. and Perlman, Mark (forthcoming), "Keynesian Economics and the Meaning of Uncertainty," in O. F. Hamouda and B. B. Price (eds) *Keynesianism and the Keynesian Revolution in America*, Cheltenham: Edward Elgar.

—— (forthcoming) "Varieties Of Uncertainty."

McGill, V. J. (1967) *The Idea of Happiness* (Concepts in Western Thought series), New York: Friedrich A. Praeger.

McKee, Arnold F. (1987) *Economics and the Christian Mind*, New York: Vantage Press.

McKeon, Richard (ed.) (1947) *Introduction to Aristotle*, New York: The Modern Library.

McNicol, Nicol (ed.) (1938) *Hindu Scriptures: Hymns from the Rigveda, Five Upanishads, the Bhagavadgita*, London: J. M. Dent.

Maehler, Herwig and Strocka, Volder Michael (eds) (1978) *Das Ptolemaïsche Aegypten: Akten der Internationale Symposions, 27–29 September 1976 in Berlin*, Mainz am Rhein: P. von Zabern.

Mahabharata (rpt. 1993), Kisari Mohan Ganguli (trans. from Sanskrit), New Dehli: Munshiram Manoharlal.

Maimonides (1947, rpt. 1978) *Guide of the Perplexed [Dalatest al-hairin]* Chaim Rabin (trans.), New York: East and West Library.

—— (1949) The Code of Maimonides [Mishneh Torah], New Haven: Yale University Press.

Maitra, S. K. (1969) "Political and Economic Literature in Sanskrit," in *The Cultural Heritage of India*, Calcutta: Sri Ramakrishna Mission, vol. V.

Malinowski, Bronislaw (1962) *Geschlechitstrieb und Verdrangung bei den Primitiven*, Hugo Seinfeld (trans.), Reinbek bei Hamburg: Rowolt.

Mandeville, Bernard (1714; 1962) *Fable of the Bees; or Private Vices, Public Benefits*, Irwin Primer (ed.), New York: Capricorn Books.

Manselli, R. (1983) "Il Pensiero Economico del Medioevo" in L. Firpo (ed.) *Storia delle Idee Politiche, Economiche e Sociali*, Torino: Unione Tipografico editrice torinese, vol. 2.

Marbod of Rennes (1100; 1974) [in] *Ein Dichterbuch des Mittelalters*, W.v.d. Steinen (ed. and trans.), Bern: Francke.

Marrou, H. I. (1965) *Histoire de l'éducation dans l'antiquité*, Paris: Editions du Seuil.

Marshall, E. (1961) *Principles of Economics*, London/New York: Macmillan.

Marx, A. (1916) "A Description of Bills of Exchange, 1559," *American Economic Review* 6: 609–614.

Matthers, John (ed.) (1981) *The River Qoueiq, Northern Syria and its Catchment: Studies Arising from the Tell Rifa'at Survey 1977–79, parts 1 and 2,* Oxford: BAR International Series 98.

Meier, Christian (1988) *Die politische Kunst der griechischen Tragodie*, Munich: C. H. Beck.

Meiggs, R. and Lewis, D. (1969) *A Selection of Greek Historical Inscriptions to the End of the Fifth Century BC,* Oxford: Clarendon Press.

Meikle, S. (1991) "Aristotle and exchange value," in F. Miller and D. Keyt (eds), *A companion to Aristotle's Politics*, Oxford: Blackwell.

Menjot, D. (1988) "La politique monetaire de Nicolas Oresme," in P. Souffrin and A. Segonds (eds), *Nicolas Oresme*, Paris: Les Belles Lettres.

Meyer, Eduard (1892) *Zur alteren grieschen Geschichte*, Halle A.S.: Max Niemeyer.

— — (1895) *Die Wirtschaftliche Entwicklung des Altertums: ein Vortraggehalten auf der dritten Versammlung, Deutscher Historiker in Frankfurt am Main, 20 April 1895,* Jena: G. Fischer.

Migeotte, L. (1984) *L'emprunt public dans les cités grecques*, Paris: Belles Lettres.

Millar, Fergus (1983) "The Phoenician Cities: A Case-Study of Hellenism," *Proceedings of the Cambridge Philiological Society*, 209: 55–71.

— — (1987) "The Problem of Hellenistic Syria," in Amélie Kuhrt and Susan Sherwin-White (eds), *Hellenism in the East: The Interaction of Greek and Non-Greek Civilizations from Syria to Central Asia after Alexander*, Berkeley: University of California Press.

Miller, C. (1925) *Studien zur Geschichte der Geldlehre*, Münchener volkswirtschaftliche Studien, 146, Stuttgart/Berlin: Cotta.

Miller, Jeanine (1974) *The Vedas Harmony, Meditation and Fulfilment*, London: Rider & Company.

Millett, P. (1990) "Sale, Credit and Exchange in Athenian Law and Society," in P. Cartledge, P. Millet and S. Todd (eds), *Nomos: Essays in Athenian Law, Politics and Society*, Cambridge: Cambridge University Press.

— — (1991) *Lending and borrowing in Ancient Athens*, Cambridge: Cambridge University Press.

Mitsis, Phillip (1988) *Epicurus' Ethical Theory: The Pleasures of Invulnerability*, Ithaca, NY: Cornell University Press.

Moerbeke, William of (1961), [Aristotle] *Politica Libri I–II. ll: translatio prior imperfecta interprete Guillelmo de Moerbeka*, Petrus Michaud-Quantin (ed.), Bruges: Desdee de Brouwer.

Moller, D. A. (1984) "The Money Economy and the Ptolemaic Peasantry," *Bulletin of the American Society of Papyrologists*, 21.

— — (1990) *Naukratis: Handel im archäischen Griechenland*, Ph.D. thesis, Freie Universität, Berlin. Berlin: Mikrofilm-Center Klein.

Montgomery, H. (1986) "Merchants Fond of Corn," *Symbolae Osloenses*, LXI.

Morris, Ian (ed.) (1994) *Classical Greece: Ancient Histories and Modern Archeologies*, Cambridge: Cambridge University Press.

Morris, Sarah P. (1992) *Daidalos and the Origins of Greek Art*, Princeton: Princeton University Press.

Morrison, K. F., (1963) "Numismatics and Carolingian Trade: A Critique of the Evidence," *Speculum*, 38: 403–432.

Murray, Alexander (1978) *Reason and Society in the Middle Ages*, Oxford: Clarendon Press.

Musti, D. (1984) "Syria and the East," in F. W. Walbank and A. E. Astin (eds), *The Cambridge Ancient History,* vol. 7, pt. 1, *The Hellenistic World,* 2nd edn., London: Cambridge University Press.

Natali, C. (1979) "L'Economia Antica: Scienza o Filosofia Pratica?," in R. Crippa (ed.), *Le dimensioni dell'economico,* Padova: Liviana.

—— (1982) "Il pensiero economico dei Romani," in L. Firpo (ed.), *Storia delle idee politiche, economiche e sociali,* vol. I, Torino: Unione tipografico-editrice torinese.

—— (1988) *L'Amministrazione della Casa de Senafonte,* Venice: Marsilio Editori.

—— (1990) "Aristote et la chrematistique," in G. Partzig (ed.), *Aristoteles' "Politik,"* Gottingen: Vandennoeck and Roprecht.

Neusner, J. (1982–) *The Talmud of the land of Israel, a preliminary translation and explanation,* Chicago: Chicago University Press.

—— (1990) *The Economics of the Mishna,* Chicago: Chicago University Press.

Nicolet, C. (1970, 1982) "Il Pensiero Economico dei Romani," in L. Firpo (ed.), *Storia delle idee politiche, economiche e sociale,* vol. I, Torino: Unione tipografico-editrice torinese.

Nicolet, C. (1988) *Rendre à Cesar: Economie et Societé dans la Rome antique,* Paris: Gallimard.

Niehans, J. (1990) *A History of Economic Theory,* Baltimore: Johns Hopkins University Press.

Nock, A. D. (1972) "Soter and euergetes," in *Essays on Religion and the Ancient World,* Z. Steward (ed.), Oxford: Clarendon Press.

Noshy, I. (1937) *The Arts in Ptolemaic Egypt,* London: Oxford University Press.

Nutton, V. (1978) "The beneficial ideology," in P. Garnsey and C. R. Whittaker (eds), *Imperialism in the Ancient World,* Cambridge: Cambridge University Press.

Oates, J. F. *et al.* (1985) *Checklist of Editions of Greek Papyri and Ostraca, Bulletin of the American Society of Papyrologists,* Supplement 4, Chico, CA: Scholars Press.

Oehler, J. (1909) "Euergetes" in Pauly, A, *Real-Encyclopädie der classischen Altertumswissenschaft,* Stuttgart: J. B. Metzler: VI: 978–981.

Ohrenstein, R. A. and Gordon, B. (1992) *Economic Analysis in Talmudic Literature – Rabbinic Thought in the Light of Modern Economics,* Leiden: E. J. Brill.

Pareto, V. (1935) *Mind and Society [Trattato di Sociologia Generale]* New York: Harcourt Brace and Co.

Patzer, H. (c. 1970) "Die dichterische Stilisierung der Lebenswirklichkeit im homerischen Epos" (mimeo)

Pauly, A., Wissowa, G., and Kroll, W. (eds), (1894–) *Real Encyclopädie der classischen Altertumswissenschaft,* Stuttgart: J. B. Metzler.

Pellegrin, P. (1982) "Monnaie et Chrematistique," in *Revue Philosophique.*

Penso, J. (1688; 1957) *Confusion de Confusiones* (parts descriptive of the Amsterdam Stock Exchange), H. Kellenbenz (ed. and trans.), Boston, Mass.: Kress Library of Business and Economics Publication No. 13.

Perlman, Mark (1980) Review of G. L. S. Shackle, *Imagination and the Nature of Choice, Journal of Economic Literature,* vol. XVIII, March: 115–118.

Petrie, W. M. F. (1888) *Tanis II. Nebesheh (Am and Defenneh (Tahpanhes)),* Egypt Exploration Fund, London: Trubner and Co.

[Phokylides] (1954) in *Elegy and Iambus,* J. M. Edmonds (ed. and trans.), 2 vols., Cambridge, MA: Harvard Unversity Press.

Pindar (1935; 1951) *Pindari carmina,* C. M. Bowra (ed.), Oxford: Clarendon Press.

BIBLIOGRAPHY

Pisa, J. N. da (1962) *Banking and Finance Among Jews in Renaissance Italy* [*Hayei Olam*], G. S. Rosenthal (ed. and trans.), New York: Bloch Publishing Co.

Plato (1926) *Laws*, R. G. Bury (trans.), Cambridge, Mass.: Harvard University Press series: Loeb Classical Library.

— — (3rd edn., 1936) *The Republic of Plato*, Benjamin Jowett (trans.), Oxford: Clarendon Press, vol. I.

— — (1991) *Protogaras*, Stanley Lombardo and Karen Bell (trans.), Indianapolis: Hackett Publishing Co.

Plutarch (1575) *Alexandri Vita* in Arrian, *Arrianou Peri anabaseos*, Geneva: Henr. Stephanus.

— — (1575) *De fortuna vel virtute Alexandri* in Arrian, *Arrianou Peri anabaseos*, Geneva: Henr. Stephanus.

Polanyi, K. (1983) *La sussistenza dell'uomo*, H. W. Pearson (ed.), Torino: Bollati Boringhieri.

Pollitt, J. J. (1986) *Art in the Hellenistic Age*, Cambridge: Cambridge University Press.

Polybius (1954) *The Histories [Historiae]*, W. R. Paton (trans.), Cambridge, Mass.: Harvard University Press.

— (1961) *Geschichte Historiae*, Hans Drexler (trans.), Zurich/Stuttgart: Artemis-Veol.

Prèaux, Claire (1939) *L'Économie Royale des Lagides*, Bruxelles: Édition de la Fondation égyptologique Reine.

— — (1966) "Sur la Stagnation de la Pensée Scientifique à l'Époque Hellénistique," in *Essays in Honor of C. Bradford Welles*, American Studies in Papyrology I. New Haven: American Society of Papyrologists, 235–250.

— — (1978) *Le monde hellénistique: La Grèce et l'Orient de la Mort d'Alexandre à la Conquête Romaine de la Grèce (323–146 av. J.-C.)*, Paris: Presses Universitaires de France.

Preuss, J. (1911) *Biblisch-Talmudische Medizin, Berlin: S. Karger; (1978) Biblical and Talmudic Medicine*, New York: Sanhedrin Press.

Price, B. B. (forthcoming), *Medieval Economic Thought*, London: Routledge.

Pius XI, Pope (1932; 1950) *Quadragesimo Anno*, Encyclical letter of Pope Pius XI on social reconstruction, Derby, New York: Daughters of St Paul, Apostolate of the Press.

Quaegebeur, J. (1979) "Documents Égyptiens et Rôle Économique du Clergé en Égypt Hellénistique," in Edward Lipinski (ed.), *State and Temple Economy in the Ancient Near East: Proceedings of the International Conference Organized by the Katholieke Universiteit Leuven from the 10th to the 14th of April, 1978*, Leuven: Departement Orientalistiek.

Raju, P. T. (1941) "Morality and Self-Realisation," in S. M. Katre and P. K. Gode (eds), *A Volume of Studies in Indology Presented to Professor P. V. Kane*, Poona: Oriental Book Agency.

Randsborg, Klaus (1991) *The First Millenium AD in Europe and the Mediterranean*, Cambridge: Cambridge University Press.

Rangaswami Aiyangar, K. V. (1941) *Rajadharma* (Dewan Bahadur K. Krishnaswamy Row Lectures), Adyar: The Adyar Library.

— — (1949) *Indian Cameralism: A Survey of Some Aspects of Arthasastra*, Adyar: Adyar Library.

— — (2nd edn., 1965) *Aspects of Ancient Indian Economic Thought*, Varanasi: Banaras Hindu University.

Rathbone, D. W. (1983) "The Grain Trade and Grain Shortages in the Hellenistic

East," in P. Garnsey and C. R. Whittaker (eds), *Trade and Famine in Classical Antiquity*, Cambridge: Cambridge Philological Society.

— — (1989) The Ancient Economy and Greco-Roman Egypt," in L. Criscuolo and G. Geraci (eds), *Egitto e Storia Antica dall'Ellenismo all'eta araba: Bilancio di un Confronto*, (Atti del colloquio internazionale, Bologna, 31 agosto–2 settembre 1987), Bologna: CLUEB 159–176.

— — (1991) *Economic Rationalism and Rural Society in Third Century Egypt. The Heroninos Archive and the Appianus Estate*, Cambridge: Cambridge University Press.

Rauh, Nickolas K. (1993) *The Sacred Bonds of Commerce. Religion, Economy, and Trade Society at Hellenistic Roman Delos*, Amsterdam: J. C. Crieben.

Reekmans, T. (1951) "The Ptolemaic Copper Inflation," in E. van't Dack and T. Reekmans (eds), *Ptolemaica, Studia Hellenistica* 7: 61–120.

Reichert, Klaus (1992) "Wucher und Wucherklischees am Ubergang zur Neuzeit," in B. Schefold (ed.) *Studien zur Entwicklung der okonomischen Theorie XI*, Berlin: Duncker & Humbolt.

Reinhold, Meyer (1946) "Historian of the Classic World: A Critique of Rostovtzeff," *Science and Society*, 10: 361–391.

Renfew, Colin (1982) "Socio-economic Change in Ranked Societies," in C. Renfew and S. Shennan (eds), *Ranking, Resource and Exchange: Aspects of the Archeology of Early European Society*, Cambridge: Cambridge University Press.

Reuter, Timothy (1985) "Plunder and Tribute in the Carolingian Empire," *Transactions of the Royal Historical Society*, 5, 35: 75–94.

Rich, J. (1989) "Patronage and Interstate Relations in the Roman Republic," in A. Wallace-Hadrill (ed.), *Patronage in Ancient Society*, London/New York: Routledge.

Riedel, M. (ed.) (1972; 1974) *Rehabilitierung der Praktischen Philosophie*, Freiburg: Rombach, 2 vols.

Robert, L. (1926) "Notes d'Epigraphie Hellénistique," in *Bulletin de Correspondance Hellénique*.

Robert, P. (1988; 2nd edn., 1989) *Dictionnaire alphabetique et analogique de la langue française*, Paris: Le Robert.

Roll, E. (rev. edn., 1961) *A History of Economic Thought*, London: Faber and Faber.

Rostovtzeff, M. (1922) *A Large Estate in Egypt in the Third Century* BC. *A Study in Economic History*, Madison: University of Wisconsin. Studies in the Social Sciences and History, 6.

— — (1928) "Syria and the East," in S. A. Cook, F. E. Adcock, and M. P. Charleswort (eds), *Cambridge Ancient History, Vol. VII: The Hellenistic Monarchies and the Rise of Rome*, Cambridge: Cambridge University Press.

— — (2nd edn., 1951) *The Social and Economic History of the Hellenistic World*, Oxford: Clarendon Press.

— — (2nd edn., 1957) *The Social and Economic History of the Roman Empire*, P. M. Frazer (ed.), Oxford: Clarendon Press, 2 vols.

Ruderman, D. (1974) *Abraham Farrisol: An Historical Study of his Life and Thought in the Context of Jewish Communal Life in Renaissance Italy*, Ph.D. thesis (in Hebrew, with English summary), Jerusalem: the Hebrew University.

Ruggiu, L. (1982) "Aristotele e la Genesi dello Spazio Economico," in L. Ruggiu (ed.), *Genesi dello Spazio Economico*, Naples: Guida Editori.

Russell, J. C., (1958) *Late Ancient and Medieval Population*, Transactions of the American Philosophical Society, N. S. 48, pt. 3, Philadephia: American Philosophical Society.

Said, Edward W. (1993) *Culture and Imperialism*, New York: Knopf.

Saller, R. P. (1982) *Personal Patronage Under the Early Empire*, Cambridge: Cambridge University Press.

Salles, J.-F. (1991) "Du Blé, de l'Huile et du Vin . . . (Notes sur les échanges commerciaux en Méditerranée orientale vers le milieu du 1er millénaire av. J.-C.)," in H. Sancisi-Weerdenburg and A. Kuhrt (eds), *Achaemenid History VI. Asia Minor and Egypt: Old Cultures in a New Empire*, Proceedings of the Groningen 1988 Achaemenid History Workshop, Leiden: Nederlands Instituut voor het Nabije Oosten, pp. 207–236.

—— (1993) "The Arab-Persian Gulf under the Seleucids," in Susan Sherwin-White and Amélie Kuhrt, *From Samarkhand to Sardis. A New Approach to the Seleucid Empire*, Hellenistic Culture and Society XIII, Berkeley: University of California Press.

Salmon, P. (1974) *Population et Dépopulation dans l'Empire Romain*, Brussels: Latomus, Collection Latomus 137.

Samuel, Alan E. (1983) *From Athens to Alexandria: Hellenism and Social Goals in Ptolemaic Egypt*, Louvan: Studia Hellenistica 26.

—— (1984) "The Money-Economy and the Ptolemaic Peasantry," *Bulletin of the American Society of Papyrologists*, 21: 187–206.

—— (1989) *The Shifting Sands of History: Interpretations of Ptolemaic Egypt*, Lanham, MD: University Press of America.

Sancisi-Weerdenburg, H. and Kuhrt, A. (eds) (1991) *Achaemenid History VI. Asia Minor and Egypt: Old Cultures in a New Empire*, Proceedings of the Groningen 1988 Achaemenid History Workshop, Leiden: Nederlands Instituut voor het Nabije Oosten.

Sappho (1944; 1954) *Sappho* [Greek and German], Max Treu (ed.), Munich: E. Heimeran.

—— and Alcaeus (1971) *Fragmenta*, E. M. Voigt (ed.), Amsterdam: Athenaeum-Polak and Van Genrep.

Sarton, George (1927) *Introduction to the History of Science: Volume I. From Homer to Omar Khayyam*, Baltimore: The Williams & Wilkins Company for the Carnegie Institution of Washington.

—— (1959) *A History of Science: Hellenistic Science and Culture in the Last Three Centuries BC*, Cambridge: Harvard University Press.

Sartre, Maurice (1989) "La Syrie sous la Domination achéménide," in Jean-Marie Dentzer and Winfried Orthmann (eds), *Archéologie et Histoire de la Syrie II. La Syrie de l'époque achéménide à l'avenement de l'Islam*, Saarbrucken: Saarbrucker Druckerei und Verlag.

Schefold, B. (1989) "Platon und Aristoteles," in J. Starbatty (ed.), *Klassiker des okonomischen Denkens*, Munich: C. H. Beck.

—— (1992) "Spiegelungen des antiken Wirtschaftsdenkens in der griechischen Dichtung," in B. Schefold (ed.), *Studien zur Entwicklung der okonomischen Theorie XI*, Berlin: Duncker & Humbolt.

Schefold, Karl and Jung, Franz (1989) *Die Sagen von den Argonauten, von Theben and Troja in der klassischen und hellenistischen Kunst*, Munich: Hirmer.

Schmitt, C. B. (1983) *Aristotle and Renaissance*, Cambridge, Mass./London: Harvard University Press.

Schumpeter, J. A. (1954) *History of Economic Analysis*, New York: Oxford University Press.

Schwartz, L. (1990) "Talmudic Approaches to the Distribution of the Tax Burden," *The Jewish Quarterly Review*, 81 (1–2): 93–113.

Scott, K. (1929) "Plutarch and the Ruler Cult," *Transactions and Proceedings of the American Philological Association*, LX: 117–135.

Seaford, R. (1994) *Reciprocity and Ritual*, Oxford: Clarendon Press.

Seneca, Lucius Annaeus (1982) *De beneficiis*, Pisa: Giardini.

Seyrig, H. (1968) "Seleucus and the Foundations of Hellenistic Syria," in W. A. Ward (ed.), *The Role of the Phoenicians in the Interaction of Mediterranean Civilizations*, Beirut: American University of Beirut.

Shackle, G. L. S. (1992) *Epistemics and Economics*, New Brunswick, New Jersey: Transaction Publishers.

Shanks, M. and Tilley, C. (2nd edn., 1992) *Re-Constructing Archeology: Theory and Practice*, London: Routledge.

Shastri, Dakshina Ranjan (1969) "Materialists, Sceptics, and Agnostics," in *The Cultural Heritage of India*, Calcutta: Sri Ramakrishna Mission.

Shaw, Brent D. and Saller, Richard P. (eds) (1981) "Editors' Introduction" in Brent D. Shaw and Richard P. Saller (eds), *Economy and Society in Ancient Greece*, London: Chatto & Windus Ltd.

Shennan, S. J. (ed.) (1989) *Archaeological Approaches to Cultural Identity*, One World Archaeology, London: Unwin Hyman.

Sherratt, Andrew (1992) "What can Archaeologists learn from Annalistes?," in A. B. Knapp (ed.), *Archaeology, Annales, and Ethnohistory*, Cambridge/New York: Cambridge University Press.

Sherwin-White, Susan and Kuhrt, Amélie (1993) *From Samarkhand to Sardis: A New Approach to the Seleucid Empire*, Hellenistic Culture and Society XIII, Berkeley: University of California Press.

Siddiqi, M. (1982) *Recent Works on the History of Economic Thought in Islam: A Survey*, Jeddah, Saudi Arabia: International Centre for Research in Islamic Economics, King Abdul Aziz University.

Singer, Kurt (1958) "Oikonomia: An Inquiry into Beginnings of Economic Thought and Language," *Kyklos*, XI: 1.

Sjoman, N. E. (1986) "The Memory Eye: An Examination of Memory in Traditional Knowledge Systems," *Journal of Indian Philosophy*, 14 (2) June: 195–213.

Slatkin, Laura (n.d.) "The poetics of exchange in the *Iliad*" (mimeo).

Smith, Adam (1759; 1986) *The Theory of Moral Sentiments*, Dusseldorf: Verlag Wirtschaft and Finanzen, Klassiker der Nationalokonomie.

— — (1776; 1976) *An Inquiry into the Nature and Causes of the Wealth of Nations*, R. H. Campbell, A. S. Skinner and W. B. Todd (eds), Oxford: Clarendon Press.

Sohn-Rethel, Alfred (1970) *Geistige und Korperliche Arbeit*, Frankfurt am Main: Suhrkamp.

Solon (1954) (in) *Elegy and Iambus*, J. M. Edmonds (ed. and trans.), Cambridge, Mass.: Harvard University Press, 2 vols.

— — (1963) (in) *Griechische Lyrik. Von den Anfangen bis zu Pindar* [Greek and German], Gerhardt Wirth (ed.), Reinbek bei Hamburg: Rowohlt.

Sombart, W. (1911; 1962) *The Jews and Modern Capitalism*, M. Epstein (trans.), New York: Colliers Books.

Sophocles (1877) [*Antigone*], *The Antigone of Sophocles* G. Dindorfii (ed.), London: Crosby Lockwood.

— — (1950) *Antigone*, Ernst Buschor (ed.), Munich: C. H. Beck.

Spengler, Joseph J. (1971) *Indian Economic Thought: A Preface to its History*, Durham, N.C.: Duke University Press.

— — (1980) *Origins of Economic Thought and Justice*, Carbondale, Illinois: Southern Illinois University Press.

Spengler, Joseph J. and Allen, William R. (ed.) (1960) *Essays in Economic Thought: Aristotle to Marshall*, Chicago: Rand McNally & Co.

Sperber, D. (1974) *Roman Palestine 700–400: Money and Prices*, Ramat-Gan: Bar-Ilan University.

Spicciani, A. (1977) *La Mercatura e la Formazione del Prezzo nella Reflessione Teologica Medioevale*, Rome: Academia Nazionale dei Lincei.

—— (1990) *Capitale e Interesse tra Mercatura e Poverta: nei Teologi e Canonisti dei Secoli*, XIII–XV, Rome: Jouvence.

Spiegel, H. W. (1971) *The Growth of Economic Thought*, Prentice-Hall, Englewood-Cliffs/Durham: Duke University Press.

Sri Aurobindo (1972) *Sri Aurobindo Birth Centenary Library*, Pondicherry: Sri Aurobindo Ashram, Vol. XII.

Stevenson, T. R. (1992) "The Ideal Benefactor and the Father Analogy in Greek and Roman Thought," *Classical Quarterly*, 42: 421–436.

Stovaios, Ioannis (1884–1912; 1958) *Anthologium*, C. Wachsmuth and O. Hense (eds), Berlin: Weidmann, 5 vols.

Sylloge Inscriptionum Graecarum, (3rd edn., 1915), G. Dittenbergero (ed.), Lipsiae: S. Hirzelium.

Tale of Ihor's Campaign, The (1963) in C. H. Andrusyschen and W. Kirkconnell (eds), *The Ukranian Poets*, Toronto: University of Toronto Press.

Tamari, Meir (1979) "Medieval Interpretations of Talmudic Economic Law," presented to the VI Annual Conference of the History of Economics Society, May 23–26.

—— (1987) *"With all your Possessions" – Jewish Ethics and Economic Life*, New York: The Free Press.

Thani Nayagam, Xavier S. (n.d.) *Indian Thought and Roman Stoicism* (Inaugural Lecture), Kuala Lumpur: University of Malaya.

Theocharis, R. D. (1961) *Early Developments in Mathematical Economics*, London: Macmillan.

[Theocritus] Theokrit (1949) "Die Chariten," in Eduard Morike (transcrib.) and M. Ninck (ed.), *Griechische Lyrik*, Basel: B. Schwabe.

[Theogonis] (1954) in *Elegy and Iambus*, J. M. Edmonds (ed. and trans.), Cambridge, MA: Harvard University Press, vol. I.

—— (1960) [in] *Griechische Lyrik*, Eduard Morike (trans.) and Uvo Holscher (ed.), Frankfurt am Main: Fischer Bucherei.

—— (1963) in *Griechische Lyrik. Von den Anfangen bis zu Pindar* [Greek and German], Gerhardt Wirth (ed.), Reinbek bei Hamburg: Rowohlt.

Thompson, D. B. (1973) *Ptolemaic Oinochoai and Portraits in Faience*, Oxford: Clarendon Press.

Thucidides (1965–1969) [History of the Peloponnesian War] [Greek and English] Charles Forster Smith (trans.), Cambridge, Mass.: Harvard University Press.

—— (1966) [Works] Johannes Classen and Juluis Step (eds) Berlin: Weidmann.

Tortajada, Roman (1992) "La Renaissance de la Scolastique, la Reforme et le Droit Naturel," in A. Beraud and G. Faccarello (eds), *Nouvelle Histoire de la Pensée Economique*, Paris, Editions La Découverte, vol. 1.

Trigger, B. G., Kemp, B. J., O'Connor, D. and Lloyd, A. B. (1983) *Ancient Egypt: A Social History*, Cambridge: Cambridge University Press.

Tsafrir, Y. and Foerster, G. (1994) "From Scythopolis to Baysan – Changing Concepts of Urbanism," in G. R. D. King and A. Cameron (eds), *The Byzantine and Early Islamic Near East II: Land Use and Settlement Patterns*, Princeton: Darwin Press.

Tulpin, C. (1991) "Darius' Suez Canal and Persian Imperialism," in H. Sancisi-

Weerdenburg and A. Kuhrt (eds), *Achaemenid History VI. Asia Minor and Egypt: Old Cultures in a New Empire*, Proceedings of the Groningen 1988 Achaemenid History Workshop, Leiden: Nederlands Instituut voor het Nabije Oosten: 237–283.

Turner, E. G. (1984) "Ptolemaic Egypt," in F. W. Walbank and A. E. Astin (eds), *The Cambridge Ancient History: vol. 7, pt. 1, The Hellenistic World*, 2nd edn., London: Cambridge University Press.

Tyrtaeus (1954) [in] *Elegy and Iambus*, J. M. Edmonds (ed. and trans.), Cambridge, Mass.: Harvard University Press.

— — (1960) [in] *Griechische Lyrik*, Eduard Morike (transcrib.), Frankfurt am Main: Reinbek bei Hamburg: Rowohlt.

— — (1968), *Tirteo*, Carlo Prato (annot.) Rome: Ateneo.

Urbain, Yves (1939), "Les Idées Economiques d'Aristophanes," *L'Antiquité Classique*, XIII, (I): 183–200.

Urvoy, D. (1990), *Ibn Rushd*, London: Routledge.

Vannier, F. (1988), *Finances Publiques et Richesses Privées dans le Discours Athenien aux Vᵉ et IVᵉ siècles*, Paris: Belles Lettres.

van't Dack, E. and Reekmans, T. (eds) (1951), *Ptolemaica, Studia Hellenistica, 7* Universitas Catholica Lovaniensis, Leiden: E. J. Brill.

[Vatsyayana] (1883, rpt 1963) *Kama Sutra*, Sir Richard Burton and E. F. Arbuthnot (trans.), London: Richard Champion.

Vegetti, M. (1982) "Il Pensiero Economico Greco," in *Storia delle idee politiche economicke e sociali*, L. Firpo (ed.), Torino: Unione typographic editrice torinese.

Verbeke, G. and Verhelst, M. (1974) *Aquinas and Problems of his Time*, Leuven: Leuven University Press.

Veyne, P. (1969) "Panem et Circenses: l'Evergetisme devant les Sciences Humaines," *Annales ESC* XXIV: 785–825.

— — (1976) *Le pain et le cirque*, Paris: Editions de Seuil.

— — (1989) " 'Humanitas': romani e no," in A. Giardini (ed.) *L'Uomo Romano*, Roma: Laterza.

Vidal-Naquet, P. (re-edn., 1983) *Le Chasseur Noir: Formes de Penseés et Formes de Societé dans le Monde Grec*, Paris: Maspero.

Vivenza, G. (1995) "Origini Classiche della Benevolenza nel Linguaggio Economico," in R. Molesti (ed.), *Tra economia e storia. Studi in memoria di Gino Barbieri*, Pisa: IPEM edizioni.

Vogelstein, H. (1894) *Die Landwirtschaft in Palastina zur Zeit der Misnah*, Berlin: Mayer und Muller.

Vorlander, K. (1963) "Philosophie des Altertums," in K. Vorlander, *Geschichte der Philosophie*, Reinbek bei Hamburg: Rowohlt I: 139–146.

Wagner, F. (1969) *Das Bild der Fruhen Okonomik*, Salzburg: Stifterbibliothek.

Walbank, F. W. and Astin, A. E. (eds) (2nd edn., 1984) *The Cambridge Ancient History*: vol. 7, pt. 1, *The Hellenistic World*, Cambridge/New York: Cambridge University Press.

Wallace, S. L. (1941) "Ptolemaic Egypt: A Planned Economy," in *The Greek Political Experience. Studies in Honor of William Kelly Prentice*, New York: Russell and Russell.

Wallace-Hadrill, A. (1989) "Introduction," in A. Wallace-Hadrill (ed.), *Patronage in Ancient Society*, London/New York: Routledge.

Ward, W. A. (ed.) (1968) *The Role of the Phoenicians in the Interaction of Mediterranean Civilizations*, Beirut: American University of Beirut.

Ward-Perkins, B. (1984) *From Classical Antiquity to the Middle Ages: Urban Public*

Building in Northern and Central Italy, AD 300–850, Oxford: Oxford University Press.

Webb, Virginia (1978) *Archaic Greek Faience: Miniature Scent Bottles and Related Objects from East Greece, 650–500 BC*, Warminster, England: Aris & Phillips.

Weber, Egon (1976) *Peasants Into Frenchmen: The Modernization of Rural France, 1870–1914*, Stanford, Calif.: Stanford University Press.

Weber, Max (1967) *Ancient Judaism*, New York: Free Press.

Weidemann, M. (1982) *Kulturgeschichte der Merowingerzeit nach dem Werken Gregors von Tours*, Mainz: Verlag des Romisch-Germanischen Zentralmuseums/ Bonn: R. Habelt, 2 vols.

Whitcomb, Donald S. and Johnson, Janet H. (1982) *Quseir al-Qadim 1980: Preliminary Report*, American Research Center in Egypt Reports 7, Malibu: Undena Publications.

White, Lynn, Jr., (1962) *Medieval Technology and Social Change*, Oxford: Oxford University Press.

White, S. A. (1992) *Sovereign Virtue: Aristotle on the Relation Between Happiness and Prosperity*, Stanford, Calif.: Stanford University Press.

Wieland, G. (1981) *Ethica, scientia practica: Die Anfänge der Philosophischen Ethik im 13. Jahrhundert*, Münster, Westfalen: Achendorff.

Wightman, E. M. (1978) "Peasants and Potentates: An Investigation of Social Structure and Land Tenure in Roman Gaul," *American Journal of Ancient History*, 3: 97–128.

Wilhelm, A. (1942) "Attische Urkunde," V. Teil, XLII, in *Sitzungsberichte der Akademie der Wissenschaften in Wien*, 220, 5.

Will, E. (1954) "Trois Quarts de Siècle de Recherches sur l'Économie Grec Antique," *Annales Économies, Sociétés, Civilisations*, 9: 7–22.

— — (1985) "Pour une 'Anthropologie Coloniale' du Monde Hellénistique," in John W. Eadie and Josiah Ober (eds), *The Craft of the Ancient Historian: Essays in Honor of Chester G Starr*, Lanham, Maryland: University Press of America.

— — (1989) "Les Villes de la Syrie à l'Époque Hellénistique et Romaine," in Jean-Marie Dentzer, and Winfreid Orthmann (eds) (1989) *Archéologie et Histoire de la Syrie II. La Syrie de l'Époque achéménide à l'Avenement de l'Islam*, Saarbrück: Saarbrücker Druckerei und Verlag.

Wipszycka, Ewa (1972) *Les Ressources et les Activités Economiques des Eglises en Égypte du IVe au VIII Siècle*, Brussels: Papyrologica Bruxellensia 10, Fondation Egyptologique Reine Elisabeth.

Wistrand, E. (1972) "Gratus, Grates, Gratia, Gratiosus," in E. Wistrand, *Opera selecta*, Stockholm/Lund: P. Astrom.

Wolkmann, H. (1954) "Griechische Rhetorik oder romische Politik? Bemerkungen zum romischen 'Imperialismus'," *Hermes*, 82.

Wood, N. (1988) *Cicero's Social and Political Thought*, Berkeley: University of California Press.

Woolley, C. Leonard (1938) "The Excavations at Al Mina, Sueidia I," *Journal of Hellenic Studies*, 58 (1–30): 133–170.

Worland, Stephen T. (1984) "Aristotle and the Neo-Classical Tradition: The Shifting Ground of Complimentarity," *History of Political Economy*, 16, (1) Spring.

Wright, Henry T. and Herbert, Sharon (1993) "Archeological Survey in the Eastern Desert of Egypt: Report of the University of Michigan/University of Asiut Project," submitted to the Egyptian Antiquities Organization, Ann Arbor: University of Michigan, Museum of Anthropology.

Wunderbar, R. J. (1859) *Biblisch-talmudische Medicin*, Riga, Leipzig: W. F. Hacker, 2 vols.

Xenophon (1968) *Memorabilia and Oecenomicus*, E. C. Marchant (trans.), Cambridge, Mass: Harvard University Press/London: Heinemann.
—— (1971) *Xenophon's Scripta Minora* [Greek and English], E. C. Marchant (ed. and trans.), Cambridge, Mass.: Harvard University Press/London: Heinemann.
—— (1992) [*Poroi*] *Okonomische-Schriften* [German and Greek], Gert Audring (trans.), Berlin: Akademie Verlag.
Yutang, Lin (1938) *My Country and My People*, London: William Heineman.
Zeyadeh, A. (1994) "Settlement Patterns, an Archeological Perspective: Case Studies from Northern Palestine and Jordan," in G. R. D. King and A. Cameron (eds), *The Byzantine and Early Islamic Near East II: Land Use and Settlement Patterns*, Princeton: Darwin Press.
Zuckermandel, M. S. (1880; 1963) *Tosephta* [Hebrew] (photo-reproduction of the 1880 edition), Jerusalem: Wahrman.

INDEX